Rom

REVISION AND ROMANTIC AUTHORSHIP

ZACHARY LEADER

OXFORD
UNIVERSITY PRESS

OXFORD

UNIVERSITY PRESS

Great Clarendon Street, Oxford OX2 6DP

Oxford University Press is a department of the University of Oxford.
It furthers the University's objective of excellence in research, scholarship,
and education by publishing worldwide in

Oxford New York

Athens Auckland Bangkok Bogotá Buenos Aires Calcutta
Cape Town Chennai Dar es Salaam Delhi Florence Hong Kong Istanbul
Karachi Kuala Lumpur Madrid Melbourne Mexico City Mumbai
Nairobi Paris São Paulo Singapore Taipei Tokyo Toronto Warsaw

with associated companies in Berlin Ibadan

Oxford is a registered trade mark of Oxford University Press
in the UK and in certain other countries

Published in the United States
by Oxford University Press Inc., New York

British Library Cataloguing in Publication Data

Data available

Library of Congress Cataloging in Publication Data
Leader, Zachary.
Revision and romantic authorship / Zachary Leader.
Includes bibliographical references.
1. English literature—19th century—Criticism, Textual.
2. Editing—History—19th century. 3. Romanticism—Great Britain.
4. Authorship. I. Title.
PR457.L43 1996 820.9'145—dc20 95-50432
ISBN 0-19-812264-0
ISBN 0-19-818634-7 (Pbk.)

3 5 7 9 10 8 6 4 2

Printed in Great Britain
on acid-free paper by
Bookcraft Ltd,
Midsomer Norton, Somerset

PREFACE

I FIRST became interested in the topic of revision while at work on William Blake's *Songs of Innocence and of Experience*, the subject of my first book. A central argument of this book is that the poems and designs of Blake's *Songs* make up a single, carefully organized volume of verbal and visual art, one more complexly structured than earlier accounts had suggested, in part because earlier accounts mostly ignored the designs Blake etched and coloured to accompany his poems, or focused only on paired but antithetical plates.

In mounting this argument I had immediately to confront an awkward fact of the publishing history of *Songs*, one that applies to most of the works Blake printed himself: that he repeatedly altered the order and appearance of its poems and designs, a practice with interesting theoretical and interpretative as well as textual implications. What exactly was Blake up to when he varied the sequence or look of individual copies? Was he 'revising' an initial concept, attempting more fully to realize it, or creating something wholly new? Blake is sometimes accused of losing touch with his audience (such as it was), or ignoring its needs. In the case of *Songs*, though, as of others of his works, he seems to have known exactly who his readers were, sometimes, it has been claimed, tailoring copies to specific customers. If, as he insisted, 'as Poetry admits not a Letter that is insignificant so Painting admits not a Grain of Sand or a Blade of Grass insignificant much less an Insignificant Blur or Mark', which version of a given work should a student of Blake or a modern publisher favour?[1] And on what grounds? Does it make sense, moreover, to use terms such as 'version' and 'variant', with their implied 'originals', in a Blakean context?[2]

[1] The quotation from Blake comes from 'A Vision of the Last Judgment' (1810), a 20-page explication of a richly detailed painting of the same name now presumed lost. See *The Poetry and Prose of William Blake*, ed. David V. Erdman (1965; repr. Garden City, NY: Doubleday, 1970), 550.

[2] These questions have been immensely complicated (simplified too) by Joseph Viscomi's *Blake and the Idea of the Book* (Princeton, NJ: Princeton University

The topic of revision also figures in my second book, on the subject of writer's block, mostly in relation to its accounts of potentially inhibiting Romantic notions of creativity—notions such as spontaneity, originality, genius. These notions are 'Romantic' because they are associated with an age in which, in Jerome J. McGann's words, 'the ideologies of Romanticism exerted an increasingly dominant influence'; they live on, again in McGann's words, in 'the scholarship and criticism of Romanticism and its works [which] are dominated by a Romantic Ideology, by an uncritical absorption in Romanticism's own self-representations'.[3] Romantic notions can block because they locate creative power in areas that lie outside conscious control; in doing so they also call revision into question, undermining

Press, 1993), which argues against individual variants as revisions. Viscomi is an experienced printmaker, and his literal reconstruction of Blake's production procedures leads him to conclude that, for the most part, the Illuminated Books were not produced singly but in small editions, though with some retouching and detailing of individual copies. For Viscomi, significant differences—revisions—occur from edition to edition:

Variants occuring among edition copies are relatively subtle and are not always by Blake's hand, and generally they do not alter the meaning of the text, but variations occurring among copies produced years apart and in different styles do. These variant book styles, however, while creating different reading experiences and thus different versions of the book, were created by changes in modes of production, changes that reflect revisions in Blake's idea of the illuminated book and not a deliberate revisioning of the particular book. (pp. xxiv–xxv)

The potential consequences of Viscomi's 'materialist' approach are far-reaching: the dating of individual Illuminated Books will have to be altered (what matters now is 'editions' or printing and colouring sessions, not dates of commission or purchase); there will be—has been—a consequent unsettling of the consensus on Blake's changing styles or 'periods'; those who celebrate the control and unity of individual books, as I do, for example, in *Reading Blake's 'Songs'* (London: Routledge & Kegan Paul, 1981), will have to think again; and the meanings of words such as 'intention' and 'difference' in respect to Blake are likely to be reconfigured.

[3] See Jerome J. McGann, *The Romantic Ideology: A Critical Investigation* (Chicago: University of Chicago Press, 1983), 19, 1. To attain a critical distance from Romantic self-representations is no easy business; according to Clifford Siskin, in *The Historicity of Romantic Discourse* (New York: Oxford University Press, 1988), 56–63, McGann himself unconsciously shares them. For a recent retrospective survey of the debate surrounding the term 'Romanticism', one which places *The Romantic Ideology* in relation to earlier essays such as Arthur O. Lovejoy's 'On the Discrimination of Romanticisms', *PMLA* 39 (1924), 229–53, and René Wellek's 'The Concept of Romanticism in Literary History', *Comparative Literature*, 1 (1949), 147–72, see Frances Ferguson, 'On the Numbers of Romanticisms', *English Literary History*, 58 (1991), 471–98.

the authority of second thoughts. This bias against cognitive or controlling aspects of creation makes blockage *as* revision (endlessly altering the text, never bringing it to conclusion or releasing it) especially painful and shaming for Romantic writers.

A number of people have helped me over the course of this book's composition. I want especially to thank Stephen Gill, Peter Manning, Jack Stillinger, John Beer, William St Clair, Christopher Ricks, J. C. C. Mays, Frances Ferguson, Robert Essick, P. N. Furbank, Jim McKusick, Michael Ferber, Grevel Lindop, Richard Sha, Josh Gidding, Maurice Hindle, Susan Matthews, Kevin Gilmartin, Frances Wilson, and Ron Bush, who read and commented on parts of the manuscript. For more general advice, encouragement, and assistance I would like also to thank Robert Brinkley, Keith Hanley, Philip Horne, Jonathan Bate, Betty T. Bennett, John Sutherland, Norman Fruman, Johanna M. Smith, Jim Woodward, David Hilbert, Mac Pigman, Cindy Weinstein, Ann Brook, Oriane Haldane, Helen Ghodbane, Judy Cobb, Emilia Di Paoli, Barbara DiPalma, Gina Morea, Erik Tarloff, Richard Dimitri, Wendy Lesser, Martin Amis, David Papineau, Rosalinde Leader, and Alice Leader. I have benefited also from the support of Martin Ridge, Roy Ritchie, and the staff of the Huntington Library; Dr Bruce Barker-Benfield and the staff of Duke Humphrey's Library, the Bodleian Library; the staff of the John Clare Collection in the Northamptonshire Central Library; David Grether, John Ledyard, and Susan Davis, of the Division of Humanities and Social Sciences at the California Institute of Technology; Neil Taylor, Dean of Arts and Humanities at the Roehampton Institute, and Ann Thompson of Roehampton's English Department; and Kim Scott Walwyn, Andrew Lockett, and Jason Freeman of Oxford University Press.

I am grateful to the Humanities Research Board of the British Academy for an award under its research leave scheme, to the Huntington Library in San Marino, California, for two Andrew Mellon Research Fellowships, and to the Roehampton Institute and the Department of English at Roehampton for sabbatical leave and research funding. Parts of Chapter 1, 'Wordsworth, Revision, and Personal Identity', appeared in *ELH* 60 (1993).

CONTENTS

INTRODUCTION

THE subject of this book is the manner in which revision calls into question and complicates Romantic attitudes to authorship, attitudes which continue to influence writers, critics, and editors. Chief among these attitudes is a preference for what comes naturally (as the leaves to a tree, says Keats), with a concomitant devaluing of secondary processes, including second thoughts.[1] Hence Coleridge's reluctance or inability to 'finish' works, or to admit to having worked at them at all; hence also the continuing debate over differing versions of *The Prelude*, or the prevailing 'primitivism' of Wordsworth's and Clare's editors, with their championing of early or 'raw' versions, regardless of the explicit wishes of the poets themselves, or the fame or familiarity of later versions.

Shelley expresses the Romantic attitude to secondary processes most clearly in the following well-known passage from *A Defence of Poetry* (1821):

Poetry is not like reasoning, a power to be exerted according to the determination of the will. A man cannot say, 'I will compose poetry.' The greatest poet even cannot say it: for the mind in creation is as a fading coal which some invisible influence, like an inconstant wind, awakens to transitory brightness. . . . [W]hen composition begins, inspiration is already on the decline, and the most glorious poetry that has ever been communicated to the world is probably a feeble shadow of the original conception of the poet. I appeal to the greatest Poets of the present day, whether it be not an error to assert that the finest passages of poetry are produced by labour and study. The toil and the delay recommended by critics can be justly interpreted to mean no more than a careful observation of the inspired moments, and an artificial connexion of the spaces between their suggestions by the

[1] See letter of 27 Feb. 1818 to John Taylor, in *The Letters of John Keats, 1814–1821*, ed. Hyder Rollins, 2 vols. (Cambridge, Mass.: Harvard University Press, 1958), i. 238–9: 'if Poetry comes not as naturally as the Leaves to a tree it had better not come at all'.

intertexture of conventional expressions; a necessity only imposed by a limitedness of the poetical faculty itself.[2]

Shelley's identification here of inspiration with 'the poetical faculty itself' is echoed by a number of Romantic writers, as is his implicit preference for an unfallen, an editor would say 'uncorrupted', 'original conception'—as immaterial, ghostly, and tantalizingly inaccessible (because of incarnation itself, presumably, if not the Fall) as the inaugurating dream vision of 'Kubla Khan'. Here and elsewhere, what the writer privileges publicly—and what gets remembered—is the primary: Wordsworth's 'spontaneous overflow', Keats's 'troops' of thoughts, De Quincey's 'unpremeditated torrents', Scott's 'something separate from the volition', Byron's 'licence' (as in 'the Soul of such writing is its licence'), Shelley's 'undisciplined overflowing of the soul'.[3]

This bias against cognitive or controlling aspects of creation feeds into two seemingly contradictory notions of writing, both of which stigmatize revision: writing is associated with the organic (by which is partly meant the whole or complete) and with process (which implies incompletion). The organic view conceives of writing as occurring in a single, seamless moment, the moment of inspiration, without superadded or 'inorganic' refinements; the work 'rises spontaneously from the vital root

---

[2] Percy Bysshe Shelley, 'A Defence of Poetry' (1821), in *Shelley's Poetry and Prose*, ed. Donald H. Reiman and Sharon B. Powers (New York: W. W. Norton, 1977), 503–4.

[3] For 'spontaneous overflow' and its surrounding complications see the preface to *Lyrical Ballads*, in *The Prose Works of William Wordsworth*, ed. W. J. B. Owen and Jane Smyser, 3 vols. (Oxford: Clarendon Press, 1974), i. 124–7; for Keats's 'troops' of thoughts see Richard Woodhouse's comment in *The Keats Circle: Letters and Papers, 1816–1878*, ed. Hyder E. Rollins, 2 vols. (Cambridge, Mass.: Harvard University Press, 1948), i. 128: '[Keats] never sits down to write unless he is full of ideas—and then thoughts come about him in troops'; for De Quincey's 'unpremeditated torrents' see *A Diary of Thomas De Quincey, 1803*, ed. Horace A. Eaton (London: Noel Douglas, 1927), 169; for Scott's 'something separate from the volition' see letter of 31 Jan. 1817 to Lady Louisa Stuart, in *The Letters of Sir Walter Scott*, ed. H. J. C. Grierson, 12 vols. (New York: Columbia University Press, 1932–7), vi. 381; for Byron's 'licence' see letter of 12 Aug. 1819 to John Murray, in *Byron's Letters and Journals*, ed. Leslie A. Marchand, 12 vols. (Cambridge, Mass.: Harvard University Press, 1973–81), vi. 206; for Shelley's 'undisciplined overflowing' see the note on 'Mont Blanc' in the preface to *History of a Six Weeks' Tour through a Part of France, Switzerland, Germany and Holland* (1817), quoted in *The Poems of Shelley*: i. *1804–1817*, ed. Geoffrey Matthews and Kelvin Everest (London: Longman, 1989), 537.

of genius; it *grows*, it is not *made*'.[4] When writing is conceived of as process, the notion of a finished work—'finished' in all its senses—is slighted. 'You must take my things as they happen to be,' says Byron, who liked to think of writing as 'a habit', elsewhere 'an occupation of mind, like play, or any other stimulus' (as opposed to a form of production, with a product, like a poem).[5] Though currently fashionable 'indeterminist' editors, for whom all versions have equal authority, associate this stress on process with their own advanced views (and implied freedom from ideology), indeterminism can be seen as no less Romantic than primitivism, with its organicist faith in an originating authorial intent.[6] 'The romantic kind of poetry', says Friedrich Schlegel in the *Athenaeum*, the periodical the Schlegels

---

[4] Edward Young, *Conjectures on Original Composition* (1759), ed. Edith J. Morley (Manchester: Manchester University Press, 1918), 7.

[5] For the first two quotations see letters of 12 Aug. 1819 to John Murray and 17 Mar. 1823 to John Hunt, in *Byron's Letters and Journals*, ed. Marchand, ii. 175 and vi. 207; for the third quotation see *Byron's 'Don Juan': A Variorum Edition*, ed. T. J. Steffan and W. W. Pratt, 4 vols. (Austin, Tex.: University of Texas Press, 1957), i. 45–6. For the distinction between literature as process and product see Northrop Frye, 'Towards Defining an Age of Sensibility', in *Fables of Identity: Studies in Poetic Mythology* (New York: Harcourt, Brace, & World, 1963), 130–7: 'In the history of literature we become aware, not only of periods, but of a recurrent opposition of two views of literature. These two views are the Aristotelian and the Longinian, the aesthetic and the psychological, the view of literature as product and the view of literature as process. . . . [O]ur age ought to feel a close kinship with the prose fiction of the age of sensibility, when the sense of literature as process was brought to a peculiarly exquisite perfection by Sterne, and in lesser degree by Richardson and Boswell' (pp. 130–1).

[6] Textual indeterminists or pluralists like to think of themselves as postmodern: open, unillusioned, anti-essentialist, externalizing function, their editions the bibliographical equivalents of postmodern buildings (as in the inside-out Centre Georges Pompidou in Paris). To Jerome J. McGann, for example, Hans Gabler's 'synoptic' (i.e. pluralist) edition of *Ulysses* (*Ulysses. A Critical and Synoptic Edition*, ed. Hans Walter Gabler with Wolfhard Steppe and Claus Melchior, 3 vols. (New York: Garland, 1984)), 'raises all the central questions that have brought such a fruitful crisis to literary work in the postmodern period' (*Social Values and Poetic Acts: The Historical Judgement of Literary Work* (Cambridge, Mass.: Harvard University Press, 1988), 174). For a survey of the theoretical orientations of current editorial practices, one which identifies the Greg-Bowers New Bibliography (with its faith in authorial 'final intentions') with 'modernism' and its eclectic or pluralist successors with 'post-modernism', see D. C. Greetham, 'Textual and Literary Theory: Redrawing the Matrix', *Studies in Bibliography*, 42 (1989), 1–13; for a more general survey of editorial theory, see Jack Stillinger, *Multiple Authorship and the Myth of Solitary Genius* (New York: Oxford University Press, 1991), 194–202. For an overview of the history of the editing of Romantic poetry see Donald H. Reiman, 'The Four Ages of Editing and the English Romantics', in *Romantic Texts and Contexts* (Columbia, Miss.: University of Missouri Press, 1987), 85–108.

founded in 1798 to serve as the voice of German Romanticism, is 'a progressive universal poetry. . . . [O]ther kinds of poetry are finished and are now capable of being fully analysed. The romantic kind of poetry is still in the state of becoming; that, in fact, is its real essence: that it should forever be becoming and never be perfected.'[7]

A comparable doubleness attends Romantic notions of the author or writer (as opposed to writing), in particular of the author's personal identity. Yeats succinctly relates these notions to revision in lines first published in 1908:

> The friends that have it I do wrong
> Whenever I remake a song,
> Should know what issue is at stake:
> It is myself that I remake.[8]

These lines are open to several readings: 'remaking' can mean making right, either bringing out or correcting, or it can mean making new. To some Romantic authors—to some people—personal identity is single and continuous, something indivisible

---

[7] The *Critical Fragments* from the *Athenaeum* are dated 1798–1800. For fragment no. 116 see *Friedrich Schlegel's Lucinde and the Fragments*, trans. Peter Firchow (Minneapolis: University of Minnesota Press, 1971), 174. For a discussion of Romanticism and process, including reference to Friedrich Schlegel, see Anne K. Mellor, *English Romantic Irony* (Cambridge, Mass.: Harvard University Press, 1980), especially 3–30. Jerome J. McGann, *The Romantic Ideology* (Chicago: University of Chicago Press, 1983), 24, praises Mellor for rectifying the supposedly 'comprehensive theory of Romanticism' erected by M. H. Abrams in *Natural Supernaturalism: Tradition and Revolution in Romantic Literature* (New York: W. W. Norton, 1971), but also sees her in turn as 'gerrymandering'. Abrams's theory of Romanticism, according to McGann, 'does not rest upon an investigation of Keats or, more crucially, of Byron. Mellor's work steps in precisely to call attention to this weakness in Abrams' theory and to rectify it. But Mellor's study raises new sets of problems. . . . In her view, whatever forms do not show "an enthusiastic response to process and change" are "something else" than Romantic.' In contrast, one might cite a range of darker or deconstructive interpreters of Romantic irony, including Paul de Man, 'The Rhetoric of Temporality', in *Blindness and Insight: Essays in the Rhetoric of Contemporary Criticism* (Minneapolis: University of Minnesota Press, 1983), David Simpson, *Irony and Authority in Romantic Poetry* (Totowa, NJ: Rowan & Littlefield, 1979), and Tilottama Rajan, *Dark Interpreter: The Discourse of Romanticism* (Ithaca, NY: Cornell University Press, 1980). For other accounts of Romantic irony see Peter L. Thorslev, Jr., *Romantic Contraries: Freedom versus Destiny* (New Haven: Yale University Press, 1984) and Frederick Garber, *Self, Text, and Romantic Irony: The Example of Byron* (Princeton: Princeton University Press, 1988).

[8] Repr. in *Variorum Edition of the Poems of W. B. Yeats*, ed. Peter Allt and Russell K. Alspach (London: Macmillan, 1957), 778.

with which we are born; and memory, as John Locke would have it, is its guarantor. To others, personal identity is a creation, the sum of a series of discrete 'selves', both over time and at any one time. When the self is thought of as inherently indivisible and continuous, revision is often seen as a simple matter of refinement or clarification, 'bringing out'. When the self is thought of as something towards which one works, an aspiration or value rather than something given, revision is as much an attempt to establish personal identity as to reveal it. As for those Romantic writers who think of the self as ultimately or inevitably discontinuous, reactions to past work can take several forms: to some, its imperfections won't matter, won't be worth revising, being the product of a past self; to others, not revising is an obligation: it would be wrong to misrepresent the self one once was by revising past work; finally, to more piratical sceptics—Byron, at times—reworking past writing becomes a form of 'making new': original intentions are simply ignored.[9]

The boundaries between these positions are often unclear, for writers as well as critics. Consider, for example, Tennyson's uncertainty in the following lines from 'Tithonus', an obviously autobiographical poem about loss first published in the *Cornhill Magazine* in 1860:

> Ay me! ay me! with what another heart
> In days far-off, and with what other eyes
> I used to watch—if I be he that watched—
> The lucid outline forming round thee; saw

[9] For Jerome J. McGann, in *A Critique of Modern Textual Criticism* (Chicago: University of Chicago Press, 1983), 32, Byron's *The Giaour* (written in 1812/13, published in 1813, revised through fourteen editions from 1813–15), 'typifies what Hans Zeller has recently suggested: that texts frequently exist in several versions no one of which itself can be said to constitute itself the "final" one. . . . [*The Giaour* is one of many works] of which it can be said that their authors demonstrated a number of different wishes and intentions about what text they wanted to be presented to the public, and that these differences reflect accommodations to changed circumstances, and sometimes to changed publics'. For Zeller see 'A New Approach to the Critical Constitution of Literary Texts', *Studies in Bibliography*, 28 (1975), 231–64, which challenges a view of textual variants as either 'teleological' (steps towards a goal, that of ideal form or perfection) or 'morphological' (part of an organic process, 'a continual process of ripening', p. 243). These theories grow out of, and are reflected in, Zeller's editorial work on the 19th-c. Swiss poet and novelist, Conrad Ferdinand Meyer (*Sämtliche Werke. Historisch-kritische Ausgabe*, ed. Hans Zeller and Alfred Zach (Berne: Benteli, 1958–63)).

The dim curls kindle into sunny rings.
Changed with thy mystic change.   (lines 50–5)

Does it help us to settle the doubts Tithonus/Tennyson expresses here about continuity of self ('if I be he that watched')
to know that over twenty-five years earlier, in 'Tithon' (1833),
the first, shorter version of the poem, this passage read

Ay me! ay me!, with what another heart,
By thy divine embraces circumfused,
Thy black curls burning into sunny rings,
With thy change changed, I felt this wondrous glow?   (41–4)

Does the knowledge that Tennyson revised these lines in 1860
confirm their message of discontinuity, partly on the grounds
that all revision is change, an expression of new self, partly
because the changes themselves emphasize change ('and with
what other eyes'), or does it challenge that message, by rein-
forcing an already-implicit counter-sense or under-meaning: that
Tithonus/Tennyson had in fact *not* changed (at least not since
the beloved's death), for all the earlier version's absence of
doubt; that he remained overcome by loss—so that, paradoxically, the interpolated 'if I be he that watched' (with its implicit
'how could I be?') suggests continuity, a still-living pain?[10] Or
was it both, as in Wordsworth's 'so wide appears | The vacancy
between me and those days | Which yet have such self-presence
in my mind' (*The Prelude*, 1850, II. 28–30)?

Whatever the answer, Tennyson's valuing of a unified and
continuous self is clear. Walt Whitman, in contrast, professed
to relish his multiple selves, as in an analogous passage about
loss (itself an interpolation, and thus a revision of sorts), written in the same year as 'Tithonus', from the 'Calamus' section
of the third edition of *Leaves of Grass* (1860):

O Love!
O dying—always dying!
O the burials of me past and present!
O me, while I stride ahead, material, visible, imperious as ever!

[10] For quotations from both 'Tithon' (1833) and 'Tithonus' (1860), see *The
Poems of Tennyson*, ed. Christopher Ricks (New York: Longman, 1969), 567,
1117. For a comparison of the two poems see Mary J. Donahue, 'Tennyson's
"Hail, Briton!" and "Tithon" in the Heath Manuscript', *PMLA* 64 (1949), 400–16.

O me, what I was for years, now dead, (I lament not—I am
  content;)
O to disengage myself from those corpses of me, which I turn
  and look at, where I cast them!
To pass on, (O living! always living!) and leave the corpses
  behind!

Such insouciance or equanimity issues in Byronic revisionary
habits; the successive alterations of *Leaves of Grass* are less a
matter of refining or perfecting meanings, of anxiously measur-
ing the present against the past, as of expressing new self, the
inevitable product of changed personal or political circumstances.
Yet with Whitman, too, there are complications. Why, for
example, if one holds such views about the self, insist upon
gathering everything one has written—all one's past selves—
under a single title, the ever-altering and expanding *Leaves of
Grass*? Why, in fact, revise at all, as opposed to issuing new
poems in new volumes?[11]

Questions such as these are illuminated—if not directly conditioned—by a long history of philosophical debate about personal identity.[12] In recent years, the moral implications of this
debate have been resurrected by modern philosophers, principally through a series of memorable thought experiments. These
experiments derive ultimately from the second or 1694 edition
of *An Essay Concerning Human Understanding* (1690), in
which, in a chapter entitled 'Of Identity and Diversity', Locke
imagines the soul of a prince being transferred to the body of
a cobbler, an example he uses to locate sameness of self in
consciousness, as opposed to substance.[13] The creation or creature resulting from this transfer, Locke concludes, would be the
same person as the prince but not the same man, a distinction
he reinforces with other thought experiments (involving talking
parrots, drunks, and madmen). These experiments or puzzles, it
has been argued, had the wholly unintended effect of throwing

[11] For an account of the revisionary history of *Leaves of Grass* see Michael
Moon, *Disseminating Whitman: Revision and Corporeality in 'Leaves of Grass'*
(Cambridge, Mass.: Harvard University Press, 1991). The lines from the 'Calamus'
section of the third edition, from no. 27, are quoted and discussed on p. 168.

[12] For an account of the main contours of this debate, at least for the 18th-c.,
see Appendix.

[13] John Locke, *An Essay Concerning Human Understanding*, ed. P. H. Nidditch
(Oxford: Clarendon Press, 1975), 340.

the unified self into question, in the process destabilizing the traditional location or centre of legal and ethical responsibility.

Recent thought experiments are comparably destabilizing, but intentionally. The best-known modern example occurs in Derek Parfit's *Reasons and Persons* (1984), and involves what Parfit calls teletransportation, a common feature in science fiction. Parfit imagines entering a machine, the Teletransporter, which exactly recreates his brain and body, beaming the resulting replica to Mars. This replica 'thinks he is me, and he seems to remember living my life' (that is, up to the moment of tele-transportation); 'if he returned to Earth, everyone would think that he was me'. One day, in the course of teletransportation, the machine malfunctions, damaging Parfit's earthly heart. 'Judging from the results so far,' a doctor tells the earthly Parfit, 'though you will be quite healthy on Mars, here on Earth you must expect cardiac failure within the next few days.'[14] When Parfit's replica learns the fate of his earthly original, he tries to console him: 'he will take up my life where I leave off. He loves my wife and together they will care for my children. And he will finish the book that I am writing. Besides having all of my drafts, he has all of my intentions.' The earthly Parfit takes little comfort in these assurances. 'Though he is exactly like me, he is one person, and I am another. When I pinch myself, he feels nothing. When I have my heart attack, he will again feel nothing. And when I am dead he will live for another forty years.'[15]

Is the original Parfit right not to be consoled? *Reasons and Persons* suggests not, thus aligning itself with the destabilization process inadvertently inaugurated by Locke and decisively seconded by David Hume in *A Treatise of Human Nature* (1739–40). 'I should regard this way of dying,' concludes Parfit, *in propria persona*, 'as being about as good as ordinary survival.' The relation such a conclusion has to the problems of revision examined in this book derives from its ethical implications. It is Parfit's aim to persuade his readers 'to cease to believe that our identity [that is, as separately existing entities] is what matters', an aim which may affect not only 'our emotions, such as our attitude to ageing and to death', but larger belief systems,

[14] Derek Parfit, *Reasons and Persons* (Oxford: Clarendon Press, 1984), 200.
[15] Ibid. 201.

including 'our views about both rationality and morality'.[16] Opponents of Locke and Hume would agree, wholly deploring the social and ethical consequences of such changes. In the words of Locke's 'common-sense' antagonist Thomas Reid, the Scottish philosopher and antagonist also of Berkeley and Hume, 'if personal identity consisted in consciousness, it would certainly follow, that no man is the same person any two moments of his life; and as the right and justice of reward and punishment is founded on personal identity, no man could be responsible for his actions'.[17]

Many writers and critics share this view. It plays a part, for instance, as we shall see, in Mary Shelley's disapproval of the personal conduct of both Byron and her husband, in respect to literary as well as literal offspring (neither of which, she felt, were properly 'parented' by their creators).[18] It underlies Coleridge's assertion, in *The Friend* (1809–10), that 'men are ungrateful to others only when they have ceased to look back on their former selves with joy and tenderness'.[19] For Parfit, though, as for other, very different sorts of thinkers (postmodernists, Buddhists), a dispersed or destabilized self can be both liberating and compatible with moral agency. When Parfit still believed in the importance of a unified and continuous personal identity,

---

[16] Ibid. 215.

[17] Thomas Reid, *Essays on the Intellectual Powers of Man* (1785; repr. New York: Garland, 1971), 336, quoted in Christopher Fox, *Locke and the Scriblerians: Identity and Consciousness in Early Eighteenth-Century Britain* (Berkeley: University of California Press, 1988), 47.

[18] For revision as a form of literary parenting see also Henry James, from the 1909 preface to the New York edition of *The Golden Bowl* (1904; repr. Harmondsworth: Penguin, 1979), 16: 'I had rather viewed the reappearance of the first born of my progeny [in a revised edition of his collected works] . . . as a descent of awkward infants from the nursery to the drawing-room under the kind appeal of inquiring, of possibly interested, visitors. I had accordingly taken for granted the common decencies of such a case—the responsible glance of some power above from one nursling to another, the rapid flash of an anxious needle, the not imperceptible effect of a certain audible splash of soap-and-water; all in consideration of the searching radiance of drawing-room lamps as compared with nursery candles. But it had been all the while present to me that from the moment a stitch should be taken or a hairbrush applied the *principle* of my making my brood more presentable under the nobler illumination would be accepted and established.'

[19] From 'The Landing-Place, or Essays Interposed for Amusement, Retrospect, and Preparation: Essay V', in Samuel Taylor Coleridge, *The Friend*, ed. Barbara E. Rooke, 2 vols. (Princeton: Princeton University Press, 1969), i. 40.

I seemed imprisoned in myself. My life seemed like a glass tunnel, through which I was moving faster every year, and at the end of which there was darkness. . . . I now live in the open air. There is still a difference between my life and the lives of other people. But the difference is less. Other people are closer. I am less concerned about the rest of my own life, and more concerned about the lives of others.[20]

Such an attitude, Parfit argues, encourages rational altruism, a value of increasing importance in complex, interdependent communities. A dispersed sense of individuality, or greater impersonality, is crucially important to the fight against such problems as 'pollution, congestion, depletion, inflation, unemployment, a recession, over-fishing, over-farming, soil-erosion, famine, and overpopulation'.[21] Thus, though the protean Byron and Shelley (for whom, 'the words *I, you, they*, are not signs of any actual difference subsisting between the assemblage of thoughts thus indicated'[22]) may have been negligent or irresponsible in their personal lives—as also, at times, in their attitude to finished work—politically and socially they might well be considered the most committed of writers, 'scattering' (a tellingly undeliberative verb) renovating words of protest and ridicule, to adapt 'Ode to the West Wind', like 'ashes and sparks'.

---

[20] Parfit, *Reasons and Persons*, 281.   [21] Ibid. 444.

[22] The immediate context of the quotation, from 'On Life' (1819), repr. in *Shelley's Poetry and Prose*, ed. Reiman and Powers, 477–8, is as follows: 'The existence of distinct individual minds similar to that which is employed in now questioning its own nature, is . . . found to be a delusion. The words, *I, you, they*, are not signs of any actual difference subsisting between the assemblage of thoughts thus indicated, but are merely marks employed to denote the different modifications of the one mind.' For more general accounts of Shelley and 'personal identity', contrast Timothy Clark, *Embodying Revolution: The Figure of the Poet in Shelley* (Oxford: Clarendon Press, 1989), 65–92, who sees references to 'the one mind' as anti-Humean, and Andrew M. Cooper, *Doubt and Identity in Romantic Poetry* (New Haven: Yale University Press, 1988), 10–18, who likens the passage from 'On Life' to Hume, concluding that 'personal identity exists for Shelley through the individual mind's attributing such identity to certain of its own "modifications," mainly for the same practical reasons Hume gives: convenience and reassurance' (p. 18). Cooper also offers (p. 193) an apt quotation from John Ashbery: 'The personal pronouns in my work often seem to be like variables in an equation. "You" can be myself or it can be another person, someone whom I'm addressing, and so can "he" and "she" for that matter and "we" . . . my point is that it doesn't really matter very much, that we are somehow all aspects of a consciousness giving rise to the poem and the fact of addressing someone, myself or someone else, is what's the important thing at that particular moment rather than the particular person involved. (Janet Bloom and Robert Losada, "Craft Interview with John Ashbery," *New York Quarterly* 9 [1972]: 224–25).'

Jonathan Glover, another recent philosopher of personal identity, takes issue with Parfit in ways that also recall Romantic attitudes to writing. In Parfit's view of the dispersed self, writes Glover, 'the episodes of a life can seem like a heap of stones. Then perhaps death is less important. It does not much matter whether some extra stones are dumped on my pile or some other one. But, if I see the stones as part of a building I am creating, being cut off with too few stones can ruin everything.'[23] For some writers, Wordsworth, for instance, just such an architectural metaphor shapes identity, often through revision. 'Wordsworth' is a work, a cathedral-like authorial edifice, as in the figurative language of the prose preface to *The Excursion* (1814).[24] So, too, for W. H. Auden, a comparably assiduous reviser. 'When a writer is dead', writes Auden, 'one ought to be able to see that his various works, taken together, make one consistent *œuvre*.'[25]

The example of Auden's revisions is worth considering in this context, since it raises questions of authorial autonomy as well as identity, questions of central importance in the second part of this book. From 1927 to 1939, the year he moved to the United States, Auden typically published his poems in a manner

[23] Jonathan Glover, *I: The Philosophy and Psychology of Personal Identity* (Harmondsworth: Penguin Books, 1988), 106. For other discussion of Parfit's work see the symposium on *Reasons and Persons* in *Ethics*, 96 (1986), ed. Brian Barry, especially Susan Wolf, 'Self-Interest and Interest in Selves', 704–20; also Peter Unger, *Identity, Consciousness, and Value* (Oxford: Oxford University Press, 1991). Personal identity is also the focus of Charles Taylor, *Sources of the Self* (Cambridge, Mass.: Harvard University Press, 1989), Bernard Williams, *Problems of the Self* (Cambridge: Cambridge University Press, 1973), Sydney Shoemaker, *Self-Knowledge and Self-Identity* (Ithaca, NY: Cornell University Press, 1963), and Amélie Rorty (ed.), *The Identities of Persons* (Berkeley: University of California Press, 1976).

[24] It is in the prose preface to *The Excursion* (1814) that *The Prelude* and *The Recluse* are said to 'have the same relation to each other . . . as the ante-chapel has to the body of a Gothic church'. At the same time, Wordsworth declares, his 'minor pieces, which have long been before the public . . . have such a connection with the main work as may give them claim to be likened to the little cells, oratories, and sepulchral recesses, ordinarily included in these edifices' (*Prose Works*, ed. Owen and Smyser, iii. 5–6). See also Wordsworth's letter of 3 June 1805 to Sir George Beaumont, in *The Letters of William and Dorothy Wordsworth*, ed. Ernest de Selincourt; *The Early Years, 1787–1805*, rev. edn. Chester L. Shaver (Oxford: Clarendon Press, 1967), 594, in which *The Prelude* is described as 'a sort of portico to the Recluse, part of the same building'.

[25] W. H. Auden, 'Writing', in *The Dyer's Hand and Other Essays* (London: Faber & Faber, 1963), 21.

reminiscent of Coleridge: that is, first in periodicals, then in initial book form, then in collected editions, revising, often radically, at each stage. These were the years, especially 1932–9, of Auden's most intense political engagement. After 1939, though, according to Edward Mendelson, his editor and literary executor, 'alarmed by his own power to bring a political meeting roaring to its feet, Auden resolved never again to speak directly about politics'.[26] He also began planning a new collected edition, one that would importantly transform a number of his best-known political poems.[27]

Auden's post-1939 revisions were a product not so much of changed political opinions as of anxiety about his audience; in particular, paradoxically, anxiety about the intensity of audience approval. His early political poems, he came to feel, in the words of the 1940 'New Year Letter', 'adopted what I would disown, | The preacher's loose immodest tone'. Hence the excision of the following well-known stanzas from 'In Memory of W. B. Yeats' (1939):

> Time that is intolerant
> Of the brave and innocent,
> And indifferent in a week
> To a beautiful physique,
>
> Worships language and forgives
> Everyone by whom it lives;
> Pardons cowardice, conceit,
> Lays its honours at their feet.
>
> Time that with this strange excuse
> Pardoned Kipling and his views,
> And will pardon Paul Claudel,
> Pardons him for writing well.

These stanzas were dropped from the version printed in the 1958 Penguin, *W. H. Auden: A Selection by the Author*, not because Auden's politics had changed, but because, in Mendelson's words, the stanzas 'assume the right-wing aristocratic views of

[26] Edward Mendelson, 'The Two Audens and the Claims of History', in George Bornstein (ed.), *Representing Modernist Texts: Editing as Interpretation* (Ann Arbor: University of Michigan Press, 1991), 157.
[27] The resulting edition was *The Collected Poetry of W. H. Auden* (New York: Random House, 1945).

Kipling, Claudel, and Yeats require the pardon of Time in order to survive, while the left-wing democratic views of Auden and those he admires implicitly do not', an 'immodest' assumption likely to encourage immodesty and self-satisfaction in like-minded readers.[28]

Auden's fear of looseness and immodesty figures also in the revision of 'Spain, 1937' (dropped completely, along with 'September 1, 1939', from the 1958 selection), especially in his famous alteration of the line, 'The conscious acceptance of guilt in the necessary murder,' which became 'The conscious acceptance of guilt in the fact of murder.' This alteration first appeared in the 1940 collection *Another Time*, and was again inspired by external factors, or audience reaction. George Orwell had praised the poem in *Inside the Whale* (1940), calling it 'one of the few decent things that have been written about the Spanish war', but he also objected strenuously to the phrase 'the necessary murder'. It could only, Orwell declared, have been written by someone 'to whom murder is at most a *word*'.[29] Auden knew of and was probably influenced by this objection (voiced in an earlier magazine publication), but the revision, he insisted, was no repudiation or disavowal. 'I was *not* excusing totalitarian crimes but only trying to say what, surely, every decent person thinks if he finds himself unable to adopt the absolutely pacifist position. If there is such a thing as a just war, then murder can be necessary for the sake of justice.'[30] The alteration was thus

[28] Mendelson, 'The Two Audens and the Claims of History', 165.
[29] George Orwell, *Inside the Whale* (London: Gollancz, 1940), 169.
[30] Quoted in Humphrey Carpenter, *W. H. Auden: A Biography* (London: George Allen & Unwin, 1981), 219. The quotation comes from a letter written to Monroe K. Spears, and quoted in Spears's *The Poetry of W. H. Auden: The Disenchanted Island* (New York: Oxford University Press, 1963), 157. As Mendelson, in *The English Auden* (London: Faber & Faber, 1977), 424–5, has pointed out, the revised version of 'Spain' was published a month before *Inside the Whale*, which appeared in late 1940. It was Bernard Crick, in *George Orwell: A Life* (London: Secker & Warburg, 1980), 435, who discovered that Orwell 'had written an earlier and cruder version of the same thing. In "Political Reflections on the Crisis," *The Adelphi* December 1938, p. 110, Orwell had attacked "this utterly irresponsible intelligentsia", the alliance of "the gangster and the pansy", had referred to Auden by name, had neither mentioned "Spain" explicitly nor quoted the two offending stanzas but had misquoted "from Auden", he said "the acceptance of guilt from the necessary murder."' Mendelson, *Early Auden* (London: Faber & Faber, 1981), 322, is good on the word 'necessary' in the original or 1937 version: 'This word can have two different meanings: either required by circumstance, as in the common phrase "a necessary evil," or inevitably fixed and determined, as in the necessary

a matter of 'tone' or tact rather than substance, was no imposition of new self.

Auden is frequently associated with Byron, who was as lordly about the hobgoblin consistency ('But if a writer should be quite consistent, | How could he possibly show things existent?'[31]) as Emerson. Auden as reviser, in contrast, cared passionately about consistency, like Wordsworth the reviser, who longed to see 'past, present, future, all . . . | In harmony united' ('Yarrow Revisited', lines 29–30). Yet Auden was not prepared, again like Wordsworth, to alter or reject poems simply because they expressed views, in Mendelson's words, 'that he entirely disbelieved later'.[32] Though he strove for continuity, he respected difference, and was alert to the temptation to disguise it. 'The ego which recalls a previous condition of a now changed Self', Auden writes in *The Dyer's Hand* (1963), 'cannot believe that it, too, has changed. The Ego fancies that it is like Zeus who could assume one bodily appearance after another, now a swan, now a bull, while all the time remaining Zeus.'[33] The poems Auden altered or rejected were ones that misrepresented original meanings and intentions, an underlying Zeus as it were. 'A dishonest poem', he wrote in 1966, of the sort of poems he revised, 'is one which expresses, no matter how well, feelings or beliefs which its author never felt or entertained', but which 'sounded to me rhetorically effective'.[34] That these poems were often political was to be expected, since 'the integrity of a writer is more threatened by appeals to his social conscience, his political or religious convictions, than by appeals to his cupidity'.[35]

obedience of matter to the laws of physics. Orwell assumed that *Spain* used the word in the first of these senses, as a casual justification of murder on the grounds of expedience. But context indicates that the word must be read in the second sense. "The *conscious* acceptance of guilt in the *necessary* murder" is a paradox, the one line in the poem in which the manifest argument about choice directly confronts the metaphoric argument about necessity. The necessary murder is the harshest of the unchosen unconscious processes associated, in the metaphoric argument, with the people's army. The poet chooses to accept guilt in this murder, but the act itself is a necessary step taken by others towards History's inevitable fulfilment.'

[31] Byron, *Don Juan*, xv. 87, in the Oxford Authors *Byron*, ed. Jerome J. McGann (Oxford: Oxford University Press, 1986), 840.

[32] Mendelson, 'The Two Audens and the Claims of History', 66.

[33] From the essay 'Hic et Ille', in Auden, *The Dyer's Hand*, 96.

[34] W. H. Auden, foreword to *Collected Shorter Poems 1927–1957* (London: Faber & Faber, 1966), 15.

[35] W. H. Auden, 'Writing', in *The Dyer's Hand*, 19.

What *is* Byronic about Auden—though Byron, as we shall see, would object—is his responsiveness to readers, including critics, a responsiveness at odds with Romantic, including Byronic, notions of solitary genius or authorial autonomy. These notions, according to Jack Stillinger, are 'so widespread as to be nearly universal'.[36] But they are simplifications. As a study of its revision suggests, the writing of the Romantic period (as of all periods) is the product of a network of literary and social relations, one in which the nominal author's contribution and authority are dominant but not exclusive.[37] Even when fiercely professing independence, the author typically draws on a range of personal and institutional collaborators, including family, friends, publishers, reviewers, and readers. It is not always the case that the contributions of these collaborators are either negligible or 'corrupting' (sometimes 'contaminating'), even when we have no explicit evidence of authorial proofing or approval. When editors privilege early, often manuscript, versions of texts, burying the contributions of collaborators (even in a bed of footnotes), they assume a thoroughly Romantic view of the relation between writers, works, publishers, and readers. Yet the indeterminist or pluralist editorial backlash, as I have suggested, is also Romantic, in that it undervalues secondary processes, the sort that 'finish' or 'perfect' works. The issues involved, that is to say, are more complicated than partisans suggest.

These issues are grouped into the second of the book's two

---

[36] Stillinger, *Multiple Authorship*, 183.

[37] Such a view recalls Foucault's theory of the discursive 'author-function' in 'What Is an Author?' (1969). This theory, says Foucault, 'is a matter of depriving the subject (or its substitute) of its role as originator, and of analyzing the subject as a variable and complex function of discourse' (trans. Josue V. Harari, in Harari (ed.), *Textual Strategies: Perspectives in Post-Structuralist Criticism* (Ithaca, NY: Cornell University Press, 1979), 148). That Foucault is willing to grant the individual author or subject some part in the creation of texts, though, in addition, that is, to his or her transmission of the 'author-function', may account for his relative appeal to theoretically inclined textualists. Michael Groden, e.g., in 'Contemporary Textual and Literary Theory', in Bornstein (ed.), *Representing Modernist Texts*, 275, approvingly cites the following passage from Foucault's 'The Discourse on Language' (1971): 'Of course, it would be ridiculous to deny the existence of individuals who write, and invent. But I think that, for some time, at least, the individual who sits down to write a text, at the edge of which lurks a possible *œuvre*, resumes the functions of the author' (*The Archaeology of Knowledge and the Discourse on Language*, trans. A. M. Sheridan Smith (New York: Pantheon, 1972), 222).

parts. In the three chapters of Part 1, entitled 'Revision and Personal Identity', the revisionary practices of Wordsworth, Byron, and Coleridge are contrasted. Wordsworth and Byron are presented as seeming opposites, a product of wholly different notions of personal identity. Coleridge is then shown to occupy a middle ground between them, being a radically divided or discontinuous apostle of unity and unified selfhood. In Part 2, 'Revision and Authorial Autonomy', the role of collaborators in the revising process is related to the questions of personal identity discussed in Part 1. Part 2 consists of chapters on Percy Shelley's revisions of Mary Shelley's *Frankenstein*, on the publisher John Taylor's revisions of the poems of John Clare, and on the role of readers and critics in the revision of Keats's poems. The focus throughout the book is on what might be called revision proper, as opposed to, say, metaphorical revisions, or revision in the Bloomian or intertextual sense (that is, of giant, inhibiting precursors). The book's larger distinction between internally imposed revisions, whether a product of unconscious compulsions or matters of conscious conviction, and revisions of external origin, involving the writer's personal and institutional affiliations, is an analytic device: revision, after all, is often multiply or variously motivated; Wordsworth and Coleridge revised in response to external as well as internal pressures, as did Keats and Clare.

PART ONE

Revision and Personal Identity

CHAPTER ONE

WORDSWORTH, REVISION, AND PERSONAL IDENTITY

IN 1984 Stephen Gill published a selection of Wordsworth's poetry and prose in the Oxford Authors series. This series aims to offer 'authoritative editions of the major English writers for the student and general reader', an especially welcome prospect in the case of Wordsworth, since in the early 1980s inexpensive one-volume alternatives were either too selective or forbiddingly bulky, inclusive, cramped, or unannotated.[1] Like other volumes in the series, Gill's edition claims to print 'the best texts available' in a selection that seeks out 'the essence of a writer's work and thinking'. But it also has other, and potentially conflicting, aims. 'Here, for the first time,' the blurb tells us, Wordsworth's poems 'are presented in order of composition and in texts in which their original identity is restored.' That is, in versions Wordsworth revised in subsequent editions.

---

[1] Like many teachers of the writing of the English Romantic period, my interest in the problem of Wordsworth's revisions began in the early 1980s, in the face of an awkward pedagogical reality: many of the upper-level undergraduates to whom I taught the poetry of the period simply could not afford the books I was assigning, particularly the bulky two-vol. Penguin Wordsworth and the parallel-text Penguin *Prelude*. The Penguin texts are *William Wordsworth: The Poems*, ed. John O. Hayden, 2 vols. (Harmondsworth: Penguin Books, 1977) and *The Prelude: A Parallel Text*, ed. J. C. Maxwell (Harmondsworth: Penguin Books, 1977), the source, unless otherwise specified, of all quotations from the poem, whether from the 1805 or 1850 version. The alternatives in the early 1980s were Geoffrey Hartman's Signet Classics edn., *The Selected Poetry and Prose of Wordsworth* (New York: New American Library, 1970), which is too selective, and Ernest de Selincourt's one-vol. *Poetical Works*, in the Oxford Standard Authors Series, rev. edn. Thomas Hutchinson (Oxford: Oxford University Press, 1950), which errs on the other (cramped and forbidding) side. Jack Stillinger's Riverside edn., *Selected Poetry and Prefaces of William Wordsworth* (Boston: Houghton Mifflin, 1965), is difficult to obtain in England, where I teach, and expensive as well—if not quite as expensive as the three-book Penguin package (now a four-book package, with the publication of a 528-page *Selected Prose Writings*, ed. John O. Hayden (Harmondsworth: Penguin Books, 1988)).

Wordsworth's career as a poet spanned sixty-five years, from 1785 to 1850. Between 1793 and 1850, Wordsworth published fifteen books of new verse, and nine collected editions, the first of which appeared in 1815. These collected editions were arranged topically rather than chronologically, and contained both fresh poems and the latest revised versions of older poems. According to Ernest de Selincourt, editor of what is still the standard edition (until, at least, the completion of the Cornell Edition, to be discussed later), 'it is probable that no poet ever paid more meticulous or prolonged attention to his text'.[2] As Gill himself puts it, in a textual note to the Oxford Authors edition, and amply documents in his richly informative 1989 biography, *Wordsworth: A Life*, 'over revision the poet expended enormous vigilance and the labour did not end until his death'.[3] That death followed hard on the heels of the publication in 1849–50 of a six-volume *Poems*, the last collected edition worked on by Wordsworth himself. Though Wordsworth was 80 when he died, and incapable of the major revisions of, for example, the 1836/7 and 1845 collections, he was, as Gill's biography puts it, 'alert enough to attend to details'.[4] There is little reason to question the edition's status as 'the poet's final authorized text',[5] or to suppose he ever changed his mind about the importance, as he wrote to Alexander Dyce in 1830, of 'following strictly the last Copy of the text of an Author'.[6]

Gill's motives for ignoring Wordsworth's final texts relate only indirectly to the aims of the Oxford Authors series. On the back of the edition, right next to the general rubric (with its talk of 'best' texts and 'the essence of a writer's work and thinking'), is a one-paragraph description beginning as follows:

---

[2] *The Poetical Works of William Wordsworth, Edited from the Manuscripts, with Textual and Critical Notes*, ed. Ernest de Selincourt and Helen Darbishire, 5 vols. (Oxford: Clarendon Press, 1941–9), i. p. v.

[3] *William Wordsworth*, ed. Stephen Gill (Oxford: Oxford University Press, 1984), p. xxx.

[4] Stephen Gill, *William Wordsworth: A Life* (Oxford: Clarendon Press, 1989), 419.

[5] *William Wordsworth*, ed. Gill, p. xxx.

[6] Letter of *c.*19 Apr. 1830 to Alexander Dyce in *The Letters of William and Dorothy Wordsworth*, ed. Ernest de Selincourt; *The Later Years, Part 2*, rev. edn., Alan G. Hill (Oxford: Clarendon Press, 1979), ii. 236. There are seven volumes of Wordsworth's *Letters*, all published by Clarendon Press. Subsequent references use the abbreviations *EY (Early Years), MY (Middle Years)*, and *LY (Later Years)*, plus editor, and part and page numbers.

This edition enables today's readers to share something of the experiences of Wordsworth's contemporaries. Keats and Shelley, Hazlitt and Lamb read his poems as they were first published, but later readers have generally been familiar only with the poems altered, often markedly, by the revisions Wordsworth made to his work throughout his long life.

The question of aesthetic value—are these versions 'best'—goes unmentioned here. What matters is Wordsworth's relation to history, specifically literary history. By restoring his poems to 'their original identity' the reader will have a more accurate sense of their immediate impact on his contemporaries.

Whether this historical sense is quite what is wanted or needed by 'the student and general reader' is not addressed in the publicity material on the back cover. Nor are such needs addressed in Gill's textual note, which offers a rather different account of his editorial procedures:

In the belief that a chronological presentation can best reveal the growth of the poet's mind (the subject, after all, of his greatest poem, *The Prelude*) and the unfolding of his imagination, this volume is ordered according to date of composition. It follows—and here I break with all of the editorial pioneers, Dowden, Knight, Hutchinson, De Selincourt, Darbishire—that one *must* print a text which comes as close as possible to the state of a poem when it was first completed.[7]

Though John O. Hayden's two-volume Penguin edition also orders the poems chronologically, its use of authorized or revised texts poses, as he himself admits, 'very complex problems' to students of Wordsworth's poetic evolution.[8] As Gill puts it: 'To place a poem under 1795 in a text encrusted with the revisions of perhaps forty years—the practice of the current Penguin edition—is, to say the least, confusing.'[9] This confusion, though, originates with Wordsworth, who 'towards the end of his life, does not even scruple to offer the present as if it were the past'. When in 1842 Wordsworth issued *Poems Chiefly of Early and Later Years*, for example, ostensibly 'to gratify the natural interest faithful readers have in all his verse', those

---

[7] *William Wordsworth*, ed. Gill, p. xxi.
[8] *William Wordsworth: The Poems*, ed. Hayden, i. 26. Hayden is not the first editor to print the poems chronologically. That distinction belongs to William Knight, editor of *The Poetical Works of William Wordsworth*, an eight-vol. edn. of 1882–6.   [9] *William Wordsworth*, ed. Gill, p. xxxi.

readers, in Gill's words, 'could not have known that what was presented as historical period pieces are in fact freshly revised poems'.[10]

But there are confusions in Gill's practice as well. On the one hand, his editorial justifications present themselves as historical or biographical; on the other, they draw on implicit aesthetic or value judgements. The privileging of chronology and original (or originally published) editions highlights Wordsworth's development. This development matters because poetical or imaginative growth is the subject-matter of Wordsworth's 'greatest' poem, *The Prelude*. But in order to highlight this subject-matter Gill prints versions of other poems, not to mention *The Prelude* itself, that Wordsworth importantly revised, ignoring long-famous and much-honoured authorized versions. Hence, in 'Resolution and Independence', a 'great' poem openly concerned with poetical or imaginative growth, Gill retains lines 59–63, in which the leech gatherer is described with a flatness Coleridge thought 'only proper in prose',[11] because they appeared in the 'original' 1807 publication (by which Gill means the first version to appear in a book of Wordsworth's poems, rather than in newspapers or periodicals). Wordsworth's excision of these lines in 1815 and all subsequent editions, along with a number of smaller changes, both in 1815 and later, is simply ignored, presumably on the grounds that what matters is our sense of Wordsworth in 1807, at the time of 'original' publication.

But 'Resolution and Independence' was mostly written five years earlier, in an already revised version of July 1802 which Jared E. Curtis, its Cornell editor, calls 'substantially the one published in 1807'.[12] As for the aim of allowing readers to 'share something of the experiences of Wordsworth's contemporaries', it is true that neither Keats nor Shelley nor Hazlitt would have known the poem before 1807, but Coleridge did, and Lamb may also have read it. Moreover, Wordsworth's contemporaries are as likely to have known the 1815 version,

[10] Stephen Gill, '"Affinities Preserved": Poetic Self-Reference in Wordsworth', *Studies in Romanticism*, 24/4 (Winter 1985), 540, 541.

[11] Samuel Taylor Coleridge, *Biographia Literaria*, ed. James Engell and W. Jackson Bate, 2 vols. (Princeton: Princeton University Press, 1981), ii. 121; also 124–5.

[12] Jared E. Curtis, *Wordsworth's Experiments with Tradition: The Lyric Poems of 1802* (Ithaca, NY: Cornell University Press, 1971), 100.

in which lines 59–63 were first excised, as that of 1807. But in either case the number of contemporaries about whom we are talking—certainly in terms of sales—is minuscule: the poem did not appear in the magazines; of the 1,000 copies of the 1807 *Poems, in Two Volumes,* 230 remained unsold by 1814; of the 500 copies of the 1815 *Poems by William Wordsworth,* also in two volumes, only 352 copies were sold by 1817, and the remaining copies only by 1820.[13] Most readers—that is, most of Wordsworth's contemporaries—would have known the poem in the later collected editions.

Gill, I am suggesting, ignores Wordsworth's explicit intentions for reasons that are not always clear or consistent—at least as stated. One might argue the aesthetic or artistic merits of different versions (about which there is no consensus), but Gill chooses not to. Nor does he do so in support of comparably noteworthy instances, such as that of 'Ode: Intimations of Immortality', here titled merely 'Ode' (its title in the 1807 printing), or 'I Wandered Lonely as a Cloud' (with its host of 'dancing' as opposed to 'golden' daffodils), or a number of early versions of importantly revised *Lyrical Ballads.*[14] In other instances—notably *Peter Bell, The Ruined Cottage,* and *The Prelude*—he even prints manuscript versions, because the time between original composition and publication is so great. But what, then, of Wordsworth's impact on his contemporaries?

The implicit aesthetic dimension of Gill's editorial rationale is suggested by another passage in the 'Note on the Text'. The 1849–50 edition is 'most unsatisfactory', writes Gill, because 'many poems have been considerably revised from their first

---

[13] See Gill, *Life,* 471 n. 79; also W. J. B. Owen, 'Costs, Sales, and Profits of Longman's Editions of Wordsworth', *Library,* 12 (1957), 93–107. Gill contrasts Wordsworth's sales with those of Byron, whose *Corsair* (1814) sold 25,000 copies in little over a month, and Scott, whose *Lord of the Isles* (1815) sold 1800 quartos in the first month of publication. (As such footnotes attest, though I take issue with Stephen Gill's editorial rationale for the Oxford Authors Wordsworth, like all students of the poet I am deeply indebted to Gill's scholarship, as biographer, critic, and bibliographer.)

[14] For debate about the aesthetic merits of the different versions of 'Resolution and Independence', see Curtis, *Wordsworth's Experiments,* 112–13. For an interesting account of the significance of the change from 'Ode' to 'Ode: Intimations of Immortality', see Peter J. Manning, 'Wordsworth's Intimations Ode and its Epigraphs', in *Reading Romantics: Texts and Contexts* (Oxford: Oxford University Press, 1991), 68–84.

published state, altered moreover not in one creative burst of revision, but at various times throughout Wordsworth's life-time'.[15] In other words, periodic and deliberated revisions are somehow less likely to be creative than those that come in a burst: poetic power and spontaneity or imagination go hand in hand, even in secondary or cognitive processes of creation, such as revision, a belief with obvious connections to the privileging of earlier over later versions.

That Wordsworth himself played a vital role in propagating such views—in championing the so-called primary-process claims of originality, spontaneity, authenticity, inspiration—is a central irony of the recent history of his texts. Wordsworth's account of the poetical process is no simple, single thing: he had almost as much to say about 'labour', 'judgement', 'finish', 'poetical pains', the necessity of having 'thought long and hard', as about 'powerful feelings' or 'unelaborated expression'. But in literary historical terms the Wordsworth who is remembered is the Wordsworth of 'spontaneous overflow', of verses 'written at a heat', 'fresh from the brain', 'piping hot', and free of any merely 'mechanical' adoption of tropes or figures.[16] In bibliographical circles, the influence of this Wordsworth has only recently, in the last fifteen or so years, held sway. Earlier, the Wordsworth who mattered to textual critics was the Wordsworth of author-ized versions, the careful reviser who wondered whether 'such thoughts as arise in the process of composition should be expressed in the first words that offer themselves, as being likely

---

[15] *William Wordsworth*, ed. Gill, p. xxx. Aesthetic reasons figure more openly in Gill's Landmarks of World Literature study, *William Wordsworth: 'The Prelude'* (Cambridge: Cambridge University Press, 1991), which discusses the 1805 version because 'it is poetically the finest version, Wordsworth in 1805 declared the poem finished, and [the poem] needs to be read in the form it took when the greatest of the Romantic poets was at the height of his powers' (p. 6).

[16] For references to 'labour' and 'poetical pains' see letter to Thomas de Quincey of 19 Mar. 1804, in *EY*, ed. Shaver, 458; for 'finish' see the recollections of Justice Coleridge in *The Prose Works of William Wordsworth*, ed. Alexander B. Grosart, 3 vols. (London: E. Moxon, Son, & Co., 1876), iii. 429; for thinking 'long and hard', 'powerful feelings', 'uninterrupted expression', 'spontaneous overflow', and 'mechanical' composition, see the preface to *Lyrical Ballads*, in *The Prose Works of William Wordsworth*, ed. W. J. B. Owen and Janet Smyser, 3 vols. (Oxford: Clarendon Press, 1974), i. 124–7; for verses 'written at a heat', see letter to Samuel Rogers of 30 July 1830, in *LY*, ed. Hill, ii. 309; for 'fresh from the brain', see letter to Dorothy Wordsworth of 8 Nov. 1830, ibid. ii. 340; for 'piping hot', see letter to Benjamin Haydon of 11 June 1831, ibid. ii. 396.

to be most energetic and natural', and then concluded that 'it is frequently true of second words as of second thoughts, that they are the best'.[17] For followers of the authorized Wordsworth, such as Edward Dowden, in his influential seven-volume edition of 1892/3, 'the latest text is the best text'.[18]

The move away from Dowden's view—from what might be called Wordsworth's practice as opposed to his theory—is most clearly marked in the opening words of the preface to Jonathan Wordsworth's 1969 critical and textual study of *The Ruined Cottage*, entitled *The Music of Humanity*. 'On the whole', writes Jonathan Wordsworth, in what looks like an allusion to Dowden, 'poets are known by the best versions of their works: Wordsworth is almost exclusively known by the worst.'[19] Today, this judgement—echoed, for example, in Stephen Maxfield Parrish's introduction to the Cornell Wordsworth editions, with its talk of 'the original, often the best, versions'—prevails among Wordsworth's editors, so that, as Jack Stillinger puts it in a powerful 'revisionist' article of 1990, 'the later Wordsworth is being forced out of the picture, and a kind of textual primitivism has taken hold, that in effect is burying, possibly forever, some of Wordsworth's most admired writing'.[20]

---

[17] Letter of 22 Dec. 1814, to R. P. Gillies, in *MY*, ed. Moorman and Hill, ii. 178.

[18] As quoted in Stephen Gill, 'Wordsworth's Poems: The Question of Text', *Review of English Studies*, 34 (May 1983), 179.

[19] Jonathan Wordsworth, *The Music of Humanity: A Critical Study of Wordsworth's 'Ruined Cottage' Incorporating Texts from a Manuscript of 1799–1800* (New York: Harper & Row, 1969), p. xiii. More recently Jonathan Wordsworth has become something of a pluralist (rather than a primitivist) in relation to *The Prelude*. See 'Revision as Making: *The Prelude* and its Peers', in Keith Hanley and Robert Brinkley (eds.), *Romantic Revisions* (Cambridge: Cambridge University Press, 1992), 18–42.

[20] Jack Stillinger, 'Textual Primitivism and the Editing of Wordsworth', *Studies in Romanticism*, 28/1 (Spring 1989), 4. A slightly expanded version of this article appears as ch. 3 of Stillinger's *Multiple Authorship and the Myth of Solitary Genius* (New York: Oxford University Press, 1991), 69–95. One sign of how widespread or pervasive the new consensus has become is the following introductory note to Peter J. Manning's 'Cleansing the Images: Wordsworth, Rome and the Rise of Historicism', in *Texas Studies in Literature and Language*, 73/2 (Summer 1991), 272: 'Because Wordsworth's participation in a cultural debate rather than the aesthetic merits of individual works is the theme of this essay,' announces Manning, one of the most sophisticated and sympathetic of late Wordsworth's readers, 'I have approached his poems through the collections he carefully planned and have treated the original notes as integral parts of the volumes'—the implication being, in part, that otherwise Manning might have read the works in earlier, unrevised, aesthetically more satisfying versions.

As I have been suggesting, Wordsworth himself helps sanction these changes—the Wordsworth whose theories of poetical power and natural virtue, in M. H. Abrams's words, 'may in all fairness be classified as a form . . . of cultural primitivism',[21] the Wordsworth for whom 'the child is father of the man'. It might even be argued—in effect, has been, by Jerome McGann—that a more general bibliographical primitivism, in which earliest is best, is also indebted to Wordsworth, or at least to the Romantic Ideology with which he is so centrally associated. When, for example, current bibliographical scholars privilege manuscripts over first editions, invariably attributing discrepancies to editorial interference, the 'practical experience' they cite in defence of these attributions is seen by McGann as coloured by unacknowledged 'Romantic' notions of poetical autonomy.[22]

THE CORNELL WORDSWORTH

Chief among the textual primitivists to whose procedures Stillinger objects are the editors of the magisterial Cornell Wordsworth, a projected twenty-volume edition which aims to supplant Ernest de Selincourt's five-volume *Poetical Works* (1941–9, revised with Helen Darbishire, 1952–9). Parrish, the series co-editor, lays out its aims in a half-page introduction at the front of each volume. It is here that he writes of recovering 'the original, often the best, versions' as the edition's first objective, quoting de Selincourt on the 'obsessive' nature of Wordsworth's revisions, and then identifying as a second, historical objective the presentation of 'a complete and accurate record of variant readings'. The resulting format of the edition is uniform: an 'original' or earliest version is designated as

[21] M. H. Abrams, *The Mirror and the Lamp: Romantic Theory and the Critical Tradition* (New York: Oxford University Press, 1953), 105.

[22] Jerome J. McGann, *A Critique of Modern Textual Criticism* (Chicago: University of Chicago Press, 1983), 40. The 'practical experience' McGann questions (with obvious respect) is that of Fredson Bowers in 'Some Principles for Scholarly Editions of Nineteenth-Century American Authors', repr. in O. M. Brack and Warner Barnes, *Bibliography and Textual Criticism* (Chicago: University of Chicago Press, 1969), 197–8. For an extreme instance of its application see Hershel Parker's account of the revision of works by Twain, James, Crane, and other American writers in *Flawed Texts and Verbal Icons: Literary Authority in American Fiction* (Evanston, Ill.: Northwestern University Press, 1984).

'reading text', even in cases of the most famous later versions, and variant readings are relegated to an *apparatus criticus*, though the 'most important variants are shown in full transcription, and photographs of the manuscript pages are also provided'. The Cornell edition is thus something of a mirror image of de Selincourt's five-volume *Poetical Works*, in which it is *early* readings that are relegated to the *apparatus*. When Stillinger complains of the loss—or 'burial'—of later versions in the Cornell edition ('some of Wordsworth's most admired verse'), he sounds like Parrish, in an early defence of the Cornell series, complaining of the 'lamentable loss . . . of whole poems that has resulted from Wordsworth's efforts coupled with de Selincourt's decision to reduce early readings to an apparatus'.[23]

Stillinger's disapproval extends to other aspects of the Cornell Wordsworth. In its annotation of facing-page editions such as John E. Jordan's *Peter Bell* volume, it is the left-hand or earlier version which receives the bulk of the annotation, in effect being treated as the main text, while the later version is treated 'as a variant having inferior status'.[24] This arrangement doubly incenses Stillinger in the case of *Peter Bell* because the 'main' or left-hand text, dated 1799, is not only in manuscript form, but is a conflation of two different manuscripts, an editorial construct. The right-hand text, moreover, is that of the *earliest* published edition of 1819, and there are no subsequent transcriptions and facing photographs. 'Later versions', writes Stillinger, 'are available *only* via the apparatus readings.'[25] As in the case of other volumes in the series, not only are Wordsworth's latest revisions ignored here, but unpublished versions are given the status of completed works, even though, as Stillinger sensibly comments (with *The Ruined Cottage* specifically in mind), 'it is doubtful . . . whether the poet himself considered any version complete before the printed text'.[26]

That the Cornell Wordsworth editors have grown nervous in the face of such criticism is suggested by an essay Parrish published in 1988 in *Text*, entitled 'The Whig Interpretation of Literature'. This essay, Parrish reveals, was originally titled 'Textual Ethics: or, the Morality of Reconstruction', and its aim

---

[23] Stephen Maxfield Parrish, 'The Worst of Wordsworth', *The Wordsworth Circle*, 7/2 (Spring 1976), 90.   [24] Stillinger, 'Textual Primitivism', 16.
[25] Ibid. 17.   [26] Ibid. 16.

is to 'justify putting together scraps and pieces of paper that the writer himself never finished or fully assembled'.[27] This it does by attacking a view of composition—the titular 'Whig' view—that sees all rejected drafts and discarded variants 'as false starts, misjudgments', mistaken versions 'happily rectified' on the road to a work's 'final form', which represents the poet's 'final intention' (pp. 344–5). What is wrong with this view, says Parrish, is that it falsifies a truth familiar to 'all teachers of writing': that 'language is prior to thought'. One consequence of this sense of the relation between language and thought is that 'intention becomes not only elusive and illusory, but irrelevant' (p. 345). These 'truths' are then linked, no less fashionably, to history:

The poet's 'final intention' chronologically supersedes his earlier intention, but for the historian not blinkered by literary bias the earlier 'intentions' will command independent interest, especially as they reveal the poet's persistent struggle to redefine, and perhaps even to understand, his purposes. That is, the language of early versions, especially when these versions are complete, will be valued not for what it contributed to the late versions, not as a step in an inevitably flowing design, but for its own sake, as an achievement separate from the later history of the text (p. 345).

Let us leave aside for a moment the matter of language as prior to thought—since Parrish himself, like everyone else who says this sort of thing, goes on to behave as if it isn't; as if 'intention' in general, which he has just called 'not only elusive and illusory, but irrelevant', could also 'command . . . interest'. It is the phrase 'for its own sake' that most strikes me in this context, since Parrish has so far presented himself as a value-free historian. Even granted the word 'achievement' (by which Parrish presumably means an intention-free accident of language, the linguistic equivalent of some natural beauty or wonder), how can each version be of value to a historian 'for its own sake'? It can only do so if the historian values something in addition to history, or the story of a work's development (whether progressive or retrograde); if she or he values the work for aesthetic reasons. This is true even if the value of

[27] Stephen M. Parrish, 'The Whig Interpretation of Literature', *Text*, 4 (1988), 343. Further references will be given by page numbers accompanying the citations.

separate versions is said to be what each tells us of Wordsworth at a given moment in his literary career.

At which point, on the page that follows, Parrish turns to what in his Cornell introduction he presents as the primary purpose of the series. In addition to preserving 'the rich profusion of variant texts' (p. 345), bringing 'into view what we call the "early Wordsworth"', the Cornell editors 'even ventured, somewhat warily, to pronounce this as "often" a better Wordsworth than the "late Wordsworth" and generally more interesting' (p. 346). By using the word 'often', we now learn, the editors were equivocating: 'not always, not even usually, but "often"' (p. 346). Despite the note of defensiveness here, Parrish is prepared to stand by this judgement, on two grounds: ' "often" we can confidently say that the early Wordsworth was a better poet than the late Wordsworth, for the plain reason that he was closer to the sources of his inspiration and less inhibited by the various orthodoxies—poetical, religious, and political—that he succumbed to in his later years' (p. 346).

Neither of these grounds seem to me self-evidently or uncomplicatedly true. On the matter of Wordsworth's gathering orthodoxy, most critics agree; as they do on its deleterious effects on his verse. But as we shall see when we come to look at specific revisions, particularly of *The Prelude* (the ultimate source, according to Stillinger, of the current primitivist consensus), the record is mixed.[28] As Philip Horne puts it, in introductory remarks about Wordsworth in his study of Henry James's revisions, 'it is likely that every revision will be felt progressive according to some criteria and retrograde according to others. More beautiful may be less vigorous; more intelligible less suggestive; more vivid less impartial.'[29]

As for the matter of Wordsworth's closeness to the sources of his inspiration, is this not a species of Romantic Ideology? One thinks of Lionel Trilling's justly famous reading of 'Ode: Intimations of Immortality': on the one hand, the lost 'visionary

[28] 'Historically', claims Stillinger, 'it is argument over *The Prelude* ... that has led to the more general textual and critical predicament I am concerned with' ('Textual Primitivism', 4). Stillinger provides a useful chronological summary of this argument on pp. 6–12. For an amusing recent manifestation see 'Waiting for the Palfreys: The Great *Prelude* Debate', *The Wordsworth Circle*, 17/1 (Winter 1986), 2–38.

[29] Philip Horne, *Henry James and Revision* (Oxford: Clarendon Press, 1990), 29.

gleam', in 'Whither is fled the visionary gleam? | Where is it now, the glory and the dream?' (ll. 56–7), is admitted by Trilling as essential to poetic power; on the other hand, it is not synonymous with it. In the Ode, writes Trilling,

Wordsworth is talking about something common to us all, the development of the sense of reality. To have once had the visionary gleam of the perfect union of the self and the universe is essential to and definitive of our human nature, and it is in that sense connected with the making of poetry. But the visionary gleam is not in itself the poetry-making power, and its diminution is right and inevitable.[30]

If by 'closeness to the sources of his inspiration', Parrish means to his youth or childhood, that time 'when meadow, grove, and stream | The earth, and every common sight, | To me did seem | Apparelled in celestial light' (ll. 1–4), then this is not, obviously, the time when he was capable of writing a poem such as 'Ode: Intimations of Immortality'. That time comes with the growth of 'the philosophic mind' mentioned in the poem's penultimate stanza, in which, as Trilling puts it, by 'philosophic' Wordsworth 'does not mean abstract . . . and does not mean apathetic'.

Wordsworth is not saying, and it is sentimental and unimaginative of us to say, that he has become less a feeling man and less a poet. He is only saying that he has become less a youth . . . [M]echanical and simple notions of the mind, and of the poetic process are all too tempting to those who speculate on Wordsworth's decline.[31]

Though some may find Trilling's sense of Freud as prophet of maturity itself 'sentimental and unimaginative', or balk at the certitude of a phrase such as 'right and inevitable', as this reading suggests, there is no necessary reason why poetry written 'closer' to the sources of Wordsworth's inspiration should be any better than poetry written 'further' from it, particularly when we are talking—as is often the case with variant readings—of very short distances in time.

   'The Whig Interpretation of Literature' is not Parrish's only defence of the Cornell Wordsworth. In fact, it is itself something

---

[30] Lionel Trilling, 'The Immortality Ode', in *The Liberal Imagination: Essays on Literature and Society* (New York: Viking Press, 1950), 148.
[31] Trilling, 'The Immortality Ode', 151.

of a revision: of an article published in 1983 entitled 'The Editor as Archeologist', itself a revision and expansion of an article of 1976 entitled 'The Worst of Wordsworth'. In all three articles the procedures of the Cornell edition are defended, arguments and illustrations (about Wordsworth's anxiety as an author) are repeated. But as a comparison of the titles suggests, early Parrish is bolder—more vivid, and thus less judicious-seeming—than late Parrish. Here there is no pussy-footing about: 'the aging Wordsworth failed to serve himself well'; the Cornell edition promises 'to make it possible at last to know the best of Wordsworth'.[32] Six or so years later, in 'The Editor as Archeologist', his second defence, Parrish has begun to trim: 'The poems that were composed by the youthful revolutionary Romantic seem to our modern taste, at least, better than the poems composed by the aging Victorian, the Tory humanist'; 'There can be no doubt that a good deal of Wordsworth's revisionary labor improved details of his verse. . . . But [such improvements] are the exception not the rule' (despite the 'good deal' of labour involved). This second defence stresses the virtue of historical immediacy, 'the passion and the pathos' of early Wordsworth, and in doing so mutes exclusively aesthetic criteria. What the Cornell edition is now said to be after is 'the real Wordsworth, the early Wordsworth, generally the best Wordsworth'.[33]

Let us suppose now that one has been asked to compile an anthology of essays by prominent editors and textual scholars. The principles of textual criticism are a hot topic, a useful way of grounding currently fashionable theoretical issues. What one is after are representative and influential accounts of editorial procedures, and some contribution from or about a project such as the Cornell Wordsworth ought to be included. Which of Parrish's defences does one choose? To include all three would be impossible. There won't be room (there's all that Jerome McGann to get in, not to mention controversy over *King Lear*) and, besides, the essays perform essentially the same function, though the later versions are increasingly balanced, moderate, concessional. In the 1988 version, Parrish devotes

---

[32] Parrish, 'The Worst of Wordsworth', 89, 91.
[33] Stephen Maxfield Parrish, 'The Editor as Archeologist', *Kentucky Review*, 4 (1983), 6, 12, 14.

half his essay's pages to a careful consideration of specific 'ethical' dilemmas faced by the Cornell editors, and in his defence of early versions questions of aesthetic value take second place both to historical considerations and to a theory of Wordsworth's texts, first voiced in the middle, 1983, defence, as unstable, 'a continuum, stretching over the poet's lifetime, terminated only by his descent into the grave'.[34] If, however, it is a *representative* document one is after, a perfect example of late-1970s textual primitivism, of secure, unselfconscious Romantic Ideology, then the 1976 version is best. Parrish himself, presumably, would favour the latest defence. Why else would he have revised the two earlier versions? But he would hardly have grounds for complaint, given his own editorial practice, if we decided that the early Parrish is the best Parrish, the real Parrish.

THE TEXT AS CONTINUUM

In both the 1983 and 1988 defences Parrish offers a theory of the Wordsworthian text as a 'continuum'. Because Wordsworth revised so obsessively, after as well as before publication, his text (or 'texts') can never be considered fixed or stable. Though in his earliest account of the Cornell edition, Parrish seemed to imply that the selection of reading texts was mostly a matter of aesthetic judgement, in the 1983 and 1988 essays—the latter in particular—what is emphasized is their relative stability. After reluctantly admitting in the 1988 essay to a 'rash' preference for early Wordsworth, and drawing attention to the equivocating 'often' in the edition's general introduction, Parrish proceeds:

In any event, we carried out our resolve by drawing up what we call Reading Texts to show the way a poem stood at a given stage of work on it. These are not, I should emphasize, efforts to create poems out of fragments. Rather, they represent something like a vertical slice cut through the continuum of text for a given poem. The slice is cut where the poet reached a stopping-place in his work, and it is generally based on a fair copy drawn up at that point by the poet or his household of amanuenses.[35]

---

[34] Ibid. 10.
[35] Parrish, 'The Whig Interpretation of Literature', 346.

Parrish conjectures a psychological motive for the obsessive rewriting that produces 'texts' of this sort. As he puts it in the 1983 article: 'After the age of 35 or 40 [Wordsworth's] creative powers began slowly to fade. . . . As he aged, his anxieties about his poems intensified, and he kept on compulsively putting in and taking out, right to the end.'[36] This is the view also of Stephen Gill, in his biography and elsewhere, for whom 'Wordsworth's revision was compulsive and . . . always brought him illness, fatigue, and sleepless nights.' But Gill also offers a potentially non-psychological interpretation of Wordsworth's behaviour, one which connects with Parrish's sense of the text as continuum: 'To republish a poem without first subjecting it to rewriting', writes Gill, 'would be to concede that it had reached a final form. But Wordsworth could not bear the idea of finality.'[37]

Fixity and finality are out of favour in modern theory and criticism, and the reluctance of both Coleridge and De Quincey to finish their works has recently been interpreted along post-structuralist (Heideggerian and Derridean) lines as a matter of principle or philosophical honesty rather than—or, at least, in addition to—personal psychology.[38] Fixity falsifies both the subject and the object. Once one realizes the inevitable inadequacies of representation, process takes precedence over product, energy over form. These are views manifest in the practice of both writers, it is claimed, and something like them may be reflected in Wordsworth's compulsive revision. Though Gill and Parrish only very vaguely suggest as much, others are more explicit. Jonathan Arac, for example, takes issue with conventional accounts of the shape of *The Prelude* by claiming that the poem simply stops rather than closing harmoniously and that its narrative structure is purposely discontinuous—that Wordsworth's revisions consciously highlight interruption, dislocation, intermediacy, frustration. Wordsworth may at first, in his plans for *The Recluse*, have intended to ' "Assume the station of a man in mental repose . . . whose principles were made

---

[36] Parrish, 'The Editor as Archeologist', 7.
[37] Gill, *Life*, 191.
[38] For Coleridge see Edward Kessler, *Coleridge's Metaphors of Being* (Princeton: Princeton University Press, 1979); for De Quincey, see Edmund Baxter, *De Quincey's Art of Autobiography* (Edinburgh: Edinburgh University Press, 1990).

up . . . prepared to deliver upon authority a system of philosophy," . . . [but he] never achieved such grounding and was therefore unwilling to "assume" it. He recognized that his life as a
poet depended upon disturbance, "shock" and "surprise," however moderated; if he could speak "upon authority," it was
derived not from the stability of truth but from the lability of
moments in which the world slipped away.'[39]

Arac quotes several passages in support of this view. 'Our
destiny, our nature, and our home', we learn in Book VI of *The
Prelude*, is not only with 'infinitude' and 'hope that can never
die', but with 'Effort, and expectation, and desire, | And some-
thing evermore about to be' (VI. 538–42, 1805 edition). 'Not
favoured spots alone, but the whole Earth,' Wordsworth proclaims of the early revolutionary period, in Book XI of *The
Prelude*,

> The beauty wore of promise—that which sets
> (As at some moments might not be unfelt
> Among the bowers of Paradise itself)
> The budding rose above the rose full blown   (1850, XI. 117–21)

To these examples one might add the phrase 'lifeless as a written
book', also from *The Prelude* (1805, VIII. 727), which equates
visionary deadness with fixed form.

Arac connects such passages to the following unpublished
fragment relating to *The Prelude*:

> Along the mazes of this song I go
> As inward motions of the wandering thought
> Lead me, or outward circumstance impels.
> Thus do I urge a never-ending way
> Year after year, with many a sleep between,
> Through joy and sorrow . . .[40]

To Arac, these lines are determined and heroic, in the manner
of 'Resolution and Independence', just as Wordsworth's perpetual rewriting is noble not neurotic, evidence not only of
'continuing liveliness of response' but of a principled refusal to

---

[39] Jonathan Arac, 'Bounding Lines: *The Prelude* and Critical Revision', *Boundary 2*, 7/3 (Spring 1979), 37. An expanded version of this essay, contextualizing
rival readings, appears in Arac's *Critical Genealogies: Historical Situations for
Postmodern Literary Studies* (New York: Columbia University Press, 1987), 57–80.
[40] Printed in *Poetical Works*, ed. de Selincourt and Darbishire, v. 347.

settle for false finality or 'closure'. 'If *The Prelude* fulfills the ambition it expresses,' Arac himself concludes, 'it is not because it has reached its goal but rather because intervening accident had intervened, because the means had become the end.'[41] This is similar to the conclusion of another recent student of Wordsworth's revisions, Susan J. Wolfson, whose account of the various versions of the 'Drowned Man of Esthwaite' episode of *The Prelude*—or rather, of its various contextualizations— also champions indeterminacy. 'Once a specter shape can be given a definite form,' she writes, both of the Drowned Man and of other figures and instances of distress and anxiety in Wordsworth,

as if stabilized into a literary artifact, the life of the imagination, which works with motion, mystery, and ferment, dies: mastery is death. But as the play of Wordsworth's revision shows, mastery is an illusion that dissolves inevitably into the mystery that is life. Revision is synonymous with the energy that postpones death, quickening the imagination with a sense of unknown, limitless possibility.[42]

What links such arguments to the current editorial consensus about Wordsworth's texts is their indifference to authorial experience and intention. Wordsworth's revisions are said to evidence a truth about writing or language or representation; this truth, though, hardly deflected Wordsworth from the goal of mastery or perfection, or the attempt to come as close to it as possible. That such an attempt was difficult, the goal elusive, was not to say that the poet's job was indeed 'never-ending', or

---

[41] Arac, '*The Prelude* and Critical Revision', 40.

[42] Susan J. Wolfson, 'The Illusion of Mastery: Wordsworth's Revisions of "The Drowned Man of Esthwaite", 1799, 1805, 1850', *PMLA* 99 (1984), 917–35. For another influential reading of the 'Drowned Man' revisions, see Peter J. Manning, 'Reading Wordsworth's Revisions: Othello and the Drowned Man', in *Reading Romantics*, 87–114. Both essays originated as contributions to a 1981 MLA convention panel entitled 'Wordsworth's Revisions and Wordsworthian Revisionism: The Case of the Drowned Man'—a veritable indeterminacist breeding-ground. The organizer of the panel was Gene W. Ruoff, Arac was the respondent, and among the other speakers were Theresa M. Kelley, whose contribution was incorporated, in modified form, into *Wordsworth's Revisionary Aesthetics* (Cambridge: Cambridge University Press, 1988), and Clifford R. Siskin, whose contribution became part of ch. 5 of *The Historicity of Romantic Discourse* (New York: Oxford University Press, 1988), 114–24, having previously appeared as 'Revision Romanticized: A Study in Literary Change', *Romanticism Past and Present*, 7/2 (Summer 1983), 1–16.

that experiences of perfection or satisfaction were impossible. In 1827, while at work on revisions for the five-volume third collected edition of *Poems*, Wordsworth composed the following sonnet, a typically mixed late effort which takes its opening lines from Cowper's *Task*:

> *There is a pleasure in poetic pains*
> *Which only Poets know;*—'twas rightly said;
> Whom could the Muses else allow to tread
> Their smoothest paths, to wear their lightest chains?
> When happiest fancy has inspired the strains,
> How oft the malice of one luckless word
> Pursues the enthusiast to the social board,
> Haunts him belated on the silent plains!
> Yet he repines not, if his thoughts stand clear,
> At last, of hindrances and obscurity,
> Fresh as the star that crowns the brow of morn;
> Bright, speckless, as a softly-moulded tear
> The moment it has left the virgin's eye,
> Or rain-drop lingering on the pointed thorn.

There is much to deplore here, in particular a bland poeticality light-years removed from the awkward, inward-looking blank verse of the 1805 *Prelude* (as, for instance, in its discussion, at the end of Book V, of how 'forms and substances . . . | . . . | . . . through the turnings intricate of verse, | Present themselves as objects recognized, | In flashes, and with a glory scarce their own,' ll. 625–9). It is hard not to blanch—hard even for someone sceptical about the 'early is best' consensus—at the prospect of this later Wordsworth dutifully 'correcting' and 'emending' youthful infelicities.

Yet the sonnet has its virtues, particularly in the sestet (dewy-eyed virgin notwithstanding). The octave introduces the theme of perfectionism with its reference to 'the malice of one luckless word', a phrase which to some might suggest the inevitable inadequacies of language or representation, impossible perfection. The sestet, on the other hand, not only imagines but enacts this perfection, or at least the feeling of its triumphant discovery. When the maliciously elusive word, obsessively pursued from 'social board' to 'silent plains', stands revealed, free 'At last, of hindrances and obscurity', pleasurable sensations of recognition are realized in the poem's best and final image: that of the 'rain-drop lingering on the pointed thorn'. Meaning, precision, control can often seem hopelessly elusive in Wordsworth, but their attainment is no necessary (either in the sense of inevitable or enabling) illusion.

Nor is perfection of form the aim only of a later, 'unspontaneous' Wordsworth. Consider, for instance, the following fragment of verse found in an autograph manuscript of *Peter Bell*, dated between 1798 and 1800. Wordsworth's subject is the difference between private effusions and true or finished composition:

> . . . I burst forth
> In verse which, with a strong and random light
> Touching an object in its prominent parts,
> Created a memorial which to me
> Was all sufficient, and, to my mind
> Recalling the whole picture, seemed to speak
> An universal language: Scattering thus
> In passion many a desultory sound,
> I deemed that I had adequately clothed
> Meanings at which I hardly hinted, thought
> And forms of which I scarcely had produced
> A monument and arbitrary sign.

What is missing from such verse, the manuscript continues after a break, is

> . . . that considerate and laborious work
> That patience which, admitting no neglect,
> By slow creation, doth impart to speach
> Outline and substance even, till it has given
> A function kindred to organic power,
> The vital spirit of a perfect form.[43]

Once again, the concluding line enacts or performs the process of creative discovery which is the verse's subject: it presents the laboriously sought-for 'perfect form' much as Milton, after a half-dozen lines of Satan's tangled, enjambed searching, discloses Eve, 'Veiled in a cloud of fragrance, where she stood' (*Paradise Lost*, 9. 425).

Revision, I am suggesting, was only rarely seen by Wordsworth

[43] Quoted in *The Prelude*, ed. Ernest de Selincourt, 2nd edn., rev. Helen Darbishire (Oxford: Clarendon Press, 1959), p. lvi n. 1.

as 'never-ending'. Though obsessive, its purpose was for the most part straightforward: the end of Wordsworth's efforts, he knew, would come with death, and he wished to be judged by the accomplishments—the final authorized versions—of his lifetime. Where Wordsworth differs from many other poets is in his refusal, with rare exceptions, to recognize earlier work as the work of an earlier self, insisting instead on 'affinities preserved | Between all stages of the life of man',[44] and constantly returning to the past to test and confirm personal identity. 'So was it when my life began,' he writes in 1802 in 'My Heart Leaps Up', 'So is it now I am a Man; | So be it when I shall grow old.' It is Wordsworth's wish, the poem concludes, that his days—that is, the stages of his life—'be bound each to each'. In like manner, in the concluding sonnet of the 1820 *River Duddon* sequence, thoughts of the River, the 'partner' and 'guide' with which his life is identified, 'as being past away', provoke immediate defiance: 'As I cast my eyes, | I see what was, and is, and will abide.' Though the sonnet accepts the fact of death, this death will be redeemed, not by any abstract 'energy' or 'continuing liveliness of response', but by a thing made:

> We Men, who in our morn of youth defied
> The elements, must vanish;—be it so.
> Enough if something from our hands has power
> To live, and act, and serve the future hour.

It is this sense of poetry as a thing made, suggested by the phrase 'from our hands', that suits ill with contemporary notions of writing as process. When Wordsworth says his way is 'never-ending', he need not mean that he thinks his works will have no fixed or final form, only that that form cannot be known until his death. When he revises a poem he does so not out of indifference to—or to repudiate—the intentions of a former self, but to assert his identity with that self. Because that self is still felt as, or needs to be felt as, *this* self, his present self, revision is no violation. When Gill complains of revised versions that they have been altered 'not in one creative burst of revision, but at various times throughout Wordsworth's life', he is implying a vision of personal identity—as the sum of a series

---

[44] Verse related to 'Michael', printed in *Poetical Works*, ed. de Selincourt and Darbishire, ii. 481.

of discrete, successive selves—that Wordsworth consistently denied. Though Arac and Wolfson are right to draw attention to the various ways *The Prelude*, in all its incarnations, resists narrative closure and cohesion, what they (and Herbert Lindenberger and Walter Pater before them) have identified in the poem is a counter-spirit not a controlling-spirit. That this counter-spirit is so prominent or pronounced is a mark of the poem's rigour; its insistence upon pattern and sense, upon the shapeliness of return and recovery, is earned. Wordsworth demands the maximum control and coherence, even as he admits everything possible that might stand in their way. He differs from De Quincey and Coleridge in always taking responsibility for his texts, even while experiencing and expressing a sense of lack of control comparable to their own.

Hence Wordsworth's insistence on a mostly thematic rather than chronological ordering of his poems in collected editions— another manifestation of his sense of the self as single and unified. 'He clearly had a strong sense of the book', writes Gill, and from 1815 onwards the presentation of his shorter poems was designed to 'assist the attentive reader in perceiving their connections with each other'. Not only did he tinker with the larger categories into which his poems were grouped—some psychological, some determined by subject or occasion or form— and with the placing of individual poems, moving them from category to category, but he also paid special attention to the ordering of poems within categories, aiming 'to make one poem smooth the way for another. . . . Miscellaneous poems ought not to be jumbled together at *random* . . . one poem should shade off happily into another.'[45] Though ostensibly what he disapproved of about chronology was its immodesty (he detected

---

[45] Gill, 'Wordsworth's Poems: The Question of Text', 174–5. The phrases Gill quotes from Wordsworth come from a letter to H. Crabb Robinson of 6 Apr. 1826, from which come the subsequent quotations. See *LY*, ed. Hill, i. 440. Wordsworth returns to these issues in a subsequent letter to Crabb Robinson of 27 Apr. 1826, ibid. 444. For an interesting account of Wordsworth's ordering of *Lyrical Ballads*, and its relation to the ordering of other influential volumes of Romantic verse, see Neal Fraistat, *The Poem and the Book: Interpreting Collections of Romantic Poetry* (Chapel Hill, NC: University of North Carolina Press, 1985), especially pp. 47–94. For a discussion of Wordsworth's various orderings of his collected volumes, including especially the ordering of 'Miscellaneous Sonnets', see Alan Liu, *Wordsworth: The Sense of History* (Stanford: Stanford University Press, 1989), 485–99, 505–9, 641 n. 43.

offensive egotism in such arrangements),[46] he also simply—
egotistically? defensively?—denied its relevance. 'No change',
he claimed in 1843, 'has taken place in my manner for the last
45 years';[47] and even those single broad chronological distinctions he was prepared to countenance—between pre-Alfoxden
(that is, pre-1797–8) juvenilia, which he either left unpublished
or identified variously as 'Written in Youth' or 'Early' (as in
Poems Chiefly Early and Late) and what came after—were
muddied by extensive revision, as if even across this divide he
saw, or wanted to see, affinities. As for the autobiographical
Prelude, it too, it has been argued, works against chronology:
beginning where it ends, structured by 'spots of time' each
reiterating the same ineffable insight. 'There is no real progres-
sion in *The Prelude*,' writes Lindenberger, 'but only restatements
of the poet's efforts to transcend the confines of the temporal
order.'[48] These efforts, I am suggesting, underlie the revision
process as well, which for the most part should be seen as
Wordsworth's way of asserting continuity, defying time, putting
to the proof the all-too-precarious-sounding affirmations—'for
such loss, I would believe, | Abundant recompense' from 'Tintern
Abbey' (ll. 87–8), 'I feel—I feel it all,' from 'Ode: Intimations
of Immortality' (l. 41)—with which he braves fears of loss.

Such defiance also helps to account for the figurative language Wordsworth uses to describe his *œuvre*. Again, what is
suggested is something single, created, built; the relations between works are spatial rather than temporal, as in the previously cited reference to *The Prelude*, in a letter of 1805, as 'a
sort of portico to the Recluse, part of the same building', or the
related, though more elaborate, architectural simile in the preface to *The Excursion* (1814), in which *The Prelude* and *The
Recluse* are said not only to 'have the same relation to each

---

[46] According to evidence cited by Edward Dowden in the preface to his *Poetical
Works of William Wordsworth*, 7 vols. (London: George Bell & Sons, 1892–3).
For example: '"I remember being surprised", writes the Rev. R. P. Graves, "by the
feeling akin to indignation which Wordsworth manifested at the suggestion [of a
chronological arrangement of his poems]. He said that such proceeding would
indicate on the part of the poet an amount of egotism, placing interest in himself
above interest in the subjects treated by him"' (i, p. xi).

[47] Quoted in *Poetical Works*, ed. de Selincourt and Darbishire, i, p. vii.

[48] Herbert Lindenberger, *On Wordsworth's 'Prelude'* (Princeton: Princeton University Press, 1963), 188.

other . . . as the ante-chapel has to the body of a Gothic church,'
but his 'minor pieces, which have long been before the
public . . . have such a connexion with the main work as may
give them claim to be likened to the little cells, oratories, and
sepulchral recesses, ordinarily included in those edifices.'[49] In
1842, in the 'Prelude, Prefixed to the Volume Entitled *Poems
Chiefly of Early and Late Years*', this architectural metaphor
gives way to a more social or organic metaphor (though of all
architectural forms, the Gothic cathedral is the most 'organic',
the least monolithic, in its growth), but again there is the same
stress on individual works as interconnected, unified. 'Go single,' he addresses the volume,

> . . . yet aspiring to be joined
> With thy forerunners that through many a year
> Have faithfully prepared each other's way. (ll. 17–19)

REVISION AS IMPOSITION

What puts the lie to, or at least complicates, such assertions of
continuity is the evidence of the poetry itself—by which is meant
its explicit preoccupation with imaginative growth and loss,
rather than actual deterioration or decline. 'I cannot paint |
What then I was,' Wordsworth declares in 'Tintern Abbey' (ll.
75–6), 'That time is past' (l. 83). 'The things which I have seen
I now can see no more,' he declares in 'Ode: Intimations of
Immortality', in a line which knowledge of its earlier incarnation ('The things which I have seen I see them now no more')
might be thought to second, given what Philip Horne calls its
aptly 'broken statement of immediate fact, with its redundant
but affecting "them"'.[50] 'The days gone by,' we learn in Book
XI of the 1805 *Prelude*,

> Come back upon me from the dawn almost
> Of life: the hiding-places of my power
> Seem open; I approach, and then they close;

---

[49] See letter of 3 June 1805 to Sir George Beaumont, in *EY*, ed. Shaver, 594; for
the preface to *The Excursion* (1814) see *Prose Works*, ed. Owen and Smyser, iii.
5–6.
[50] Horne, *Henry James and Revision*, 27.

> I see by glimpses now; when age comes on,
> May scarcely see at all.   (XL. 334–8)

The revision of these lines is difficult to read as self-fulfilling prophecy. When Wordsworth changes 'the hiding-places of my power | Seem open: I approach, and then they close' to 'the hiding-places of man's power | Open, I would approach them, but they close,' it might be argued that drama and immediacy give way to a generalizing correctness—from 'my' power to 'man's' power, from 'approach' to 'would approach' (though 'open', as opposed to 'would open', moves the other way); but these changes hardly 'prove' Wordsworth's fears. What is interesting and characteristic about this revision is that the anxieties of the original, of a poet in his mid-30s (the lines do not, of course, appear in the 1799 manuscript), are both identified with, or reimagined, *and* subtly modified (in particular by the changes from 'my' to 'man's'). The older, revising poet continues to see himself in the earlier poet—even when that earlier poet doubts his (that is, the revising poet's) powers; he is merely bringing into focus, clarifying, an original meaning or intention, not altering or denying it.

This sort of revision, in which 'affinities' are preserved, is characteristically Wordsworthian. Though there are instances in which Wordsworth seems to be repudiating past work, or altering it to fit changed circumstances or standards—as in certain passages of *The Prelude* or the recasting of 'The Ruined Cottage' manuscript of 1799 for Book I of *The Excursion*[51]— for the most part the revisions respect original meanings and effects even when they seem to be serving new ones. For example, in a letter of 1801 to Anne Taylor, Wordsworth details a rationale for revision of *The Female Vagrant* which Stephen Gill characterizes as imposition. Wordsworth sent Anne Taylor his list of revisions to *The Female Vagrant* 'because that poem, he said, did not conform to the principle he had laid down in the Preface that he had "at all times endeavoured to look steadily at my subject." Here his practice is revealed. *The Female*

---

[51] For defences of the revisions of 'The Ruined Cottage', see Peter J. Manning, 'Wordsworth, Margaret, and The Pedlar', in *Reading Romantics*, 9–37, and Philip Cohen, 'Narrative and Persuasion in *The Ruined Cottage*', *Journal of Narrative Technique*, 8 (1978), 185–99.

Vagrant, an early poem, is to be revised into supposed conformity with a principle Wordsworth had not articulated when he originally wrote it. And this was his usual practice.'[52]

This example is complicated. To call *The Female Vagrant* 'an early poem' is, in this context, somewhat misleading. In 1793/4 Wordsworth composed a poem he called 'Salisbury Plain'. Within the next few years this poem had been altered, expanded, and retitled 'Adventures on Salisbury Plain'. Neither of these versions was ever published, though, and it was not until 1841 that Wordsworth returned to the manuscripts, revised the material again, and published it in 1842, under the title *Guilt and Sorrow; or Incidents upon Salisbury Plain*. *The Female Vagrant*, first published in 1798 in the *Lyrical Ballads*, was a version of parts of the initially revised 'Adventures' (stanzas 226–324, 352–94). It is these stanzas—this poem—about which Wordsworth writes to Anne Taylor in 1801.

Wordsworth introduces the revisions by openly admitting that there are important differences between his early and late poems. *Descriptive Sketches* and *An Evening Walk*, both published in 1793, 'are juvenile productions, inflated and obscure', he tells her, but 'they would perhaps interest you, by showing how very widely different my former opinions must have been from those which I hold at present'. He concurs with—is flattered by—Miss Taylor's description of his present style as 'distinguished by a genuine simplicity', and claims to have attained this simplicity 'solely by endeavouring to look, as I have said in my preface, steadily at my subject'. He then offers *The Female Vagrant*, which he calls the 'first written' of the *Lyrical Ballads*, as an example of inferior early work: 'The diction of that poem is often vicious, and the descriptions are often false giving proofs of a mind inattentive to the true nature of the subject on which it was employed.' Wordsworth at this point offers his corrections, designed 'to bring the language nearer to truth'.[53]

I take issue with Gill when he suggests that the aim of these revisions was 'supposed conformity with a principle Wordsworth had not articulated when he originally wrote [*The Female*

---

[52] Gill, *Life*, 191.
[53] Letter of 9 Apr. 1801 to Anne Taylor, in *EY*, ed. Shaver, 327–8.

Vagrant]'. To begin with, though most of its lines do indeed come from the early 1790s, *The Female Vagrant* does not exist as a separate poem until 1798, when it was 'created' (out of the earlier manuscripts) as such. Second, though Wordsworth's phrase about endeavouring 'to look steadily at my subject' comes from the 1800 preface to the second edition, there is little question that the 1798 first edition was animated by just this aim. In the advertisement to the first edition Wordsworth warns his readers not to 'suffer the solitary word Poetry, a word of very disputed meaning, to stand in the way of their gratification; but that, while they are perusing this book, they should ask themselves if it contains a natural delineation of human passions, human characters, and human incidents'[54]—that is, the sort of delineation possible only for a mind free of 'false' refinement and attentive 'to the true nature of the subject'.

The Female Vagrant, like the manuscript poems from which it derives, aims in part to make us 'look steadily' at what we might otherwise overlook or look away from, perhaps out of a sense of false refinement. The importance of looking behind the ordered façade of English society, of looking directly at figures of suffering such as the female vagrant, accounts in part for the direction of the revisions, which Gill, in his Cornell edition of the poems, characterizes (uncharacteristically) as revealing 'the progress of a great mind from indebtedness of various kinds to the more original exercise of its powers'[55] (though he still prints the original 1793/4 version in his Oxford Authors edition). Though the Salisbury Plain poems owe much to an eighteenth-century tradition of 'pathetic' poetry, the poetry of human suffering, or what Wordsworth himself characterized to Coleridge, apropos of the 'Adventures' revisions, as 'pretty moving accident[s]',[56] even in the early 1790s Wordsworth laid great stress on the importance of the thing seen.

Consider a second figure of female suffering, encountered by Wordsworth in Book IX of *The Prelude*, during the poet's first residence in France in 1791. After a passage in which Wordsworth recalls what might be termed the 'Romantic' hold ancient

---

[54] See *Prose Works*, ed. Owen and Smyser, i. 116.
[55] *The Salisbury Plain Poems of William Wordsworth*, ed. Stephen Gill (Ithaca, NY: Cornell University Press, 1975), 16.
[56] Letter of 27 Feb. 1799 to Samuel Taylor Coleridge, in *EY*, ed. Shaver, 256–7.

buildings had over him at the time, their power to 'mitigate the force | Of inner prejudice, the bigotry, | So call it, of a youthful patriot's mind' (1805, IX. 498–500) by stimulating or 'inflaming' his imagination with dreams of chivalry, he and his friend Beaupuy

>   . . . chanced
> One day to meet a hunger-bitten girl
> Who crept along fitting her languid self
> Unto a heifer's motion, by a cord
> Tied to her arm, and picking thus from the lane
> Its sustenance, while the girl with her two hands
> Was busy knitting in a heartless mood
> Of solitude, and at the sight my friend
> In agitation said, ''Tis against *that*
> Which we are fighting' . . . (ll. 510–19)

'*That.*' In other words, '*Look*'; as opposed to dream, or, as in the few lines that follow his talk of dreaming, reason (as Wordsworth reasons himself back to 'hatred of absolute rule' by line 503). Look as steadily as possible at the object. Let its actual properties—the cord tied to the arm, the languid movement—register. This sense of a thing—a person—looked at, or seen, is for the most part reinforced by subsequent revision. The 'languid self' becomes a 'languid gait', for it is more particularly the gait one sees as languid; 'her two hands' become 'two lean hands', then 'pallid hands'. In some manuscripts, the powerful ''Tis against *that* | Which we are fighting' becomes 'There it is, there | That which we fight against,' an awkward variant but one if anything *more* committed to the importance of the thing seen, looked at steadily, than the lines it might have replaced.[57] The whole episode, of course, was only turned into poetry after 1800, but the attitudes and experiences it describes are meant to derive from a period before any of the Salisbury Plain manuscripts. Though it is impossible to be certain that Wordsworth's

---

[57] The manuscript variants are identified in *The Prelude*, ed. de Selincourt, rev. edn. Darbishire, 340–1. Paul D. Sheats, in *The Making of Wordsworth's Poetry, 1785–1798* (Cambridge, Mass.: Harvard University Press, 1973), 85, has also noted the resemblance between the Salisbury Plain poems and this episode from Book IX of *The Prelude*: 'The explicit mode of the poem', he writes of the 1793–4 version, 'may be described as an indignant realism . . . [Wordsworth's] spirit is Beaupuy's: "it is against *that* | Which we are fighting"' (p. 85).

actual experience of the hunger-bitten girl in 1791 was as he depicted it in Book IX, if it was, then it would be inaccurate to imply of the proposed 1801 revisions to *The Female Vagrant* that they were occasioned by new principles. Here, too, revision would be a matter not of new intentions imposed on old ones, but of an attempt to ensure the latter's—the original's—more precise and powerful realization.

REVISION AND THE THEME OF RETURN

Wordsworth's textual revisions are for the most part continuous with—conform to—his treatment of the theme of return or re-vision in the poetry, for here too, and not only in the most famous poems, such as *The Prelude* and 'Ode: Intimations of Immortality', his concern is unity or continuity, asserted in the face of loss and difference. 'Wordsworth never relinquished anything that had really mattered to him,' writes Gill in his biography, 'the memory of a place, a few lines of poetry, a friendship.'[58] But the poetry is neither ahistorical nor delusional: it admits, unlike occasional moments of bland defiance in the letters, that time has passed and things change. Consider, for example, the following lines from Book II of *The Prelude*:

> Of all mankind, who does not sometimes wish
> For things which cannot be, who would not give,
> If so he might, to duty and to truth
> The eagerness of infantine desire?
> A tranquillizing spirit presses now
> On my corporeal frame: so wide appears
> The vacancy between me and those days,
> Which yet have such self-presence in my mind
> That, sometimes, when I think of them, I seem
> Two consciousnesses, conscious of myself
> And of some other Being . . .   (1805, ll. 23–33)

This passage both does and does not relinquish past strength. What Wordsworth wishes for are 'things which cannot be', by which he means, as the 1850 revision makes clear; 'union which cannot be' (l. 24), or union with past strength. *The Prelude* is an attempt to re-establish contact with—to regain the ardour

---

[58] Gill, *Life*, 205.

of—a past self, one unencumbered by the 'tranquillizing spirit' of adulthood. On the one hand, Wordsworth admits a wide gap or 'vacancy' between youthful eagerness and adult dutifulness, on the other hand, 'those days I . . . have such self-presence in my mind I That, sometimes . . . I seem I Two consciousnesses, conscious of myself I And of some other being.' Here, the youth and the adult are united, but also separate; the youthful poet lives on in the older poet, yet they are two separate beings or consciousnesses as much as one.

A similar doubleness appears later in *The Prelude*, in a comparably well-known passage, from Book IV, a passage occasioned by a new self-consciousness in the young Wordsworth. Wordsworth describes his youthful, Cambridge self as overcome by a new pensiveness, in which apprehensions of the sublime—'scatterings I Of awe or tremulous dread' (1850, ll. 252–3)—give way to something less fierce, 'yearnings of a love I Enthusiastic, to delight and hope' (ll. 254–5). The change is felt as a loss, but only obliquely or implicitly, and is immediately followed—in a familiar gesture of compensation—by a passage in which Wordsworth reflects on the activity of recollection:

> As one who hangs down-bending from the side
> Of a slow-moving boat, upon the breast
> Of a still water, solacing himself
> With such discoveries as his eye can make
> Beneath him in the bottom of the deep,
> Sees many beauteous sights—weeds, fishes, flowers,
> Grots, pebbles, roots of trees, and fancies more,
> Yet often is perplexed and cannot part
> The shadow from the substance, rocks and sky,
> Mountains and clouds, reflected in the depth
> Of the clear flood, from things which there abide
> In their true dwelling; now is crossed by gleam
> Of his own image, by a sunbeam now,
> And wavering motions sent he knows not whence,
> Impediments that make his task more sweet;
> Such pleasant office have we long pursued
> Incumbent o'er the surface of past time
> With like success, nor often have appeared
> Shapes fairer or less doubtfully discovered
> Than these to which the Tale, indulgent Friend!
> Would now direct thy notice   (1850, IV. 256–76)

Here again, past self and present self are simultaneously inter-
twined and independent. That the attempt to discern a past self
is impeded by the present self is less a source of irritation to
Wordsworth than of pleasure. When 'things which there abide'
(that is, in the past, 'the bottom of the deep') are 'crossed by
gleam | Of his own image' (that is, by a present self), as well as
by other 'impediments', this interference or complication only
makes the task of recollection or re-envisioning 'more sweet', a
'pleasant office'. The very process of return effects the sought-
for unity, even as it acknowledges difference.

This is precisely what happens in Wordsworth's textual revi-
sions, where 'the days gone by | Come back', as he puts it in
Book XI (1805), lines 334–5 (lines already discussed), and while
yet he can—that is, before 'age comes on' (l. 338)—he seeks to
'give, | . . . as far as words can give, | A substance and a life to
what I feel: | . . . would enshrine the spirit of the past | For
future restoration' (ll. 339–43). What Wordsworth means here
by 'restoration', according to Philip Horne, is activity of two
sorts: 'probably of *him*, poetry as a restoration, but it may also
refer to his rehandling of *it*, the poet as restorer of his poems'.[59]
The act of revision, when entered into in the spirit here specified, maintains unity of identity even as it also acknowledges
differences—acknowledges, for example, that what early
Wordsworth meant by 'things which cannot be', but for some
reason did not or could not specify, was 'union that cannot be'.
Of course, it is impossible to tell for certain if the sense of unity
expressed in such passages, the pleasurable or untroubled lay-
ering of past and present 'selves', is ultimately *constructed* in
the act of writing rather than reconstructed—just as the 'truth'
of psychoanalytic narrative may be merely the analysand's
willingness to claim, and subsequently to inhabit, a certain story
about the self as true. 'Seem', in the passage from Book II (l.
31), keeps this possibility open. But mostly Wordsworth shows
little inclination to see or depict experiences of unity as mere
'unity effects', present creations only—or even to entertain the
possibility.

Return, or re-vision, is, of course, an important literal as well
as literary feature of Wordsworth's life: his adulthood was

---

[59] Horne, *Henry James and Revision*, 28.

almost as full of revisitings as rewritings. To begin with (ex-
cepting the July 1798 Wye Valley revisit), there was the crucial,
liberating return to his childhood home in the Lake District in
November 1798, after the period in Goslar in Germany with
Coleridge and Dorothy. In Goslar, the newly reunited Wordsworth and Dorothy were isolated by bad weather, ill health,
and lack of German, and consequently retreated into a world
of shared memories. The result was a flood of poetry about
childhood experiences, including the earliest *Prelude* passages.
Gill calls Wordsworth's subsequent—consequent?—return to
the Lake District 'the fulfilment of a schoolboy dream, a resumption of continuity with an earlier self', and cites Dorothy's
recollection of John Wordsworth, William's beloved sailor
brother, the 'never-resting Pilgrim of the Sea', 'exulting within
his noble heart that his father's children had once again a home
together'.⁶⁰ As for lesser returns, a representative example is
Wordsworth's retracing in 1820 of his formative 1790 walking
tour of the Alps. From the 1790 tour came not only *Descriptive
Sketches* (1793), but the experiences recounted in the climactic
Simplon Pass episode in Book VI of *The Prelude*. Robert Jones,
Wordsworth's original companion on the tour, was prevented
from joining the 1820 retracing by parish duties and poor health,
but perfectly understood—and shared—its aims. 'It would have
been a singular and memorable incident in our lives', Jones
wrote to Wordsworth on 23 February 1821, 'to have gone over
the same ground together after an interval of thirty years.' What
the absent Jones was particularly keen to know from Wordsworth—'whether the things you saw in Switzerland in 1820
brought to your recollection sometimes . . . the objects which
you saw with far different eyes in 1790'⁶¹—Wordsworth was
himself keen to know, though he would have demurred at 'far
different eyes'. Whatever the answer, though, the result, as in
other such returns, would be poetry—as Wordsworth well knew.
The 1820 retracing, like the 1798 return to Grasmere, was partly
undertaken to recharge poetical batteries, to produce new work,

---

⁶⁰ Gill, *Life*, 180, 183. The description of John Wordsworth as 'Pilgrim of the
Sea' comes from *Home at Grasmere*, MS B, l. 866, ed. Beth Darlington (Ithaca,
NY: Cornell University Press, 1977), 381. Dorothy's recollection can be found in
a letter to Lady Beaumont of 29 Nov. 1805, in *EY*, ed. Shaver, 649.
⁶¹ Quoted by Gill, *Life*, 338, from a letter in the Wordsworth Library in Grasmere.

and the consequent *Memorials of a Tour on the Continent* (1822) was not unexpected.

One measure of the importance the theme or fact of return had for Wordsworth is the often unexpected or oddly intrusive prominence he gives it in his poetry. Consider 'Nutting', for example, which was written in Goslar in 1798 and included in the second edition of the *Lyrical Ballads*. It is not enough for Wordsworth to record an unexpected moment of violence in the poem, the episode must be thrown into retrospect, so that the speaker's (and reader's) attention is diverted at the poem's conclusion to Wordsworth's wondering whether 'I now | Confound my present feelings with the past' (ll. 48–9), and to the familiar assertion—qualified, as in all Wordsworth's best poems—of personal continuity, of 'even then' (a phrase from an earlier draft) feeling what now he feels (in this case, 'a sense of pain', l. 52). That 'Nutting' was originally intended as part of *The Prelude* hardly invalidates this reading: Wordsworth was perfectly at liberty to alter the poem before its incarnation as a separate work in *Lyrical Ballads*. Or consider an instance from *The Prelude* itself, its account of London in Book VII. This account opens with a phrase ('Five years are vanished since', which becomes 'Six changeful years' in revision) that recalls the opening lines of 'Tintern Abbey', the most famous Wordsworthian instance of literal re-visioning ('Once Again | Do I behold') leading to speculation about personal identity, loss, the continuity of personality. Immediately, London itself, Book VII's nominal concern, takes second place—or shares billing with—just such speculation; the poem's present—its account of 'Residence in London'—is of interest as much for its connection with the past, and thus with the nature of the poet's identity, as for its own qualities.

Nowhere is the connection between literal return and literary return, by which is meant thematic return as well as revision proper, clearer than in the case of Wordsworth's three poems on the River Yarrow.[62] In 1803, during their walking tour of

---

[62] Among less obvious literary 'returns' one might mention 'Resolution and Independence', which, it has been argued, returns to the themes of such earlier poems as 'The Sailor's Mother' (also 1802) and 'A Narrow Girdle of Rough Stones and Crags' (1800); or 'Ode, Composed Upon an Evening of Extraordinary Splendour and Beauty' (1820), which even more clearly returns to 'Ode: Intimations of

Scotland, Wordsworth and Dorothy came close to visiting the River Yarrow but never did. Wordsworth composed a poem about this near miss, entitled 'Yarrow Unvisited', which was published in 1807. When he finally did visit the river in 1814, with his wife Mary and James Hogg, among others, Wordsworth immediately composed a second poem, 'Yarrow Visited', characteristically devoted almost as much to the discrepancy between imagined (or past) and actual (or present) reality as to the present reality itself. It begins,

> And is this—Yarrow?—*This* the stream
> Of which my fancy cherished,
> So faithfully, a waking dream?
> An image that hath perished!

Similarly, when Wordsworth recalls this poem, and the circumstances of its composition, in the Fenwick Notes (themselves, of course, a form of return or re-vision), the pleasure he imagines Dorothy Wordsworth would have taken in the 1814 visit, were she present, is predominately recollective: 'I seldom read or think of this poem', Wordsworth declares of 'Yarrow Visited', 'without regretting that my dear Sister was not of the party, as she would have had so much delight in recalling the time when, travelling together in Scotland, we declined going in search of this celebrated stream.'[63] When the stream itself is

---

Immortality'. For 'Resolution and Independence' as a 'revision' of 'The Sailor's Mother' see Parrish, *The Art of 'Lyrical Ballads'* (Cambridge, Mass.: Harvard University Press, 1973), 213–21; for its relation to 'A Narrow Girdle' see Peter J. Manning, '"My Former Thoughts Returned": Wordsworth's "Resolution and Independence"', *The Wordsworth Circle*, 9 (1978), 398–400; also Gene W. Ruoff, *Wordsworth and Coleridge: The Making of the Major Lyrics, 1802–1804* (New Brunswick, NJ: Rutgers University Press, 1989), 111–19, 135–6.

[63] Quoted in *Poetical Works*, ed. de Selincourt and Darbishire, iii. 451. The Fenwick Notes were dictated to Isabella Fenwick by Wordsworth in 1842 and 1843 and detail 'the origin and composition of his poems'. The idea for these notes first came to Wordsworth in 1841, once again in the course of a return—to Alfoxden. 'He pointed out the spots where he had written many of his early poems,' Fenwick recalls, 'and told us how they had been suggested.' Over the winter of 1842/3 they 'were augmented by whatever he could recollect that seemed worth recording about the poetry from Hawkshead days to the present'. Stephen Gill, from whom these quotations derive, thinks the notes 'need to be read alongside *The Prelude* and with *Biographia Literaria* in mind. They matter because they are a great poet's last attempt at what has been his lifelong endeavour—to record, interpret, and harmonize disparate experience' (see *Life*, 408–9).

finally, directly encountered, the pleasure it affords derives in part from recollection:

> I see—but not by sight alone,
>   Loved Yarrow, have I won thee;
> A ray of fancy still survives—
>   Her sunshine plays upon thee! (ll. 73–6)

As in cases of revision proper, thematic return knits past to present (past 'fancy' to present actuality), asserts unity and continuity in the face of difference.

Finally, in 1831, Wordsworth saw Yarrow a second time, travelling with his daughter Dora to visit Sir Walter Scott at Abbotsford, and the result was 'Yarrow Revisited', published in 1835. Here the theme of continuity, of preserved affinities, is explicitly sounded in several ways. The poem begins by noting a 'gallant Youth' (l. 1) who 'Was but an Infant in the lap | When first I looked on Yarrow' (ll. 3–4). It then immediately throws the present visit into the past: 'Once more, by Newark's Castle-gate | . . . | I stood, looked, listened' (ll. 5–7), so that all subsequent description is recollective—recollective, moreover, of recollections, as in 'We made a day of happy hours, | Our happy days recalling' (ll. 23–4). Recalling in the poem functions as a counterweight to loss and ageing, themes struck not only by the juxtaposition in stanza 1 of Scott's presence on the trip (and Scott, as we shall see, stands for Wordsworth) with that of the 'gallant Youth', and with an immediately subsequent reference to 'sere leaves' (l. 12), but by more explicit lines to follow:

> Brisk Youth appeared, the Morn of youth,
>   With freaks of graceful folly,—
> Life's temperate Noon, her sober Eve,
>   Her Night not melancholy;
> Past, present, future all appeared
>   In harmony united,
> Like guests that meet, and some from far,
>   By cordial love invited.
>
> And if, as Yarrow, through the woods
>   And down the meadow ranging,
> Did meet me with unaltered face,
>   Though we were changed and changing;

> If, *then*, some natural shadows spread
> Our inward prospect over,
> The soul's deep valley was not slow
> Its brightness to recover. (ll. 25–40)

It is through revisiting or recollection that 'Morn', 'Noon', 'Eve', and 'Night' can be seen as connected, that 'Past, present, future, all appeared | In harmony united'; it is revisiting or recollection that allows Wordsworth to register continuities in the midst of loss, as in the phrase about Yarrow 'with unaltered face, | Though we were changed and changing'. Loss is inevitable: the shadows that spread over 'our' inward prospect are 'natural'; but that inward prospect—our soul—is also 'deep' (the figurative language grows a bit complicated here), as if filled with restorative memories, the sort capable of allowing the soul 'Its brightness to recover'.

In the lines that follow, Wordsworth implies a close connection between recollection and the poetical faculty. The Muse brings 'hope and calm enjoyment' (l. 44) in the face of 'sickness' (l. 45), just as memories of Yarrow, inspired by the revisit, bring 'brightness' in the face of 'natural shadows', the 'changed and changing'. 'Fancy', we later learn, like 'Memory', is a 'linking' (l. 54) faculty. Or more explicitly, four stanzas later:

> And what, for this frail world, were all
> That mortals do or suffer,
> Did no responsive harp, no pen,
> Memorial tribute offer? (ll. 81–4)

And later on, in lines that refer only in part to the effect of 'Romance' (l. 89):

> ... the visions of the past
> Sustain the heart in feeling
> Life as she is—our changeful Life,
> With friends and kindred dealing. (ll. 93–6)

Again, Wordsworth insists that recollection (already linked to 'fancy', and thus to 'Romance', the immediate sources of this stanza's 'visions of the past') is sustaining but not falsifying: 'visions of the past | Sustain the heart in feeling | Life as she is— our changeful Life'. And this is true also, I have been arguing, of most Wordsworthian textual revision. Both activities—literary revision proper and return or re-vision—are connected to poetry-making, both are restorative, establishing unity and continuity in the face of loss and change. This sense of imaginative or recollective power as redemptive is, as I have suggested, quite contrary to the bias of much recent criticism, whether deconstructive or new historicist, and was already being challenged in Geoffrey Hartman's *Wordworth's Poetry 1787–1814* (1964), with its stress on the imagination's dangers, its negativity;[64] but evidence for it—evidence that it was Wordsworth's view—is abundant. Wordsworth returns to his poems as he returns to the Yarrow or the Alps or Calais or London: to test his powers, while also attempting to confirm and test the integrity and continuity of the self. And in doing so, he is like Scott, whose novels explicitly attempt to reconcile history with created form, conferring a shape on inchoate change while also acknowledging such change. No two writers, for all the acuteness of their sense of discontinuity and contingency, more clearly exemplify Coleridge's account of the crucial meaning and function of return in narrative, and of the importance of the poet's or novelist's shaping power. As Coleridge puts it, in a letter of 7 March 1815, to Joseph Cottle, 'the common end of all *narrative*, nay of all, Poems is to convert a series into a *Whole*, to make those events which in real or imagined History move on a *strait* line, assume to our Understandings a *circular* motion—the snake with it's Tail in it's Mouth'.[65]

'Yarrow Revisited' concludes with an exhortation that the river 'Flow on forever' (l. 105), suggesting an image of time as flux. But immediately this image provokes a counter-image:

> Flow on forever, Yarrow Stream!
>   Fulfil thy pensive duty,
> Well pleased that future Bards should chant
>   For simple hearts thy beauty;
> To dream-light dear while yet unseen,
>   Dear to the common sunshine,
> And dearer still as now I feel,
>   To memory's shadowy moonshine! (ll. 105–12)

[64] See David Simpson, 'Criticism, Politics, and Style in Wordsworth's Poetry', *Critical Inquiry*, 2 (1984), 52–81.

[65] See *Collected Letters of Samuel Taylor Coleridge*, ed. E. L. Griggs, 6 vols. (Oxford: Oxford University Press, 1956–71), iv. 545.

In place of ceaseless linearity, or, rather, superimposed upon it, we have form, pattern, continuity. Yarrow remains 'dear' to the poet in all stages of his relation to it; the poet remains unchanged, as capable of registering the river as dear in 'memory' (that is, in his 60s, in a potentially diminished present), as in 'common sunshine' or reality (that of the first visit of 1814, when he was a middle-aged man of 44), or in fancy-rich youth, that time when he 'saw' the river only in 'dream-light'. Though a traditional symbol of change, of mutability, of history, for Wordsworth the river is also a token of personal integrity. This is a truth return discloses—or is meant to disclose—just as revision, conventionally conceived of as alteration, is for Wordsworth also a way of affirming continuity.

Such links—between return and revision, personal continuity or integrity and poetical power—are suggested also in the Fenwick Notes to 'Yarrow Revisited', which detail the circumstances of the poem's composition. In 1831, the year of Wordsworth's revisit, Sir Walter Scott was preparing a visit of his own, to Italy, via Malta. This visit, urged on him by his doctors, was for Scott a return to origins (the origins of romance, not only in Italy, the land of Tasso and Ariosto, but in Malta, with its obvious connections with the Crusades), as well as a testing, both of creative powers, and, as this was a first visit, of the relative strengths of the imagined and the real—an important theme of the Yarrow poems. On the eve of his departure for Italy, Scott complained in his diary of ill-health, mental fatigue, and a host of worries, including the expense of the coming journey: 'Yet these heavy burdens could be easily borne if I were to be the Walter Scott I once was—but the change is great.' By the time he got to Malta, his spirits had recovered: 'It will be hard if I cannot make something of this,' he declared before leaving for Italy itself.[66]

Wordsworth was 61 when he went to visit Scott on the eve of the latter's departure; Scott was 60. Wordsworth's visit, the Fenwick Notes tell us, had been delayed by illness, an inflammation of the eyes: 'I was then scarcely able to lift up my eyes to the light.' Scott himself, when finally encountered, was in

---

[66] Quoted in John Gibson Lockhart, *Memoirs of the Life of Sir Walter Scott*, 10 vols. (Boston: Houghton Mifflin, 1901), x. 85, 108.

even worse shape: 'How sadly changed did I find him from the
man I had seen so healthy, gay, and hopeful a few years before,
when he said at the inn at Paterdale, in my presence ... "I
mean to live till I am *eighty*, and shall write as long as I live."'
Scott's confidence at the Paterdale meeting made a deep impression on Wordsworth: 'I was startled and almost shocked at that
bold saying which could scarcely be uttered by such a man
sanguine as he was without a momentary forgetfulness of the
instability of human life'—a view Scott's present enfeebled state,
the product of a stroke, seemed only to corroborate.

Scott here, in the Fenwick Notes, resembles the leech-gatherer
of 'Resolution and Independence', an obvious example for, as
well as something of a projection of, Wordsworth himself. Like
the leech-gatherer, he is as much a figure of hope or resolution
as of decline. The impression is indirectly reinforced later in the
Notes when Wordsworth expresses sympathy and admiration
for Scott's son, Major Walter Scott, another figure of heroic
endurance, who 'had much to suffer from the sight of his
father's infirmities'. Like the leech-gatherer, the Major is
commended for his resolute demeanour: 'What struck me most
was the patient kindness with which he supported himself under the many fretful expressions that his sister Anne addressed
to him or uttered in his hearing.' This sister, Wordsworth tells
us, 'as mistress of that house [Abbotsford, which Scott was
about to lose], had been subject, after her mother's death, to a
heavier load of care and responsibility and greater sacrifice of
time than one of such a constitution of body and mind was able
to bear'. Both Wordsworth and his daughter came away from
Abbotsford with the apprehension 'that her brain would fail
and she would go out of her mind', a fate that might well have
suggested to the Wordsworth of the Fenwick Notes the fate of
Dorothy Wordsworth two years later, when she began a decline
into dementia.[67]

Wordsworth, I am suggesting, saw himself in Scott. 'These
two great poets', writes Lockhart in his *Life of Scott* (1837–8),
'who had through life loved each other well ... appreciated
each other's genius more justly than inferior spirits ever did.'[68]

[67] The Fenwick Note from which I have been quoting is found in *Poetical Works*,
ed. de Selincourt and Darbishire, iii. 524–6.
[68] Lockhart, *Memoirs of the Life of Sir Walter Scott*, x. 78.

When in the Fenwick Notes to 'Yarrow Revisited' Scott is described accompanying Wordsworth and his daughter to the Yarrow, Wordsworth notes the sick man's still 'stout' walk and his 'great pleasure in revisiting'. At the end of the description Wordsworth also recalls Scott's gallant gesture of transcribing a poem for Dora, which he did with great mechanical difficulty, calling it 'probably the last verses I shall write'. Wordsworth's sympathetic identification with Scott may help account for his description of the verses: 'They show how much his mind was impaired, not by the strain of thought but by the execution'— as if Wordsworth were pleading Scott's case. The Note ends by recounting Scott's behaviour in Italy, which recalls Wordsworth's own behaviour in Germany, the turn into himself and to the past. 'I heard from several quarters while abroad, both at Rome and elsewhere, that little seemed to interest him but what he could collect or heard of the fugitive Stuarts.' Scott's stay in Italy threw him back to previous work, as Wordsworth's stay in Germany had also involved a return of sorts. Wordsworth reports in Scott the same stubborn refusal to give up on an older (that is, 'younger') self—'the Walter Scott I once was'— as we have noted in Wordsworth himself. Finally, it should be mentioned that in 1831, Scott, as Wordsworth knew full well, was engaged in a massive revision of his novels for a new standard edition.[69] Thus, in both the Yarrow poems themselves and Wordsworth's account of the circumstances out of which they grew, in particular those involving Sir Walter Scott, the recollective impulse—the impulse also of return—is depicted as recuperative, creative, and integrative, precisely the qualities I have ascribed to Wordsworth's revising practice.

THE PRELUDE AND REVISION

The text to which Wordsworth's critics and editors point first in justifying both the privileging of earlier versions over later ones, and a conception of Wordsworth's revisionary practice as imposition, importation, betrayal, rather than refinement, recuperation, restoration, is, of course, *The Prelude*. From the time

---

[69] See letter of 7 June 1830 to Sir Walter Scott, in *LY*, ed. Hill, ii. 276–8.

of the poem's publication in 1850, three months after Wordsworth's death, from a manuscript 'left ready for the Press by
the Author',[70] to 1926, when de Selincourt first made public, in
a facing-text edition, the thirteen-book version Wordsworth
completed in 1805, *The Prelude* was known in its authorized
or 1850 version, the result of thirty-four years of painstaking
but intermittent revision, including three full-scale revisions (in
1816–19, 1832, and 1839) as well as numerous smaller alterations. Ultimately, these revisions involved nearly half of the 1805
version's 8000 or so lines.

The 1926 de Selincourt facing-page edition marks a key
moment in the relative fortunes of the two versions of *The
Prelude*, but its effect was hardly galvanic. It was not until
1970, round about the time Gill edited the first separately
published text of the 1805 version, that the earliest-is-best
consensus began fully to emerge. In 1979, Gill and Jonathan
Wordsworth, following along lines suggested by Helen
Darbishire and J. R. MacGillivray,[71] produced a text of a 1799
two-part *Prelude* for the third edition of the *Norton Anthology*.
This edition, though extremely useful to teachers of the sort of
undergraduate survey for which the *Norton Anthology* is intended, is none the less symptomatic of the larger 'predicament'
Stillinger deplores. (That the Norton's rival, the *Oxford Anthology*, edited by Harold Bloom and Lionel Trilling, excerpts
passages from the 1850 rather than the 1805 version, is but one
of several signs of its prevailing eccentricity or unorthodoxy;
typically—that is, unsystematically—it also publishes Jonathan
Wordsworth's reconstruction of 'The Ruined Cottage'.) In 1977,
Jonathan Wordsworth 'discovered' a five-book scheme of 1804,
though this revision, he admits, 'does not survive as a whole in
fair copy and cannot be printed, as can 1799 and 1805'.[72] Two

---

[70] This phrase comes from a letter by Wordsworth's brother, Christopher, to Joshua
Watson, on 14 June 1850 (Wordsworth died on 23 Apr.), as quoted in *The Prelude
1799, 1805, 1850*, ed. Jonathan Wordsworth, M. H. Abrams, and Stephen Gill
(New York: W. W. Norton, 1979), 539. Henceforward cited as the 'Norton *Prelude*'.

[71] See ibid. 512, which refers to Helen Darbishire's 'passing remark' of 1958 on
the writing of a two-part poem and then to J. R. MacGillivray's 'The Three Forms
of *The Prelude*' (1964), repr. in *Wordsworth, 'The Prelude': A Casebook*, ed. W. J.
Harvey and Richard Gravil (London: Macmillan, 1972), 99–115.

[72] Jonathan Wordsworth, 'The Five Book *Prelude* of Early Spring 1804', *Journal
of English and German Philology*, 76 (1977), 25. For a challenge to this article see
Robin Jarvis, 'The Five-Book *Prelude*: A Reconsideration', *Journal of English and
German Philology*, 80 (1981), 528–51.

years later, he, Gill, and M. H. Abrams published the Norton Critical Edition *Prelude*, a book of immense usefulness to advanced students and teachers, containing texts of the 1799, 1805, and 1850 versions. Stillinger also reports Mark Reed's forthcoming documentation of an 'intermediate' version of the poem from the period between 1805 and the 'final' text of the late 1830s, a version that also cannot be fair-copied but 'exists as a distinctive level of revision all through the thirteen books'.[73] Finally, and no doubt only partly to annoy, Jonathan Wordsworth claims to have uncovered sixteen separate pre-1850 drafts.[74]

De Selincourt is a key figure in this history not only for first printing the 1805 version, but for the strong, judiciously phrased stand he takes in the edition's introduction in favour of the earlier text. This stand encompasses both 'changes of idea' and 'changes of style'. 'When his poetry was commended for the purity of its morals', concludes the introduction, in a section on changes of idea, Wordsworth 'insisted that he, on the other hand, valued it according to the power of the mind which it presupposed in the writer and excited in the hearer. The work of his which most triumphantly stands this test belongs to the years 1798–1807; and of the vital source and hiding-places of its power the original *Prelude* is the frankest and most direct confession.' A similar conclusion is drawn about stylistic changes. 'Sincerity', de Selincourt argues, is 'the true Wordsworthian spirit'; in post-1805 revisions an 'anxiety to write up his poem, and give it a more definitely literary flavour creates in places the impression of pompous phrase-making'.[75]

These judgements have been much disputed, but in the present context they require only two comments in response. First, that many of even the most notorious of the poem's revisions can be understood—were understood by Wordsworth—as refinements, or recuperations of meaning, rather than as impositions or assertions of what Philip Horne calls '*new* self',[76] a more conservative and religious self in particular. Second, that the virtues

[73] Quoted in Stillinger, 'Textual Primitivism', 6. Details of this 'intermediate' version appear in Mark Reed's 1805 or *Thirteen-Book 'Prelude'* in the Cornell Edition, 2 vols. (Ithaca, NY: Cornell University Press, 1991), i. 62–89.

[74] According to Duncan Wu, 'Editing Intentions', *Essays in Criticism*, 41/1 (Jan. 1991), 3.

[75] *Prelude*, ed. de Selincourt, rev. edn. Darbishire, pp. lxii, xlix.

[76] Horne, *Henry James and Revision*, 30.

of many of Wordsworth's alterations have been undervalued. This is not to argue that the poem remains unchanged by revision, or that some revisions are not in the end impositions, merely that Wordsworth's aim or impulse was for the most part respectful of the material he revised. For example, the 1850 *Prelude* is frequently quarried for evidence of political apostasy, of ageing Tory overcoming or rewriting youthful radical. Chief among the passages cited in support of this view— it is the last and most 'significant'[77] of the examples offered by de Selincourt in his discussion of Wordsworth's changing attitudes to the French Revolution—is the insertion sometime in the 1820s in Book VII of a passage in praise of Edmund Burke (1850, ll. 512–43). But as James Chandler and others have argued, Wordsworth's attitudes to Burke, both in 1804 and earlier, were by no means solely negative.[78] De Selincourt himself concedes that Wordsworth could have written the Burke passage as early as 1804, and recalls that the stated 'theme' of the poem's account of the Revolution was 'juvenile errors' (1805, X. 638).[79]

Of the charge of political apostasy, Wordsworth was consistently scornful, and in terms which bear interestingly on his more general revisionary practice. 'I would think that I had lived to little purpose', he writes to his friend, the radical barrister James Losh in 1821,

if my notions on the subject of Government had undergone no modification—my youth must, in that case, have been without enthusiasm, and my manhood endued with small capacity of profiting by reflexion. If I were addressing those who have dealt so liberally with the words Renegade, Apostate etc. I would retort the charge upon them, and say, *you* have been deluded by Places and Persons, while I have stuck to Principles—I abandoned France, and her Rulers, when they abandoned the struggle for Liberty, gave themselves up to Tyranny, and endeavoured to enslave the world. I disapproved of the war against France at its commencement, thinking, which was perhaps an error, that it might have been avoided—but after Buonaparte had violated the Independence of Switzerland, my heart turned against him.[80]

[77] *Prelude*, ed. de Selincourt, rev. edn. Darbishire, p. lxviii.
[78] See James Chandler, *Wordsworth's Second Nature: A Study of the Poetry and Politics* (Chicago: University of Chicago Press, 1984). The 'Genius of Burke' passage is discussed by Chandler on pp. 25–8, 32–42.
[79] See *Prelude*, ed. de Selincourt, rev. edn. Darbishire, pp. lxv–lxviii.
[80] Letter of 4 Dec. 1821 to James Losh, in *LY*, ed. Hill, i. 97.

As in the ordering of his poetical works, Wordsworth is prepared to countenance a single broad change in political outlook: his early support of the Revolution is, in effect, bracketed
as 'juvenilia' ('juvenile errors'), and at much the same date—
sometime in the mid-1790s—that separates 'poems of youth'
from those of maturity.[81] Otherwise, Wordsworth insists on
continuity, an underlying coherence of purpose such as I have
argued motivates his revisions in general. For Wordsworth, the
Burke passage is a species of clarification by amplification rather
than correction, which in part explains its apologetic opening.
'Genius of Burke! forgive the pen seduced | By specious won-
ders, and too slow to tell' (1850, VII. 512–13)—as if to say, 'I
should, of course, have mentioned', or 'Obviously.' The in-
serted lines, Wordsworth seems to imply, might have been
deduced.

De Selincourt's objection to the Burke passage is as follows:
'Burke's oratory would, doubtless, have stirred the poet on his
visits to London in either 1791 or 1793, but it would have
stirred him to very different emotions from those which inspired the added lines.'[82] But is this true? As we have seen, even
in the midst of 'virtuous wrath and noble scorn' (1805, IX.
497)—a phrase of obvious irony—the 'juvenile' Wordsworth
could lapse into chivalric reverie. In 1791 he pockets a relic
from the fallen Bastille 'in the *guise* | Of an enthusiast' (1805,
IX. 66–7, my italics), 'Affecting more emotion than I felt' (l.
71). Nothing in revolutionary Paris moves him more than 'a
single painting' (l. 77), 'the Magdalene of Le Brun' (l. 78), the
power of which has nothing to do, he implies, with the times.
Even when most enthusiastic, Wordsworth 'rejoiced | Less than
might well befit my youth' (ll. 249–50). On his second visit to
Paris in October 1792, such rejoicing was further muted by the

[81] This is the view also of James K. Chandler, 'Wordsworth after Waterloo', in
Kenneth R. Johnston and Gene W. Ruoff (eds.), *The Age of William Wordsworth*
(New Brunswick, NJ: Rutgers University Press, 1987), 99. Chandler sees
Wordsworth's decision to publish *Peter Bell* in 1818 as the 'ultimate act of drama-
tizing the continuity he asserted in his thought and work' (p. 99): 'In the case of
Peter Bell,' he concludes, 'an older conservative poet goes out of his way to publish
a poem from what is thought to be his own early radical period, acknowledging
it as his own both by the constant attention he has given it and by saying as
much—as if to insist that, radical or otherwise in 1798, he had not undergone
significant change in his principles since then' (p. 100).
[82] *Prelude*, ed. de Selincourt, rev. edn. Darbishire, p. lxviii.

evidence of the September massacres, and in the account of his return to London at the end of the year he admits that political debate (specifically abolitionist debate) 'had ne'er | Fastened on my affections' (1805, X. 219–20). This is not to say that the Wordsworth of 1791 or 1793 was incapable of radical passion or had failed to consider the great issues of the day; one look at the 1793 *Letter to the Bishop of Llandaff*, written in part out of furious disappointment at Britain's joining of 'the confederated host' (1805, X. 229) in February 1793, would prove otherwise (though the *Letter* was neither finished nor published). It is only to suggest that Wordsworth was never—even when most radical—the sort of ideologue incapable of registering, for example, the power of Burke's anti-radical rhetoric. Was it indeed impossible, as de Selincourt claims, that to the Wordsworth of 1791 or 1793 Burke could be, as the 1850 passage suggests, impressive and inspiring? 'Could a youth,' Wordsworth asks, 'and one in ancient story versed, whose breast had heaved | Under the weight of classic eloquence, | Sit, see, and hear, unthankful, uninspired?' (1850, VII. 540–3).

This question, I am suggesting, is asked precisely to meet the context (in fact, 'contexts', given the differences between Wordsworth in 1791 and 1793) de Selincourt invokes; as if to say, 'even granted my radical sympathies, how could a young man such as I was—that is, of my education and background—not be moved and inspired not only by the power of Burke's "armour of resplendent words" (l. 539) but by his appeals to custom, common-sense (over upstart "Theory", l. 529), Englishness (Burke stands "like an oak", l. 520)?' It is, of course, possible that the subtly mixed or qualified portrait we are given in the 1805 *Prelude* of the politics of the young Wordsworth is inaccurate, already toned down, but those who suspect as much—Nicholas Roe, for instance—provide little in the way of corroborating evidence. Roe even fair-mindedly admits not only that Wordsworth's 'active commitment to political life was never so extensive or consistent as Coleridge's', but that he 'did not share his friend's sense of personal failing as a motive for disguising his revolutionary self; rather the reverse'.[83] In fact,

[83] Nicholas Roe, *Wordsworth and Coleridge: The Radical Years* (Oxford: Clarendon Press, 1988), 6. Certainly the poem's Victorian audience saw Wordsworth's radicalism clearly, even in the 1850 version. 'Wordsworth's narrative of his

Wordsworth is quite explicit about the importance of accurately recalling his past, even when he finds that past embarrassing. As he proclaims at the end of Book X,

> Through times of honour, and through times of shame,
> Have I descended, tracing faithfully
> The workings of a youthful mind, beneath
> The breath of great events, its hopes no less
> Than universal, and its boundless love— (1805, x. 940–5)

As for the evidence of Wordsworth's few surviving letters from the years 1791 to 1793, it is perfectly consistent with the portrait offered in *The Prelude*. Here, too, Wordsworth is capable of moments of indignation, but his sympathy for France or liberty is rarely more than an incidental feature in any letter, and often his tone neatly recalls the apolitical—tourist-like— wonder of his depiction in the poem. Writing to Dorothy in September 1790, Wordsworth comments on the good spirits of the French people: 'We had also perpetual occasion to observe that chearfulness and sprightliness for which the French have always been remarkable. But I must remind you that we crossed it at the time when the whole nation was mad with joy, in consequence of the revolution. It was a most interesting period to be in France, and we had many delightful scenes when the interest of the picture was owing solely to this cause.'[84] These are exactly the accents of the 'coasting' tourist of Book IX of the 1805 version, and they are sounded in the letters from the 1791/2 visit as well, although in these letters Wordsworth's tone is also at times wary and worldly—distant in a more sombre fashion.[85]

Still, even granted that the 'Genius of Burke' insertion misrepresents Wordsworth's feelings in 1791 or 1793—which I am arguing it need not—it hardly misrepresents Wordsworth's feelings in 1804. De Selincourt himself, as I have already noted, can imagine the passage being written in 1804, and even Chandler,

political odyssey', writes Stephen Gill of the poem's reception among Victorian readers, 'could not be absorbed without shock. Macaulay's "The poem is to the last degree Jacobinical, indeed Socialist," might have seemed overstated to some, but no one could ignore its core of truth' (*William Wordsworth: 'The Prelude'*, 95).

[84] Letter of 6 and 16 Sept. 1790 to Dorothy Wordsworth, in *EY*, ed. Shaver, 36.
[85] See letter of 18 Dec. 1791 to Richard Wordsworth, ibid. 70, and letter of 19 May 1792 to William Mathews, ibid. 77–8.

who cannot, claims that the poem 'is Burkean from the start', at the same time noting as 'a fact too often overlooked that when [Wordsworth] did write the tribute he thought it ideologically suited to the completed poem'.[86] This is a point—the central question of intention—with which de Selincourt concurs. Though to de Selincourt Wordsworth's revisions represent or effect political self-betrayal, apostasy, he imagines Wordsworth as unaware of their effect. Conservatism triumphs 'gradually, insensibly to himself'.[87]

The revisions of a religious nature—those which express a newly explicit orthodoxy—are somewhat harder to see as attempted amplifications or clarifications, though in some respects they do not directly contradict the views expressed in 1805. As Jonathan Wordsworth puts it, in the Norton *Prelude*: 'It is doubtful if [Wordsworth] ever rejected his pantheist or near-pantheist beliefs of 1798–1805. He came to see them, however, in a new context; and he became increasingly self-conscious about how such beliefs might seem to the orthodox.'[88] Seeing past beliefs 'in a new context' conforms to Wordsworth's practice in general. For example, in Book I of the 1805 *Prelude*, Wordsworth remembers how even at age 10,

> . . . even then,
> A child, I held unconscious intercourse
> With the eternal beauty, drinking in
> A pure organic pleasure from the lines
> Of curling mist, or from the level plain
> Of waters coloured by the steady clouds.   (I. 588–93)

In the 1850 version this becomes

> . . . even then
> I held unconscious intercourse with beauty
> Old as creation, drinking in a pure
> Organic pleasure . . .   (I. 561–4)

By substituting 'beauty | Old as creation' for 'the eternal beauty' Wordsworth, according to Jonathan Wordsworth, removes 'the possibility of transcendental interpretation', a possibility he sees

---

[86] Chandler, *Wordsworth's Second Nature*, 42.
[87] *Prelude*, ed. de Selincourt, rev. edn. Darbishire, p. lxvi.
[88] 'Norton *Prelude*', ed. Wordsworth, Abrams, Gill, 524 n.

as supported by MS. JJ, the earliest of the poem's manuscripts, drafted in Germany in October 1798, which he calls 'a short version of 1799, I, as a whole'.[89] But the lines to which Jonathan Wordsworth refers are complicated and might well be taken as support for the 1850 version. The relevant passage begins with Wordsworth hoping to paint not only

> How Nature by collateral interest
> And by extrinsic passion peopled first
> My mind with beauteous objects. (ll. 100-3)

but also how it performed a higher, more than merely aesthetic function, a task which

> ... might demand a loftier song,
> How oft the eternal spirit—he that has
> His life in unimaginable things,
> And he who painting what he is in all
> The visible imagery of all the worlds
> Is yet apparent chiefly as the soul
> Of our first sympathies ... (ll. 103-9)

Here 'Nature' (l. 100) is clearly distinguished from that 'eternal spirit' (l. 105)—a 'he' (l. 104)—who lives not only in 'unimaginable things' (l. 105), and in 'all | The visible imagery of all the worlds' (ll. 106-7), but who is 'chiefly' (l. 109) manifest 'as the soul | Of our first sympathies' (ll. 108-9). The passage sees what Wordsworth will later more comfortably call God *in* nature not *as* nature. When, therefore, Wordsworth changes 'the eternal beauty' of 1805 to 'beauty | Old as creation', he may be seeking more fully to realize an inadequately realized intention of 1805 rather than imposing a new meaning on the poem. The 1788 passage is as likely to support the 1850 revision as the more 'transcendental' 1805 version, since what 1805 lacks is precisely the distinction 1798 so carefully delineates. It is not true that only later Wordsworth distinguishes between divine source and earthly manifestation. 'Among the more awful scenes of the Alps,' he writes to Dorothy, in a letter of 1790, 'I had not a thought of man, or a single created being: my whole soul was turned to him who produced the terrible majesty before

[89] Ibid. 61 n., 485.

me.'[90] Nor is it sufficient to say that he never rejected his pantheist and near-pantheist beliefs of 1798–1805; one must also say that he was never fully comfortable with them.

Here is another example of only apparent imposition, at least from the perspective of MS. JJ. In 1805, Wordsworth asks his reader to

> . . . Wonder not
> If such my transports were; for in all things
> I saw one life, and felt that it was joy. (1805, II. 428–30)

In 1850, this becomes

> . . . Wonder not
> If high the transport, great the joy I felt,
> Communing in this sort through earth and heaven
> With every form of creature, as it looked
> Towards the Uncreated with a countenance
> Of adoration, with an eye of love. (1850, II. 409–13)

As in MS. JJ, Wordsworth is careful in the 1850 version to distinguish between 'creature' and 'Uncreated'. Yet as the 1850 version suggests, the joy he derives from 'every form of creature', itself derives from every creature's obvious devotion to God, the Uncreated; the Uncreated is detectable in the love of the created, which is what 'in all things | I saw one life' may be, less precisely, saying. What *is* troubling and new about the 1850 version, product of a late revision of 1839, is not so much its distinction between God and Nature, the 'Uncreated' and creation—a distinction I believe Wordsworth is newly punctilious about rather than newly aware of or accepting—as the 'countenance | Of adoration' with which creation turns to the creator. The note of abject piety here—the grovelling note—is a new one in Wordsworth, and sounded in other revisions. In 1805 man is called 'of all visible nature crown, and first | In capability' (VIII. 634–5); in 1850, after a revision of 1838/9, he is 'of all visible nature, crown, though born | Of dust, and kindred to the worm' (VIII. 487–8). In both versions, Wordsworth goes on to call man 'more than anything we know, instinct | With godhead' (1805, VIII. 638–9; 1850, VIII. 493–4), so in this instance the revision does not wholly negate the meaning of the original; but it offers a context for that meaning

---

[90] Letter of 6 and 16 Sept. 1790 to Dorothy Wordsworth, in *EY*, ed. Shaver, 36.

which is wholly new, alien to the Wordsworth not only of the 1790s but of 1805. In like manner, when 'The mind of man is framed even like the breath | And harmony of music' (1805, I. 352–3) becomes, in a revision dating from 1832, 'Dust as we are, the immortal spirit grows | Like harmony in music' (1850, I. 340–1), the change is imposition pure and simple. The pietistic note of abasement here is wholly foreign both to the 1805 version and to the version of 1799.

Such revisions are corrections, not clarifications. Though Wordsworth had always, in Gill's words, 'been moved by the fabric of the Church visible',[91] as in the lines on Hawkshead church in Book IV of the 1805 *Prelude*—the 'snow-white church upon its hill | . . . sending out | A gracious look all over its domain' (ll. 13–15)—strict adherence both to church doctrine and to fashionable evangelical notions of sinfulness was new, a late development. Wordsworth's early fearlessness about such matters had always been a distinguishing feature of his poetry, especially when compared to that of Coleridge; in the post-1820 revisions this fearlessness, and the deep faith in natural goodness from which it derives, is sometimes betrayed. When Wordsworth writes in 1805 of 'Nature's self which is the breath of God' (v. 222) and then adds in 1850 'Or his pure word by miracle revealed' (l. 223), the revision can be seen as a clarification. So too when 'sanctified | By reason and by truth' (1805, XIII. 443–4) becomes 'sanctified | By reason, blest by faith' (1850, XIV. 448). But when the power of nature that 'lifts | The being into magnanimity' in 1805 (XII. 31–2) in 1850 'trains | To meekness, and exalts by humble faith' (XIII. 27–8), something new is being added; Wordsworth is not now writing 'as my soul bade me' (1805, XI. 234), but, in the words of the very phrase's revision, 'as piety ordained' (1850, XII. 185). It is impossible to imagine such a change occurring to him 'insensibly'.

What is remarkable about such instances of imposition is how few of them there are—given, for example, the melancholy history traced in the so-called crisis poems, from 'Resolution and Independence' and 'Ode: Intimations of Immortality' to 'Elegaic Stanzas' and 'Ode to Duty'. The rigidity towards which this sequence gathers might have resulted in more drastic rewriting. Instead, earlier, more hopeful, and self-reliant poems

---

[91] Gill, *Life*, 344.

are respected in revision and reprinted (alongside new poems quite different in tone and outlook), perhaps because even early Wordsworth can be said to contain doubts and dark undersongs, points of contact with a late 'undeluded' self; perhaps because the extremity of poems such as 'Elegiac Stanzas' and 'Ode to Duty' derives in part from particular circumstances, from the 'deep distress' ('Elegiac Stanzas', l. 36) of John Wordsworth's drowning. Wordsworth's need, in 'Ode to Duty', for 'control' (l. 35) in the place of 'unchartered freedom' (l. 37), his longing 'for a repose which ever is the same' (l. 40), or his recourse, in 'Elegiac Stanzas', to 'unfeeling armour' (l. 51), remain with and help to explain the later poetry, including its weaknesses; the impulse to repudiate, though, fades. The crisis poems register a change, one connected to the note of pietistic abasement in *The Prelude* revisions, but Wordsworth retains the ability to identify with earlier work: there is no continuing rejection or self-hatred.

In the case of the style and structure of *The Prelude*, matters are comparably mixed. The principal charge against the style of the 1850 version is that, in Norman Fruman's words, it 'regularly ... substitute[s] a formal, harmfully predictable language for the urgency of genuine speech. ... The speaker is no longer inside the materials *as a participant*, but he is now the detached observer Coleridge so wanted him to be.'[92] Among numerous examples Fruman cites, not all of them especially damaging, are several manifest absurdities. What in 1805 are called 'two horses' in Book XI (l. 348) become in 1850 'led palfreys' (XII. 291). 'Did anyone suppose that the creatures would arrive alone?' asks Fruman. 'And had anyone in England during Wordsworth's lifetime ever called a horse a palfrey? Is it not significant that even the most ardent admirers of 1850 have never dared refer to this spot of time as "waiting for the Palfreys"? Or, as Jonathan Wordsworth murmured when I mentioned this to him ... "Attending Upon the Palfreys?"'[93]

There are other such instances, some almost as silly.[94] But

[92] From Fruman's contribution to 'Waiting for the Palfreys', 7.

[93] Ibid. 10.

[94] For extreme formulations of the case against the 1850 version see especially Fruman and supporting examples from Herbert Lindenberger's less combative contribution to 'Waiting for the Palfreys'; also Philip Hobsbaum, *Tradition and Experiment in English Poetry* (London: Macmillan, 1979), 180–205.

there are also, of course, manifest improvements, revisions of obvious good sense. Sometimes Wordsworth's syntax is convoluted in the 1805 version for no discernible reason, as in several fairly ridiculous passages cited by de Selincourt. For example, in Book VIII, the following lines

> Yet do not deem, my Friend! though thus I speak
> Of Man as having taken in my mind
> A place thus early which might almost seem
> Pre-eminent, that it was really so,   (ll. 472–5)

become, in the 1850 revision, simply

> Yet deem not, Friend! that human kind with me
> Thus early took a place pre-eminent.   (ll. 340–1)

In Book IX, the awkward

> . . . Officers
> That to a regiment appertained which then
> Was stationed in the city   (ll. 126–8)

becomes (as de Selincourt puts it, 'with no loss of sense')[95] 'Officers, | Then stationed in the city' (ll. 125–6). In 1805 Coleridge is called 'In many things, my brother, chiefly here | In this my deep devotion' (II. 478–9). In 1839, the last line is aptly revised—the original sentiment more fully realized—when 'my deep devotion' becomes 'our deep devotion' (1850, II. 466). Similarly, in Book XIV of 1850 Coleridge is apostrophied as 'most capacious soul' (l. 273), a thoughtful improvement over 1805's 'most loving soul' (XIII. 248). Weak transitions are tightened up, as when the authorial bridging lines between the two spots of time in Book XI—'Yet another | Of these to me affecting incidents, | With which we will conclude' (ll. 342–5)—becomes simply 'Yet another | Of these memorials—' (1850, XII. 286–7). Vaudracour and Julia are dropped from Book IX, in Book VI the Grande Chartreuse passage is added—two improvements, even to champions of the earlier version.[96] Important linking touches are added: the Arab of Book V in 1850 is

---

[95] *Prelude*, ed. de Selincourt, rev. edn. Darbishire, p. lvii. Neither of these instances, it is worth noting, are drawn to the reader's attention in Jonathan Wordsworth's annotations to the 'Norton *Prelude*'.
[96] See Lindenberger's contribution to 'Waiting for the Palfreys', 4.

called an 'uncouth shape' (l. 75), precisely the term used for the discharged soldier in Book IV (1805, l. 402; 1850, l. 386). There are obvious improvements in sense, as when Wordsworth's time at Cambridge is described as a 'second act | In this new life' (1850, III. 259–60) rather than its 'opening act' (1805, III. 259), since it comes after the childhood experiences described in Books I and II. At times, revision even improves—vivifies—the experience itself, rather than our understanding of it (said by detractors of the 1850 version to be late Wordsworth's sole concern), as when the following lines describing entry to Cambridge at the beginning of Book III, 'Onward we drove beneath the castle, down | By Magdalene Bridge and crossed the Cam' (1805, III. 14–15), become the more performative 'Onward we drove beneath the castle; caught, | While crossing Magdalene Bridge, a glimpse of Cam' (1850, III. 15–16); or when, in the skating episode in Book I, young Wordsworth retires from the 'tumultuous throng' of fellow skaters to cut across what in 1799 is called the 'shadow' (l. 174) of a star, in 1805 the 'image' of a star, and in 1850, in what Jonathan Wordsworth calls a revision of 'indefinable rightness', the 'reflex' of a star. Such alterations belong with the memorable added lines on the bust of Newton in Trinity College Chapel in Book III—'The marble index of a mind for ever | Voyaging through strange seas of Thought, alone' (ll. 62–3)—or the transformation of the more generalized 'mountain pomp | Of autumn and its beauty' in 1805 (VI. 10–11) to 'caves and heights | Clothed in the sunshine of the withering fern' (VI. 10–11).

These and other instances should be recalled when particularly egregious examples of what Jonathan Wordsworth calls 'gratuitous poetic elaboration' are cited, for they make clear that late Wordsworth was neither senile, servile (to a once scorned poetic convention), nor tone deaf. Yet the larger question of a new, more public, and generalizing voice remains. Again and again the revisions clarify and simplify an earlier performative or experiential style, in the process obscuring the experience itself, if not 'the thought processes it had been Wordworth's original intention to invoke'.[97] For example, in Book XI of the 1805 version, Wordsworth proclaims: 'I felt,

---

[97] 'Norton *Prelude*', ed. Wordsworth, Abrams, Gill, 287 n., 523 n.

and nothing else; I did not judge, I I never thought of judging' (ll. 237–8). In 1850, this becomes 'I felt, observed, and pondered; did not judge, I Yea, never thought of judging' (ll. 188–9). The revision, it could be argued, is representative: on the one hand, it falsifies, by making more deliberative or ruminative Wordsworth's earlier, feeling self; on the other hand, the youth described, in the 1805 version as well as that of 1850, was hardly a being of mere 'glad animal movements' ('Tintern Abbey', l. 75). 'I felt, and nothing else' is vivid and dramatic, but in what sense is it truer than 'I felt, observed, and pondered'? The revision is doubtless more accurate as an account of Wordsworth's mental processes—as the *anatomy* of an experience—than the original, but something of the power of the experience, the truth of what it felt like, has been lost.

The question I want to pose is whether this trade-off is a betrayal. To Norman Fruman, the consciousness of the Wordsworth of the later revision was 'alien'; late Wordsworth 'no longer approved of much in his former self, and did not wish to be remembered as a youth who sought to drink wild water, pluck green herbs . . . for their *own* sake, and not because they were "consecrated" for some other purpose'.[98] This judgement seems to me doubly wrong: first, in its implication that Wordsworth's former self was unaware of the 'consecrated' nature of his most vivid experiences, or that their vividness derived from something consecrated—'A presence' ('Tintern Abbey', l. 95), for example, or 'the sense of God, or whatso'er is dim I Or vast in its own being' (1805, VIII. 67–8)—in 1850, simply 'God' (precisely the sort of emendation supporters of 1805 deplore); and second, in its implication that later Wordsworth was somehow embarrassed by, or disapproved of, his earlier intensities, especially those which seemed at first to be matters of pure sensation. The 1850 version still allows us to see the young Wordsworth, in Fruman's words, as 'truly baffled, exalted, and frightened by his uncanny intuitions and intimations, and his utterances', even when it also generalizes beyond individual experience about their meaning, sometimes in conventionally religious terms. Though Fruman is right to say that the 1850 revision 'narrows the force of [Wordsworth's]

---

[98] See Fruman's contribution to 'Waiting for the Palfreys', 4.

spiritual experience',[99] it does so in the service of understanding, as the expression of a truth latent—not fully realized—in the early version.

THE EDITOR'S OBLIGATION

What, then, to return to the editorial questions with which this chapter begins, are the grounds for ignoring Wordsworth's explicit authorial instructions, for printing early over revised editions? To begin with, there are aesthetic grounds: but about these, unsurprisingly, there is no stable consensus. Early versions—unrevised versions—are more vivid, claims the current fashion, than late versions; but late versions are clearer. Early versions, it is claimed, are more original than late versions; but late versions are more correct. Moreover, as I have tried to show, these oppositions are rarely as clear-cut as partisans would have us believe.

What, then, of other grounds? It is not so much, one might argue, that early Wordsworth is better—or worse—than late Wordsworth, as that he is different. To ignore revised versions is to slight one Wordsworth, late Wordsworth, in order to honour another, early Wordsworth—say on historical or political grounds (those of his importance to the revolutionary or early Romantic period, for example, or of his more congenial—or congenially expressed—politics). Wordsworth, however, spent his life defying and denying the conception of self that underlies such a view, in both original works and revision—though few poets have written as feelingly about loss and change, about 'all the persons, down to palsied age, | That life brings with her in her equipage' ('Ode: Intimations of Immortality', ll. 105–6). Though not identical with the person he once was, late Wordsworth continues to brave his doubts and fears and to insist upon an essential or underlying continuity of personality. This insistence, I have tried to show, is not quite as groundless as some would have us believe. Leaving aside the obvious difference *any* revision produces, it is the case—at least, this is what I have been arguing—that Wordsworth the revising poet

<hr>

[99] Ibid. 11.

not only thought of himself as clarifying or refining an original and still-living intention rather than altering or overturning it, but that often—as later Stephen Parrish might put it—he was right to think so. In addition to wishing to be a single and continuous person over time, in some respects—certainly more than are today acknowledged—he reveals himself in his revisions to have been one, continuing to identify with the aims, aspirations, thoughts, and feelings of earlier poems, by attempting to bring them to a more perfect expression.

To some textual scholars, the dilemma I am worrying over is a false one. Why not, they respond, simply print all versions? This is Stillinger's view, which is close to that of McGann and the textual theorists—James Thorpe, Hans Zeller—McGann cites not only in support of a move away from the privileging of earliest or manuscript versions but of what might be called 'textual pluralism'.[100] After a detailed comparison of the Snowdon episode in both the 1805 and 1850 versions of *The Prelude*—chosen because for Jonathan Wordsworth its revision 'does not merely destroy one of [Wordsworth's] greatest pieces of poetry, [it] weakens those aspects which had made it the fitting climax to his poem'[101]—Stillinger argues that both versions have comparably weighted strengths and weaknesses. Instead of picking one over another, he concludes, 'A healthier reaction would be to stop this nonsense about "the worst of Wordsworth" and grant the legitimacy and interest . . . of *all* versions of *The Prelude* and the rest of the poems in the canon.'[102] In the words of another recent pluralist, Duncan Wu, 'The only remaining obstacle to publishing sixteen different versions of *The Prelude* is likely to be the publisher's bank account.'[103]

One does not have to be a Luddite to demur. The new technology may very well soon make widely available all sixteen

---

[100] See James Thorpe, *Principles of Textual Criticism* (San Marino, Calif.: Huntington Library, 1972), and Hans Zeller, 'A New Approach to the Critical Constitution of Literary Texts', *Studies in Bibliography*, 28 (1975), 231–64.

[101] Jonathan Wordsworth, *William Wordsworth: The Borders of Vision* (Oxford: Clarendon Press, 1982), 328.

[102] Stillinger, 'Textual Primitivism', 27.

[103] Wu, 'Editing Intentions', 8. Those who object to this view are accused by Wu of 'intellectual Ludditism', in 'Acts of Butchery: Wordsworth as Editor', *The Wordsworth Circle*, 23 (Summer 1992), 157.

'versions' of *The Prelude*; and these versions will be of interest
to the scholar and critic. But what student or non-specialist
reader is going to read them all? Though the larger issues of
Wordsworth's conception of personal identity, and of its deter-
mining influence on revision, do not, of course, depend upon or
revolve around practical questions of reception (whether or not
the general reader is able or willing to pay attention to a
'pluralized' text), the question of which version should be read
reflects interestingly upon Wordsworth's own revisionary practices. This is why I began the chapter talking about Gill's Oxford
Authors *Wordsworth* rather than the Cornell edition, which is
clearly aimed at specialists. To object that the choice of a single
text is artificial, that there are all kinds of pedagogical purposes
and all kinds of students, is both wrong (in respect to the
choice, which is and was perfectly real) and evasive. The choice
Gill was faced with was stark: he could print only one text,
without textual notes. Nor was his dilemma either exceptional
or unimportant. The market for a series like the Oxford Authors is a genuine one, and such single-volume selections play
a crucial role in producing not only the sorts of readers, more
advanced readers, who will go on to need other editions—
eventually, a whole range of editions—but the culture's larger
sense of the subject. No edition will more widely disperse its
sense—*a* sense—of Wordsworth's 'essence' than Gill's. Editors
of affordable texts for students and general readers—and if the
general reader is a pious fiction the student certainly is not—
have to make a choice. It is my contention that the grounds for
this choice relate directly to the concerns authors themselves
weigh when they come to revise their works: in both cases,
what is being pondered is the nature of the self or person, and
the relative claims of truth, beauty, history, and authorship.

To print early over late Wordsworth is more often than not
to ignore—or override—Wordsworth's explicit instructions: we
almost always know the forms of the works he wished the
public to have.[104] As a reviser, he was neither mad nor senile,
nor did he conceive of revision as the creation of new works.

---

[104] To some editorial theorists such knowledge is the goal of all editors. 'Scholarly
editors may disagree about many things,' writes G. Thomas Tanselle, in 'The Editorial Problem of Final Authorial Intention', 'but they are in general agreement that
their goal is to determine exactly what an author meant and to determine what form
of his work he wished the public to have' (*Studies in Bibliography*, 29 (1976), 167).

He was respectful of original meanings, which he sought to clarify or more fully realize, to perfect. 'Certainly, a man's last will and testament we honour,' declares Herbert Lindenberger, 'even if he gives his money to a prostitute instead of to his wife. I don't think we have the same obligation to the poet.'[105] Why? In the case of a last will and testament there comes a time when legality—obligation—is determined. Was the deceased of sound mind? If the answer is yes, the will is observed, regardless of whether we think it ill-advised, unfair, foolish. Nor does it matter that a year previously there was a different will or that it might well have changed had its author lived on. We don't pick what we think is the best of the deceased's wills on the grounds that he changed his mind a lot, or that for him will-writing was 'a continuum'.

To Wordsworth, the rights of literary and material property were—or ought to have been—related, which in part explains his attitude to copyright. 'As it now stands', he writes in 1838, the statute law of copyright

is a composition or compromise between two opinions; the extreme point of one being, that, by giving his thoughts to the world, an author abandons all right to consider the vehicle as private property; and of the other, that he has the right in perpetuity.... This right I hold to be more deeply inherent in that species of property than in any other, though I am aware that many persons, perceiving wherein it differs from acquisitions made in trade and commerce, etc., have contended that the law in respect to literature ought to remain upon the same footing as that which regards the profits of mechanical inventions and chemical discoveries; but... this is an utter fallacy.

Nor are financial considerations the sole motive for such views. A fair copyright law must ensure that 'the printing of works should be made the control of their authors' representatives, however long those works may have been before the public, in order to secure copies correctly printed, and to preclude the sending forth without the author's recent or last additions or emendations, by those publishers who are ready to seize upon expiring copyrights'.[106]

[105] See Lindenberger's contribution to 'Waiting for the Palfreys', 28.
[106] The first quotation comes from Wordsworth's letter 'To the Editor of the *Kendal Mercury*', dated 12 Apr. 1838 and printed 14 Apr. 1838. The second quotation comes from a public petition to the Select Committee of the House of Commons, appended to the Seventh Report, 27 Feb.–1 Mar. 1839. Both documents

Wordsworth's latest 'additions or emendations'—expressions of his last will, as it were—might not be to an editor's taste or purpose (as in Gill's announced historical purpose with the Oxford Authors *Wordsworth*), but why grant the editor authority over the poet on such matters? Because we can, is one answer. Because the poet is dead and, besides, our responsibility is to something higher than any mere person. Our responsibility is, variously, to history, truth, beauty. Moreover, in most cases the superseded early versions we are talking of were published in editions authorized by Wordsworth himself, were placed in the public domain by their author. The editor is perfectly free to pick whichever edition best suits his or her interests and standards.

The irony of such a position is that those who print early versions over revised ones—who override or ignore the author's last, explicit instructions—often do so on the grounds of a comparable betrayal or high-handedness on Wordsworth's part. Were these grounds fair in Wordsworth's case, I might view them with more sympathy. An author's explicit instruction is not a law, at least not in the Anglo-American tradition;[107] we are not obliged always to follow it. Nor would we wish to. No one would wish Virgil's friends Marius and Varro to have followed his instructions and burned *The Aeneid*, or Max Brod to have burned Kafka's writings—even were it possible to determine that both authors were of sound mind, not engulfed in depression or death-bed despair. Nevertheless, ignoring or denying authorial agency and intention means ignoring or denying one's

are printed in *Prose Works*, ed. Owen and Smyser, iii. 313–14, which also contains a useful introduction to Wordsworth's writings on copyright and to the law in general (see iii. 303–6). For a thorough and often suggestive meditation on Wordsworth's 'extraordinary' efforts on behalf of copyright reform see Susan Eilenberg, 'Mortal Pages: Wordsworth and the Reform of Copyright', *English Literary History*, 56 (1989), 351–74, repr. in Eilenberg's *Strange Power of Speech: Wordsworth, Coleridge and Literary Possession* (Oxford: Oxford University Press, 1992), 192–215. Though Eilenberg speculates widely on Wordsworth's sense of the 'material' nature of poetry and language, she has relatively little to say about the importance to Wordsworth of copyright's capacity to control and fix the final forms of his works.

[107] Consider, e.g., the rival traditions of copyright, and the larger theories of intellectual property underlying them, as laid out by Edward M. Plowman and L. Clark Hamilton, in *Copyright: Intellectual Property* (London: Routledge & Kegan Paul, 1980), 26–46. More generally, see Mark Rose, *Authors and Owners: The Invention of Copyright* (Cambridge, Mass.: Harvard University Press, 1993).

responsibility to persons. As the example of Wordsworth's revisions so intelligently and honourably suggests, this responsibility ought to apply as much to dead persons—or the person one once was—as to the living.

CHAPTER TWO

BYRON, REVISION, AND THE STABLE SELF

THE first point to make about Byron's revisions is that there are so few of them, at least in comparison with those of Wordsworth. This is a point Byron himself makes much of in his correspondence. As he reminds his publisher, John Murray, in a letter of 6 June 1822, often his poems 'were written as fast as I could put pen to paper—and printed from the *original* M.S.S. & never revised but in the proofs'. 'Don't ask me to alter for I can't,' he elsewhere informs Murray, in a much-quoted letter of 12 August 1819, 'I am obstinate and lazy—and that's the truth.' And most famously, in a simile repeated elsewhere: 'I can't *furbish*.—I am like the tyger (in poesy) if I miss my first spring—I go growling back to my Jungle.—There is no second.—I can't correct—I can't—& I won't.' Later, in the same letter, Byron elaborates: 'Nobody ever succeeds [in revision] great or small.—Tasso remade the whole of his Jerusalem but who ever reads that version?—all the world goes to the first.— Pope *added* to the "Rape of the Lock"—but did not reduce it.—You must take my things as they happen to be . . . I would rather give them away than hack and hew them.'[1]

In many instances, the manuscripts bear out such assertions, which is as one would expect given Byron's astonishing fluency. *Lara* (1814), an Eastern tale of 1272 lines, was composed in four weeks, 'while undressing after balls and masquerades'.[2]

---

[1] Letters of 6 June 1822 and 12 Aug. 1819, both to Murray, are printed in *Byron's Letters and Journals*, ed. Leslie A. Marchand, 12 vols. (Cambridge, Mass.: Harvard University Press, 1973–81), ix. 166, vi. 207. See also ix. 54 where the 'tyger' simile is repeated in reference to *Cain* (1822). That Byron hated revision and rarely 'hacked or hewed' quickly became legend. 'He does not prepare any plan beforehand,' declares Hazlitt in *The Spirit of the Age* (1825), 'nor revise and retouch what he has written' (*The Complete Works of William Hazlitt*, ed. P. P. Howe, 21 vols. (London: J. M. Dent & Sons, 1932), xi. 72). Subsequent references to Byron's letters and journals abbreviated *BLJ*, ed. Marchand.

[2] Letter of 6 June 1822 to John Murray, *BLJ*, ed. Marchand, ix. 168.

Among other Eastern tales, *The Bride of Abydos* (1813), a poem of similar length (1215 lines), took four *nights*; *The Corsair* (1814), a much longer poem (1864 lines), took two weeks. The ninety *ottava rima* stanzas of Canto XI of *Don Juan* were completed by Byron in eleven days; Canto XIII, which is longer (111 stanzas), took a week. In a dozen turbulent years, Byron produced almost as many lines of verse as Wordsworth, whose much longer poetical career was largely free of distraction. Byron 'could not have produced the great bulk that he did', writes T. J. Steffan in the Variorum *Don Juan*, 'if he had not written with phenomenal speed and ease and for the most part without thoughtful revision'. Even in the most heavily revised of Byron's works, such as the opening cantos of *Don Juan*, there is 'no evidence . . . that he ever labored tediously . . . the handwriting shows that he was scrawling very fast'; nor did Byron ever radically reconstruct any of the cantos or even any large part of one.[3] It is also hard to see Byron's more metaphoric literary 'returns' as revisionary. Unlike Wordsworth, when Byron returns to old character types, situations, styles, *topoi*, it is not so much to perfect what has been imperfectly realized, as to exploit a winning formula. The Eastern tales that follow *Childe Harold's Pilgrimage* I and II (1812) are, in Peter Manning's phrase, 'repetitions-with-variations', attempts to find more room within the genre, to squeeze out material.[4] They are not the works of a writer worrying at a problem to get it right.

---

[3] *Byron's 'Don Juan': A Variorum Edition*, ed. T. J. Steffan and W. W. Pratt, 4 vols. (Austin, Tex.: University of Texas Press, 1957), i. 103, 105. For lengths of composition see i. 103. Vol. i of the Variorum edition, entitled *The Making of a Masterpiece*, is by Steffan alone. Vol. iv, containing notes on the edition, is by Pratt alone. For a rare example of the sort of large-scale structural recasting absent from *Don Juan*, see Maria Hogan Butler, 'An Examination of Byron's Revision of *Manfred*, Act III', in *Studies in Philology*, 7/4 (Oct. 1963), 627–36. Byron, Butler shows, was clear from the start about the inadequacy of the drama's original ending of 1816 and radically revised it a year later.

[4] Peter J. Manning, '*Don Juan* and the Revisionary Self', in Robert Brinkley and Keith Hanley (eds.), *Romantic Revisions* (Cambridge: Cambridge University Press, 1992), 216. For a view of Byron's poetical repetitions as a 'postmodern' defiance of origins, see Jerome Christensen, 'Perversion, Parody, and Cultural Hegemony: Lord Byron's Oriental Tales', in *The South Atlantic Quarterly*, 88/3 (Summer 1989), 569–603. Peter L. Thorslev, Jr., in *The Byronic Hero: Types and Prototypes* (Minneapolis: University of Minnesota Press, 1962), 147, claims that the Eastern tales (he calls them 'romances') 'depend primarily on their protagonists, rather than on plot or verse, for their effect', and that they 'do not show much advance in the development of the hero beyond *Childe Harold*'.

ON NOT REVISING

'I am obstinate and lazy.' These are the main reasons Byron gives for not revising, and they are worth pondering. 'Obstinate' raises questions of context: often when Byron claims in his letters that he won't or can't revise, he is responding to pressure, both direct, from Murray and the circle of friends and literary advisers who made up Murray's 'Utican Senate' or 'Synod', and indirect, from the larger reading public whose tastes the Synod sought to anticipate. Byron can't and won't revise potentially libellous or offensive passages, because he can't or won't be pressured (also, at times, because his acute feel for the market—his sense of what it would take—caused him to doubt Murray's judgement). To revise under such circumstances would be cowardly: 'As to Beppo I will not alter or suppress a syllable for any man's pleasure but my own';[5] *Don Juan* 'shall be an entire horse or none';[6] 'You shan't make *Canticles* of my Cantos. . . . I will have none of your damned cutting & slashing';[7] 'I will have no gelding.'[8] As language like this suggests, revision, especially 'cutting', was equated by Byron with loss of manhood or emasculation, a connection to be taken up more fully later in the chapter.

Byron not only 'won't' revise his poems, he claims he 'can't' revise them, not just because he is lazy, but because to write his poems at all, particularly the later comic poems, requires absolute freedom. 'Why Man,' he tells Murray later in the letter of 12 August 1819, after declaring he 'can't' revise, 'the Soul of such writing is its licence.' And not just its soul, its very existence. 'If like Tony Lumpkin I am "to be snubbed so when I am

---

[5] Letter of 23 Apr. 1818 to John Murray, in *BLJ*, ed. Marchand, vi. 35. Byron's resistance to pressure was real and noble (in several senses), but it was not suicidal. For a catalogue of prudent or diplomatic retreats (some conceded *after* victory) see Ian Jack, *The Poet and His Audience* (Cambridge: Cambridge University Press, 1987), 64–5 (for *Childe Harold*), 76–7 (for *Don Juan*). As for stylistic alterations, Byron was always amenable: 'I cannot alter the sentiments, but if there are any alterations in the structure of the versification you would wish to be made, I will tag rhymes, and turn stanzas, as much as you please' (letter of 5 Sept. 1811 to John Murray, in *BLJ*, ed. Marchand, ii. 91).
[6] Letter of 5 Jan. 1819 to Count Giuseppino Albreizzi, in *BLJ*, ed. Marchand, vi. 91.   [7] Letter of 6 Apr. 1819 to John Murray, ibid. 105.
[8] Letter of 6 Apr. 1819 to John Cam Hobhouse, ibid. 107.

in spirits" the poem will be naught—and the poet turn serious again.'[9] For Byron, as for Blake, the many forms of 'licence' are interconnected: *Don Juan*'s compositional licence, its improvisational manner, is explicitly linked at several places in the poem both to Juan's adult promiscuity and to political freedom, most notably at the end of Canto XI, when Byron declares that he 'would not change my free thoughts for a throne' (st. 90).[10] 'Free thoughts' here refers not only to the poem's sexual and political daring, but to the teasing 'looseness' of its narrative, its freedom, as in the immediately preceding lines, to go wherever it pleases:

89

Whether he married with the third or fourth
   Offspring of some sage, husband-hunting Countess,
Or whether with some virgin of more worth
   (I mean in Fortune's matrimonial bounties)
He took to regularly peopling Earth,
   Of which your lawful awful wedlock fount is,—   710
Or whether he was taken in for damages,
For being too excursive in his homages,—

90

Is yet within the unread events of time.
   Thus far, go forth, thou Lay! which I will back
Against the same given quantity of rhyme,
   For being as much the subject of attack
As ever yet was any work sublime,
   By those who love to say that white is black.
So much the better!—I may stand alone,
And would not change my free thoughts for a throne. 720

Behind these lines lies a single noteworthy revision: 'lawful wedlock' in the original becomes 'lawful awful wedlock' (l. 710), a thoroughly Lumpkin-like alteration, one which *serves* licence.[11]

   That so productive a poet could be lazy is hard at first to

---

[9] Letter of 12 Aug. 1819 to John Murray, ibid. 206.
[10] I quote from *Lord Byron: The Complete Poetical Works*, ed. Jerome J. McGann, v. *Don Juan* (Oxford: Clarendon Press, 1986), and hereafter cite its various volumes (there are 7) as *Complete Poetical Works*. Subsequent quotations cite canto, stanza, or line numbers parenthetically in the text.
[11] See *Complete Poetical Works*, ed. McGann, v. 492.

credit—until, that is, one recalls Byron's working habits. Byron found copying a bore; nor was he always keen on proofreading, whether of transcripts or of printed text.[12] This was not because he was indifferent to textual accuracy: the 'eternal blunders' of Murray's printers could drive him to distraction, and as McGann reminds us, 'before he left England in 1816 he always paid scrupulous attention to the printing of his works, all legend to the contrary notwithstanding';[13] it was just that, after 1816, he could not always be bothered to recopy or labour through proofs.[14] So strong was his aversion to recopying that, at times, when unable to find suitable amanuenses while abroad, he risked sending Murray uncopied holographs.[15] It is, for example, no accident that the much-revised first five cantos of *Don Juan* were produced in a period when he was without suitable copyists; or that the least revised cantos, the latest ones, were transcribed by Mary Shelley.

Jerome McGann sees Byron's collaboration with Mary Shelley as exemplary (rather than exploitative), paradigmatic of the mixed or social origins of texts. Though Mary Shelley sometimes revised Byron's poems in the act of transcribing them, Byron was 'well aware of her interventions: he sometimes converted back to his initial readings, he sometimes accepted her readings, and occasionally he produced a new reading altogether'.[16] For Steffan, though, Byron's revision of Shelley's transcripts is so infrequent and widely spread as to suggest that he 'must have only skimmed over'[17] them. Perhaps what McGann sees as considered assent is simple obliviousness, the product of laziness. Still, what is worth noting here, as also in his masterly

[12] For complaints about copying see letter of 16 Apr. 1820 to John Murray, and for complaints about proofreading see letters of 22 Aug. and 28 Sept. 1820, also to Murray, in *BLJ*, ed. Marchand, vii. 77, 161, 182.

[13] For 'eternal blunders' see letter of 19 Jan. 1818 to Murray, in *BLJ*, ed. Marchand, vi. 8; McGann's comment comes from 'Editing Byron's Poetry', *The Byron Journal*, 1/1 (1973), 7.

[14] 'The corruptions of *Manfred*, for example, are a direct result of Byron's eventual loss of patience at the end of a complex printing history. *Manfred* was written and elaborately revised in 1816 and 1817, and Byron corrected proof early in 1817. But the whole process carried on for so long that, in the end, Byron refused to look at Murray's final, crucial proof' (McGann, ibid. 7).

[15] See *Byron's 'Don Juan'*, ed. Steffan and Pratt, i. 101.

[16] Jerome J. McGann, *A Critique of Modern Textual Criticism* (Chicago: University of Chicago Press, 1983), 52.

[17] *Byron's 'Don Juan'*, ed. Steffan and Pratt, i. 112.

edition of Byron's works, is how McGann, who has done so much to emphasize the poet's 'mobility', his principled inconsistency, as well as the socially constructed nature of texts in general, gives authorial control its due (in this case, perhaps, more than its due). McGann the editor takes seriously expressed authorial intentions—much more so, certainly, than Wordsworth's Cornell editors. In, for example, his textual note to the 'Ode to Napoleon Buonaparte' (1814), McGann relegates stanzas 17–19, a new ending to the poem which Byron eventually rejected, to the position of 'Additional Stanzas'—despite the fact that they had been printed as part of the poem since 1832. Though McGann approves Byron's aesthetic grounds for excluding the stanzas,[18] grounds subsequent editors ignored, his own grounds are quite different: 'however one feels about this aesthetic question, the editorial question is clear and admits of only one answer, given Byron's explicit instructions to his publisher'.[19]

REVISION AND 'PROFESSIONAL' AUTHORSHIP

A question remains about Byron's 'laziness': Why lazy over some activities—proofreading or revision, for example—and not others? Because proofreading and revision were for Byron 'work', in a way original composition was not, though for

---

[18] See letters of 25 and 29 Apr. 1814 to Murray, in *BLJ*, ed. Marchand, iv. 103–4, 107.

[19] *Complete Poetical Works*, ed. McGann, iii. 456–7. Jack Stillinger, in his review of vol. i of *Complete Poetical Works*, in *Journal of English and German Philology*, 81/1 (Jan. 1982), 126, says of McGann's copy-texts that they are 'chosen, as they should be, on a poem-by-poem basis—early editions when they are the most authoritative versions, but also manuscripts and printer's proofs when these are judged superior representations of the author's intentions—and they are substantially amended when Byron's marked copies and other evidences of authorial revision warrant the alterations.' Only on rare occasions does McGann depart from this admirable policy, as when he retains, as part of the text of *English Bards and Scotch Reviewers*, the preface and prose postscript, which Byron had deleted before authorizing the suppressed fifth edition of the poem. As Donald H. Reiman, another admirer of the edition (though one with severe reservations about some aspects of its format and annotation), puts it, in 'The Oxford Byron', a review reprinted in *Romantic Texts and Contexts* (Columbia, Miss.: University of Missouri Press, 1987), 162: 'Here the best expedient might have been to reprint this prose (which Byron obviously considered obsolescent by 1811–1812) either in the notes or (better) after the text of the poem as "Prose Associated with *EBSR*," as McGann has handled certain important poetic passages eventually rejected by Byron.'

many writers, Wordsworth among them, the reverse is true. There is a class element involved here. Byron's carelessness—or relative carelessness—about finished work, his flaunting casualness ('Hail, Muse! *et cetera*', *Don Juan*, III. 1), signal upperclass hauteur—disdain for effort, graft, anything that smacks of the artisan or labourer. Such disdain is of a piece with Byron's scorn for Leigh Hunt's references to poetry as a 'profession' (one headed by Wordsworth, of all men): 'I thought that Poetry was an *art*, or an *attribute*, and not a *profession*.'[20] 'One hates an author that's *all author*,' ends his attack on the minor poet and 'man of letters' William Sotheby, thinly disguised as 'Botherby' in *Beppo* (1817). Such 'authors' are mere 'shreds of paper, |... unquenched snuffings of the midnight taper' (st. 75), 'professionals' who live off literary odd-jobbery, including journalism, translation, drama ('sweating plays so middling, bad were better', a line which itself entailed some sweating[21]). Nor was Sotheby alone of his kind. Only Walter Scott, Henry Gifford, and Thomas Moore among Byron's contemporaries were free of 'professional' affectations: 'as for the rest whom I have known—there was always more or less of the author about them—the pen peeping from behind the ear—and the thumbs a little inky or so'.[22] As Marilyn Butler matter-of-factly asserts: 'any upper-class author of the period resented being called "author" to his face, because the occupation was socially degrading'.[23] And as Scott himself notes, Byron avoided such a title by 'managing his pen with the careless and negligent ease of a man of quality'.[24] Revising, like other forms of authorial 'sweating' or 'midnight taper' burning, was simply not something gentlemen did.

Nor was it something done by men of action, those in *Beppo* called 'men of the world, who know the world like men' (LXXVI. 602), and whom Byron explicitly contrasts with 'authors' such

[20] Letter of 1 June 1818 to Thomas Moore, in *BLJ*, ed. Marchand, vi. 47.

[21] 'Sweating' was Byron's distinct improvement on 'writing', in stanza 74 of *Beppo*. See *Complete Poetical Works*, ed. McGann, iv. 152.

[22] Letter of 25 Mar. 1817 to John Murray, in *BLJ*, ed. Marchand, v. 192.

[23] Marilyn Butler, 'One Man in His Time', review of Jerome McGann, '*Don Juan*' *in Context*, in *Essays in Criticism*, 28/1 (Jan. 1978), 55.

[24] See Scott's unsigned review of *Childe Harold* III in the *Quarterly Review* of Feb. 1817, repr. in Andrew Rutherford (ed.), *Byron: The Critical Heritage* (New York: Barnes & Noble, 1970), 91.

as Botherby. Why are the Lake Poets 'despicable impostors', asks Byron in a letter of 24 March 1814? Because 'they know nothing of the world'.[25] As George Watson puts it, 'a claim to be ready to act—to be just about to hurry off to a war—is implicit in much of his verse',[26] and this claim does not sit well with an image of composition as craftsmanship, as honing, refining, polishing. Byron may attack Keats for disparaging Pope in 'Sleep and Poetry' (1817), but he too had little time for poets who 'smooth, inlay, and clip, and fit', those 'thousand handicraftsmen [who] wore the mask | Of poesy' (ll. 197, 200-1). His own life—obviously yet teasingly reflected in his verse— was one of broad strokes, of conspicuous glamour and adventure, qualities crucial to the best-selling appeal of his poems. No man could have written *Don Juan*, he famously declared, who had not 'lived in the world'.[27] To think such living incompatible with authorial graft may, indeed, be 'vulgar', as Watson claims, but Byron himself seems to have thought it so;[28] just as he sometimes seems to have thought reflection in general—first thoughts as well as second—both unmanly and *déclassé*. Byron professes himself reluctant to 'hack into the roots of things'. As long as 'the branch a goodly verdure flings, | I reck not if an acorn gave it birth' (*Don Juan*, XIV. 59). Revision was for him a form both of hacking ('I refuse to hack and hew') and reflecting; original composition alone was doing or 'flinging', a phrase which associates writing with sexual release, and also recalls the connection between revision and 'cutting' or emasculation.

Byron's sense of the poem was almost as important a source of his reluctance to revise as his sense of the poet, and here too class considerations play their part. 'I continue to compose', Byron tells John Hunt in a letter of 17 March 1823, 'for the

[25] Letter of 24 Mar. 1814 to James Hogg, in *BLJ*, ed. Marchand, iv. 85.
[26] George Watson, 'The Accuracy of Lord Byron', *Critical Quarterly*, 17/2 (Summer 1975), 137.
[27] Letter of 26 Oct. 1819 to Douglas Kinnaird, in *BLJ*, ed. Marchand, vi. 232.
[28] For Watson's claim about vulgarity see 'The Accuracy of Lord Byron', 137. The incompatibility of authorial graft and a life of action is implied in e.g. the following passage from a letter of 28 Febr. 1817 to Thomas Moore, in *BLJ*, ed. Marchand, v. 177: 'If I live ten years longer, you will see, however, that it is not over with me—I don't mean in literature, for that is nothing; and it may seem odd enough to say, I do not think it my vocation.'

same reason that I ride, or read, or bathe, or travel—it is a habit.'[29] And a habit of no special import: 'the mighty stir made about scribbling and scribes', writes Byron in a journal entry of 24 November 1813, is 'a sign of effeminacy, degeneracy, and weakness. Who would write who had anything better to do?'[30] Elsewhere, he calls writing 'an occupation of mind, like play, or any other stimulus'.[31] 'You know or don't know,' writes Byron in Canto XIV of *Don Juan*,

> . . . that great Bacon saith,
> 'Fling up a straw, 'twill show the way the wind blows;'
> And such a straw, borne on by human breath,
> Is Poesy, according as the mind glows;
> A paper kite, which flies 'twixt life and death,
> A shadow which the onward Soul behind throws:
> And mine's a bubble not blown up for praise,
> But just to play with as an infant plays.   (XIV. 8)

Two stanzas later Byron declares himself addicted to poetry. For all the damage, the 'thunders' and 'pious libels' it has brought him,

> . . . yet I can't help scribbling once a week,
> Tiring old readers, nor discovering new.
> In youth I wrote, because my mind was full,
> And now because I feel it growing dull.   (XIV. 10)

Here, as in the previously quoted letters, the end result of writing, the finished product or poem, goes unmentioned. It is writing that matters to Byron.

'Why then publish?' (XIV. 11). Byron's answer in *Don Juan* is no answer at all (confirming what he elsewhere admits: that 'I do not think publishing at all creditable either to men or women . . . and very often feel ashamed of it myself'[32]). Though publishing once brought him 'rewards | Of fame or profit' (XIV. 11), these no longer figure.

> I ask in turn,—why do you play at cards?
> Why drink? Why read?—To make some hour less dreary.

---

[29] Letter of 17 Mar. 1823 to John Hunt, in *BLJ*, ed. Marchand, x. 123.
[30] Journal entry of 24 Nov. 1813, ibid. iii. 220.
[31] See *Byron's 'Don Juan'*, ed. Steffan and Pratt, i. 45–6.
[32] Letter of 1 May 1812 to Lady Caroline Lamb, in *BLJ*, ed. Marchand, ii. 175.

It occupies me to turn back regards
  On what I've seen or ponder'd, sad or cheery;
And that I write I cast upon the stream
To swim or sink—I have had at least my dream. (XIV. 11)

What occupies Byron is the writing, the dreaming, the recollecting (there is a Wordsworthian note here, as in the previous stanza's reference to the mind 'growing dull'); casting what is written 'upon the stream' is an afterthought, its fate of little import. 'In play,' he continues in stanza 12, 'there are two pleasures for your choosing— | The one is winning, and the other losing.' Again, the outcome, the writing's fate, does not much matter. Unlike Wordsworth, Byron seeks to create the impression that he really does value process over finished product, and the terms he uses to describe process—or writing—have class implications. Writing is associated with a life of leisure, with riding, bathing, travelling, playing; it is a way of staving off the sort of boredom so amusingly depicted in the English cantos of *Don Juan*. That writing can sometimes 'show the way the wind blows' (XIV. 8), like Bacon's straw, or bring 'fame or profit', are secondary considerations at best. The poem itself, though, is invariably seen as commodity or product.

For example, in 1821 Byron records the following reflection in his Ravenna journal:

I was out of spirits—read the papers—thought what *fame* was, on reading, in a case of murder, that 'Mr. Wych, grocer, at Tunbridge, sold some bacon, flour, cheese, and it is believed, some plums, to some gypsy woman accused. He had on his counter (I quote faithfully) a *book*, the Life of *Pamela*, which he was *tearing* for *waste* paper, &c., &c. In the cheese was found, &c., and a *leaf* of *Pamela wrapt round the bacon*.' . . . What would he [Richardson] have said? What can anybody say, save what Solomon said long before us? After all, it is but passing from one counter to another, from the bookseller's to the other tradesman's—grocer or pastry-cook. For my part, I have met with most poetry upon trunks; so I am apt to consider the trunk-maker as the sexton of authorship.[33]

Sonia Hofkosh has written suggestively about this passage, particularly about the fact that Richardson's *Pamela* is the book in question. As she reminds us, 'in his dual role as author and

---

[33] Journal entry of 4 Jan. 1821, ibid. viii. 11–12.

publisher, Richardson enacted for the eighteenth century what many already perceived as the alarming debasement of literature into commerce'. Moreover, 'the publication of *Pamela* occasioned the recognition of new voices in the literary marketplace—the voice of prose, of a literate middle class, and of women as both consumers and producers of literature'.[34] For our purposes, though, the mere conjunction of 'book' and 'bacon' (or 'flour' or 'cheese'), or the seamless passage from 'one counter to another, from the bookseller's to the other tradesman's', is enough. For if the finished poem or book is a product, revision is analogous to sifting, cleaning, clipping, fitting, turning on a lathe.

The revisions themselves support such views of writing and the written. Consider the evolution of stanza 96 in Canto I of *Don Juan*, which describes Juan's lovesick moonings:

> Thus would he while his lonely hours away
>   Dissatisfied, nor knowing what he wanted;
> Nor glowing reverie, nor poet's lay,
>   Could yield his spirit that for which it panted,
> A Bosom whereon he his head might lay,
>   And hear the heart beat with the love it granted,
> With——several other things, which I forget,
> Or which, at least, I need not mention yet.   (I. 96)

Byron had little trouble arriving at the first six lines of the stanza. His difficulties began in line 7, with the couplet, which seems originally to have been intended as a crescendo of sorts. After line 6, 'And hear the heart beat with the love it granted', Byron at first wrote, 'And feel the nameless tumult', a fragment he crossed out. This initial false start was followed by a second: 'An eye for once might'—also crossed out. Attempt number three, the incomplete 'That heart which', became 'That heart which he'—and both were scrapped. Byron then tried 'And feel the joy of loving doubled', which was also found wanting. Finally, on a new line, he managed only the word 'That', also crossed out, before at last arriving at

---

[34] Sonia Hofkosh, 'The Writer's Ravishment: Women and the Romantic Author—The Example of Byron', in Anne K. Mellor (ed.), *Romanticism and Feminism* (Bloomington, Ind.: Indiana University Press, 1988), 95–6.

> And—several other things which I forget—
> Or which at least I need not mention yet.

Here is how the revising process looks in manuscript:

> And hear the heart beat with the love it granted—
> ~~And feel the nameless tumult~~
> ~~An eye for once might~~
> ~~Which he~~
> ~~That heart which~~
> ~~And feel the joy of loving doubled~~
> ~~That~~
> And—several other things which I forget—
> Or which at least I need not mention yet.

The end result of all this labour, the finished couplet, is genuinely amusing: but mostly if one knows its compositional context, the series of false starts from which Byron turns in comic defeat. These contexts are unavailable to the reader, though, and as printed the couplet is accurately described by Steffan as 'lame' (though, I suppose, it could be read, less damagingly, as euphemistic, a sort of conspiratorial wink to the reader; as if to say, *you* fill in what else Juan wanted besides laying his head on Julia's bosom).[35] Byron seems not to have cared: here and elsewhere in revision his concern is less the finished product than the compositional process itself; the joke is for himself only, or perhaps also for readers of the manuscript.

That the activity of writing was more important to Byron than the finished work is suggested also in the best-known of his poetical self-explanations, from the beginning of Canto III of *Childe Harold's Pilgrimage* (1816). Why write?

> 'Tis to create, and in creating live
> A being more intense, that we endow
> With form our fancy, gaining as we give
> The life we image, even as I do now.
> What am I? Nothing; but not so art thou,
> Soul of my thought! with whom I traverse earth,
> Invisible but gazing, as I glow
> Mix'd with thy spirit, blended with thy birth,
> And feeling still with thee in my crush'd feelings' dearth. (III. 6)

---

[35] See *Byron's 'Don Juan'*, ed. Steffan and Pratt, i. 120.

What matters here is *Byron's* existence, the kind of life writing gives him; Harold matters because he gives Byron (not the reader) life, because in the act of composition Byron can travel with him, mix and blend with him, feel what he feels. It is the process that matters.

So, too, a year later, when we are told at the beginning of Canto IV that

> The beings of the mind are not of clay;
> Essentially immortal, they create
> And multiply in us a brighter ray
> And more beloved existence: that which Fate
> Prohibits to dull life, in this our state
> Of mortal bondage, by these spirits supplied
> First exiles, then replaces what we hate;
> Watering the heart whose early flowers have died,
> And with a fresher growth replenishing the void.   (IV. 5)

Immediately, in these lines, Byron moves from the nature of imaginative characters—never, of course, either here or in Canto III, of the work itself—to their effect on 'us', by which he mostly means 'me', given the familiar Byronic litany of 'mortal bondage', withered hopes, 'the void'. The 'more beloved existence' of the stanza's fourth line exists within the poet (in this case, the reader as well), not the work; it is the effect of the work on the poet or reader. Even if we think of the stanza as more concerned with the purpose of works than the purpose of writing (in comparison to its counterpart in Canto III), it is *purpose* that concerns Byron. Neither passage communicates much sense of the poem as finished work.

BYRON AND THE MARKET

That Byron's class position was unsure often made him *more* rather than less insistent upon the gentlemanly or non-professional character of poetical composition. 'In England', Byron proclaims in a letter of 10 January 1820 to Richard Hoppner, 'none are strictly noble but peers—not even peers' Sons.'[36] Byron's own title, though, came to him indirectly, in

---

[36] Letter of 10 Jan. 1820 to Richard Hoppner, in *BLJ*, ed. Marchand, vii. 25.

Jerome Christensen's phrase, was 'contingent',[37] breeding a sensitivity exacerbated by the relative poverty and obscurity of his early years, and by subsequent slights, as when his relation, Lord Carlisle, refused to participate in Byron's induction into the House of Lords. As Lord Holland remarked to Thomas Moore: 'It was *not* from his birth that Lord Byron had taken the station he held in society, for till his talents became known, he was, in spite of his birth, in any thing but good society, and *but* for his talents would never, perhaps, have been in any better.'[38] From attitudes such as these—or, rather, from the desire to combat them—came, in part, the uneasy ancestor-mongering of *Hours of Idleness* (1807), so cruelly skewered by Henry Brougham in the *Edinburgh Review*. They must also have been a source of Byron's extreme personal touchiness about rank and due. In reaction—both to his own insecurities and to the larger issue of hereditary excellence—Byron sometimes grew meritocratic, rudely dismissing society as '*fatal* to all original undertakings of every kind'.[39]

Christensen sees such wavering or uncertainty as representative: like many in his age, Byron was caught between conflicting visions of aristocracy, one 'integrative and economic', in which peerage and gentry combine, the other 'by and large cultural and political', in which peerage and gentry are distinguished by 'the incompatible and irrepressible claim that existence is hereditary, colored by the blood that flows, and that excellence is merited, tinctured by the blood one sheds'.[40] Hazlitt makes much the same point, at least implicitly, in anatomizing Byron's 'egotism'. 'A mere nobleman', he writes in *The Spirit of the Age*, 'is, in [Byron's] estimation, but "the tenth transmitter of a foolish face": a mere man of genius is no better than a worm.'[41] This point is also seconded by Lady Blessington, who said of Byron that 'he seemed to think that the bays of the author ought to be entwined with a coronet to render either valuable,

---

[37] Jerome Christensen, 'Theorizing Byron's Practice: The Performance of Lordship and the Poet's Career', *Studies in Romanticism*, 27/4 (Winter 1988), 482.
[38] Quoted in Leslie A. Marchand, *Byron: A Biography*, 3 vols. (New York: Alfred A. Knopf, 1957), i. 32.
[39] Letter of 4 Mar. 1822 to Thomas Moore, *BLJ*, ed. Marchand, ix. 119.
[40] Christensen, 'Theorizing Byron's Practice', 482.
[41] William Hazlitt, *The Spirit of the Age*, in *Complete Works*, ed. Howe, xi. 77.

as, singly, they were not sufficiently attractive'.[42] Even in *Hours of Idleness* it was not enough for Byron, as the preface implies, merely to rank 'amongst "the mob of gentlemen who write" ', or to have his name recorded only 'on a posthumous page in "The Catalogue of Royal and Noble Authors" '.[43] Yet when tempted by an inclusive conception of nobility as achievement, the achievement in question was rarely thought of as a 'product'; merit was always for Byron a matter of shedding not sweating blood.

At least that is the image—the poet as man of action, the poet born—Byron would project. The reality, of course, was more complex. Early Byron, in Manning's words, 'was unusually sensitive to the reception of his poetry',[44] and some part of the vehemence and ostentation of his subsequent defiance of commercial pressures may derive from a sense of prior complicity. When Byron told Murray he would write no more 'Ladies books' (the Eastern tales), in Steffan's paraphrase, 'to court their praise',[45] he was admitting as much. Manning writes of Murray 'resourcefully cajoling Byron to continue in genres he calculated would sell . . . incurring accusations of negligence in order to discourage others, surreptitiously circulating or adroitly publicizing some poems while suppressing or excising others', but he also points to instances of authorial compliance, again for commercial reasons, as when, upon request, Byron furnished the previously discussed three additional stanzas to the 'Ode to Napoleon Buonaparte' expressly to avoid stamp duty for pamphlets of less than a sheet.[46] Manning even cites a letter from Murray suggesting that the crucial shift from sublime to comic styles was commercially motivated. 'Give me a poem,' Murray wrote Byron in January 1817, 'a good Venetian tale describing manners formerly from the story itself, and now from your

---

[42] Ernest J. Lovell (ed.), *Lady Blessington's Conversations of Lord Byron* (Princeton: Princeton University Press, 1969), 97–8.

[43] See *Complete Poetical Works*, ed. McGann, i. 34.

[44] Manning, '*Don Juan* and the Revisionary Self', 210.

[45] For 'Ladies books' see letter of 6 Apr. 1819 to Murray, in *BLJ*, ed. Marchand, vi. 107; for Steffan's paraphrase see *Byron's 'Don Juan'*, ed. Steffan and Pratt, i. 24.

[46] See Peter J. Manning, 'The Nameless Broken Dandy and the Structure of Authorship', in *Reading Romantics: Texts and Contexts* (New York: Oxford University Press, 1990), 147.

own observations, and call it "Marianna".[47] 'Marianna Segati was Byron's mistress,' comments Manning, and 'the following August Byron heard from her husband the anecdote which became the basis for *Beppo*, written in October'. As for *Don Juan* itself, 'its publication over several years enabled Byron repeatedly to situate his writing against the criticisms passed on earlier cantos'.[48]

None of which is to minimize Byron's later defiance of market considerations; the comic poems would neither have been written nor published—at least not in anything like their present form—without tenacious resistance to commercial or editorial pressure. It is only to suggest that often Byron's remarks about revision and composition are not to be trusted. 'It is ironic', comments Steffan of the composition of the first cantos of *Don Juan*, that Byron 'exercised most caution with the manuscripts ... when he pretended to take *Juan* lightly and that when opposition later drove him to protest his seriousness he then preceded to dash off canto after canto with extraordinary facility'.[49] Though it is hard to see that Byron ever, as Christensen maintains, 'relinquished his pose of gifted, indifferent amateur',[50] it is certainly true that his relations with the market were more complex and varied than his correspondence or public statements would suggest. It could even be argued that his relatively untroubled reaction to literary piracy—what Manning calls the 'Hone-ing' of his texts, after the radical publisher and literary pirate, William Hone—was calculated rather than unconcerned (notable exceptions to this equanimity include his genuine fury at the staging of *Marino Faliero* against his wishes, his refusal to co-operate with Galignani on a French edition, and his anger over the piracy of *Cain*). Byron's notoriety owed much to Hone's thefts, and Byron cultivated notoriety. Ian Jack conjectures that

---

[47] Quoted by Manning in '*Don Juan* and the Revisionary Self', 219. Manning's source is Samuel Smiles, *A Publisher and His Friends: Memoir and Correspondence of the Late John Murray*, 2 vols. (London: John Murray, 1891), i. 396.

[48] Manning, '*Don Juan* and the Revisionary Self', 219, 221.

[49] *Byron's 'Don Juan'*, ed. Steffan and Pratt, i. 114.

[50] Jerome Christensen, 'Byron's Career: The Speculative Stage', *English Literary History*, 52/1 (Spring 1985), 66. Christensen divides Byron's relations with Murray into 'four phases of self-abandonment' (p. 64), the 'speculative' one, when Byron supposedly ceased posing as a literary amateur, being 'pivotal' (p. 64).

Byron's willingness privately to circulate poetry Murray and his advisers disapproved of sometimes derived from a sense that such material was bound, therefore, to get pirated and more widely circulated.[51] Byron, I am suggesting, was always more commercially aware than he wished others to think.

BYRONIC REVISION AND 'ROMANTICISM'

There is a literary historical dimension to Byron's reluctance to revise, or to be thought to revise, one which feeds into the temperamental and class factors already discussed. Later Byron self-consciously set himself against 'vasty' (a phrase from the dedication to *Don Juan*, stanza 4) or 'Romantic' conceptions of poetic composition, the sorts of conceptions found in Wordsworth's prefaces and poems (and used by contemporary editors to override his explicit instructions about ordering and versions), in Coleridge's Shakespeare lectures and the *Biographia Literaria* (1817), in Keats's 'Sleep and Poetry'. As M. H. Abrams puts it, by way of explaining Byron's absence from *Natural Supernaturalism* (1971), his influential study of Romantic narrative, 'in his greatest work he speaks with an ironic countervoice and deliberately opens a satirical perspective on the vatic stance of his Romantic contemporaries'.[52] Yet in respect to revision, Byron's theory and practice were if anything *more* Romantic than those of other figures discussed in this book. Like Lady Adeline in Canto XVI of *Don Juan*, Byron is always 'acted on by what is nearest' (XVI. 97): 'When I once take pen in hand—I *must* say what comes uppermost.'[53] As both Steffan and George Ridenour, among others, have been at pains to emphasize, when it comes to energy, of which spontaneity is a manifestation, Byron is as keen as, for example, Blake.[54]

---

[51] For Hone see Peter J. Manning, 'The Hone-ing of Byron's *Corsair*', in *Reading Romantics*, 216–37. See also Jerome J. McGann, *The Textual Condition* (Princeton: Princeton University Press, 1991), 58, and Hugh J. Luke, Jr., 'The Publishing of Byron's *Don Juan*', *PMLA* 80 (1965), 198–209. For Ian Jack's conjectures see *The Poet and His Audience*, 72–5.

[52] M. H. Abrams, *Natural Supernaturalism: Tradition and Revolution in Romantic Literature* (New York: W. W. Norton, 1971), 13.

[53] Letter of 6 June 1822 to Murray, in *BLJ*, ed. Marchand, ix. 168.

[54] See *Byron's 'Don Juan'*, ed. Steffan and Pratt, i. esp. 130–8, and George Ridenour, *The Style of Don Juan* (New Haven: Yale University Press, 1960), and 'Don Juan and the Romantics', *Studies in Romanticism*, 16/3 (Fall 1977), 563–71.

Romantic notions affect Byron's revisions in several ways. For Coleridge and Wordsworth, as we have seen, a prime purpose of narrative is to convert sequences into wholes. But for Byron, as McGann argues, 'the true significance of sequential events is not that they confirm a wonderful, harmonious order in the world but that they reveal the equally wonderful, apparently endless, and yet finite possibilities of order and disorder'.[55] Variety becomes an aesthetic criterion, as in the description of Lord Amundeville's Norman Abbey (modelled on Byron's own Newstead Abbey), which was 'irregular in parts | Yet left a grand impression on the mind' (XIII. 67), or the shifting, flickering glory of the Northern Lights, with their 'thousand and a thousand colours' (VII. 1). *Don Juan* is a literary equivalent of such phenomena, an 'ever-varying rhyme, | A versified Aurora Borealis' (VII. 2). Like Lord Amundeville's or any other 'Gothic' structure, it is added to rather than develops.[56] Organic unity, the aesthetic benchmark of High Romanticism, is, thus, openly flouted (though a preference for the Gothic is, in other contexts, also 'Romantic'); the poem, in McGann's words, 'is radically, aggressively episodic and meandering. . . . However it would have stopped, Byron would still have wanted to say: "I leave the thing a problem, like all things" (XVII. 13).'[57] Manning makes a related point about the thematic implications of the poem's narrative. He sees both Donna Julia and Haidée as representing possible closures for both Juan and the poem, closures which are false and falsifying, a Byronic equivalent of Blake's Beulah. 'Byron's refusal to linger over the episode of Juan and Haidée is a refusal of fixation, a refusal of the seductions of completion and finality. He writes their story not as a self-contained heroico-pathetic romance like his own earlier tales, but as part of an ongoing narrative whose rhythms undo the authority both of its dreams of bliss and of its conclusion.'[58]

Given such an aesthetic, Byron is unlikely to have troubled much about consistency and coherence, primary objectives of revision proper. Hence, as McGann points out, his self-conscious ease with transitions, often sites of extensive alteration

---

[55] McGann, *'Don Juan' in Context*, 101.
[56] See ibid. 34.   [57] Ibid. 3–4.
[58] Peter J. Manning, 'Byron's Imperceptiveness to the English Word', in *Reading Romantics*, 128.

for more conventional Romantics, particularly Wordsworth.[59] Except for a few nervous additions in the opening cantos of *Don Juan*, which Steffan calls 'neither very attractive or successful',[60] Byron is perfectly content not only to accept but often to draw attention to sudden or discordant alterations of mood or register; such awkwardnesses are part of the poem's famously planless plan. 'I *have* no plan—I *had* no plan—but I had or have materials', Byron declares shortly after completing Cantos I and II;[61] 'the fact is that I have nothing plann'd', the narrator tells us towards the opening of Canto IV (stanza 5); 'I know not,'[62] was Byron's serious answer about the number of cantos the poem would contain. Whereas Wordsworth is made anxious by the absence of plans, as in the agitated rhythms of the 'Glad Preamble' of *The Prelude*, Byron is perfectly at home without one. Though eventually he offered several schemes for the poem, including one which involved Juan in the French Revolution and its aftermath, another in the fight for Greek independence, and a third in an eventual return to Spain after expulsion from England (thus recalling the shape of *The Prelude*, which also returns the poem to its starting point), none stuck. In February 1821 Byron outlined one scheme for Murray and a different one for Thomas Medwin; later, in Greece, he called the poem's first sixteen cantos an 'introduction', hinting mischievously at a finished poem of 150 cantos (other projected numbers were 24 and 100).[63] One consequence of this unplanned or improvised mode of procedure, as has been suggested, is a relative minimum of structural or tonal refining. If something does not fit, that's part of the poem's point or meaning; so too if a prominent character simply disappears (Manning mentions the English adventurer Johnson);[64] or if plot points or possible connections are missed (as in Byron's complete failure to explain how Juan gets out of the harem in Canto VI or to identify

[59] See McGann, *'Don Juan' in Context*, 91–3.
[60] *Byron's 'Don Juan'*, ed. Steffan and Pratt, 87.
[61] Letter of 12 Aug. 1819 to John Murray, in *BLJ*, ed. Marchand, vi. 207.
[62] Letter of 16 Feb. 1821 to John Murray, ibid. viii. 78.
[63] Ibid.; for Medwin see Ernest J. Lovell, Jr. (ed.), *Medwin's Conversations of Lord Byron* (Princeton: Princeton University Press, 1966), 164–5; the 24 and 100 canto plans are mentioned in *Don Juan* xii. 55.
[64] Peter J. Manning, *Byron and His Fictions* (Detroit: Wayne State University Press, 1978), 190.

the women who show up with him at the Russian camp in Canto VII). These, of course, are the traditional concerns of revision.

REVISION AND SCEPTICISM

Behind Byron's attack on organic unity lies a thoroughgoing scepticism, one that works to undermine hopes not only of perfection but of improvement. 'I leave the thing a problem, like all things' (XVII. 12): the search for perfection in art is wrong as well as futile, at least to a poet of Byron's mimetic (as opposed to 'vatic' or 'vasty') character. Moreover, 'if a writer should be quite consistent, | How could he possibly show things existent?' (XV. 87)—a question which leads directly to doubts about veracity *per se*:

> If people contradict themselves, can I
>   Help contradicting them, and every body,
> Even my veracious self?—But that's a lie;
>   I never did so, never will—how should I?
> He who doubts all things, nothing can deny;
>   Truth's fountains may be clear—her streams are muddy.
>   (XV. 88)

Here, as so often in *Don Juan*, revision or second thought ('But that's a lie') lies out in the open; the stanza incorporates it as it goes along, which may be why, as elsewhere, the first draft of the stanza was printed without alteration. Compare Wordsworth's wholly serious allusion to Book XII of *Paradise Lost*, 'the road lies plain before me' (*The Prelude*, 1850, I. 640), with *Don Juan's* 'The world is all before me—or behind' (XIV. 9). Wordsworth's line is both an expression of hope and an act of will. In fact, as *The Prelude* itself makes clear, he is everywhere assaulted by paths or tropes for his poem, as well as by inhibiting predecessors such as Milton; this is why he has such trouble getting the poem started—though in the end he will, indeed, choose one plain (autobiographical) road. The line is finally, subtly ironic. Byron's allusion is more openly ironic, and doubly mimetic: not only does it insist upon a larger truth of multiplicity (and the corresponding 'lie' of single ways), but it does so performatively, again openly incorporating second thoughts ('or behind'), and thus obviating revision proper. 'It is through its many forms of contradiction', claims McGann, 'that the poem declares its truth-function to consist in the setting of problems and not the presentation of solutions.'[65] When Byron does revise, as we shall see, it is often precisely in this direction: seeming solutions are problematized, single tones, moods, and styles are consistently complicated, undercut, overturned.

George Watson points to a related feature of Byron's scepticism, one that concerns language. 'There are many moments', he writes of *Don Juan*, 'when Byron seems to surrender himself to the language, in a sort of joking despair, as to something he cannot resist but may, after all, confide in.'[66] This sense—whether thought of as mature or defeatist—connects to a more general conservatism, inspiring impatience with Romantic innovation and its claims both of autonomy, as in Southey's 'insolent wish', shared by the other 'Lakers', 'to supersede all warblers here below' (dedication to *Don Juan*, stanza 3), and of theoretical rigour, as in the age's 'wrong revolutionary poetical system— or systems', from which, among current poets, 'none but Rogers and Crabbe are free'.[67] Byron's acceptance of what is given— in language and literary convention—relates directly to his freedom from thoughts of 'perfecting' things. It may also reflect a class antipathy, given that the 'system' in question, in Hazlitt's words, 'gets rid of all the high plains of poetry. . . . [T]he distinctions of rank, birth, wealth, power . . . are not to be found here.'[68] 'No poetry is *generally* good', Byron writes to Murray on 23 April 1820, 'only by fits and starts—and you are lucky to get a sparkle here and there—you might as well want a Midnight *all stars*—as rhyme all perfect.'[69] 'When Pegasus seems winning | The race', we are told at the beginning of Canto IV of *Don Juan*, 'he sprains a wing, and down we tend' (IV. 1). Such falls are inevitable, human. As Byron writes to Moore on 5 July 1821: ' I can never get people to understand that poetry

---

[65] Jerome J. McGann, 'Byron's Twin Opposites of Truth', in *Towards a Literature of Knowledge* (Chicago: University of Chicago Press, 1989), 57.

[66] Watson, 'The Accuracy of Lord Byron', 143.

[67] Letter of 15 Sept. 1817 to John Murray, in *BLJ*, ed. Marchand, v. 265.

[68] William Hazlitt, *The Spirit of the Age*, in *Complete Works*, ed. Howe, xi. 87.

[69] Letter of 23 Apr. 1820 to John Murray, in *BLJ*, ed. Marchand, vii. 84.

is the expression of *excited passion*, and that there is no such thing as a life of passion any more than a continuous earthquake, or an eternal fever.'[70]

A good example of the 'maturity' of Byron's attitude to compositional perfection is provided by lines from *Beppo*. On 11 April 1818 Byron wrote to Murray explaining his motives for a particular revision, something he did even less frequently than revising itself. The lines in question are those previously cited from stanza 74, in which 'professional' poets are disparaged. In the original version Botherby is described as follows:

A stalking oracle of awful phrase
    The approving '*Good*' (by no means GOOD in Law)
Humming like flies around the newest blaze,
    The bluest of bluebottles you e'er saw,
Teasing with blame excruciating with praise,
    Gorging the little fame he gets all raw
Translating tongues he knows not even by letter,
And sweating plays so middling, bad were better.   (74. 585–92)

Byron declares that he wants to alter the line 'Gorging the little fame he gets all raw' (l. 590) to 'Gorging the slightest slice of flattery raw' for stylistic reasons; he is worried about the presence of the word 'fame' in the previous stanza, and a consequent distracting echo. The alteration, though, continues to bother him: it lacks something of the strength of the original, and for Byron, 'anything is better than weakening an expression, or a thought. I would rather be as booming as Nat Lee—than wishy-washy.' In the end, Byron leaves the decision about which version to print up to William Gifford, Murray's chief editor, to whom, after he'd left England in 1816, Byron frequently delegated the responsibility for seeing his poems through the press. 'Ask Mr. Gifford', he tells Murray, 'and Mr. Hobhouse, and, as they think, so let it be.'[71] This willingness to let others decide is no mere matter of detail; it is also, for example, extended to larger questions of attribution. As Byron writes to Murray, of *Beppo*: 'If you think that it will do *you* or the work—or *works* any good—you may—or may not put my name

---

[70] Letter of 5 July 1821 to Thomas Moore, ibid. viii. 146.
[71] Letter of 11 Apr. 1818 to John Murray, ibid. vi. 27.

to it—*but first consult the knowing ones.*'[72] Byron was, in one sense, not joking—or rather, not *only* joking—when he declared in Canto IV of *Don Juan,* apropos pressure from his publisher to alter the poem's direction and character, that "Tis all the same to me; I'm fond of yielding' (IV. 98).

Yielding such as this arises neither from laziness nor insecurity, but from a sense of the ultimate impossibility of the sort of control and surety Wordsworth aspired to in revision. The world is mixed, various, 'mobile', and Byron can't choose; maybe others will see particular issues—the alteration of a line, the effect on a reputation—more clearly. Byron refuses an authorial 'totalizing fantasy', one of perfect control, as surely as *Don Juan* rolls past the Haidée episode, with its promise of perfect bliss. He simply has too vivid a sense of the part played by contingency in composition, as in all human affairs. 'Ah!——what should follow slips from my reflection,' is how he begins Canto XV of *Don Juan,*

> Whatever follows ne'ertheless may be
> As apropos of hope or retrospection,
> As though the lurking thought had follow'd free.   (XV. 1)

Plans, in other words, are illusions, one as good as another. Or, as the next stanza continues,

> . . . more or less the whole's a syncopé
> Or a singultus—emblems of Emotion,
> The grand Antithesis to great Ennui,
> Wherewith we break our bubbles on the ocean,
> That Watery Outline of Eternity.   (XV. 2)

The 'whole' here means the whole of human effort, including all of human utterance, which reduces to emotion—a swoon, a sob. That poetry is what Byron has in mind in the passage is suggested by the implied function of such 'emblems' (the swoon, the sob): to combat boredom, to be 'the grand Antithesis to great Ennui'. Here, too, poetical utterance is likened to a bubble, as in a previously quoted passage from Canto XIV ('mine's a bubble not blown up for praise | But just to play with as an infant plays'), the very opposite of Wordsworth's metaphor of

---

[72] Letter of 25 Mar. 1818 to John Murray, ibid. 25.

poems as monuments. And, again, why bother revising ephemera, froth, foam?

Byron's fetish for literal accuracy seems at first to contradict this scepticism about improvement and perfection. As Steffan points out, Byron's revisions reveal him to be 'finical about qualifications of degree, minute differences in time, number, and quantity':[73] 'six flasks of wine', for example, rather than 'five quarts of rum' (*Don Juan*, II. 47); 'twelve' days not 'ten' (II. 49); 'five' not 'three' bits of lead (V. 39). But such particularity—or particularizing—can be seen as an ally of scepticism. The impression it conveys is that for Byron the world is a place of irreducible individuality and multitudinousness; the sort of place that mocks theory, explanation, the search for essential properties. As McGann puts it, '*Don Juan* argues that while the world is the subject *of* our understanding, it is not subject *to* our understanding.'[74] Hence related remarks about human powerlessness, such as the assertion that 'few mortals know what end they would be at' (*Don Juan*, I. 133), or the advice to Hobhouse to 'above all recollect that it is all luck in this world'.[75] Such views are reinforced, it could be argued, by the plot of *Don Juan*, in which the hero is as passive, as acted upon, as Waverley. In the opening episode of Canto I, characteristically, 'nothing turns out as any of [the characters] had hoped or expected . . . and in the second episode, Nature's large forces stand as the very symbol of the unforeseen factor in life'.[76]

Such a view of human contingency is unlikely to encourage obsessive revision, just as a passion for discordant local detail hardly harmonizes with the aims of shapeliness and order, for example. 'My Muse by no means deals in fiction,' Byron declares in Canto XIV of *Don Juan*, 'she gathers a repertory of facts' (XIV. 13)—a repertory which, because it contains or constitutes 'too much truth, at first sight, ne'er attracts' (XIV. 13). Consider the poem's famous digressiveness and the consequent distortion or disfiguring of narrative and tone. Often the poem's digressions create—cultivate—the impression that Byron is willing to forgo 'art' (as he elsewhere forgoes or undermines

---

[73] See *Byron's 'Don Juan'*, ed. Steffan and Pratt, i. 154.
[74] McGann, *'Don Juan' in Context*, 112.
[75] Letter of 19 June 1819 to John Hobhouse, in *BLJ*, ed. Marchand, vi. 93.
[76] McGann, *'Don Juan' in Context*, 101.

'system') for the sake of awkward particulars. His compositional liberties 'some irregularity may make | In the design', so that he feels it necessary to beg pardon, 'as I have a high sense | Of Aristotle and the Rules' (*Don Juan*, I. 120)—though it is the rules and regularity which yield. The digressive impulse is as much 'On the other hand, of course,' or 'But that's not right,' as 'It just occurs to me'; it too, in other words, can be seen as a form of internal revision, obviating revision proper. The world, such digressiveness implies, is simply too various and mobile for either simple, single assertions or art. When Francis Cohen famously objects to the poem's changes in tone, its simultaneous scorching and drenching, Byron defends himself by referring to examples drawn from common human experience, from the nature of the world.[77]

REVISION AND THE BYRONIC SELF

The subject, or self, as well as the object, partakes of this mobility or inconstancy, with comparable implications for revision. Unlike Wordsworth, Byron, it has been argued, had no illusions about the single and continuous nature of personal identity. 'I hate inconstancy', he mockingly declares towards the end of Canto II, 'I loathe, detest, | Abhor, condemn, abjure the mortal made | Of such quicksilver clay that in his breast | No permanent foundation can be laid' (II. 209)—at which point he himself strays. 'Opinions are made to be changed,' he tells Murray in a letter of 9 May 1818, 'or how is truth to be got at?'[78] So full of easy contradiction is Byron's life and character, 'that I almost think that the same skin | For one without—has two or three within' (*Don Juan*, XVII. 11). This sense of Byron's that his identity was fluid or multiple others shared as well. His friend Lady Blessington called him 'a perfect chameleon', and was convinced 'that if ten individuals undertook the task of describing Byron, no two, of the ten, would agree'.[79] As for the discrete moments or episodes that make up a life—or the narrative of *Don Juan* —these remain discrete, unlike, for example,

---

[77] See letter of 12 Aug. 1819 to John Murray, in *BLJ*, ed. Marchand, vi. 207–8.
[78] Letter of 9 May 1818 to John Murray, ibid. v. 221.
[79] See Lovell (ed.), *Lady Blessington's Conversations of Lord Byron*, 72.

Wordsworth's 'spots of time', which implicitly disclose a single, larger truth, and with it a correspondingly single subjectivity. The moments in Juan's life seem as individual as the selves that experience them; they are neither epiphanal nor disclose any ordering principle (though their dissimilarity could be said to reinforce the poem's prominant *ubi sunt* or elegiac strain). Manning makes a related point about the poem's aimlessness: 'Byron's refusal to treat [Juan's] life according to the familiar pattern of crisis autobiography is a dissent from the notion of a fixed identity, of a life stiffening into shape once and for all.'[80]

Byron was fully prepared to admit, as Wordsworth would only reluctantly, that both his style and his ideas—the self he projects in his writing—changed not only over time but within individual works; he also felt little need to go back to past works, or previous parts of a work, to make them consistent with new work—that is, to revise, as did Wordsworth, after publication. Once the work is gone into press for Byron, it makes its own way in the world, is a mere 'product', no longer connected to him in the way, for example, Wordsworth continued to feel himself connected with published work. If Cantos III and IV of *Childe Harold's Pilgrimage* appear to differ importantly from Cantos I and II, in terms of both narrative strategy (the relation of poet to protagonist) and metaphysics, so be it: no attempt is made to revise the earlier cantos into conformity with the new ones. The disappearance of Childe Harold as a character 'speaking in his own person' is blithely explained away in the preface to Canto IV: 'I had become weary of drawing a line which everyone seemed determined not to perceive.'[81] Byron was also quite candid about wishing to dissociate himself from the earlier 'Byronic' mode. As he put it in a letter of 15 September 1817 to Murray, his intellect was 'progressive', and would grow out of the limiting habits of his previous verse. Change of style for Byron meant growth, a chance 'to repel the charge of monotony and mannerism';[82] for Wordsworth, change of style mostly meant loss and decay. As for memory, the

[80] Manning, 'Byron's Imperceptiveness to the English Word', in *Reading Romantics*, 133.
[81] *Complete Poetical Works*, ed. McGann, ii. 122.
[82] Letters of 15 Sept. 1817 and 25 Mar. 1818 to John Murray, in *BLJ*, ed. Marchand, v. 265 and vi. 25.

guarantor of the self's integrity, for Wordsworth as for Locke before him, Byron held out no great hopes. 'It is singular,' he writes in one of his 'Detached Thoughts', 'how soon we lose the impression of what ceases to be *constantly* before us.—A year impairs, a lustre obliterates.—There is little distinct left without an *effort* of memory,—then indeed the lights are rekindled for a moment—but who can be sure that the Imagination is not the torch-bearer?' (a truth *The Prelude* also discovers, though only, as I've argued, to resist).[83]

There may well be an unconscious class element involved in attitudes such as these. Thinking of oneself as possessed of a single, continuous identity over time, a coherent interiority established by memory, could be—has been—seen as serving a larger social function. A unified interior self offered the emergent middle classes of the late seventeenth and eighteenth centuries—the rising classes, that is—an escape from traditional and restrictive structures of self-definition (e.g. 'region or birth or . . . communal rituals').[84] Byron might well have seen too overt a preoccupation with personal identity—the sort of preoccupation which makes a project like *The Prelude* thinkable—'bourgeois'. While a man of Wordsworth's class position, the son of a nobleman's steward, might be keen to escape an identity determined in large measure by traditional or 'impersonal' forms of social differentiation, an aristocrat, even one as 'contingent' as Byron, might not. What is clear, though, is that the moral implications of different notions of identity had class inflections. Wordsworth implicitly connects the disconnectedness of *Don Juan* with immorality; Byron's ostentatiously easy or offhand denial of wholeness, both in the work and the self, is seen from a thoroughly bourgeois perspective. *Don Juan*, 'that infamous publication', contributes to the moral weakening of the nation, 'not so much as a *Book*', but in the form of 'choice

[83] See 'Detached Thoughts', no. 51, ibid. ix. 29.

[84] See Felicity Nussbaum, *The Autobiographical Subject: Gender and Ideology in Eighteenth-Century England* (Baltimore: Johns Hopkins University Press, 1989), 54, and more generally ch. 2, 'The Politics of Subjectivity', 30–57. Asa Briggs also discusses the relation of middle-class self-consciousness to traditional forms of social differentiation in two somewhat overlapping essays: 'Middle-Class Consciousness in English Politics', *Past and Present*, 9 (Apr. 1956), 65–74, and 'The Language of "Class" in Early Nineteenth-Century England', in M. W. Flinn and T. C. Smout (eds.), *Essays on Social History* (Oxford: Clarendon Press, 1974), 154–77.

bits', 'extracts'. The poem is an attack both on 'the institutions of the country' and 'the English character'.[85] As for Byron, he was not only well aware of but cultivated, even as he professed to deny, such charges. Censure like Wordsworth's was mere 'prudery'; whenever possible the poem's enemies were depicted as gauche and small-minded. In defending the poem, Byron's tone is tauntingly *de haut en bas*. As Hazlitt puts it, of Byron's satire in general: 'If a great man meets with a rebuff which he does not like, he turns on his heel, and this passes for repartee. . . . So, his Lordship, in a "Letter to the Editor of My Grandmother's Review," addresses him fifty times as *"my dear Robarts"*.'[86]

REVISING *DON JUAN*

As has been mentioned, the opening cantos of *Don Juan* are among the most heavily revised of Byron's writings. So worked over was Canto I that 'only Byron himself could have unscrambled its disorder'. The additions and excisions began 'as soon as the first draft was finished, and continued after the fair copy had been sent off'. Steffan, from whom I have been quoting, calls the holographs of Canto I 'astonishing refutations of the generally accepted view not only of Byron's working habits but of Byron himself as he wished others to see him'.[87] In Canto I, over 40 per cent of the lines show some reworking; in the fair copy, 124 lines are altered, 13 completely rewritten; a total of 46 per cent of the lines (628 by Steffan's calculation) underwent correction at some stage of composition. In the later cantos, these percentages drop off dramatically. As for time of composition, the dedication and Canto I took Byron four months to complete, Canto II took a month, Cantos III and IV together took three months. With later cantos, time of composition is measured in weeks or days. What such figures suggest is that once Byron had arrived at the poem's style or manner—in effect,

---

[85] See Edith J. Morley (ed.), *The Correspondence of H. C. Crabb Robinson with the Wordsworth Circle*, 2 vols. (Oxford: Clarendon Press, 1927), ii. 850–1.

[86] Hazlitt, *The Spirit of the Age*, in *Complete Works*, ed. Howe, ii. 74.

[87] *Byron's 'Don Juan'*, ed. Steffan and Pratt, i. 13, 14, 104. Steffan is the source, also, of the ensuing statistics.

'set it going'—it pretty much ran itself. Though one might argue that later cantos were less heavily revised because Byron himself ceased to copy them, it could also be countered that he seems no longer to have felt such copying necessary.

Most of Byron's revisions in *Don Juan* take the form of additions rather than excisions or alterations (though there are also a surprising number of perfectly straightforward stylistic improvements). These additions were frequently copied crosswise onto, or interleaved with, first drafts, though some emerge mysteriously in fair copies. The work grew like *The Giaour* (1813), Byron's 'snake' of a poem, constantly 'lengthening its rattles'.[88] Altogether Byron added 166 stanzas to the various first drafts, 134 of which were added to the first eight cantos (half to Canto I alone). All but three cantos (VI, VII, XVII) had stanzas added after the final draft. Such additions count as revision not just because addition *per se* 'revises' a text. When Wordsworth expanded *The Prelude* from two to five to thirteen to fourteen books he was revising the poem with each expansion; the expansions took place within an already determined conceptual and narrative structure, one in which the poem rounds back to its beginning. Such expansions could be thought of as interpolations. So, too, with *Don Juan*: when Byron turns his manuscript sideways and adds two or three stanzas to an already extant sequence, this too is a revision. When, though, Byron adds Canto III, and then IV, to the two original cantos of *Childe Harold's Pilgrimage*, as he added Cantos III and IV to *Don Juan* I and II, he is doing something different, as he is in all further added cantos to *Don Juan*. *Childe Harold* I–IV, 'completed' in 1818, is a separate work from *Childe Harold* I–II, published in 1812, not a revised version of the earlier work;[89] though the two later cantos carry forward the narrative as it existed in Cantos I–II, the Childe Harold who emerges from I–IV is, for example, different in kind from the hero of I–II, is a different and more ambiguous species of fictional character. As for revising (interpolating, excising, substituting), the latest

[88] Letter of 26 Aug. 1813 to John Murray, in *BLJ*, ed. Marchand, iii. 100.
[89] *Complete Poetical Works*, ed. McGann, i. 264, thinks of *Childe Harold* as assuming three possible forms: 'as a single, integral poem, as two loosely related units (Cantos I–II and Cantos III–IV), or as three separate parts of one changing poetic project (Cantos I–II, Canto III, Canto IV)'.

substantial alterations Byron made to Cantos I–II were in the seventh edition of 1814, before the publication of subsequent cantos. The creation of *Childe Harold* I–IV entailed addition to, not revision of, I–II. When Byron protests to Murray that 'Pope *added* to the "Rape of the Lock"—but did not reduce it,' he seems to have had in mind some such distinction.

One characteristic function of a number of the interpolated additions to the early cantos of *Don Juan* is to complicate or overturn moods, whether sombre or light. The aim, in part, is to keep readers off balance. In Canto II the shipwrecked seamen see a rainbow, 'a good omen' (ii. 93), and then 'a beautiful white bird' (ii. 94). This bird

> ... pass'd oft before their eyes,
> And tried to perch, although it saw and heard
>   The men within the boat, and in this guise
> It came and went, and flutter'd round them till
> Night fell:—this seem'd a better omen still.   (ii. 94)

In the original, twilight follows, the stars shine out, and the wind begins to blow again. In revision, though, Byron interpolates a crosswise stanza which deliberately undercuts the bird's spiritual or aesthetic associations (while also echoing earlier grotesquerie, the demise of Juan's tutor, Pedrillo). Had it been imprudent enough to perch upon 'our shatter'd bark' (ii. 95), the bird would not have survived. Even

> ... had it been the dove from Noah's ark,
>   Returning from her successful search,
> Which in their way that moment chanced to fall,
> They would have eat her, olive-branch and all.   (ii. 95)

Here, as throughout the poem, the bodily or material triumphs, a central theme in Canto II in particular. But also unsettled or overturned is the gathering mood of quiet seriousness in stanzas 93–4.

Similarly, in Canto I, after Julia 'succumbs' ('A little still she strove, and much repented, | And whispering "I will ne'er consent"—consented', i. 117), Byron provides a digressive catalogue of sweets, including moonlit gondola rides, rainbows (again), homecomings, wine, rural mirth, laurels won 'by blood or ink' (i. 126), and, finally, 'first and passionate love' (i. 126). In the next stanza, Byron declares,

> ... life yields nothing further to recall
> Worthy of this ambrosial sin, so shown,
> No doubt in fable, as the unforgiven
> Fire which Prometheus filch'd for us from heaven.   (1. 127)

In the original, the digression ended at this point, and the story itself resumed. The catalogue of pleasures had its occasional levity ('the death of some old lady | Or gentleman . . . | Who've made "us youth" wait too—too long already | For an estate', 1. 125), but even these half-conformed to a prevailing 'fallen', almost post-coital, wistfulness. That Byron was chafing under all this 'weak-sidedness' is suggested by an emendation to the last line of the above passage, the substitution of 'filch'd for us' for 'gave us all',[90] a characteristically energetic or hard-edged change.

The debunking spirit of such an alteration animates the interpolation of stanzas 128–33, a 'revision' which again aims to unsettle. The reference to Prometheus in stanza 127 leads to another catalogue, this time of useless inventions or 'impostures' (1. 128), medical, scientific, commercial, military. The catalogue ends with some sharp reflections on the way the world treats human passion:

> Man's a phenomenon, one knows not what,
>   And wonderful beyond all wondrous measure;
> 'Tis pity though, in this sublime world, that
>   Pleasure's a sin, and sometimes sin's a pleasure;
> Few mortals know what end they would be at,
>   But whether glory, power, or love, or treasure,
> The path is through perplexing ways, and when
> The goal is gain'd, we die, you know—and then.   (1. 133)

Man's 'Promethean' inventions and impostures lead Byron to a sense of inevitable powerlessness ('few mortals know what end they would be at') as well as folly. The sharpness of the passage is achieved by subtle touches, as in the substitution of 'this sublime world' for 'this fine old world'[91] ('sublime' recalling the

---

[90] See *Complete Poetical Works*, ed. McGann, v. 49. The phrase 'weak-sidedness' comes from Keats on *Isabella; or, the Pot of Basil* (1820): 'What I should call were I a reviewer "A weak-sided Poem" with an amusing sober-sadness about it' (letter of 21–2 Sept. 1819 to Richard Woodhouse, in *The Letters of John Keats, 1814–1821*, ed. Hyder E. Rollins, 2 vols. (Cambridge, Mass.: Harvard University Press, 1958), ii. 174).   [91] Ibid. v. 51.

pretentions of 'vasty' poets, and neatly picking up on 'wonderful beyond all wondrous measure'). The success of the revision lies not just in its overturning of solemnity, but in its doing so while still retaining something of the wistfulness of the preceding catalogue of sweets.

Other moments of revisionary counterbalance serve a similarly complex aim, both unsettling the reader and enriching the poem's moods. Most famously there is the episode in Canto II in which the eating of Pedrillo, a passage of comic grotesqueness, is immediately followed by four interpolated stanzas of a quite different character, in which two fathers witness the contrasting deaths of their sons, one of whom is physically robust but passive, the other spirited but sickly. The last we hear of Pedrillo, in stanza 82, is of some sailors making 'a little supper' of him, until 'at length they caught two boobies, and a noddy, | And then they left off eating the dead body.' These lines are followed by an interpolated stanza (83), originally unnumbered and written on a small addendum sheet, expanding on the mood of the preceding stanzas; in this stanza, Dante's Ugolino is cited in exculpation, as comparably grotesque or 'horrible'. There then follows, in stanzas 84–6, a newly grim but no less *guignolesque* description of storm and dire thirst ('their baked lips, with many a bloody crack, | Suck'd in the moisture', ll. 86), that in the original is overturned by the very rainbow discussed earlier. In revision, though, Byron adds stanzas 87–90, which aim directly for the heartstrings (as when the brave but weaker son smiles up at his distraught parent, 'as if to win a part from off the weight, | He saw increasing on his father's heart', ll. 88). Here, indeed, is scorching and drenching—an effect achieved through second thoughts. The grotesqueness of the preceding cannibalism episode takes on a retrospective gloom because of the interpolated stanzas, just as the pathos of the interpolated stanzas is 'placed' by the comic abnormality that precedes them.

One final example of revisionary unsettling is provided earlier in the canto when Juan's seasickness spoils his professions of undying devotion in stanza 19 ('if e'er I should forget, I swear—| But that's impossible'), resulting in full-blown comic deflation in stanza 20, which ends, ' "Beloved Julia, hear me still beseeching! | (Here he grew inarticulate with reaching)'.

In the first draft, Byron sticks with this manner through two stanzas which catalogue physical frailty, love's inability to withstand 'a cough and cold', a 'quinsy', a 'sneeze', 'inflammations' (stanza 22), 'nausea', 'a pain | About the lower region of the bowels' (stanza 23). On second thought, though, he interpolates a stanza which complicates the sequence's deflating corporeality. Juan is said to feel

> . . . that chilling heaviness of heart
> Or rather stomach, which, alas! attends,
> Beyond the best apothecary's art,
> The loss of love, the treachery of friends,
> Or death of those we dote on, when a part
> Of us dies with them as each fond hope ends:
> No doubt he would have been much more pathetic,
> But the sea acted as a strong emetic.   (II. 21)

Here the mood of blunt physicality is leavened by a less dismissive attitude to sentiment. 'The loss of love' is associated with 'the treachery of friends, | Or death of those we dote on.' The poem takes on a sudden seriousness and only returns to the prevailing mood with the concluding couplet. Once again revision works to counterbalance and unsettle.

'MOBILITY' AND THE STABLE SELF

On the surface, revisions such as these might seem anomalous, the antithesis of refining, smoothing, polishing. But they can also be seen as conventional, as Byron's attempts to shape—to perfect—a single and coherent narrative voice or persona, though one whose message is of inevitable imperfection and inconsistency. Disruption is, thus, in the case of the *Don Juan* revisions, a form of smoothing or polishing. This is why so many of the poem's revisions proper, as opposed to interpolated stanzas, occur in the concluding couplets, which frequently reverse or puncture what has gone before (two-thirds of the couplets in the first canto, for example, were revised, forty-three of them completely rewritten). The effect of such reversals or deflations is not only to reveal a truth about the world (its mobility, inconstancy, incoherence, etc.) but to affirm the narrator's cool, smooth control, the distance that marks the narrator as equal to—equable in the face of—anything.

Christopher Ricks has written best about Byron's coolness, shrewdly contrasting it with Keats's very different persona. 'The antagonism was a true one,' he writes, 'a clash of whole systems of thinking and feeling.' What Keats objected to in Byron was 'an affected coolness, a manner or code which would think it a betrayal to be awkward and to blush'.[92] Hence Keats's fierce denunciation of the shipwreck scene in *Don Juan*. Joseph Severn reports him as declaring: 'this gives me the most horrid idea of human nature, that a man like Byron should have exhausted all the pleasures of the world so compleatly that there was nothing left for him but to laugh and gloat over the most solemn and heart rending since [scenes] of human misery'.[93] The dying Keats is not fair to Byron here, who hardly *gloats* at suffering in the shipwreck episode, and whose laughter is decidedly mixed. Ricks points to Pedrillo's actual death in stanza 76 by way of refutation:

> He but requested to be bled to death.
>   The surgeon had his instruments and bled
> Pedrillo, and so gently ebbed his breath
>   You hardly could perceive when he was dead.
> He died as born, a Catholic in faith,
>   Like most in the belief in which they're bred,
> And first a little crucifix he kissed
> And then held out his jugular and wrist.   (II. 76)

Pedrillo's calm, Ricks comments, is 'at once admirable and sheeplike; Byron's lines vacillate yet never lurch here, since they are truly perplexed by such simplicity and faith',[94] an impression, it should be added, created in part by revision, as in the replacing of 'He died a staunch good Catholic' with the more solemn and measured 'He died as born, a Catholic in faith'[95]— an alteration precisely analogous in effect to that of the addition

[92] Christopher Ricks, *Keats and Embarrassment* (Oxford: Clarendon Press, 1974), 75, 77.
[93] See Hyder E. Rollins (ed.), *The Keats Circle: Letters and Papers 1816–1878*, 2 vols. (1948; Cambridge, Mass.: Harvard University Press, 1965), ii. 134–5.
[94] Ricks, *Keats and Embarrassment*, 82.
[95] See *Complete Poetical Works*, ed. McGann, v. 112; also *Byron's 'Don Juan'*, ed. Steffan and Pratt, ii. 197.

of stanzas 87–90 to the episode as a whole. Such revisions complicate (one can't just laugh) even as they refine, by helping to create the narrator's persona, which is unembarrassable (though 'perplexed', the narrator retains his poise, does not 'lurch') yet attentive to feeling, especially embarrassing feeling. 'Blushes and embarrassment are frequent in *Don Juan*,' writes Ricks, 'but they never work upon us, as Keats's do, by implicating us in the hot tinglings of sensation; they are always seen from outside, and the feeling that is induced in us as we read is not of sharing others' embarrassment but of being for once permitted to feel no such thing.'[96]

Embarrassment involves doubleness. Ricks quotes Erving Goffman on the embarrassed individual: 'while he cannot present a sustainable and coherent self . . . he is at least disturbed by the fact'.[97] The voice or persona of Byron's comic poems, as of the letters, exposes doubleness in others, but is always itself single: cool, controlled, undisturbed. Because no topic or situation can threaten the narrator's poise, can make him self-conscious (and thus 'double'), the very dangers the comic style was meant to avoid (monotony, mannerism) re-emerge. As George Ridenour puts it, commenting on McGann's *'Don Juan' in Context*: 'McGann rightly insists on the frequency of what seem random or chance (or at least unexpected) occurrences in the poem. But the very frequency of the unpredictable creates a kind of predictability—that the unpredictable will happen.' The poem's ultimate singleness of view is a matter of 'unity of temper, the way things are taken, the kinds of attitudes'.[98] The very security Byron's comic poems seek to evade and expose—as illusion, childish fantasy, what Manning calls 'totalization'—returns in the narrator's perpetual poise. The result—perfect poise in a world of perpetual flux—is as much an illusion as the promise of perfect and perpetual bliss with Haidée. In the case of Haidée, though, Byron is aware of the illusion.

The revisions help to create an illusion of mastery—even at those moments when the narrator casually professes bafflement or defeat. By puncturing moods, whether cynical or sentimental, they ensure (or restore) authorial balance or poise. The voice of

---

[96] Ricks, *Keats and Embarrassment*, 83.
[97] Erving Goffman, 'Embarrassment and Social Organization', *American Journal of Sociology*, 62 (1956), 264–75, quoted by Ricks in *Keats and Embarrassment*, 2.
[98] Ridenour, *'Don Juan* and the Romantics', 569, 571.

the comic poems may be more 'natural' to Byron than that of his 'heroico-pathetic' poetry—than that of the 'Byronic' Byron; it is closer, for example, to the prevailing tones of the letters.[99] But it, too, the revisions remind us (by ensuring that Byron never lapses wholly into pathos or cynicism, remains always outside, composed), is a creation. Byron turned to the comic style because he came to agree with criticisms such as the following, from an April 1816 review of *Hebrew Melodies* in the *Critical Review*: 'that an individual who publishes so much and so repeatedly, ought to have a larger stock of true poetical feeling than is possessed by the author of these melodies'.[100] The early manner begins to seem mechanical, artificial, as much to Byron as to his critics. Manning connects this sense of artificiality (and strain) with what Byron's later poems suggest is a false sense of single and coherent selfhood, false both in general and for Byron in particular. 'The tales', Manning writes, 'record the terrible cost of trying to preserve unity by rigid repression of disruptive forces. The multiple roles Byron relishes in Adeline are the sign of a more expansive view of the self.'[101] As the word 'relishes' suggests, what Manning thinks is recorded is a terrible cost for poet as well as characters. Byron is as much a victim as Lara, Conrad, Manfred—of the rigidities of their characters. Manning makes a similar point in another context, in regard to the successive female figures—really types of a single figure—Juan encounters and evades over the course of the poem: 'this potentially deadly woman, mother and lover, is a figure of desire and therefore Juan's freedom consists only of this endless chain of disruptions and losses'. If Lambro is 'the avatar of the hero who fills Byron's earlier work', a failed hero of 'absolute masculine will' who 'destroys the peace of his home' by seeking to impose his authority on Haidée, Juan, in contrast, affirms 'the vital multiplicity of his own independent existence'.[102]

---

[99] According to Jack, in *The Poet and his Audience*, Byron's letters from Italy 'helped him to form and develop the new persona which had in fact appeared in his earlier letters before he had been able to express it in verse. The letters to Murray and others were not intended to be private' (p. 73).

[100] Repr. in Donald H. Reiman, *The Romantics Reviewed: Contemporary Reviews of British Romantic Writers*, part B, *Byron and Regency Society Poets*, 5 vols. (New York: Garland, 1972), ii. 647.

[101] Manning, *Byron and His Fictions*, 255.

[102] Manning, 'Byron's Imperceptiveness to the English Word', in *Reading Romantics*, 125–8.

Manning, like McGann and others, sees the comic voice of *Don Juan* as a release. The 'heroico-pathetic' or Byronic poems grew rigidly repetitive not only because their heroes were so fixed and single in character but because Byron himself became locked in a false and falsifying mode. The comic poet is conventionally thought of as easy, relaxed, the very opposite of mannered. Christensen, for example, thinks of Byron's 'true' character—of character in general, no doubt—as split and oscillating, posing to the early poems 'a constant threat to the stability of the Byronic poetic subject . . . until in *Don Juan* the undecidable priority between "Padrone" and "Amica" becomes the whirligig on which character and narrator ride in outlandish parody of chivalrization and its discontents'.[103] The later poetry, in other words, represents a relaxation into the truth, a truth of diversity, mobility, inconstancy, flux—a 'whirligig'. But whirligigs, too, can grow monotonous. *Don Juan* is 'about' everything, or could be about everything, since it means to abide by no fixed order, plan, narrative return; all subjects and climes are grist for its comic mill. Mills, though, grind to a common consistency, and nothing the poem turns to, nothing the poetic voice describes, can touch or affect the narrator; everything is contained in the 'system' of the poem, as expressed in the poet's imperturbability or poise. The result is that everything the poem touches upon is oddly 'the same'. England and English society hold no more surprises (i.e. none) than Greece and Greek society or Spain and Spanish society or Russia and Russian society. 'To the mind | Which is itself', writes Byron at the beginning of Canto IV of *Childe Harold's Pilgrimage*, 'no changes bring surprise' (stanza 8). And the reader knows this; knows, I would claim, very early in the reading of *Don Juan*, that, though a 'whirligig', capable of going anywhere, saying anything, the poem also will hold no surprises. Though, in one sense, it is true, as McGann claims, that 'the poem's contradictions . . . deconstruct all truth-functions which are founded either in (metaphysical) Identity or (psychological) Integrity [and in their place] . . . set a truth-function founded (negatively) in contradiction itself, and (positively) in

[103] Jerome Christensen, 'Byron: Class, Sexuality, and the Poet', in Elaine Scarry (ed.), *Literature and the Body: Essays on Populations and Persons* (Baltimore: Johns Hopkins University Press, 1988), 134.

metonomy',[104] the source of these deconstructions is a voice or persona of for the most part flawless Identity and Integrity, one capable of communicating the most embarrassing inconsistencies and contradictions with perfect and, it could be argued, monotonous sang-froid.[105]

Late Byron, then, is also prone to rigidity, monotony, mannerism; the supposed opposition between Wordsworth as poet of coherent and unified selfhood, and Byron as poet of selves, is misleading; as misleading as the supposed anomalous character of Byron's revisions, their disruptive rather than refining function. It could even be argued that Byron's sense of self was if anything *more* rigid than Wordsworth's. Consider the famous Wordsworthian passages of Canto III of *Childe Harold*. What these passages reveal is the deep incompatibility between Byron's temperament and Wordsworthian or idealist conceptions of interdependence, of the marriage of subject and object.

> I live not in myself, but I become
> Portion of that around me; and to me,
> High mountains are a feeling, but the hum
> Of human cities torture. (III. 72)

What is missing here is any of the performative dislocation found in the passage's Wordsworthian—or Shelleyan—models. The poetical voice is clear and distinct, even as it talks of merging; the sublimity of nature—'high mountains'—is unthreateningly other, matter-of-factly registered. When Wordsworth recalls in

---

[104] McGann, 'Byron's Twin Opposites of Truth', 56–7.

[105] In a recent study of that most 'thoroughly dead' of Byron's contemporaries, his friend, mentor, and literary model, Samuel Rogers, Peter T. Murphy distinguishes between 'struggling poems', such as Wordsworth's 'An Evening Walk', and the smoothness of Rogers's *The Pleasures of Memory*: 'A struggling poem needs critics because it is in some ways telling a story that it doesn't know' ('Climbing Parnassus, and Falling Off', p. 16 of the unpublished typescript of a talk given at the 1992 MLA convention in New York). Byron's poems, like Rogers's, don't struggle, for all their pretence of not knowing what's coming next; their smooth poise excludes the reader, leaves the reader little to do. As for moments in *Don Juan* which challenge the poem's prevailing sang-froid, the most notable involve the persistence of what might be called a *Childe Harold* tone, as in the melodramatic stanza at the end of Canto XV, a stanza which is anything but urbane; or, to take an opposite extreme, the bafflement of the two stanzas at the end of Canto XIV, stanzas which face the inner life in a manner quite different from that of the poem's prevailing satiric comprehension or distance. Moments like these, though, remain exceptions.

'Tintern Abbey' how 'the sounding cataract | Haunted me like a passion' (ll. 76–7), the uncertainty of the indeterminate article (*whose* 'passion'?) is performative, just as the poem's circling abstractions ('a presence that disturbs', 'a sense sublime | Of something far more deeply interfused', 'a motion and a spirit', ll. 94, 95–6, 100) communicate a sense of mystical striving, the sort of striving found also in Shelley, whose verse likewise struggles to communicate 'the vanishing apparitions which haunt the interlunations of life'.[106] Byron's 'to me | High mountains are a feeling', in contrast, has a declarative solidity (indeterminate article notwithstanding) wholly alien to the state it is meant to describe.

So, too, in the following lines from stanza 75:

> Are not the mountains, waves, and skies, a part
> Of me and of my soul, as I of them?
> Is not the love of these deep in my heart
> With a pure passion?   (III. 75)

'*These*'? The slack pronoun does not convince. Byron is supremely the poet of unclouded distinctions, especially between self and other, subject and object. In stanzas 72 and 75, writes Frederick Garber, 'the self foregoes none of its autonomy (we are looking forward to Manfred's compulsions) . . . the self is in no sense unmade, its integrity is in no sense qualified'.[107] Or, as Hazlitt puts it, with characteristic vigour, Byron either 'raises his subject to himself, or tramples on it; he neither stoops to, nor loses himself in it'.[108] I agree: autonomy and integrity (that is, wholeness, completeness) are crucial elements of Byron's poetic temperament. The rigidity of the Byronic hero finds its complement in the impermeable or imperturbable assurance of the narrator of the later comic poems; both are creations of a poet constitutionally incapable of letting down his guard, softening or effacing the boundaries of the self. Wordsworth was a conscious apostle of the unified and coherent self, but much in his temperament responded to a very different and more

---

[106] Shelley, *A Defence of Poetry* (1821), in *Shelley's Prose or the Trumpet of a Prophecy*, ed. David Lee Clark (Albuquerque: University of New Mexico Press, 1966), 294.

[107] Frederick Garber, *Self, Text, and Romantic Irony: The Example of Byron* (Princeton: Princeton University Press, 1988), 108.

[108] Hazlitt, *The Spirit of the Age*, in *Complete Works*, ed. Howe, xi. 69.

fluid notion of personal identity. Byron made constant reference to this fluidity—thought the fixed or stable self an illusion—yet could only, in the end, present himself as unified and autonomous. As Marlon Ross puts it, Byron 'never disarms himself, never makes himself vulnerable to his public by revealing the bard as a naked hero. He always unmasks himself by self-consciously displaying the masks within himself.'[109] That is, he reserves from view an essential, singular, and irreducible identity, the 'self' ('stance' to the fastidiously postmodern) doing the unmasking. It is this self or stance that many of the revisions in *Don Juan* function to protect and perfect.

REVISION AND MASCULINITY

The ambiguities of Byron's sense of self find their complement in related questions of gender. For many critics, Byron is a supremely masculine figure. His supposedly 'male' force of self-definition is often, for example, contrasted with Keats's 'feminine' flexibility of ego—sometimes favourably, sometimes not. In Hazlitt's 'On Effeminacy of Character' (1822), Keats is cited for 'deficiency in masculine energy of style', as opposed to 'manly firmness and decision of character',[110] qualities Keats himself associates with Byron. Byron, Keats famously declared, 'cuts a figure'; Keats himself has 'no self . . . no identity'.[111] To Margaret Homans, Keats's obscure origins and relative poverty, in contrast to Byron's more elevated station, suggest 'certain aspects of women's experience as outsiders relative to the major literary

[109] Marlon B. Ross, 'Romantic Quest and Conquest: Troping Masculine Power in the Crisis of Poetic Identity', in Mellor (ed.), *Romanticism and Feminism*, 37.
[110] The essay was first collected in *Table Talk: Opinions on Books, Men, Things* (1822). See Hazlitt, *Complete Works*, ed. Howe, viii. 254: 'We may observe an effeminacy of style, in some degree corresponding to effeminacy of character . . . I cannot help thinking that the fault of Mr. Keats's poems was a deficiency in masculine energy of style. He had beauty, tenderness, delicacy in an uncommon degree, but there was a want of strength and substance.'
[111] Letter of 19 Feb. 1819 to the George Keatses, in *The Letters of John Keats*, ed. Rollins, ii. 67. For a more thorough account of Keats's anxieties about gender and creativity see Margaret Homans's later article, 'Keats Reading Women, Women Reading Keats', *Studies in Romanticism*, 29 (Autumn 1990), 341–71.

tradition'.[112] Byron, implicitly, represents masculine entitlement
and privilege.

Yet the conventional account of Byron's masculinity is easily
complicated—and not just by his sexuality. In recent criticism,
much has been made of Byron's 'mobility', a term associated in
Don Juan with the feminine (definitively in the portrait of Lady
Adeline in Canto XVI), and with feminine writing in particular.
'The earth has nothing like a She epistle,' Byron declares in
Canto XIII of *Don Juan*,

> And hardly heaven—because it never ends.
> I love the mystery of a female missal,
> Which, like a creed, ne'er says all it intends,
>   But full of cunning as Ulysses' whistle,
> When he allured poor Dolon . . .   (XIII. 105)

As Manning points out, such writing, like the digressive manner of *Don Juan*, 'bespeaks a relaxation of will which permits
ominous material to surface: instead of repression, whose indefinite force heightens the sublime, the associative chains of
Don Juan work toward expression and neutralization. Sym-
bolic and metaphoric poetry achieves its richness through compression and ambiguity. *Don Juan*, which like women's letters,
also "ne'er says all it intends," creates its vitality by extended
meanings.' Looseness, incompletion, inconsistency are seen here
as feminine qualities and as virtues. Byron is a poet of 'inex-
haustible sequences rather than pregnant points',[113] a view which
fits neatly with earlier remarks about his reluctance to 'finish'
works. When Christensen calls *Don Juan* a 'whirligig', in
Byron's terms he is associating it with female formlessness
and fecundity. 'What a whirlwind is her head', writes Byron in
Don Juan of woman's 'strangeness',

> And what a whirlpool full of depth and danger
> Is all the rest about her.   (IX. 64)

---

[112] Margaret Homans, *Women Writers and Poetic Identity* (Princeton: Princeton
University Press, 1980), 240.

[113] Manning, 'Byron's Imperceptiveness to the English Word', in *Reading Romantics*, 132. For a thorough and thoughtful account of Byron's mixed attitudes
to conventional notions of sexual difference see Susan J. Wolfson, '"Their She
Condition": Cross-Dressing and the Politics of Gender in *Don Juan*', *English Literary History*, 54/3 (Fall 1987), 585–617.

The poem's inconstancy and discontinuity can also be seen to fit with conventionally 'female' waywardness.

Manning stresses the liberating power of the feminine in *Don Juan*. The 'spontaneous, ceaselessly proliferating process' of the poem's composition produces a work of 'surprising conjunctions and momentary delights'. But does it also, as Manning contends, produce a work 'that can continually surprise its author'?[114] Lady Adeline is a figure of astonishing changeableness, but she is also unsurprisable, already a master of that quality Juan is meant to grow into over the course of the poem, a quality especially associated with 'manliness' (XV. 11): 'The art of living in all climes with ease.' In this, changeable Adeline, herself 'half a poetess' (XVI. 39), one who 'rated such accomplishment | As the mere pastime of an idle day' (XVI. 42) and 'was weak enough to deem Pope a great poet, | And what was worse was not ashamed to show it' (XVI. 47), is a figure of Byron, or rather of the comic narrator of *Don Juan*, a work which 'treats all things, and ne'er retreats | From any thing' (XVI. 3)—that is, is equal to all things. In Byron's 1823 note on 'mobility', the key to Adeline's temperament, he defines the quality as 'an excessive susceptibility of immediate impressions—at the same time without *losing* the past'.[115] When Moore and others comment on Byron's own mobility (e.g. Moore: 'he was fully aware not only of the abundance of this quality in his own nature, but of the danger in which it placed consistency and singleness of character'[116]), they forget the second half of the note. What Byron means by 'without *losing* the past', is 'without *losing* the self': both he and Adeline retain mastery, control, singularity.

It is Byron's controlling side that disparages the feminine, often by associating it with the 'professional'. In the words of *English Bards and Scotch Reviewers* (1809), professional writers are servants of a 'prostituted Muse' (l. 182), 'sons of song [who] descend to trade' (l. 175). This conjunction of literal and literary prostitute—both of whom are 'at it' all the time, but

[114] Manning, 'Byron's Imperceptiveness to the English Word', in *Reading Romantics*, 132, 133, 132.
[115] *Complete Poetical Works*, ed. McGann, v. 769.
[116] See *Byron's 'Don Juan'*, ed. Steffan and Pratt, i. 285–6, for Moore's and other comments on Byron's 'mobility'.

produce no real offspring, either in the form of children or works of literary value—is of ancient provenance.[117] In Byron, it is accompanied by harsh defensiveness, for Byron sees the feminine/professional milieu not only as having brought him to a dead end (in the mannered monotony of the early 'Ladies books', or 'Byronic' poems, what John Gibson Lockhart, in his anonymous *John Bull's Letter to Lord Byron,* 1821, called 'all your humbug Harolds'[118]), but as hovering over his proposed way out. As Manning puts it, 'the virulence of Byron's attack on Sotheby and the bluestockings [in *Beppo*] is a reflex of the fear that the male sex is rendered precarious by the woman-dominated society of salons and cavaliere servente'.[119] Such precariousness is importantly a matter of the self. Though Byron is drawn to and energized by the ever-varying female, by 're-laxation of will', he also finds it threatening. Much of the power of the comic poems derives from Byron's tapping of 'feminine' resources; *Beppo* and *Don Juan* are 'woman-dominated poems', in stylistic as well as narrative or plot terms. But as the revisions to *Don Juan* show, they are also the work of a no less obvious 'masculine' wilfulness and singularity. The exposure of inevitable inconstancy or 'mobility' in others, like the exposure of ideology, requires a point of vantage, a controlling and some-how exempt perspective. In other words, it requires the very unified subjectivity or personal identity it denies. This personal identity may be less a matter of atomistic individuality or con-scious subjectivity, as in Wordsworth's 'points . . . within our souls | Where all stand single' (*The Prelude,* 1850, 3. 188–9), than of a socially legitimated role (Byron the Aristocrat, Byron the Genius, Byron the Man of Action); but in either case its status as construction or 'product' is clear, for all Byron's seem-ing disdain for labour or craft.

[117] See Catherine Gallagher, 'George Eliot and *Daniel Deronda*: The Prostitute and the Jewish Question', in Ruth Bernard Yeazell (ed.), *Sex, Politics, and Science in the Nineteenth-Century Novel* (Baltimore: Johns Hopkins University Press, 1986), 39–62.

[118] Excerpts from Lockhart's *Letter* are reprinted in Rutherford (ed.), *Byron: The Critical Heritage,* 182–91. For 'humbug Harolds' see p. 183; see also pp. 182–3 for Lockhart's witty parody of early Byron's audience (as composed of the female characters of Jane Austen's *Emma*).

[119] Manning, 'The Nameless Broken Dandy and the Structure of Authorship', in *Reading Romantics,* 155.

CHAPTER THREE

COLERIDGE'S REVISIONARY
COMPLEXITY

THE older or established view of Coleridge's revisions is that
he knew what he was doing when he revised, and that his
revisions serve wholeness, coherence, perfection of form—in
short, unity, called by Coleridge the 'ultimate end of human
Thought and human Feeling'.[1] This, of course, is precisely the
aesthetic ideal Coleridge himself championed in his criticism,
along with those qualities of mind (control, will, coherence of
self both in time and over time) from which it is conventionally
thought to derive. One well-known example of a revision which
conforms to the established view is the cutting of the last six
lines of 'Frost at Midnight' (lines 'marvellously describing
Hartley', according to Richard Holmes), so as to end the poem
with the image of 'silent icicles, | Quietly shining to the quiet
moon'.[2] As Coleridge puts it in a manuscript note, the original
ending lacked or obscured 'the rondo, and return upon itself of
the Poem',[3] a comment which recalls not only his remark, quoted
earlier in reference to Wordsworth, that the common end or
shape of all narrative ('nay of all, Poems') is circular, 'the snake
with it's Tail in it's Mouth',[4] but the remark's personal or
poetical application: the pattern of journey or excursion and

[1] Entry of 1808/11 in *The Notebooks of Samuel Taylor Coleridge*, ed. Kathleen
Coburn, 3 vols. (Princeton: Princeton University Press, 1957–73), iii. 3247; henceforth cited as *CN*, ed. Coburn.
[2] Richard Holmes, *Coleridge: Early Visions* (London: Hodder and Stoughton,
1989), 184.
[3] Note of *c*.1807–8, quoted in John Beer, *Coleridge's Poetic Intelligence* (London: Macmillan, 1977), 142–3. The note itself comes from Coleridge's copy of
'Fears in Solitude', discussed by B. Ifor Evans in 'Coleridge's Copy of "Fears in
Solitude"', *Times Literary Supplement*, 18 April 1935, 255.
[4] Samuel Taylor Coleridge to Joseph Cottle, 7 Mar. 1815, in *The Collected
Letters of Samuel Taylor Coleridge*, ed. Earl L. Griggs, 6 vols. (Oxford: Clarendon
Press, 1956–71), iv. 545; henceforth cited as *CL*, ed. Griggs.

return found in so many of his poems, including 'The Ancient Mariner', 'The Eolian Harp', and 'This Lime-tree Bower My Prison'.

Or consider B. J. McElderry's still influential 1932 defence of Coleridge's revisions to 'The Ancient Mariner', a defence which agrees with the poem's initial detractors, argues that Coleridge, too, agreed with them, systematically improving the poem by addressing specific objections in revision (modernizing archaic words and spellings, toning down the poem's more extreme Gothic passages), and chastises later critics who ignorantly ridicule the poem's first critics 'for not seeing virtues which the poem of 1798 did not have as fully as the version most familiar to us.'[5] Southey and Wordsworth were probably the most influential of the poem's initial critics (with Coleridge, that is): Southey, writing in October 1798 in *The Critical Review*, called many of the poem's stanzas 'laboriously beautiful; but in connection . . . absurd or unintelligible';[6] Wordsworth, echoing this criticism in a casually hurtful note to the second edition of *Lyrical Ballads* (1800), identifies as the most prominent of the poem's 'great defects' that 'the events having no necessary connection do not produce each other, and . . . that the imagery is somewhat laboriously accumulated'.[7] The effect these objections had on Coleridge is clear not only from the revisions themselves but from an epigram he includes in chapter 1 of the *Biographia Literaria* entitled 'To the author of the Ancient Mariner', an epigram he identifies as of his own composition:

[5] B. J. McElderry, 'Coleridge's Revisions of "The Ancient Mariner"', *Studies in Philology*, 29 (1932), 69.
[6] For Robert Southey's review see the *Critical Review*, 24 (Oct. 1798), 200–1, repr. in Donald H. Reiman, *The Romantics Reviewed: Contemporary Reviews of Romantic Writers*, 9 vols. (New York: Garland Press, 1972), i. 307–10. Lamb took Southey to task for his review's unfavourable notice of 'The Ancient Mariner' in a letter of 8 Nov. 1798: 'You have selected a passage fertile in unmeaning miracles, but have passed by fifty passages as miraculous as the miracles they celebrate.' See *The Life and Works of Charles Lamb*, ed. Alfred Ainger, 12 vols. (London: Macmillan, 1900), ix. 140.
[7] The note is oddly omitted by W. J. B. Owen and Jane W. Smyser (eds.), *The Prose Works of William Wordsworth*, 3 vols. (Oxford: Clarendon Press, 1974), but can be found, among other places, in Stephen Gill, *William Wordsworth: A Life* (Oxford: Clarendon Press, 1989), 186, and in Wordsworth and Coleridge, *Lyrical Ballads*, ed. R. L. Brett and A. R. Jones (London: Methuen, 1963), 276–7.

> Your poem must eternal be,
> Dear sir! it cannot fail,
> For 'tis incomprehensible,
> And without head or tail.

As Lawrence Lipking has pointed out, this epigram first appeared in the *Morning Post* on 24 January 1800 in reference to another poet, Henry James Pye, the poet laureate: 'The change of attribution shows how much he had internalized Wordsworth's criticism.'[8]

And rightly—at least according to those who defend later versions. The supernatural hokery of parts V and VI of the 1798 version, argues McElderry, *was* confusing or 'not quite intelligible' (in the words of the *British Critic*), especially the proliferation of bodies rising and falling and flaming red; the middle section of the poem was both obscure and overdone, and cutting (forty-six lines out of the original 263 of parts V and VI) brought straightforward improvement—just as the addition of the gloss in 1817 brought added narrative and thematic clarity.[9] Moreover, as McElderry also claims, revision produced a host of smaller, local felicities. For example, in the 1798 version of the poem, just before the phantom ship's departure, Life-in-Death wins her game of dice with Death, and a 'gust of wind' starts up and 'thro' the holes' of Death's eyes

> and the hole of his mouth
> Half-whistles and half-groans.
>
> With never a whisper in the Sea
> Off darts the Spectre-ship. (ll. 197–200)

In 1817 Coleridge cuts and alters these lines to produce a more oblique and mysterious transition:

> The sun's rim dips; the stars rush out;
> At one stride comes the dark;

---

[8] Lawrence Lipking, 'The Marginal Gloss', *Critical Inquiry*, 3 (Summer 1977), 614. For the epigram as applied 'To the author of the Ancient Mariner', see ch. 1 of the *Biographia Literaria*, ed. James Engell and W. Jackson Bate, in *The Collected Works of Samuel Taylor Coleridge* (a projected 16-vol. work), ed. Kathleen Coburn (London: Routledge & Kegan Paul, 1983), book 1 of vii. 28; henceforth cited as CW, ed. Coburn.

[9] See unsigned article in *The British Critic* (Oct. 1799), 365, quoted and approved of by McElderry, in 'Coleridge's Revisions of "The Ancient Mariner"', 71.

With far-heard whisper, o'er the sea,
Off shot the spectre-bark   (ll. 199–202)

Like McElderry, I think this revision a straightforward improvement—and a representative one. Nor am I alone among modern readers in approving such revisions. Though Jack Stillinger argues for the independent and equal authority of *all* versions of Coleridge's poems, if forced to pick single texts, 'for example, in a standardized edition or in an anthology', 'the editorial choice of the latest texts may well be artistically justifiable; Coleridge, just like Wordsworth, seems to have been an amazingly shrewd reviser, and I think most critics would agree, even if they couldn't logically defend their preferences, that the later versions are almost always richer, more complex, better structured, more pleasing aesthetically'.[10] Even among more 'advanced' or theoretically minded critics, later or revised versions have their champions. Jean-Pierre Mileur, for example, views additions such as the preface to 'Kubla Khan', the gloss to 'The Ancient Mariner', and the conclusion to part 2 of 'Christabel', as controlled and successful attempts to bring closure to the poems. Revision allows Coleridge 'to see himself not so much as the creator or generator of poems but as the prophetic reader of his own poetry. In this context, the proof of the poet's election resides not in his ability to generate poems but in his ability, in each act of poetic creation, to re-enact the transformation of poet-as-creator into poet-as-reader.'[11] Or, in Max Schulz's words, revision allows Coleridge 'to redefine his intellectual development from poet to critic in keeping with his perception that literature needs a critic-reader to complete his meaning'[12]—a perception no doubt related to explicit statements in the letters about being stronger in 'judgement', a secondary process, than creative genius or 'execution'.[13] When in 1815

---

[10] Jack Stillinger, 'The Multiple Versions of Coleridge's Poems: How Many *Mariners* did Coleridge Write?', *Studies in Romanticism*, 31/2 (Summer 1992), 140, 141.

[11] Jean-Pierre Mileur, *Vision and Revision: Coleridge's Art of Immanence* (Berkeley: University of California Press, 1982), 33.

[12] Max F. Schulz, 'Samuel Taylor Coleridge', in Frank Jordan (ed.), *The English Romantic Poets: A Review of Research* (New York: Modern Language Association of America, 1985), 378.

[13] Samuel Taylor Coleridge to Daniel Stuart, 7 Oct. 1800, in *CL*, ed. Griggs, i. 629.

Coleridge thinks of reissuing a collected *Friend*, for example, his aim is to produce 'a compleat and circular work',[14] in this case by adding eight to ten papers to the original or 1812 collection. In a letter of early April 1797, again to Cottle, Coleridge outlines a twenty-year plan for an epic poem: ten years collecting materials, five years drafting the poem, five years for revision; that is, the attempt 'to complete his meaning' is viewed as no less important and involving than initial composition.[15]

REVISION AS IMPOSITION

Those who disapprove of Coleridge's revisions do so for a variety of reasons. To begin with, some critics believe that the revisions consciously and calculatedly betray earlier views and attitudes, whether religious, political, or sexual. In the religious sphere, it is said they show a poet 'instinctively distancing himself from an unpredictable, active universe in favor of the comforting orthodoxy of a Christian explanation'.[16] In the earliest text of 'This Lime-tree Bower My Prison', for example, in a letter of 9 July 1797 to Southey, nature is called 'a living thing | Which acts upon the mind, and with such hues | As clothe th'Almighty Spirit,' an image dropped in subsequent versions, presumably because of its pantheist overtones.[17] William Empson, among the first of more recent anti-revisionists, thinks early Coleridge believed in nature spirits, and that revised versions of the poem, those without the 'living thing' passage, obscure this belief by making us read 'Spirits' (l. 40) as 'men', which is strained (though with characteristic honesty, Empson also offers counter-instances, in which Coleridge uses 'spirits' and 'men' as synonyms). Empson is also, therefore, particularly exercised about comparable alterations to 'The Ancient Mariner' ('a splendid poem much mangled by its author for reasons of conscience'), especially the substitution of 'angels' for 'spirits of the air' in

[14] See Samuel Taylor Coleridge to Joseph Cottle, 10 (11) Mar. 1815, ibid. iv. 551–2.
[15] Samuel Taylor Coleridge to Joseph Cottle, early Apr. 1797, ibid. i. 320–1 and vi. 1009.   [16] Schulz, 'Samuel Taylor Coleridge', 374–5.
[17] See Samuel Taylor Coleridge to Robert Southey, 9 July 1797, in *CL*, ed. Griggs, i. 334–6.

the 1817 gloss on the animation of the shipmates' corpses. In addition, he disapproves of the alterations for political reasons: the gloss, he argues, occludes the poem's initial political dimension by directing attention to religious or spiritual meanings, at the same time distorting those meanings by making them more orthodox and coherent than they were in the original.[18]

As for other alterations of a political nature, again according to Empson, 'Mr. C. R. Woodring reports (*Politics in the Poetry of Coleridge*, 1961) that under the dangerous but constitutionally limited police terror of Pitt it was an effective legal protection, as well as a familiar joke, to print in the errata: "for *murder* read *defence of the king*" and suchlike'.[19] For example, in *Sibylline Leaves* and all subsequent editions, Coleridge cut the last three stanzas of 'Lines Composed in a Concert-Room', a poem first printed on 24 September 1799 in the *Morning Post*, because of their radical-sounding celebration of 'the shame and absolute rout I Unhealable of Freedom's latest foe'—among other things. The motive here, in David Pirie's words, was straightforward 'ideological embarrassment'.[20] More famously, there is the change in 'To a Young Ass' from the imprudent 'Handel's softest airs that soothe to rest I The tumult of a scoundrel Monarch's Breast,' in the original 1794 manuscript, to the anodyne 'warble melodies that soothe to rest I The aching of pale Fashion's vacant breast,' in the first magazine publication, also of 1794.

Norman Fruman offers several examples of alterations of a prudish (as opposed to merely prudent) character. In the first edition of 'Christabel' of 1816, the heroine suffers 'Dreams, that made her moan and leap, I As on her bed she lay in sleep.' In subsequent editions the lines were removed. In the original version of 'An Effusion at Evening', the poet's beloved has 'dewy brilliance dancing in her eyes' (l. 16); in subsequent versions 'Chaste Joyance' does the dancing. In like manner, the revisions to 'The Pains of Sleep', a poem which first comes to light in a letter of 11 September 1802, but was not published

---

[18] See Empson's introduction to *Coleridge's Verse: A Selection*, ed. William Empson and David Pirie (New York: Schocken Books, 1972), 23–6 (for discussion of 'This Lime-tree Bower My Prison'), and 27 (for 'The Ancient Mariner').

[19] Empson, in *Coleridge's Verse*, ed. Empson and Pirie, 14.

[20] Pirie, ibid. 250.

until fourteen years later, 'almost all represent suppressions and concealments'. As Fruman reminds us, though, this prudishness was no late development: in 'Honour', for example, a very early poem, the 'Enchantress Pleasure' is already 'A Hideous hag' (l. 59), and 'a slave to pleasure' is said to be 'a slave to smoke'![21] Finally, Coleridge's prudishness is by no means exclusively sexual. In 1815, in response to earlier critical reaction, Coleridge cut lines 198 ff. from 'The Ancient Mariner', lines in which knowledge of their fate causes the mariner's shipmates to groan. 'The idea that it is somehow artistic not to let the sailors groan', comments Empson, 'strikes me as Eng. lit. at its worst'[22]—that is, as the worst kind of 'refinement', a kind that would also excise all things sexual or bodily.

These negative views of Coleridge's revisions recall the champions of early Wordsworth: later Coleridge, like later Wordsworth, is simply thought by critics of the revisions to have grown unacceptably orthodox. One difficulty with this view, though, is that Coleridge's supposed religious, political, and socio-cultural apostasies are not accompanied by poetical apostasy or 'decline'. Though Coleridge deplored what he called the 'vicious affectation in the phraseology'[23] of his early poems, particularly the slim volume of *Poems on Various Subjects* (1796), as the *Biographia* suggests, he never fully entered into the Wordsworthian spirit of plain-spoken experiment. Even in the *Lyrical Ballads* period, Coleridge was never an especially radical *poet*, a flouter of poetical decorum or propriety. As a consequence, arguments in favour of early Coleridge are more transparently political or ideological than those for early Wordsworth; the early versions are said to be better because the views they contain are more enlightened or acceptable or uninhibited, as when Pirie deplores the revisions to 'The Pains of Sleep' for having 'polished away' the original 'rawness' of its guilt-obsessed nightmares.[24]

---

[21] Norman Fruman, 'Creative Process and Concealment in Coleridge's Poetry', in Robert Brinkley and Keith Hanley (eds.), *Romantic Revisions* (Cambridge: Cambridge University Press, 1992), 159.
[22] Empson in *Coleridge's Verse*, ed. Empson and Pirie, 52.
[23] Samuel Taylor Coleridge to Thomas Poole, 5 May 1796, in *CL*, ed. Griggs, i. 207.　　　　　[24] Pirie, in *Coleridge's Verse*, ed. Empson and Pirie, 252.

REVISION AND NEUROSIS

Others object to the revisions on the grounds that they express a neurotic insecurity rather than any falsifying politico-religious agenda or controlling aesthetic. In the case of Wordsworth, few critics are prepared, quite, to call the revisions neurotic (though Stephen Gill comes close in his biography); with Coleridge, though, one often feels one is dealing with a figure who is not in control—and who knows he's not in control. 'The bottom line of this kind of thinking', writes Stillinger, 'is that Coleridge the famous advocate of unity may in fact have been one of the most scattered and *dis*unified poets in all of English literature.'[25] Also one of the least confident. 'Coleridge was very uneasy about print', writes Empson, 'and kept altering the text to meet the real or supposed demands of his public',[26] demands which, more often than for Wordsworth, ignore or clash with earlier intentions; his 'over-riding impulse' in preparing *Sibylline Leaves*, continues Empson, 'was an anxiety not to be jeered at any more, and not to give any handle to insinuation'.[27] When Coleridge himself worries that neurotic insecurity or anxiety may be the cause of his constant tinkering, he sounds like Wordsworth at the opening of *The Prelude*, frightened that he is 'self-baffling'. 'I do nothing', he confesses to Stuart in a letter of 7 October 1800, 'but almost instantly it's defects and sillinesses come upon my mind, and haunt me'[28]—leading, among other things, to revision. 'To think meanly of what I have written almost immediately after the hot fit of composition', he confesses to John Rickman in a letter of 28 February 1804, 'is ever a disease of my mind.'[29] 'I torture the poem and myself with corrections', he writes to Joseph Cottle in a letter of early February 1797, 'and what I write in an hour, I sometimes take two or three days in correcting ... The Religious Musings I have altered monstrously.'[30] As he warns other authors

---

[25] Stillinger, *Coleridge and Textual Instability: The Multiple Versions of the Major Poems* (New York: Oxford University Press, 1994), 117.
[26] Empson, in *Coleridge's Verse*, ed. Empson and Pirie, 14.
[27] Ibid. 51–2.
[28] Samuel Taylor Coleridge to Daniel Stuart, 7 Oct. 1800, in *CL*, ed. Griggs, i. 629.
[29] Samuel Taylor Coleridge to John Rickman, 28 Feb. 1804, ibid. ii. 1074–5.
[30] Samuel Taylor Coleridge to Joseph Cottle, early Feb. 1797, ibid. i. 309.

in chapter 11 of the *Biographia*, such compulsiveness may well be a mere factitious precision, the exact opposite of what it appears (as in the overuse of such phrases as 'sort of' or 'kind of', in which simple laziness passes as scrupulosity): 'strict scrutiny should always be made, whether indolence, restlessness, or vanity impatient for immediate gratification, have not tampered with the judgement and assumed the vizard of humility for the purposes of self-delusion'.[31] Again, such fears carry to an extreme what Coleridge elsewhere admits more easily: that his strength, such as it is, lies in judgement, in the so-called secondary processes, rather than in creative or primary processes. Revision is thus seen as disfiguring, like the disfiguring accretions of Blake's later prophetic books or some of his designs.

It is also seen as dishonest, in part because at times Coleridge went to some trouble to disguise his tinkerings. As Richard Holmes puts it, 'Coleridge would often hold over, and meticulously rework, several poems that would later be presented as "spontaneous" productions belonging to specific dates—the sonnet to 1793, the "Retirement" poem to the winter of 1795.'[32] As Fruman points out, *Religious Musings* was 'labored upon for over a year, but published as the production of a single night'.[33] In the preface to 'Kubla Khan', as Fruman elsewhere reminds us, Coleridge claimed to be publishing exactly what he had written down after his revery, 'without any sensation or consciousness of effort', yet the manuscript shows many variants from the published text.[34] Such dishonesty is often motivated by the desire for personal unity or identity rather than—or as well as—a reputation for genius. In chapter 23 of the *Biographia Literaria* Coleridge reprints a polemic against German 'Jacobinical' drama from 'Satyrane's Letters', which he claims was written in Germany in 1798. He then prints an 1816 criticism of Maturin's play *Bertram* which takes a similar line to the 1798 polemic. What the two pieces are meant to show is that 'I have been . . . falsely charged with any fickleness

---

[31] *Biographia Literaria*, ed. Engell and Bate, i. 226.
[32] Holmes, *Coleridge: Early Visions*, 113.
[33] Fruman, 'Creative Process and Concealment', 154. Whether many readers imagined the 400-plus-line *Religious Musings* a 'production' of a single night is uncertain; they are as likely to have thought Coleridge produced a substantial draft on Christmas Eve rather than the finished work.
[34] Ibid. 8.

in my principles of taste.' Nor, he claims, has he changed his
political views. In 1818, in *The Friend*, he continues in the
Biographia, he was able, seamlessly, to insert 'extracts from the
Conciones ad Populum, printed . . . in the year 1795, in the very
heat and height of my anti-ministerial enthusiasm: there is proof
that my principles of *politics* have sustained no change'.[35] In
fact, though, the attack on German drama in 'Satyrane's Letters',
as Bate and Engell point out, was 'written afterwards, probably
for the 1808 Lectures or for *The Friend* (1809) no. 16',[36] while
the republication of portions of the 'Conciones', as Nigel Leask
has shown, involves the omission of 250 lines of the original
1795 text 'on account of their unpalatable radicalism'.[37]

Even when Coleridge is straightforward about a poem's
compositional history, some critics see the revisions as dishonest in another sense—Coleridge's neurotic compulsion to tinker
is thought simply to override original and often quite different
intentions. For example, several scholars see the alterations to
'The Eolian Harp' as substantially changing the character and
meaning of the work. To Stillinger, who claims to have uncovered 'sixteen different versions of the poem', the revisions 'change
the tone, the philosophical and religious ideas, and the basic
structure. . . . The first recoverable version . . . recounts an amusing incident of early married life, while the later version is a
much more serious affair.'[38] For J. C. C. Mays, 'the poem heads
in different directions at different times—as Coleridge's intellectual commitments changed'.[39] For David Pirie, the addition in
1817 of the 'one Life' passage (it first appeared in the errata
notes to *Sibylline Leaves*, remaining in all subsequent editions)
'does not suit the poem to which it is attached. The addition
makes Sara inconsistently reject a passionate and serious belief.'[40] To each of these critics the revisions to the poem are seen
as impositions rather than realizations or clarifications—the
original is altered because Coleridge himself has changed, or
lost sight of his original intentions, or fallen victim to a neurotic
compulsion to tinker.

[35] *Biographia Literaria*, ed. Engell and Bate, ii. 208.   [36] Ibid. 180.
[37] Nigel Leask, *The Politics of Imagination in Coleridge's Critical Thought* (London: Macmillan, 1988), 159.   [38] Stillinger, 'Multiple Versions', 132.
[39] Personal correspondence of 30 Nov. 1992.
[40] Pirie, in *Coleridge's Verse*, ed. Empson and Pirie, 218.

Stillinger, who presents himself as in some respects neutral over such judgements (that is, once the 'textual fact' of multiple versions is granted), also tends to see the revisions as implicitly protective (and as such impositions), though he does not call them neurotic: 'I suggest Coleridge changed his texts at least partly in order to create the very instability that would make his poems and their meanings elusive'; in his proliferating prefatory excuses and apologetic subtitles, 'Coleridge intentionally presents himself to the public as a writer who is not wholly serious in his endeavours and perhaps not even competent; the emphasis is on the amateur qualities of the performance, its rough and unfinished character—the transitory, provisional nature of the work that the reader is holding in hand.'[41] Consider, most famously, the account of the additions to 'Kubla Khan' in its prose preface—think, that is, of the preface itself, as well as the concluding lines about the 'damsel with a dulcimer' (l. 37). If the preface is to be believed, these additions have the effect of turning an initial opium revery (about the exotic Khan and his domains)—or the poet's fragmentary recollection of this revery—into a meditation on writing or the poetic process, something we have no reason to believe it was in the original, whether that original is conceived of as the revery itself or its fragmentary reconstruction.

This view of Coleridge's revisions as neurotic impositions is widespread, as is the view that his personality was deeply inconsistent or incoherent. But it is not always fair. Everyone can be said to change over time, just as every alteration to a poem, however minor, can be said to make the poem 'new'. But it is also perfectly sensible to see almost all the alterations to 'The Eolian Harp', for example, as working towards intentions—thematic and formal—present from the poem's inception. The pantheist overtones of the 'one Life' passage, say, sound also in such lines as

> And what if all of animated nature
> Be but organic Harps diversely fram'd
> That tremble into thought, as o'er them sweeps
> Plastic and vast, one intellectual breeze,
> At once the Soul of each, and God of all?

[41] Stillinger, 'Multiple Versions', 146, 138, 139.

These lines appear in all extant versions of the poem, including the very earliest. When, therefore, Sara rebukes Coleridge in the lines immediately following, her 'mild reproof' is addressing serious issues; it is misleading to characterize the earliest version of the poem as merely 'an amusing incident of early married life', as does Stillinger, just as it is misleading for Pirie to argue that the 'one Life' passage 'does not suit the poem to which it is attached'.[42] The 'one Life' passage suits the poem because it is consistent with the above-quoted lines, for it is to these lines that Sara is objecting. The 'one Life' passage does, it is true, make it somewhat harder to accept Coleridge's characterization of his thoughts as 'idle flitting phantasies' (l. 40), but even in the original this line was odd, a problem. Pirie's decision to print the 1803 version because it 'allows the poem's conclusion to be at least logical'[43] is untrue to the spirit of the original as much as to that of later versions: from the start, the incident the poem means to relate and memorialize involves 'illogical' or inconsistent feelings and thoughts; that is, it was always in part *about* the oddity or discordancy both of Sara's reproof and of Coleridge's capitulation.

REVISION AND INDETERMINACY

There are those who agree that the revisions work against conventional aesthetic values, Coleridgean values,[44] but who think of their doing so not as neurotic but as a virtue. The revisions complicate and call into question the unity or coherence of the poems, and the authorial identity from which they are meant to derive, because neither the world nor the self is simple or single. The revisions work against unity, but in the service of truth or principle—along lines laid out earlier in discussion both of Wordsworth and Byron. In the process, in

---

[42] Pirie, in *Coleridge's Verse*, ed. Empson and Pirie, 218.

[43] Ibid.

[44] As J. C. C. Mays puts it, 'many assumptions about poetry which Coleridge helped to establish bear an oblique relation to his own practice and partly misrepresent it': Mays, 'Reflections on Having Edited Coleridge's Poems', in Brinkley and Hanley (eds.), *Romantic Revisions*, 150.

Stillinger's words, Coleridge 'undermines the concept of a stable text by his continuous revising'. 'Coleridge's conspicuous featuring of his poetry's instability', again in Stillinger's words, may be meant to suggest 'that the perfect poem was a chimera and that authority itself was therefore a fiction. He may, that is to say, have been . . . a deconstructionist.'[45] As Susan Eilenberg puts it, 'what Wordsworth believes in—the naturalness, expressiveness, and substantiality of words—Coleridge doubts'.[46]

This doubt is said to be expressed in individual revisions as well as in the broad fact of their frequency. Eilenberg, for example, points to that moment in 'The Ancient Mariner' in which the mariner and the reanimated body of his nephew silently tug at the same rope, causing the mariner, in the 1798 edition, to recoil in horror: 'And I quak'd to think of my own voice | How frightful it would be' (ll. 344–5). In 1800, these lines are altered to ' "I fear thee, ancient Mariner!" | Be calm, thou Wedding-Guest!' (ll. 345–6). At first, this alteration seems to allay the mariner's fears of 1798—fears of uncontrolled utterance and self-division. The mariner calms or reassures the wedding guest. But as Eilenberg points out, 'fearing at that moment the sound of his own voice, lest it *not* be his, the Mariner hears instead the Wedding Guest's, whose ventriloquy gives voice and fulfillment to the Mariner's fears . . . the relationship between the revised and the original text lends support to the possibility that the words of 1800 deny . . . the spirit of the Mariner speaks through the Wedding Guest. Both men become functions of the tale whose telling they must endure and to whose impersonal power they must bear witness.'[47] Here, revision only seems like fearful imposition, the sort of thing Fruman might deplore; in fact, thanks to the ingenuities of deconstruction, it remains true to the original by realizing the mariner's fears implicitly or performatively—as does Coleridge himself. In Eilenberg's words, 'as the Mariner is subject to a "strange power of speech" that forces him to repeat his tale endlessly, so the poet himself lay under a similar though more limited compulsion to repeat himself, revising the poem in 1800 and again in 1817'.[48] These

---

[45] Stillinger, 'Multiple Versions', 138, 146.
[46] Susan Eilenberg, *Strange Power of Speech: Wordsworth, Coleridge and Literary Possession* (New York: Oxford University Press, 1992), p. x.
[47] Ibid. 36   [48] Ibid. 39

revisions, moreover, took the form of additions—of gloss, Argument—that were also, ironically, repetitions.

Though to Eilenberg and other deconstructively minded readers *anything* written can be used to corroborate the subversiveness, the impersonal power, of language—its power, that is, to 'haunt' or 'possess'—in the case of Coleridge, fear of such power is obvious. Again and again the poems present us with speakers whose utterances are inexplicable, unreliable, uncontrolled, blocked—thus recalling the many motiveless crimes that litter the poems, as well as correspondingly inexplicable moments of personal redemption, as when 'a spring of love' (l. 284) gushes from the heart of the mariner and he blesses the water snakes 'unawares' (l. 285). In Coleridge's late despairing lyrics in particular, this unreliability is seen as a product not only of personal division or disarray, but of the untrustworthiness of language or representation *per se*. To Edward Kessler, for example, Coleridge's 'inability to conclude can be viewed as a deliberate (if not fully acknowledged) act of registering the limitations of what the poet called "confining form"'.[49] Finished works, like all things written, have a self-contained or autonomous, and hence falsifying, character. Coleridge's perpetual revisions may derive from just this sense of the falsifying nature of the finished, from a sense that 'Form is factitious *Being*.'[50] 'Words,' he writes in another entry, 'what are they but a subtle *matter*? And the meanness of Matter must they have, and the Soul must pine in them, even as the lover who can press kisses only . . . [on] the garment of one indeed beloved.'[51] Such doubts—about the possibility of ever establishing the self and its utterances as independent or autonomous—may underlie Coleridge's plagiarisms, as well as his revisions. Coleridge's borrowings might well be seen as extreme manifestations of an habitual distrust—and despair—of any assertion of independent selfhood. He knew plagiarism to be a lie, but he may also have seen it (if not quite consciously) as the admission of a dispiriting truth about all claims to autonomy.

If the revisions fail fully to perfect the poems, to bring them

[49] Edward Kessler, *Coleridge's Metaphors of Being* (Princeton: Princeton University Press, 1979), 5.
[50] Entry of Sept. 1807, in *CN*, ed. Coburn, ii. 3158.
[51] Entry of Feb. 1797, ibid. 2998.

under control, to 'redeem' them (as the gloss to 'The Ancient Mariner' aims to 'redeem' the supposed incoherence of the poem's original narrative and moral), they still, by their very failure, complement, or contribute to, the vision of the poems themselves—by exfoliating rather than channelling or containing meaning. In doing so, they recall the mariner's own inability to be rid of his tale, to tell it once and for all, to lift the curse. In the prose works, too, there is a similarly 'haunted' quality. Though the aim of the *Biographia*, in Eilenberg's words, is to 'defend the freedom of the self from the attacks of Hartley and the mechanistic school of philosophy', the work itself 'flouts the ideal it expounds. This exposition of the freedom and integrity of the self is a magpie's nest of topics and a Babel of voices ... the *Biographia* suffers the problem that is its theme: the impossible need for identity, the irremediable compromising of the self by the other.'[52] In Jerome Christensen's words, all aspects of the work reinforce or reflect 'Coleridge's doubt of the ultimate propriety of the self ... his fear that in the course of his literary life he has become a mere man of letters.'[53] This is why both Eilenberg and Christensen make so much of the episode in chapter 7 of the *Biographia*, an episode of great dramatic power, of the girl apparently possessed by a polyglot devil. This girl, who appears just after the exposition of Hartley's philosophy in chapters 5 and 6, is, according to Eilenberg, what Coleridge 'feared he might become.... The diasparactive nature of her utterance, the failure of her learned quotations to form coherent sense, seems to mock the chaotic work in which the story is embedded.'[54]

Christensen reads *The Friend* in a similar manner, as revealing that 'the writer's possession of his language is precisely what Coleridge's prose puts in question'.[55] In fact, what Christensen calls the 'marginal' method of all Coleridge's critical prose, as much as what he and the deconstructionists see as its ultimate or underlying content, could be said to reflect this conscious but doomed search for autonomy, for a stable 'will' or 'self'. According to Christensen's account of the method,

[52] Eilenberg, *Strange Power*, 139.
[53] Jerome Christensen, *Coleridge's Blessed Machine of Language* (Ithaca, NY: Cornell University Press, 1981), 21.   [54] Eilenberg, *Strange Power*, 144.
[55] Christensen, *Coleridge's Blessed Machine*, 21.

Coleridge 'does not *use* [the writings of particular philosophers] to make an argument so much as he annexes the body of thought—Maass's text, Mackintosh's lectures—into his manuscript to supply a sustaining text that he can cover with marginalia: notes, interpolations, revisions'.[56] In other words, the prose method itself implies the impossibility of ever controlling one's words, or freeing oneself from others' words, an impossibility that helps to account for Coleridge's obsessive revisions—and one that is also figured in the revisions themselves, in their tendency to open up rather than settle or perfect meanings.

The sheer multiplicity of such motivating factors leads to a more general reservation or caveat. As J. C. C. Mays reminds us, Coleridge's revisions fit no single pattern.

Some [works], like the 'Ode to Chatterton', moved through separate stages each of which in effect constitutes a different poem. It was clear that a large number of political poems was toned down when they were reprinted; other poems were re-directed; personal poems were generalized. Some poems were improved up to a point when Coleridge appears to have lost interest in them and allowed printer's errors to accumulate—for instance, 'The Garden of Boccaccio'. Others, like 'Frost at Midnight', underwent continuous improvement.[57]

Moreover, these differences can occur *within* individual poems. Though Empson thinks the basic themes of 'The Ancient Mariner' of 1798 'much mangled' by its revisions, for example, revisions motivated in part by growing political and religious orthodoxy, he also thinks Coleridge 'kept on improving it in detail, even to the first posthumous edition (1834)'—which is why he and Pirie print an 'eclectic' text (something they do in other instances as well).[58] The point Mays makes about Coleridge 'losing interest' in his poems needs also to be emphasized. Coleridgean indolence and Byronic laziness were different in character and origin, but their effect on revision was similar: some poems were simply more carefully copied, revised, proofed, than others.

---

[56] Ibid. 104.   [57] Mays, 'Reflections', 138.
[58] Empson, in *Coleridge's Verse*, ed. Empson and Pirie, 27.

COLERIDGE, DE QUINCEY, AND THE PUBLISHING MOMENT

Mays's caveat notwithstanding, there is a broad pattern to Coleridge's revisions, one that occupies a middle ground between the positions outlined above. Coleridge is, indeed, an apostle of unity and works to unify his poems; but he is also radically divided, though neither as openly as some of his deconstructionist champions imply, nor as neurotically and unconsciously as Fruman and others would claim. His poems much more directly question the autonomy of the self, language, 'possession' (that is, the 'owning' or authorship of one's writing) than do Wordsworth's, but they are rarely as explicitly indeterminist as, for example, Byron's. The poet himself is, at best, a reluctant, even despairing, indeterminist—quite unlike Byron. In Tilottama Rajan's words, 'to see through the phantasms of hope is not necessarily to renounce them', or in Max Schulz's paraphrase (of Rajan's argument), 'although semi-aware of the gap between his perceptions and his imagination and of the tenuous mediation that words provide between thought and thing . . . Coleridge persists in logocentric belief in the transcendent truth of his poetic self-projections'.[59] Mays makes a similar point in a recent interpretation of Coleridge's 'Love', which he sees as embodying

a dilemma which makes Coleridge a proleptic contemporary of Beckett and Derrida but a reluctant one. While at one level his is a poetry of postponement and an undecidable authorial voice, a canon without margins, he does not like a Postmodernist celebrate his sense of *différence, aporia, mise-en-abîme.* . . . Coleridge's pervasive sense of failure is psychological and metaphysical—his word is dejection—and has to do not with what we call Theory but with what he called Principles. It is suffused with regret.[60]

Poetic composition, according to this view, is no mere 'activity' or play of signifiers to Coleridge; it remains, for all Coleridge's

[59] Tilottama Rajan, *Dark Interpreter: The Discourse of Romanticism* (Ithaca, NY: Cornell University Press, 1980), 239, and more generally, 204–59; for Schulz's paraphrase of Rajan see 'Samuel Taylor Coleridge', 378.

[60] J. C. C. Mays, 'Coleridge's "Love": "All he can manage, more than he could" ', in Tim Fulford and Morton D. Paley (eds.), *Coleridge's Visionary Languages* (Cambridge: D. S. Brewer Press, 1993), 66.

sense of belatedness and of the impossibility of authorial autonomy, a way of making not only things or poems, but a self, it is an expression of 'logocentric belief'. The revisions, for the most part, are attempts to ready poems for publication, or republication, and in the process to establish the self as coherent both in time and over time. In chapter 4 of *Biographia Literaria* Coleridge warns against confusing *ego contemplans*, that is, the mere act or fact of self-consciousness, with *ego contemplatus*, 'the visual image or object by which the mind represents to itself its past condition, or rather its personal identity under the form in which it imagined itself previously to have existed'.[61] Personal identity, in other words, is conceived of by Coleridge as something one makes or creates; for example, say champions of Coleridge's alterations, through the act of revision, or through an autobiographical effort such as the *Biographia Literaria*.

It is precisely this sense of the importance of publication in the creation of a coherent self, an *ego contemplatus*, that proponents of early versions—Empson and Pirie, for example— sometimes slight. Nor is the slighting of publication, or the equal weighting of published and unpublished versions, common only among Coleridge's critics and editors; it features also, of course, among proponents of early Wordsworth. Duncan Wu, to cite one recent instance, in defending Wordsworth's editors against Jonathan Bate's accusation of 'modern Butchery', of having, for example, 'extricated the heart of book one [of *The Excursion*] and implied that "The Ruined Cottage" is the only part of [the poem] with which we need concern ourselves',[62] claims that 'The Ruined Cottage' as an independent poem predates *The Excursion* by over ten years. This he claims because 'The Ruined Cottage' exists in two complete fair-copy manuscripts of 1798 and 1799, was read as an independent work to Lamb and Coleridge in July 1797, and offered by Coleridge to Joseph Cottle for publication on 17 March 1798.[63] But as Wu himself admits, the poem was never published, either in 1798 or any of the intervening years up until 1804, years

---

[61] *Biographia Literaria*, ed. Engell and Bate, i. 72.
[62] Jonathan Bate, *Romantic Ecology* (London: Routledge & Kegan Paul, 1992), 63.
[63] Samuel Taylor Coleridge to Joseph Cottle, 17 Mar. 1798, in *CL*, ed. Griggs, i. 399–400.

during which 'Wordsworth continued to work on it as a discrete manuscript'.[64] 'Butchery', I agree, is hardly the right term for Jonathan Wordsworth's discriminating 'extrication' (or 'excavation') of the poem in *The Music of Humanity* (1969). What reader is not grateful for his rescue of the work? But Wu, like Jonathan Wordsworth himself, as well as other authorities Wu cites, makes too little of the fact that Wordsworth never tried to publish the poem after 1798; that we have no evidence that he ever subsequently wished it to be published as a discrete poem; or that, in Gill's words, any discrete version ever 'entirely satisfied' him, 'as if throughout its composition Wordsworth found that his material raised questions and presented difficulties which resisted resolution into a satisfying final form'.[65] *We* may think 'The Ruined Cottage' an independent poem, but the fact of its non-publication outweighs the reasons Wu gives for thinking Wordsworth did.

As for Coleridge's critics, consider Empson's account of the revisions of 'To a Young Ass', in particular the excision of lines 28–34 of the 1794 manuscript. The lines in question begin just after Coleridge has hailed the titular 'Poor despondent young ass' (l. 1) as 'Brother' (l. 26), inviting it to accompany him

> Where high-soul'd Pantisocracy shall dwell!
> Where Mirth shall tickle Plenty's ribless side,
> And smiles from Beauty's Lip on sunbeams glide,
> Where Toil shall wed young Health that charming Lass!
> And use his sleek cows for a looking-glass —
> Where Rats shall mess with Terriers hand-in-glove
> And Mice with Pussy's Whiskers sport in Love.

In these lines, Empson argues, Coleridge pokes fun at the ideal aspirations of Pantisocracy, 'a political scheme to which he was still intensely attached'. The lines signal confidence or commitment: 'he would feel that, among friends, to recognize the absurdity of the scheme only praised its high-mindedness and intellectual rigour'. To print the jokey lines, though, 'might encourage the coarse public to jeer'. That these lines would be laughed at, Empson contends, Coleridge knew from the start: he wanted them laughed at. He just did not want them laughed

---

[64] Duncan Wu, 'Acts of Butchery: Wordsworth as Editor', *The Wordsworth Circle*, 23/3 (Summer 1992), 156.   [65] Gill, *Wordsworth: A Life*, 133.

at the wrong way. Empson's decision to restore the lines in his and Pirie's selection is based on a belief that when Coleridge 'made this alteration, he would want the original text to be put back as soon as it could do no harm'.[66]

Why, though, did Coleridge not himself restore the lines in subsequent editions? When, moreover, except after Coleridge had abandoned Pantisocracy and its ideals, or the rest of the world miraculously embraced them, would the wrong kind of laughter—that is, laughter from a general audience as opposed to close friends and fellow Pantisocrats—ever be avoided? The poem as a whole was risky (the critics had a field day with it), but the lines in question, particularly the later lines, even Coleridge recognized as excessive, risible. Nor is it true to say, as does Pirie, that lines 28–34 alone communicate the original manuscript's 'blend of sincere social protest with humorous hyperbole'[67]; there is gently humorous hyperbole throughout the poem. All printed versions, moreover, retain the lines 'Toil shall call the charmer Health his bride, | And laughter tickle Plenty's ribless side.' In other words, Empson is wrong to consider the excision of lines 28–34 of the original extraordinary, the product of external 'imposition' (as in cuts that derive from fear of libel, for example, or imprisonment). The only 'imposition' involved in the excision is that of the imagined or anticipated needs and interests of an audience—something writers have always to consider, such consideration being a perfectly ordinary feature of the compositional process, of the process of turning a manuscript draft into a poem or novel or essay. What Empson underestimates is the integral or constitutive role of publication—with its implied general audience—in the creation of poetry.

Consider an analogous instance, from William Godwin's revision of the *Enquiry Concerning Political Justice* (1793). Perhaps the most notorious passage in the *Enquiry* occurs in chapter 2 of the second book, entitled 'Of Justice', in which Godwin's extreme rationalism is illustrated by a proposition involving Fénelon, the distinguished Archbishop of Cambrai and author of *Télémaque* (1699). If Fénelon and his valet were caught in a fire, 'and the life of only one of them could be preserved', it

[66] *Coleridge's Verse*, ed. Empson and Pirie, 16, 17.   [67] Ibid. 218.

is Fénelon's life, Godwin famously argues, we should preserve, since 'that life ought to be preferred which will be most conducive to the general good'. This conclusion would hold, continues Godwin in the third or 1798 edition, even if 'I had been myself the valet', or the valet 'had been my brother, my father, or my benefactor'.[68] Here, perfectly exemplified, is what Wordsworth saw as the age's tendency, as he puts it in Book 11 of *The Prelude*, 'to abstract the hopes of Man | Out of his feelings, to be fixed thenceforth | For ever in a purer element' (ll. 225–7, 1850 version).

Yet the 1798 or third edition offers a comparatively 'moderate' version of the passage. In the original or 1793 edition the discrepancy between head and heart was more extreme, for the relations over whom Fénelon was to be preferred were 'my wife or mother'. The switch from 'wife or mother' (as servant) to 'my brother, my father' (as valet) in 1798 is analogous to Coleridge's cutting of lines 28–34 from the manuscript of 'To a Young Ass'. In any of its forms, to be sure, the passage displays, as Marilyn Butler puts it, 'a curious failure of proportion or of common sense'—a damaging failure, too, since it clearly distracted readers from the book's larger arguments. As is the case with the manuscript version of 'To a Young Ass' (some would argue, with the published version as well), such failures of literary tact or judgement 'emerged, surely, in the trustful, sympathetic atmosphere engendered within a group of idealists'.[69] Revising 'wife or mother' to 'my brother, my father' made the passage marginally more tactful, the result of a perfectly straightforward calculation or recollection of the nature— the fact—of the book's wide audience, an audience beyond Godwin's immediate circle, one the book's initial notoriety taught Godwin to attend to more closely in second and third editions. Though the revision was in this case of a published text rather than a manuscript, it is still hard to see it as a product of what Empson calls 'imposition'; nor have subsequent editors, including Butler, felt moved to restore the original reading.

---

[68] William Godwin, *Enquiry Concerning Political Justice*, ed. Isaac Kramnick (Harmondsworth: Penguin Books, 1976), 170.

[69] Marilyn Butler (ed.), *Burke, Paine, Godwin and the Revolution Controversy* (Cambridge: Cambridge University Press, 1984), 150.

Related objections attend Stillinger's hypothetical reconstruction of the Coleridgean composing process, a reconstruction
that recalls Mileur's account of how Coleridge completes the
meanings of his poems. 'Initially . . . we may posit that Coleridge
drafted his poems pretty much the way Keats did: thoughts and
images came "about him in troops" . . . and he selected as best
he could, wrote down the results, and was as surprised and
pleased as anyone else at what he had done.' Unlike Keats,
though, Coleridge then went on to rework the poem: 'Coleridge
the poet metamorphosed into Coleridge the critic, as if someone
else had written his poems. He became, that is, critic *and interpreter* of what he had initially created without a plan, and now,
in these subsequent stages of writing, *added authorial intention*
that was never present in the original composition.'[70] What is
troublesome here is Stillinger's implicit assumption that the
primary process alone, the conjectured 'original composition',
is or makes poetry, or that secondary stages of composition are
somehow not poetical—by virtue of being 'critical'. This sounds
like 'Romanticism', and calls to mind Trilling's shrewd weighting of the 'visionary gleam' in his essay on 'The Immortality
Ode'.

To be a poem, I would suggest, the poet's initial thoughts,
images, and feelings need to be nominated by him or her *as* a
poem, to be nominated, that is, by the poet's judgement, as
when she or he *finds* a poem in (or *constructs* a poem out of,
if one prefers) primary process material—Keats's 'troops' of
thoughts and images. Nomination, of course, can take many
subsequent forms, as in the decision to title or recopy or read
out or reproduce in correspondence, but nowhere is it clearer
or more emphatic than in publication. This is not to say that
the mere fact of publication guarantees poetical nomination—
the author in question, as Hans Zeller puts it, must have 'desired or approved' the production of his or her published texts,
must have 'influenced the texts by supplying the printer's copy
or by personal revision, or by revision undertaken at his request
during the printing process'[71]—it is only to suggest that, with
Zeller's qualifications, no other moment more surely signals

---

[70] Stillinger, *Textual Instability*, 106, 107.
[71] Hans Zeller, 'A New Approach to the Critical Constitution of Literary Texts',
Studies in Bibliography, 28 (1975), 260, quoted ibid. 278.

creative completion or birth, for Coleridge as for many other writers.

For example, nowhere in Coleridge (or Wordsworth, for that matter) does one get a passage such as the following, from De Quincey, another compulsive reviser, and in other ways Coleridge's seeming double. De Quincey is apologizing in advance for any errors he might have made in the text of the revised *Confessions*, while also announcing the inevitability of error:

Endless are the openings for such kinds of mistake—that is, of mistakes not fully seen *as* such. But even in a case of unequivocal mistake, seen and acknowledged, yet when it is open to remedy only through a sudden and energetic act, then or never,—the press being for twenty minutes, suppose, free to receive an alteration, but beyond that time closed and sealed inexorably: such being supposed the circumstances, the humane reader will allow for the infirmity which ever wilfully and consciously surrenders itself to the error, acquiescing in it deliberately, rather than face the cruel exertion of correcting it most elaborately at a moment of sickening misery, and with the prevision that the main correction must draw after it half-a-dozen others for the sake of decent consistency.[72]

Though Coleridge, too, was prepared to acknowledge the collaborative nature of publication, rarely did he let a consequent sense of delimited authority licence this sort of defeat, this pessimism and release. For De Quincey, the contingencies of the 'press', or what McGann calls 'institutional affiliation' (such contingencies, that is, as 'the press being for twenty minutes, suppose, free to receive an alteration'), feed into a larger pessimism about creative or compositional perfection.[73] De Quincey more consciously links the two than does Coleridge; like Byron, and unlike Wordsworth, he is prepared to admit both the inevitability of error, and the impossibility of control. This lack of control, moreover, extends for De Quincey to questions of reception as well as production, as in the following

---

[72] Thomas De Quincey, *Confessions of an English Opium-Eater*, in *Selections Grave and Gay, from Writings, Published and Unpublished, of Thomas De Quincey, Revised and Arranged by Himself*, 14 vols. (Edinburgh: James Hogg, 1853–60), v. p. xii. Quoted also in an appendix to the Penguin edn. of the *Confessions*, edited by Alethea Hayter (Harmondsworth: Penguin, 1971), 138.

[73] For 'institutional affiliation' see Jerome J. McGann, *A Critique of Modern Textual Criticism* (Chicago: University of Chicago Press, 1983), 54.

excerpt from a letter written during the 1856 revision of *Confessions* for the collected edition:

I am much afraid—that in consequence of the very imperfect means for communicating with the Press which I now possess or ever *have* possessed (being at all times reduced to the single resource of *writing* —which, to evade misinterpretation and constant ambiguity, requires a redundancy of words—and, after all that is done on *my* part, requires in addition a *Reader* that is not only singularly attentive, but also has a surplus stock of *leisure time* [)]—*Premising* all this, I am and *have* been at all stages of this nominal reprint (but virtually *rifacimento*) of the Confession, in terror of mutual misunderstandings —consequetly [*sic*] of each party unintentionally thwarting or embarrassing the other by movements at *cross purposes*.[74]

Here the press's inability to understand De Quincey's instructions—because he is 'reduced to the single resource of *writing*', because the compositor or publisher (called a *'Reader'*) is not 'singularly attentive'—obviously alludes to the vicissitudes of reception in general, the published work's reception by a general audience. De Quincey is no more able to control reader response than he is the publishing process, in both cases because writing is involved, as though lack of control were an inevitable feature of writing.

Nor is it only the inevitable inadequacies of language or representation—writing—that are figured in De Quincey's account of the limitations of publication or the press. So, too, is the larger question of the possibility of *any* sort of control or agency in human behaviour. Consider, for example, one final extended quotation, again from the revised *Confessions*:

In fact, every intricate and untried path in life, where it was from the first a matter of arbitrary choice to enter upon it or avoid it, is effectually a path through a vast Hercynian forest, unexplored and unmapped, where each several turn in your advance leaves you open to new anticipations of what is next to be expected, and consequently open to altered valuations of all that has been already traversed. Even the character of your own absolute experience, past and gone, which (if anything in this world) you might surely answer for as sealed and settled forever—even this you must submit to hold in suspense, as a

---

[74] Letter of 18 Sept. 1856 to James Hogg, quoted in Edmund Baxter, *De Quincey's Art of Autobiography* (Edinburgh: Edinburgh University Press, 1990), 17.

thing conditional and contingent upon what is yet to come—liable to have its provisional character affirmed or reversed, according to the new combinations into which it may enter with elements only yet perhaps in the earliest stages of development.[75]

This passage is simultaneously about De Quincey's life and the writing and revising of that life, and in each case the conclusion is the same—that the sort of control sought by Wordsworth, for example, both as man and writer, is impossible, as impossible as attempts to express or construct a stable identity over time. This is why, as John Barrell puts it, 'we can make no assumptions about the relation between the chronological order of De Quincey's writings and rewritings and the development of his psychic life'; it is also why Barrell treats the writings 'as constituting together a synchronic myth whose different versions are not themselves easily susceptible of narrativization'.[76] De Quincey cannot and will not turn his life into a story, construct an identity. Though 'man', according to De Quincey, in the 'Autobiographic Sketches', 'is doubtless *one* by some subtle *nexus*, some system of links, that we cannot perceive, extending from the newborn infant to the superannuated dotard . . . as regards many affections and passions incident to his nature at different stages, he is *not* one, but an intermitting creature, ending and beginning anew'.[77] Coleridge resists or evades conclusions like these, just as he resists De Quincey's frank acceptance of writing as a trade (like his frank acceptance of opium-eating)[78]—in part, as we shall see, by denying or deferring the fact of publication, refusing, in a variety of ingenious

[75] De Quincey, *Confessions*, from *Selections Grave and Gay*, v. 113–14.

[76] John Barrell, *The Infection of Thomas De Quincey* (New Haven: Yale University Press, 1991), 22.

[77] 'The Autobiographic Sketches' comprise the first and part of the second volume of De Quincey's *Selections Grave and Gay*. It begins with seven newly revised versions of the thirty-three essays published intermittently between Feb. 1834 and Feb. 1841 in *Tait's Edinburgh Magazine* under the general title 'Sketches of Life and Manners; from the Autobiography of an English Opium Eater'. The first sketch was originally published in *Tait's Edinburgh Magazine* in Feb. 1834. See *Selections Grave and Gay*, i. 18.

[78] Nigel Leask, in *British Romantic Writers and the East: Anxieties of Empire* (Cambridge: Cambridge University Press, 1993), 201, tellingly quotes Coleridge's assertion in the *Biographia* that 'the *necessity* of acquiring [money and reputation] will in all works of genius convert the stimulus into a *narcotic*' (*Biographia Literaria*, ed. Engell and Bate, i. 244).

ways, to acknowledge it as 'real'. Unlike De Quincey, he never 'wilfully and consciously' surrenders to inevitable error, for all his comparable sense of fallibility.

THE DOUBLENESS OF THE MARGINAL GLOSS

This difference notwithstanding, Coleridge's compulsion to revise is every bit as intense as De Quincey's, and only in part a product of 'unresolved gaps of one sort or another in his psyche, vision, and experience'.[79] Coleridge also, in other words, though less openly than De Quincey, refuses to exclude—at least as possibilities—the larger truths these gaps suggest. For example, in the case of 'The Ancient Mariner' revisions, as is frequently argued, Coleridge's main intention is unity of effect—the very coherence or consistency the poem's earliest critics felt it lacked. No revision, runs the argument, more fully realizes this intention than the addition of the prose gloss for the 1817 *Sibylline Leaves* edition. What the gloss does, in Lipking's words, is familiarize 'every supernatural event; it assures us, in spite of the wedding-guest's fears, that the mariner is alive, sustained by a world of facts . . . it interprets the narrative by reading it as a parable. In the world of the gloss, actions have causes and consequences, parts fit into wholes, and human motives are not arbitrary.'[80] As Frances Ferguson puts it: 'The Gloss, in assuming that things must be significant and interpretable, finds significance and interpretability, but only by reading ahead of—or beyond—the main text.'[81]

Here are some obvious examples. When in Part III Death and Life-in-Death are described casting dice on the deck of the phantom ship, the text reads: 'The game is done! I've won! I've won! | Quoth she, and whistles thrice.' *What* Life-in-Death has won (that is, the ancient mariner) we are not told until much later in the text. It is only with the addition of the gloss that we learn that 'Death and Life-in-Death have diced for the ship's crew, and she (the latter) winneth the ancient Mariner.' Here

[79] Schulz, 'Samuel Taylor Coleridge', 375.
[80] Lipking, 'The Marginal Gloss', 615.
[81] Frances Ferguson, 'Coleridge and the Deluded Reader: "The Rime of the Ancient Mariner"', *Georgia Review* (1977), 623.

the gloss straightforwardly clarifies the poem itself. Elsewhere, narrative clarity is accompanied by moral clarity, argue the gloss's defenders. When, for example, his shipmates justify the mariner's shooting of the albatross—an act the mariner recounts in the text with uncomprehending neutrality—it is the gloss that tells us they 'thus make themselves accomplices in the crime'. When the poem says simply that the ship is becalmed, it is the gloss that adds 'And the albatross begins to be avenged.'

Lipking provides an ingenious defence of the gloss's seeming impositions. The discrepancy between poem and gloss, he argues, is not only a strength, but a peculiarly Coleridgean strength. In chapter 14 of the *Biographia*, Coleridge argues that in a true or successful poem, 'the reader should be carried forward, not merely or chiefly by the mechanical impulse of curiosity, or by a restless desire to arrive at the final solution; but by the pleasurable activity of mind excited by the attractions of the journey itself. Like the motion of a serpent, which the Egyptians made the emblem of intellectual power, or like the path of sound through the air, at every step he pauses and half recedes, and from the retrogressive movement collects the force which again carries him onward.' This experience, comments Lipking, is 'not unlike reading a ballad of wonders with a marginal gloss'.[82] In other words, though gloss and text differ, this difference is no necessary aesthetic weakness or blemish; Coleridge's aesthetic is more complex and inclusive than it sometimes sounds or is said to be. It is certainly clear that Coleridge accepted more heterogeneity in his writing than some of the more famous of his critical pronouncements would lead one to believe. His works were organized, but loosely—after the manner of *The Friend*, with its assorted 'landing places' and subtitles. Moreover, it was always, one might argue, 'Multeity in Unity' (a phrase from 'On the Principles of Genial Criticism') Coleridge valued.[83]

Jerome J. McGann, building in part on Lipking's account of the gloss, including its richly informative exegesis of the history of glossing, and in part on a much earlier article by Huntington

---

[82] Lipking, 'The Marginal Gloss', 621. The Coleridge quotation is from *Biographia Literaria*, ed. Engell and Bate, ii. 14.

[83] Repr. in *Biographia Literaria*, ed. John Shawcross, 2 vols. (Oxford: Clarendon Press, 1907), ii. 232.

Brown, sees its addition to the poem somewhat differently, in a manner that recalls deconstructionist readings. Brown was the first critic to draw attention to the differences between the language of the gloss and the language of the ballad, arguing that the latter comes from around the time of Henry VII, and the former from a later period, that of Shakespeare. The effect of this distinction is twofold: first, 'it serves to emphasize the remoteness of the story and its teller', and second, it emphasizes the poem's multiple points of view, including those of 'the Mariner who reports [the voyage] . . . the Wedding-Guest who listens [to the story] . . . the minstrel [who authors the verse] and, finally . . . the pious antiquarian [who edits the ballad]'.[84] McGann's contribution to Brown's reading is to see the 'finished' poem, that is the post-1817 or glossed version, as illustrating 'a special theory of the historical interpretation of texts', which is also a 'religious theory of interpretation which has its roots in the Higher Critical tradition [i.e. of biblical interpretation]'.[85]

What the poem offers, according to McGann, is a higher or 'whole' vision of a truth, a vision larger than that of its constituent voices or points-of-view, and this vision McGann summarizes as follows: '(*a*) that there is a whole truth which justifies and is the ground of all the fragments of the truth; and (*b*) that the whole truth is in a perpetual process of becoming—indeed, that its being is *the process of its being*'.[86] In other words, the gloss exfoliates and unfixes meaning, as the deconstructionists would have it, rather than clarifying or refining it, and in doing so it offers us our only available truth. As Frances Ferguson puts it, in an analogous reading, 'Coleridge could sort information from knowledge, delusion from truth, with no more certainty than anyone else who has lived long enough to have a memory and, thus, prejudice. He said, in the *Aids to Reflection*, that "original sin is not hereditary sin; it is original with the sinner and of his will" (p. 227). And for Coleridge this original sin was interpretation from a limited perspective that had disproportionate consequences, for the peril was that any apparent extension or reversal might, always, be merely a disguised

---

[84] Huntington Brown, 'The Gloss to the Ancient Mariner', *Modern Language Quarterly*, 6 (1945), 322, 324.
[85] Jerome J. McGann, 'The Meaning of "The Ancient Mariner"', *Critical Inquiry*, 8 (Autumn 1981), 50.   [86] Ibid. 52.

entrenchment of that particular limitation or prejudice.'[87] For Ferguson, the sort of certainty or perfection the older critics misguidedly attribute to the gloss is even, somehow, related to the crimes the ballad itself narrates. The poem's 'message', according to this line, is the danger as well as the impossibility of claims of certitude, perfection, autonomy, agency, personal identity, or integrity of self.

This message is no mere advanced invention. The discrepancy between gloss and ballad is obvious, as is the conclusion that Coleridge cannot quite bring himself to revise away—to efface or explain—the ultimate evil and incoherence of the mariner's world; that the gloss itself does not 'redeem' the text.[88] The Coleridge who refuses this redemption is the Coleridge for whom 'The Ancient Mariner' had too *much* (rather than too little) moral; it is the Coleridge who is reported in *Table Talk* to have countered Mrs Barbauld's charges that the poem was morally incoherent by referring her to an *Arabian Nights* story of random or senseless punishment, a story which recalls the dicing apparitions of 'The Ancient Mariner' (in that the mariner's and shipmates' fates are also a matter of pure contingency). The story in question is that of an Arab who is punished for accidentally putting out the eye of a spirit when tossing a date-stone down a well; the story, in other words, is flatly incompatible with the more positive or sacramental moments in the poem, and by alluding to it Coleridge is calling into question the moral of the poem *per se*, as opposed to its mere obtrusiveness.[89] At the same time, the poem's saving intimations of unity or interrelation are genuine; it would be wrong to deny or weaken such moments, or the concluding moral to which they point (even if Coleridge could bring himself to do so), just as it would be wrong to deny the many moments, artfully interpreted by critics from McElderry to Robert Penn Warren

---

[87] Ferguson, 'Coleridge and the Deluded Reader', 635.

[88] It has even been argued, by John Beer, that the gloss serves 'to *emphasize* the existence of evil in the Mariner's world' (personal correspondence, 1994), a view suggested also in an appendix ('The 1798 and 1817 Versions of The Rime of the Ancient Mariner') to Beer's rev. 2nd edn. of his Everyman edn. of Coleridge's *Poems*, 491–4.

[89] See entry of 31 Mar. 1832 in Samuel Taylor Coleridge, *Table Talk*, ed. Carl Woodring, 2 vols. (Princeton: Princeton University Press, 1990), i. 272–3. *Table Talk* is the 14th title in CW, ed. Coburn.

to Lipking, in which the gloss clarifies and unifies.[90] The poem, in other words, is genuinely double—as are the revisions—and this doubleness is characteristically Coleridgean.

FORMS OF 'DEJECTION'

A comparable doubleness is suggested by the revisionary history of 'Dejection: An Ode'. On 4 October 1802, the seventh anniversary of his own marriage and the day Wordsworth married Mary Hutchinson, Coleridge published a poem in the *Morning Post* entitled 'Dejection: An Ode. Written April 4 1802', the earliest printed version of the poem he would later call 'Dejection: An Ode'. This poem was a shortened, sanitized adaptation of an earlier, more personal poem, 'Letter to——', which Coleridge had sent to Mary Hutchinson's sister, Sara, on the date the newspaper version commemorates in its title. The unpublished 'Letter' was in part a despairing declaration of love from the unhappily married Coleridge, a poem full of doom, longing, self-revelation, guilt, and self-pity. Coleridge was close to separation from his wife, was ill, impoverished, addicted to opium, and unable to work or visit the Wordsworths; he had also at last realized both the hopelessness of his love for Sara (whom he had begun to think of as a sort of muse) and the deleterious effect his attentions were having on her health. At the same time, he had begun to call into question his and Wordsworth's earlier faith in the benevolence and beneficial interaction of nature and the imagination. In addition, at this time Wordsworth (who retained his 'faith') was not only at his most productive, but about to marry Sara's sister, with whom he, Dorothy, and Sara herself had been living for some months. Though the published 'Dejection, &c' expunged all romantic or amatory motives for despondency—that is, all the material 'of a private nature'[91]—in several ways (e.g. by giving the original date of composition of the 'Letter', and by indicating the

---

[90] Robert Penn Warren's much-reprinted interpretation, 'A Poem of Pure Imagination: An Experiment in Reading' (1945–6), in *Selected Essays* (1941; repr. New York: Random House, 1958), 198–306.

[91] Samuel Taylor Coleridge to William Sotheby, 19 July 1802, in *CL*, ed. Griggs, ii. 815.

supposed omission of stanzas 6 and 7—though no intervening stanzas exist in the earlier work), it also gestured towards a prior poem. Why did Coleridge draw attention to the earlier work? Had he simply numbered the stanzas consecutively, for example, as he did in later versions, no one would have realized the poem had an earlier incarnation.[92]

Coleridge clearly wanted to keep the earlier, more personal poem out of the public arena, and not only because of its romantic (if not adulterous) intimations. Much has been made— by Pirie most powerfully—of the successful combination in the 'Letter' of personal and philosophical elements: 'the problems of philosophy and of poetic creation become part of a statement of loneliness, and the resolution is that of a great love poem'.[93] Yet a case can be made that the earlier version, which also seeks to anatomize as well as articulate the poet's dejection, is inadequately analytical—that it fails to distinguish between symptoms and causes of dejection. Moreover, Coleridge could sometimes sound positively Johnsonian in his disdain for personal particulars, as in the following comment on an early version of 'To William Wordsworth', in a letter of 30 May 1815 to Wordsworth: 'It is for the Biographer not the Poet, to give the *accidents* of *individual* Life. Whatever is not representative, generic, may be indeed most poetically exprest but is not Poetry.'[94] Something of this feeling may lie behind the revisions to the original 'Letter'. Also, it must be admitted, there

---

[92] According to David Pirie, in 'A Letter to [Asra]', in Jonathan Wordsworth (ed.), *Bicentennial Wordsworth Essays in Memory of John Alban Finch* (Ithaca, NY: Cornell University Press, 1970), 334, 'it is hard to know what Coleridge meant by this claim. No form of the poem contains two other stanzas at this point, though later versions do insert seven more lines. It cannot, of course, refer to any omissions from *A Letter* since in the original poem the storm passage which now follows preceded the lines that here make up Stanza 5. The most likely explanation is that Coleridge was aware of creating a clumsy transition and decided that a little deceit would make it more acceptable. Stanza 6 (numbered 8) opens enigmatically with

> O wherefore did I let it haunt my mind
> This dark distressful dream

This had been a reasonable reaction to the vision of Sara lying ill, which preceded it in *A Letter*, but it is hard to see how the loss of Imagination could fittingly be called a dream. One can understand Coleridge's decision to ask his readers to supply some suitable nightmare at this point, but it is an admission of failure.'
[93] Ibid. 325.
[94] Samuel Taylor Coleridge to William Wordsworth, 30 May 1815, in *CL*, ed. Griggs, iv. 572.

is a whining, childish quality to the 'Letter', as in stanza 17, in which, creepily, Coleridge seems not merely to resent his children (though he professes concern for their welfare), but unconsciously to wish them harm—perhaps because it is precisely their position as dependents he himself craves.

Yet Coleridge could not quite let the earlier version go, which suggests not only the centrality of the absent love element—its causative rather than symptomatic character—but his sense, shared by a number of critics, that its presence in the poem results in greater immediacy and emotional force. In a letter to Southey, written between the original and first printed versions, the former suggestion is implicitly confirmed. In this letter, Coleridge quotes two short extracts from the 'Letter', saying nothing of Sara Hutchinson or the romantic entanglements which were its occasion. He introduces the extracts after famously questioning whether he possesses genius (as opposed to 'a more general *aptitude* of Talent, & quickness in Imitation').[95] What immediately follows the extracts, though, is an announcement that relations with his wife have improved. In other words, Coleridge continued to associate his dejection with romantic or amatory difficulties (as he would even after publication, as in a letter of 20 October 1802 to Thomas Wedgwood, in which he introduces seven unpublished lines from the 'Letter', lines immediately following an admission of marital woes and lack of sympathy, with complaints about 'domestic distresses'[96]). By gesturing towards the earlier and unknown 'Letter', then, the first printed version sought to retain something of its truth (as an account of the poet's condition) as well as its force. Coleridge could not quite bring himself to see the published poem as a new and separate work, one freed from obligation to the earlier, unpublished poem and its real-life occasion. The new poem was new, but it was also a revision, and Coleridge continued to feel loyalty to the original; that is, he continued to value the process of writing for personal, in addition to public, reasons. His attitude to revision was neither strictly Wordsworthian nor Byronic.

The editorial response to the complex compositional history

[95] Samuel Taylor Coleridge to Robert Southey, 29 July 1802, ibid. ii. 449.
[96] Samuel Taylor Coleridge to Thomas Wedgwood, 20 Oct. 1802, ibid. 464.

of 'Dejection' has been interestingly varied.[97] John Beer, in the first edition of his Everyman selection of Coleridge's poems, publishes both the 'Letter' and the 1817 *Sibylline Leaves* version of 'Dejection', as though they were indeed separate works. (In the second edition he publishes the two poems on facing pages.) Pirie and Empson publish only the 'Letter', on the grounds that successive revisions, from 1802 to 1816, resulted not in improvement but in 'gradual disintegration'.[98] E. H. Coleridge, in the Oxford Standard Authors *Poetical Works*, publishes the later version, but also prints the 4 October 1802 *Morning Post* edition in an appendix, collated with the text of the poem as sent to William Sotheby in the 19 July 1802 letter. H. J. Jackson, in the Oxford Authors *Samuel Taylor Coleridge*, publishes only the later version. Holmes summarizes the problems at issue with characteristic pungency. What the different versions of the poem reveal is

the split between Coleridge's inner world of tempestuous emotions, and the outer persona of the public philosopher-poet who wrote for the *Morning Post* . . . Coleridge moved from the one to the other by a process of supreme artistic self-discipline, cutting, editing, and self-censoring. Both versions carry their central themes with absolute conviction; but the split between the two suggests an ongoing division of spiritual life, almost a kind of schizophrenia . . . The first version overwhelms the reader with its intimacy, its torrent of lament and letting-go, which is both shocking and compulsive. The final version holds the reader in an act of high, rhetorical attention, around the proposition that external nature cannot heal the poet (as Wordsworth believed it could) whose own powers are fading . . . however much 'Dejection' is to be preferred as a finished work of art, the 'Letter' draws more directly on Coleridge's true imaginative life. It is richer in, and closer to, those irrepressible sources of imagery which fill his Notebooks and private correspondence.

Yet, confusingly, 'it is still arguable that "Dejection", in its reduced and disciplined form, is the more universal work'.[99]

With the demise of all interested parties, a strong case can be made for publishing both versions—actually, 'works', since, as

[97] For a detailed account of this history see *Coleridge's 'Dejection': The Earliest Manuscripts and the Earliest Printings*, ed. Stephen Parrish (Ithaca, NY: Cornell University Press, 1988).
[98] Pirie, 'A Letter', 294.   [99] Holmes, *Early Visions*, 318–19, 320.

Stillinger suggests, the differences between the two are so extreme—though, perhaps, the 'Letter' should appear in an appendix. Nor is the 'Letter' of value only for historical or biographical reasons—for its truth to the particular circumstances of the condition described. Though Holmes makes much of the raw emotion of the 'Letter', it should also be noted that the private material it contains is carefully shaped and ordered—is no mere 'torrent' or 'letting go'. In subsequent, supposedly more 'disciplined' versions, argues Pirie, the concluding imagery of marriage is 'just decorative; and Nature's wedding garment becomes the most straightforward kind of metaphor. The "poor loveless ever-anxious crowd" seems to be patronized by a poet who has not demonstrated any anxiety about being unloved himself . . . Coleridge . . . sounds as if he wishes to keep himself at a reverent distance from Wordsworth; whereas in *A Letter* the struggle to feel at one with Nature was part of a struggle to feel close to Sara.'[100] In other words, in addition to being a different work, the 'Letter', though still less 'tidy' than 'Dejection: An Ode', also meets Coleridgean aesthetic standards, its reliance on 'accidents of individual Life' notwithstanding.

REVISION AND PUBLICATION

That the compositional history of 'Dejection: An Ode' is exceptional, certainly among Coleridge's better-known poems, is suggested by a revealing moment in J. C. C. Mays's defence of the synoptic format of the second or 'central' volume of his forthcoming Bollingen edition of Coleridge's poems. It is Mays's contention that the synoptic method of display 'communicates a different supposition about what is going on than would the choice of one text rested on a pile of footnotes. The display communicates a process in which a number of versions have separate validity . . . Poems like *The Destiny of Nations* and *Religious Musings* are in fact several poems.'[101] Perhaps, but why single out these particular poems, both of which underwent obvious political recolourings? Why not mention the different

---

[100] Pirie, 'A Letter', 328–9.   [101] Mays, 'Reflections', 147.

versions of better-known titles such as 'The Ancient Mariner', or 'Frost at Midnight', or 'The Eolian Harp'—or a host of less obviously political poems? Are the different versions of *these* titles 'in fact several poems'?

One suspects not, or at least not meaningfully, and such suspicions raise more general questions, in particular 'What constitutes a "work"?' and 'What constitutes a "version"?' 'Is the *Ancient Mariner* a single version of the work,' asks Stillinger, 'or all the versions taken together?—and if it is all the versions taken together, is the work constituted by the *process* of its revisions, one after another, or by all the versions considered as existing simultaneously?'[102] (Stillinger's ultimate answer, in *Coleridge and Textual Instability*, is that a 'work' is constituted 'by all known versions of the work'.[103]) As for 'version', Stillinger cites Peter L. Shillingsburg's roomy definition in *Scholarly Editing in the Computer Age: Theory and Practice* (1986): 'A version has no substantial existence, but is represented more or less well or completely by a single text as found in a manuscript, proof, book, or some other written or printed form.'[104] After distancing himself from the phrase 'no substantial existence', Stillinger then extrapolates from Shillingsburg's definition to conclude that 'every separate version is a work in its own right and . . . all authoritative versions are equally authoritative',[105] a judgement that draws in part upon Hans Zeller's assertion, in 'A New Approach to the Critical Constitution of Literary Texts' (1975), that 'in the most extreme case a version is constituted by a single variant . . . fundamentally, whether the variants are numerous and of far-reaching effect is not a necessary condition for the constitution of a version'.[106] In the end, Stillinger concludes, 'the degree of textual difference necessary to *distinguish one version of a work from another* is entirely arbitrary', and the authority of any particular version rests ultimately 'on someone's arbitrary definition of what constitutes authority'.[107]

But *are* all distinctions between versions 'entirely arbitrary'?

---

[102] Stillinger, *Textual Instability*, p. v.   [103] Ibid. 132.
[104] Peter L. Shillingsburg, *Scholarly Editing in the Computer Age: Theory and Practice* (Athens, Ga.: University of Georgia Press, 1986), 47.
[105] Stillinger, *Textual Instability*, 136.
[106] Zeller, 'A New Approach', 241.
[107] Stillinger, *Textual Instability*, 132.

Without getting too complicatedly or rigorously categorical, as in attempts to determine which variants produce 'a changed aesthetic effect' (James Thorpe) or which are 'horizontal' rather than 'vertical'—that is, alter 'the purpose, direction or character of a work' (Thomas Tanselle)[108]—can one not distinguish between published versions, or versions clearly intended for publication, and extracts copied out in letters, or occasional alterations in individual copies sent out to friends (except, perhaps, when there are no subsequent printed versions or versions intended for publication)? And are not such distinctions both clear and useful? When Coleridge extracts lines 38–43 of 'This Lime-tree Bower My Prison' in a letter to John Thelwall of 14 October 1797, without even mentioning the name of the poem from which they come, can this extract constitute a *version?*[109] When William Frederick Mylius reprints the poem in *The Poetical Class-book* (1810), 'in a text . . . with only very minor changes' (changes we do not even know were Coleridge's), does such a reprinting constitute a version? When Stillinger talks of the first two texts of the poem, in letters to Southey (17 July 1797) and Charles Lloyd (also July 1797), as interesting because in both 'the exquisitely detailed description of the roaring dell . . . is mostly left out and the wide prospect—the second of the three landscapes described in the standard text—is entirely missing', what guarantee has he that these passages had even been composed at the time?[110] And if they hadn't been composed (and we have no evidence of prior existence) how could they have been 'left out'? These letters are not 'revisions' of an existing poem, they are drafts towards it.

Similarly, how can Stillinger describe the 'substantial set of variants [of "Frost at Midnight"] in a letter that Coleridge wrote in 1820' as a 'distinct version' of the poem?[111] The text in question consists of a fifteen-line extract contained in a letter

---

[108] For 'changed aesthetic effect,' see James Thorpe, *Principles of Textual Criticism* (San Marino, Calif.: Huntington Library, 1972), 185; for 'horizontal' and 'vertical' variants, see Thomas Tanselle, 'The Editorial Problem of Final Authorial Intention', in *Selected Studies in Bibliography* (Charlottesville: University Press of Virginia, 1979), 334–6. Tanselle's essay first appeared in *Studies in Bibliography*, 29 (1976), 167–211. Both are discussed by Stillinger in *Textual Instability*, 243–4.
[109] Samuel Taylor Coleridge to John Thelwall, 14 Oct. 1797, in *CL*, ed. Griggs, i. 349–50.   [110] Stillinger, 'Multiple Versions', 132–3.
[111] Ibid. 133.

of *circa* 11 October 1820 to Edward Copleston. When it differs from the corrected text of *Sibylline Leaves*, the differences are either inconsequential mistranscriptions or misrememberings— e.g. 'slumber'st' for 'sleepest', 'breathings' for 'Breathings', 'That' for 'Which', 'intervals' for 'pauses'. The only alteration of substance—changing 'But *thou*, my babe! shalt wander like a breeze' to 'But thou, my Babe! *shalt wander like a Breeze'*—is clearly made to meet a local context. The reason Coleridge quotes the poem in the first place is that he has been comparing his son Hartley's boyhood and infancy with that of a fictional character 'as indifferent to all . . . as a blossom whirling in a May-gale'.[112] To call the result of such alterations a version makes sense according to Stillinger's definition, but obscures useful distinctions.

As for 'annotated' works, when Coleridge sends Thomas Poole 'corrected' copies of the *Biographia* and *Sibylline Leaves* in July 1817, for example, it is not in this instance because he has already begun to have second thoughts about them, or because revision was for him a continuous process; he does so because he thinks the works have been printed 'so wildly . . . that a corrected Copy is of some value to those, to whom the works themselves are of any'.[113] What J. C. C. Mays says about annotated versions of such prose works as *The Watchman* and *Lay Sermons*—that the revisions they contain 'can be considered accretions to or commentary on the base text'—might also be said of other annotated works, including the *Biographia* and *Sibylline Leaves*, though 'in the case of *Biographia Literaria*, as Norman Fruman has argued, there are grounds for a fuller display of alternative readings, even for a different choice of base-text'.[114] It also seems to me unhelpful to count as two separate versions those poems in *Sibylline Leaves* that are altered by errata slips, as Stillinger does (even though the corrections and revisions date from over a year after the original setting and printing of the texts). The publishing moment—not the printing moment or the typesetting moment—establishes the version. This is not to deny authority of some sort to each

---

[112] Samuel Taylor Coleridge to Edward Copleston, *c*.11 Oct. 1820, in *CL*, ed. Griggs, v. 111.
[113] Samuel Taylor Coleridge to Thomas Poole, 22 July 1817, ibid. iv. 754.
[114] Mays, 'Reflections', 137, 136.

such 'version'; it is only to suggest the possibility of more than merely arbitrary distinctions between degrees of authority.

Coleridge, to reiterate, had a sense of the publishing occasion. Though he sometimes immediately sent out 'corrected' copies of his works to friends (J. C. C. Mays has located two dozen annotated copies of *Sibylline Leaves* alone), these copies were not for him merely alternatives, versions of equal authority; they were, for the most part, intended as improvements, to be incorporated, if possible, in later published editions. What he published in newspapers, moreover, he mostly thought of as provisional, put before the public out of financial need rather than any considered sense of achievement or completion. 'I dedicate three days in the week to the Morning Post,' he tells Thomas Wedgwood in a letter of 20 October 1802, 'and shall hereafter write for the far greater part such things as will be of as permanent Interest, as any thing I can hope to write. . . . The Poetry, which I have sent, has been merely the emptying out of my Desk. The Epigrams are wretched indeed; but they answered Stuart's purpose better than better things—/. I ought not to have given any signature to them whatsoever / I never dreamt of acknowledging either them or the Ode to the Rain.'[115] Earlier, in a letter of 26 August 1802 to Sotheby (Byron's 'professional' *bête noire*), he announced that the 'greater number' of the occasional verses to be sent to the *Morning Post* under the signature Εστησε 'will be such as were never meant for anything else but the peritura charta of the M. Post'.[116] A good proportion of the more than 700 poems Mays will print in his Bollingen edition fit this category (the exceptions in the case of the *Morning Post* are 'Dejection: An Ode', 'The Day Dream', 'Chamouny', even, *pace* the August 1802 letter to Sotheby, the 'Ode to the Rain'). Hence Mays's reference to 'the few poems Coleridge wrote which aspire purely to literature',[117] a category which excludes, presumably, not only desk-emptying or pot-boiling poems, but poems that, though deemed worthy of re-printing in book form, are hedged about by nervous disclaimers and prefatory apologies. 'At all times', Coleridge complains in

---

[115] Samuel Taylor Coleridge to Thomas Wedgwood, 20 Oct. 1802, in *CL*, ed. Griggs, ii. 876.
[116] Samuel Taylor Coleridge to William Sotheby, 26 Aug. 1802, ibid. 856–7.
[117] Mays, 'Reflections', 149.

a letter of 22 October 1815 to Byron, by way of explaining his relative lack of poetical productivity, 'I have been forced in bitterness of Soul to turn off from the pursuits of my choice to earn the week's food by the week's Labor for the Newspaper & the like.'[118] Poems Coleridge might claim to have published under such circumstances, either anonymously or under *noms de plume*, are inevitable candidates for revision.

They are also, in some sense, fair game for scavenging or recycling. What on 21 December 1799 apears in the *Morning Post* as a fragmentary 'Introduction to the Tale of the Dark Ladie', reappears in the 1800 *Lyrical Ballads*, minus four preliminary and three concluding stanzas, as 'Love', a poem importantly changed—not least by appearing whole—by the excisions. The magazine provenance of the first printing licensed such bold revision; in 1810, moreover, the *Morning Post* text was recycled for a volume entitled *English Minstrelsy*. It seems to me wrong for Pirie to claim subterfuge in the 1800 *Lyrical Ballads* version, talking of 'the pretence Coleridge later made that this was not the beginning of an incomplete poem, but a poem in its own right called *Love*', and of his 'suppressing' the opening four stanzas and the last three.'[119] These were different poems. As is clear from chapter 11 of the *Biographia*, entitled 'An affectionate exhortation to those who in early life feel themselves disposed to become authors', Coleridge clearly distinguished between the work of 'a *mere* literary man', for whom literature is a 'profession' or 'trade', 'and what is truly *genial*', the product of inspiration or unforced labour—of, say, 'three hours of leisure [per day, that is], unannoyed by any alien anxiety'.[120] Finally, it might be argued that even the poems printed in the first edition of the *Lyrical Ballads* were in some sense not yet fixed in form or 'published', because they appeared anonymously. A poem is only one's poem, Coleridge might rationalize, when it appears in a book with one's name on it. And so, too, with a piece of prose. In a footnote to the *Biographia*, for example, Coleridge justifies extended self-quotation from *The Friend* on the grounds that in its first appearance in book form it 'was printed on stampt sheets, and

[118] Samuel Taylor Coleridge to Lord Byron, 22 Oct. 1815, in *CL*, ed. Griggs, iv. 604–05.   [119] Pirie, in *Coleridge's Verse*, ed. Empson and Pirie, 250.
[120] *Biographia Literaria*, ed. Engell and Bate, i. 228, 224.

sent only by the post to a very limited number of subscribers
... To the public at large indeed it is the same as a volume in
manuscript' (though it should be noted that even as he wrote
this, he knew *The Friend* was going to be republished).[121]

The publishing (as opposed to composing) histories of
Coleridge's poems and prose works lend support to such a
view—while also providing a rough pattern for the revisions,
one which works against the notion that composing was for
him a 'continuum'. The pattern, typically, is as follows: a first
grouping of revisions works towards the initial appearance of
a poem or piece of prose in the magazines (or in a letter); a
second grouping or cluster works towards first publication in
book form; a third works towards a second publication in one
or other of Coleridge's larger collections.[122] This is the pattern
for 'Dejection', 'The Ancient Mariner', 'Christabel', and a
number of other well-known poems, and it corresponds roughly
to Mays's grouping of the manuscripts. It is also, roughly, the
pattern of the revisions to *The Friend*, which appeared first in
magazine form in 1809–10, was revised for an initial single-
volume collection published by Gale and Curtis in 1812 (an
enterprise Coleridge was later, in a letter of 8 July 1816, to
disparage, claiming, in reference to a possible second, revised
edition, 'that a work which was never in any proper sense of
the word *published* could scarcely be said to be republished'[123]),
and revised a second time and expanded, after Coleridge took
up residence in the Gillman household in 1816, in the more
substantial edition of 1818.

In some cases the pattern is even simpler. Take, for example,
the revision of 'The Eolian Harp', which for Stillinger exists in
sixteen different versions 'ranging from 51 to 64 lines in length—

[121] Ibid. i. 60 n., 147 n., 164 n.

[122] Coleridge's death, from hypertension, was not sudden; though Coleridge was
only 61 when he died, he was not at the height of his powers in the last year or
two of his life. Yet he continued to take publication seriously, as is suggested by
some final words he dictated to Joseph Green on 24 July 1834, the night before he
died, words in which he entreats Green to 'be thou sure in whatever may be
published of my posthumous works to remember that, first of all is the Absolute
Good whose self-affirmation is the "I am", as the eternal reality in itself, and the
ground and source of all other reality'. See Walter Jackson Bate, *Coleridge* (New
York: Macmillan, 1968), 236.

[123] Samuel Taylor Coleridge to John Gale, 8 July 1816, in *CL*, ed. Griggs, iv.
650.

sometimes written or printed as a single paragraph and sometimes divided into 3, 4, or 5 paragraphs—and variously titled
"Effusion XXXV," or "Composed at Clevedon, Somersetshire"
or "The Eolian Harp."' Each of these versions, Stillinger implies, 'change[s] the tone, the philosophical and religious ideas,
and the basic structure' of the poem.[124] But these differences
seem to me neither as important nor as varied as Stillinger
suggests. Stillinger's sixteen 'versions' can be grouped into two
broad categories: versions written before the addition of the
'one Life' passage in the 1817 errata list for *Sibylline Leaves*,
and versions written after it—the former being comparatively
less serious in tone and substance than the latter. Not only are
other variants relatively minor or local, but even these broad
groupings need some modifying, since the earlier versions are
themselves not without serious moments, as in lines 43–8, which
anticipate the 'one Life' passage. While wholly sympathetic to
Stillinger's larger aims as a textual theorist—that is, to challenge the prevailing indifference of critics to the instability of
Coleridge's texts, in the process drawing out important theoretical and practical problems raised by that instability—I think
he overstates his case, here and elsewhere, presenting too complicated or indeterminist an account of Coleridge's practice as
a writer.

Stillinger himself acknowledges the possibility of a degree of
pattern in the revisions (though he also lays out the case for
compulsive revision). Though Coleridge changed his poems
throughout his life,

he did some especially significant revising in 1815, when he was preparing his works for publication in *Sibylline Leaves*. The date coin-
cides neatly with two important publications by Wordsworth around
the same time: first, *The Excursion*, perhaps just a few months earlier
(August 1814), with the highly publicized preface in which Wordsworth
explains the unity and interrelatedness of all his works together; and
then Wordsworth's first collected *Poems* (April 1815) with another
preface explaining the principles by which the poems were classified
and arranged into categories.

Perhaps Coleridge 'revises to achieve in his own work the same
kind of unity of effect that Wordsworth was in the process of

---

[124] Stillinger, 'Multiple Versions', 132.

accomplishing in his'.[125] Precisely—though with less consistency, conviction, and success.

A look at the letters written around the time of *Sibylline Leaves* and the first edition of the later collected *Poetical Works* lends support to this view. The first full account of Coleridge's plans for *Sibylline Leaves* comes in a petitionary letter to Byron dated Easter Week 1815 (though some such collection had been envisaged several years before). In this letter Coleridge explains that 'circumstances' (he means lack of money) and the urging of friends 'now compel me to publish in two Volumes all the poems composed by me from the year 1795 to the present Date, that are sanctioned by my mature judgement, all that I would consent to have called mine, if it depend on my own will'.[126] Coleridge makes a similar claim in a letter of 2 July 1816 to John Hookham Frere, in which he calls *Sibylline Leaves* 'a collection of such poems as I dare consent to be known as of my own Will as well as Authorship'.[127] More than half these poems, claims Coleridge, exist only in manuscript (earlier, in a letter of 7 October 1815 to Daniel Stuart, the number is 'little more' than a third),[128] the rest appear either in the *Lyrical Ballads*, long out of print, the 'Second Edition of my Juvenile Poems', or 'different Newspapers, London and Provincial, and in other yet more obscure and equally perishable vehicles, most of them without my consent and previous knowledge, many imperfectly, all of them incorrectly'.[129]

Though money is, in part, his motive, Coleridge certainly sounds here as if he has a sense not only of the importance of such a collection—such a publishing occasion—but of the need for accurate (corrected, perfected) texts. 'The whole have been corrected throughout', he tells Byron, 'with very considerable alterations and additions, some indeed almost rewritten.' The letter to Byron is also the place where we first learn of what will eventually become the *Biographia Literaria*: 'A general Preface [to the collection] . . . on the Principles of philosophic and genial

[125] Ibid. 144.
[126] Samuel Taylor Coleridge to Lord Byron, Easter Week 1815, in *CL*, ed. Griggs, iv. 560
[127] Samuel Taylor Coleridge to John Hookham Frere, 2 July 1816, ibid. 646.
[128] Samuel Taylor Coleridge to Daniel Stuart, 7 Oct. 1815, ibid. 591.
[129] Samuel Taylor Coleridge to John Hookham Frere, 2 July 1816, ibid. 646.

criticism relatively to the Fine Arts in general; but especially to Poetry: and a Particular Preface to the Ancient Mariner and the Ballads, on the employment of the Supernatural in Poetry and the laws which regulate it.'[130] The poems are to appear, in other words, under the aegis of, and in conformance to, Coleridge's conscious poetical principles. Work from throughout his poetical career is to be included—if worthy of those principles. The collection will make the life whole, just as the *Biographia* attempted to do, just as so many of the revisions attempted to do. It is hard to conceive of a writer with a less naïve or unillusioned sense of the impediments to such wholeness than Coleridge, but it is also hard to conceive of a writer who strove so tenaciously to ignore or defy those impediments.

[130] Samuel Taylor Coleridge to Lord Byron, Easter Week 1815, ibid. 560, 561.

PART TWO

Revision and Authorial Autonomy

CHAPTER FOUR

PARENTING FRANKENSTEIN

MARY SHELLEY'S *Frankenstein* might well be cited in the debate about editions and personal identity at the centre of Part 1 of this book. The novel was begun in June 1816 and finished eleven months later, in May 1817. After two rejections (from John Murray and Charles Ollier), it was published anonymously in March 1818 by Lackington, Hughes, Harding, Mavor, and Jones of Finsbury Square, London, and in 1823 a two-volume reprint was issued, this time under the author's name. The year 1823 was also when Mary Shelley presented a hand-corrected first-edition copy (including additions, marginal notes, excisions, and substitutions) to an acquaintance from Italy, a Mrs Thomas.[1] It was not, however, until 1831 that corrections from this copy, together with other revisions, were incorporated into the version known to most Victorian and twentieth-century readers, the Colburn and Bentley 'Standard Novels' edition. It is often argued that the differences between the first or 1818 and the third or 1831 editions are analagous to the differences between the 1805 and 1850 versions of *The Prelude*; both have their champions, and the arguments adduced for earlier or later versions—growing orthodoxy, energy versus clarity—are familiarly Wordsworthian. My concern in this chapter, though, is with a prior moment in the novel's history, one which questions authorial autonomy and identity in new ways, opening the topic of revision out to encompass issues of collaboration or dual authorship.[2] This 'moment' occurs when Mary Shelley turns to Percy Shelley in the course of the novel's composition and allows him to revise it—rather as Walton allows

---

[1] This copy is now located in the Pierpont Morgan Library, New York.

[2] These issues Jack Stillinger, in *Multiple Authorship and the Myth of Solitary Genius* (New York: Oxford University Press, 1991), 20, calls 'situations where someone other than the nominal author is essentially and inextricably a part of the authorship'.

Frankenstein to correct the notes he has made of Frankenstein's 'narration'.[3]

Recent feminist scholars have come to see Percy Shelley's revisions—as many as five or six a page, virtually all of them incorporated in the published editions—as impositions. They see Mary Shelley as cripplingly insecure about her status as author, frightened not only of producing fictional 'monsters' or 'abortions', but of herself becoming monstrous, a fear compounded partly of a prejudice against 'forward' women in general, partly of particular experiences such as Percy's dream of 18 June 1816 (the second of the famous ghost-story nights), in which Mary appears as a hideous villainness with nipples for eyes.[4] The argument, in short, is that her circumstances—as an unpublished 18-year-old, an unmarried mother, a woman cut off from her family, dependent financially and personally on an older, male writer, published author of novels, essays, and poems—deprived Mary of freedom of choice.[5] The novelist or poet who willingly accedes to a friend's or editor's suggested revisions takes responsibility for those revisions, remains in some sense their author. Mary Shelley, however, was in no position to reject Percy Shelley's suggestions. Like any woman writing in the late eighteenth century, as Johanna M. Smith puts it, she was '*conditioned* to think she needed a man's help'. Moreover, Smith continues, with uncharacteristic hyperbole, 'collaboration forced by a more dominant writer on a less powerful and perhaps unwilling "partner" is a kind of rape'.[6]

---

[3] Unless otherwise specified, all references to *Frankenstein* come from the 1818 edn., ed. James Rieger (New York: Bobbs-Merrill, 1974). See p. 207 for the correction of Walton's notes. The 1818 version is available in two other editions: it is the version preferred by *The Mary Shelley Reader*, ed. Betty T. Bennett and Charles E. Robinson (New York: Oxford University Press, 1990), and by *Frankenstein: or the Modern Prometheus: The 1818 Text*, ed. Marilyn Butler (London: William Pickering, 1993).

[4] See entry of 18 June 1816 in John William Polidori, *The Diary of Dr. John William Polidori, 1816, Relating to Byron, Shelley, etc.*, ed. William Michael Rossetti (London: Elkin Mathews, 1911), 125.

[5] It is easy in retrospect to exaggerate Shelley's relative standing as an author at this time. *Queen Mab* (1813), *Alastor* (1816), and *Laon and Cythna* (1818) had, indeed, all been published, but at their author's expense. The first edition of *Frankenstein*, of course, quickly made Mary Shelley a more commercially successful writer than her husband; the book sold out and made a profit.

[6] Mary Shelley, *Frankenstein*, ed. Johanna M. Smith, in the series Case Studies in Contemporary Criticism (Boston: Bedford Books of St Martin's Press, 1992),

This view of the young Mary Shelley's helplessness or passivity relies importantly on Mary's habit, after Percy's death, of
exaggerating her meekness and dependency, a habit which, as
Ellen Moers puts it, 'contributed to the generally held opinion
that she was not so much an author in her own right as a
transparent medium through which passed the ideas of those
around her'.[7] It also undervalues contemporary accounts—those
of Leigh Hunt, Keats, Mary's doctors[8]—which stress quite different qualities: directness, precision, irony, command, qualities
frequently found in the early journal entries (those written before
Shelley's death), as in the laconic concision of, for example,
'correct F[rankenstein]. S[helley] reads Alcestes—a little turmoil
in the evening'.[9] The evidence points both ways, often within
individual instances. For example, here is how Mary describes
herself to Edward John Trelawny in 1829, in the course of
refusing to supply him with anecdotes about Percy Shelley:

You know me—or you do not, in which case I will tell you what I
am—a silly goose—who far from wishing to stand forward to assert
myself in any way, now than [sic] I am alone in the world, have but
the desire to wrap night and the obscurity of insignificance around me.
This is weakness—but I cannot help it—to be in print—the subject of
men's observations—of the bitter hard world's commentaries, to be
attacked or defended! this ill becomes one who knows how little she
possesses worthy to attract attention—and whose chief merit—if it be
one—is a love of that privacy which no woman can emerge from

275, 274. Smith is usually more reticent and qualified in her accounts of Percy's
revisions. Their principal, and most influential, feminist critic is Anne K. Mellor,
in *Mary Shelley: Her Life, Her Fiction, Her Monsters* (New York: Routledge,
1988).

[7] Ellen Moers, 'Female Gothic', in *Literary Women* (Garden City, NY: Doubleday,
1976), 94. U. C. Knoepflmacher, in 'Thoughts on the Aggression of Daughters', in
Levine and Knoepflmacher (eds.), *The Endurance of Frankenstein* (Berkeley: University of California Press, 1982), 95, explains Mary's passivity as follows: 'fearful
of releasing hostilities which—without a maternal model—she regarded (or wanted
to regard) as exclusively male attributes, Mary Shelley could resort only to passivity
as a safer mode of resistance'.

[8] See Emily W. Sunstein, *Mary Shelley: Romance and Reality* (Boston: Little
Brown, 1989), 139. Also Mary Poovey, *The Proper Lady and the Woman Writer:
Ideology as Style in the Works of Mary Wollstonecraft, Mary Shelley, and Jane
Austen* (Chicago: University of Chicago Press, 1984), 143.

[9] Entry of 10 Apr. 1817 in *The Journals of Mary Shelley 1814–1844*, ed. Paula
R. Feldman and Diana Scott-Kilvert, 2 vols. (Oxford: Clarendon Press, 1987), i.
166.

without regret—Shelley's life must be written—I hope one day to do it myself, but it must not be published now.[10]

James P. Carson has written shrewdly about this passage:

What I find interesting in this fear of publicity is not whether Shelley is telling the truth or whether she strategically evokes a conventional ideal of femininity in order to justify a refusal that seems inconsistent with friendship and professional generosity. Rather, I am struck by the hope which Mary Shelley expresses in the final sentence, a hope to write Percy Shelley's life herself, a hope which reflects belief in her own authorial talents that is not wholly consistent with her fear of appearing before the public in writing.[11]

What Carson identifies here as Mary Shelley's belief in herself as an author, and what it implies more generally about the strength of her character, is corroborated elsewhere. 'Shelley agreed with me', writes Mary of her early favourable assessment of Trelawny, 'as he always did, or rather I with him.'[12] The note of calculation here recalls a somewhat later, comparably clear-sighted, account of the origins of Byron's approval of her, 'which stands greatly I believe on my known admiration of his writings and my docility in attending him'.[13] 'I have sent my novel to Papa,' Mary writes to the same correspondent, Maria Gisborne, in reference to *Valperga* (1823), 'I long to hear some news of it . . . as with an author's vanity I want to see it in print and hear the praises of my friends.'[14] When *Valperga* finally appears, Mary writes to Leigh Hunt asking for

[10] Mary Shelley to Edward John Trelawny, Apr. 1829, in *The Letters of Mary Wollstonecraft Shelley*, ed. Betty T. Bennett, 3 vols. (Baltimore: Johns Hopkins University Press, 1983), ii. 72.

[11] James P. Carson, 'Bringing the Author Forward: *Frankenstein* through Mary Shelley's Letters', *Criticism*, 30/4 (Autumn 1988), 431.

[12] Mary Shelley to Maria Gisborne, c.27 Apr. 1822, in *Letters*, ed. Bennett, i. 253. For a comparable later instance of ambivalence, again involving Percy Shelley, see the following parenthetical turn at the end of Mary Shelley's negotiations with Edward Moxon, from whom she rightly claimed a fee and possession of copyright for her work as editor of Percy's *Posthumous Poems*: 'The M.S. from which it was printed consisted of fragments of paper which in the hands of an indifferent person would never have been decyphered—the labour of putting it together was immense—the papers were in my possession & in no other person's (for the most part) the volume might be all my writing (except that I could not write it)' (Mary Shelley to Edward Moxon, 7 Dec. 1838, ibid. ii. 300).

[13] Mary Shelley to Jane Williams, 10 Apr. 1823, ibid. i. 328.

[14] Mary Shelley to Maria Gisborne, 9 Feb. 1822, ibid. 318.

a review, again in a manner both modest and ambitious: though *Valperga* is 'merely a book of promise', it is also 'another landing place in the staircase I am climbing'.[15]

Moments like these encourage one to oppose the argument of constraint, arguing instead that Mary Shelley consciously, willingly welcomed Percy Shelley's contributions; that this welcoming was not only, paradoxically, an expression of authorial ambition (he would improve her novel), but an enactment or performance, a living out, of the novel's central themes; and that underlying these themes is a vision of authorship different in kind from those of the writers discussed in Part 1 of this book, a vision that, for example, calls into question the supposedly inevitable conflict, in Mary Poovey's words, 'between the self-denial demanded by domestic activity and the self-assertiveness essential to artistic creation'.[16] Here, at last, is the sort of revisionary practice wrongly attributed (in various ways, as I have been arguing) to Wordsworth, Coleridge, and Byron: one that consciously—and successfully—resists the conventional image of the authorial self as single and autonomous. Mary Shelley would be offended—it would violate her principles— were the text to be returned to its pre-Percy form.

THE 'PROMETHEAN' WRITER

Frankenstein is an implicit attack on the Romantic writer, a type figured in Frankenstein himself, the monster's 'author' (a phrase applied to Frankenstein three times in the first edition, in each case, it has been argued, in a revision by Percy Shelley[17]), and in the explorer, Robert Walton, who only turns to exploring

---

[15] Mary Shelley to Leigh Hunt, 3 Aug. [5 Aug.] 1823, ibid. 361.
[16] Poovey, *Proper Lady*, 138.
[17] The references occur on p. 87 and twice on p. 96 of the Rieger edn. As far as I can tell, after examining the originals (Abinger Dep. c. 477/1 and c. 534, constituting in the Rieger edn. p. 30 l. 12 to 97 l. 16 and pp. 97 l. 17 to 109 l. 8, plus p. 117 ll. 17 to end), they do indeed seem to be in Percy Shelley's hand, but Johanna M. Smith, in '"Cooped Up": Feminine Domesticity in *Frankenstein*', her contribution to the 'Case Studies' in her edition of the novel, is probably right to caution reserve: 'The manuscript evidence for this assertion does not seem to me conclusive; moreover, even if it were he who introduced the word, surely Mary Shelley would have had her own ideas of what it connoted' (p. 274 n.).

after aspiring to poetic fame.[18] 'I also became a poet,' Walton confesses at the novel's outset, 'and for one year lived in a Paradise of my own creation; I imagined that I also might obtain a niche in the temple where the names of Homer and Shakespeare are consecrated' (p. 11). To mount this argument, though, one must first distinguish between different strains of Romanticism. *Frankenstein* is anti-Romantic in its rejection of what might be called the 'Promethean' vision of the artist (as God-like, autonomous, transgressive), and of the goal of perfection, as in William Godwin's ultra-rationalist prescriptions for social renovation, his attempts, as Wordsworth puts it, 'to abstract the hopes of Man | Out of his feelings, to be fixed thenceforth | For ever in a purer element' (*The Prelude*, 1850, XI. 225–7), or Percy Shelley's vision of a perfect future in Canto 3 of *Queen Mab* (1813) or his quest for the perfect mate, in life as in verse (for instance, in 'Alastor' or 'Epipsychidion').[19] In the months preceding the dream vision which inspired *Frankenstein*, Mary and Percy Shelley worked together on a French translation of Godwin's *Enquiry Concerning Political Justice*, and Mary was also present during Percy's subsequent debates with Byron over human perfectibility, though 'incapacity and timidity'[20] prevented her from saying much. The theme of human perfectibility, moreover, was sometimes connected in these debates with discussions of galvanic electricity and the possibility of reanimating corpses. When Frankenstein hopes, like God, to 'bestow animation upon lifeless matter . . . renew

---

[18] I am obviously not alone in this belief. Paul Cantor, e.g. in *Creator and Creation: Myth-making and English Romanticism* (Cambridge: Cambridge University Press, 1984), 109, calls *Frankenstein* 'a nightmare of Romantic idealism, revealing the dark underside to all the visionary dreams of remaking man that fired the imaginations of Romantic myth-makers'.

[19] Chris Baldick, *In Frankenstein's Shadow: Myth, Monstrosity, and Nineteenth-Century Writing* (Oxford: Clarendon Press, 1987), usefully points to moments in Godwin's *Enquiry Concerning Political Justice* which explicitly deny the possibility of 'perfectibility', which Godwin calls 'pregnant with absurdity and contradiction'. 'By perfectible is not meant that he [man] is capable of being brought to perfection,' insists Godwin, but 'continually made better and receiving perpetual improvement' (quotes from *Enquiry Concerning Political Justice*, ed. Isaac Kramnick (Harmondsworth: Penguin Books, 1976), 144–5). Though the often 'rarified rationalism' of the *Enquiry*, Baldick admits, 'smacks of Frankensteinian irresponsibility', such rationalism is 'qualified by important warnings against the detachment of science from social ties' (p. 28).

[20] Entry of 19 Oct. 1822, in *Journals*, ed. Feldman and Scott-Kilvert, i. 184.

life where death had apparently devoted the body to corruption' (p. 49), his ambition is more than a mere figurative expression of Romantic idealism, it is also a literal concern of Romantic poets and writers.

At the same time, the novel is Romantic (this is particularly true of the 1818 version) in its vision of a benevolent, Wordsworthian or Thomsonian—also Rousseauistic or Godwinian— nature, the measure of all truth and goodness. The monster is monstrous because it is 'unnatural', both in conception and as a result of its upbringing. To create the monster, Victor tells us, he was obliged 'to procrastinate all my feelings of affection until the great object, which swallowed up every habit of my nature, should be completed' (p. 56). While Victor shuts himself off in his laboratory, 'winter, spring, and summer, passed away during my labours; but I did not watch the blossom or the expanding leaves ... so deeply was I engrossed in my occupation' (p. 51); earlier, he tells us, his eyes were 'insensible to the charms of nature. And the same feelings which made me neglect the scenes around me caused me also to neglect those friends who were so many miles absent' (p. 50). These defects recall Wordsworth's 'Enough of Science and of Art; | Close up those barren leaves; | Come forth, and bring with you a heart | That watches and receives' ('The Tables Turned') or the subtitle of Book 8 of *The Prelude*: 'Love of Nature Leading to Love of Mankind'.

The sources of Mary Shelley's critique of the 'Promethean' writer are easily traced. To begin with, there is the example of her father, William Godwin, to whom the novel is dedicated. Godwin's idealism was no mere matter of theory; in his private life, too, the personal or familial was sacrificed to the public, parental responsibility was neglected (though not at first, both for Mary and her illegitimate half-sister, Fanny Imlay[21]), money scrounged, in the interests of 'principle'. 'Children are a sort of

---

[21] According to Sunstein, *Romance and Reality*, 23, there is evidence that Godwin 'began by treating Mary as a great experimental opportunity', but eventually developed for her 'the strongest attachment that was in his nature'. She was educated at home, by Godwin himself, who gave her 'access to his many books, directing her reading, and in due course taking her to public lectures. He encouraged her literary abilities, in 1808 publishing her light verses "Mounseer Nongtongpaw; or the Discoveries of John Bull in a trip to Paris" in the Godwin Juvenile Library' (Butler (ed.), *Frankenstein*, p. x).

raw material put into our hands,' writes Godwin in the *En-quiry*, 'a ductile and yielding substance, which, if we do not ultimately mould in conformity to our wishes, it is because we throw away the power committed to us, by the folly with which we are accustomed to exert it.'[22] The most notorious examples of this 'experimental' or 'scientific' habit of mind, of unfeeling 'principle' (as in the Fénelon revisions discussed in the previous chapter), created a public image of Godwin, in De Quincey's words, as 'monstrous': 'most people felt of Mr. Godwin with the same alienation and horror as of a ghoul, or a bloodless vampire, or the monster created by Frankenstein'.[23]

Though unfair and exaggerated, this picture of Mary's father was fed by moments of real-life adamancy and obtuseness. Godwin was not, especially in the 1810s, a man easily crossed. 'When people disagreed with him,' writes a recent commentator, 'or, worse, disobeyed him, he simply cut them off—as he did, for instance, with Mary's beloved childhood nanny, whom she never saw again after the age of 3. When . . . Fanny committed suicide (this happened in October of 1816, during the composition of *Frankenstein*), Godwin refused to have her body brought back to the house, and insisted that this once-favoured child be buried in a pauper's grave.'[24] Earlier, of course, Godwin in effect abandoned Mary, exiling her when she and Percy Shelley, who was already married, ran off together. Such rigidity obviously plays its part in the character of Frankenstein, whose wilfulness or single-mindedness also removes him from personal or familial realms. 'If no man allowed any pursuit whatsoever to interfere with the tranquillity of his domestic affections,' declares Victor, in a telling comparison of scientist and imperialist, 'Greece had not been enslaved, Caesar would have spared his country, America would have been discovered more gradually, and the empires of Mexico and Peru had not

[22] Godwin, *Enquiry*, 112.
[23] Quoted in Mary Shelley, *Frankenstein*, ed. Maurice Hindle (Harmondsworth: Penguin Books, 1992), p. xl. The comment comes from one of De Quincey's 'Autobiographical Sketches' originally published in *Tait's Edinburgh Magazine*, 4 (March 1837), 173–4. See *The Collected Writings of Thomas De Quincey*, ed. David Masson, 14 vols. (Edinburgh: Adam & Charles Black, 1896–7), iii. 35.
[24] Wendy Lesser, in the introduction to the recently reprinted Everyman's Library edn. of Mary Shelley, *Frankenstein* (New York: Alfred A. Knopf, 1992), pp. ix–x.

been destroyed' (p. 51). D. H. Lawrence famously saw the connection between the reputedly controlling or perfectionist aspirations of Godwin and Frankenstein by way of Benjamin Franklin: 'if on the one hand Benjamin Franklin is the perfect human being of Godwin, on the other hand he is a monster, not exactly as the monster in *Frankenstein*, but for the same reason, viz., that he is the production or fabrication of the will, which projects itself upon a living being and automizes that being according to a given precept.'[25]

Jean-Jacques Rousseau provides a second major source for Mary Shelley's critique of 'Promethean' Romanticism. Rousseau, of course, was an influence on both Mary Shelley's parents: Godwin's debt to him throughout his writings is clear and explicit; so, too, is Mary Wollstonecraft's, one of whose characters, in *The Wrongs of Woman: or Maria. A Fragment* (1798), describes Rousseau as 'the true Prometheus of sentiment'.[26]

[25] Quoted in ibid., p. xiv. Coleridge, Godwin's friend and frequent visitor, is another obvious model for the 'Promethean' writer. Mary Shelley not only knew Coleridge personally—knew the reality of his dependencies and irresponsibilities ('as if', in Wordsworth's words from 'Resolution and Independence', 'life's business were a summer mood', one in which 'others should | Build for him, sow for him, and at his call | Love him')—but was much influenced by the image of the writer projected in his writings, particularly in the essays in *The Friend*, with their stress on individual genius (an image also projected in Madame de Staël's account in *De l'Allemagne* of Schlegel's distinction between the classical and the romantic, an account from which Coleridge borrows, and one Mary read in the autumn of 1815). Moreover, two of Coleridge's most famous poems, 'The Ancient Mariner' and 'Kubla Khan', are obvious and important presences in *Frankenstein*. In the opening pages of the novel, Captain Walton writes to his sister of journeying 'to unexplored regions, to "the land of mist and snow"' (p. 15), and in ch. 4 Frankenstein himself likens his haunted, fearful steps to those of the mariner, quoting ll. 446–51 (p. 54). Both Frankenstein and his creation, moreover, are outcasts, like the mariner, and the icy landscapes over which they despairingly journey ironically comment on the Khan's caves of ice, as if denying the poet-maker's capacity to ally them—magically, divinely—with the sunny pleasure dome.

Though Byron was also, obviously, a 'Promethean' figure (and much like Godwin, Shelley, and Coleridge in terms of personal or familial irresponsibility), he not only shared Mary Shelley's sceptical attitudes towards political and philosophical radicalism, but his example seems to have helped or emboldened her in resisting and questioning it. As Jane Blumberg puts it: 'Byron represented an alternative approach to the question of reform, one that was no less thrilling or attractive than PBS's, but which, beneath its iconoclasm, was somewhat more tolerant of conventional social and political structures' (*Mary Shelley's Early Novels: 'This Child of Imagination and Misery'* (London: Macmillan, 1993), 63).

[26] Mary Wollstonecraft, *The Wrongs of Woman: or Maria. A Fragment*, in *Mary and The Wrongs of Woman*, ed. Gary Kelley (Oxford: Oxford University Press, 1976), 89.

Immediately before and during the months in which *Frankenstein* was composed, Mary Shelley read the *Confessions* (Part I (1782), Part II (1789), written 1765–70), *Émile* (1762), and *Rêveries du promeneur solitaire* (1782, written 1776–78), and the Lake Geneva and Alpine scenes in the novel have long been recognized as indebted to *La Nouvelle Héloïse* (1761).[27] 'Write—and read the reveries of Rousseau,' reads a typical journal entry of the period.[28]

The precise nature of Rousseau's influence on *Frankenstein* is complicated. To begin with, the monster can be seen as a sort of noble savage, a victim, like Rousseau, of society; he, too, is an outcast, exile, and wanderer, 'author' also of a sort of autobiography or confession. More importantly, there are connections between Rousseau and the monster's creator. In particular, as David Marshall puts it, 'Frankenstein is guilty of a crime that Rousseau was notorious for throughout Europe: he is a parent who abandons his child. . . . [Rousseau] made orphans of the five infants born to him and Thérèse Lavasseur.'[29] Rousseau's children are imagined by Mary Shelley, in words that apply equally to Frankenstein's creature, as 'brutified by their situation, or depressed by the burden, ever weighing at the heart, that they have not inherited the commonest right of humanity, a parent's care'; like Victor, Rousseau 'neglected the first duty of man by abandoning his children'.[30]

Percy Shelley, though, was the Romantic writer who mattered most to *Frankenstein*, and has long been acknowledged as

[27] See Peter Dale Scott, 'Vital Artifice: Mary, Percy, and the Psychopolitical Integrity of *Frankenstein*', in Levine and Knoeplfmacher (eds.), *Endurance*, 174, for whom 'one might say that "The Modern Prometheus" is a pendant to *Émile* and *La Nouvelle Héloïse*'.

[28] Entry of 1 Aug. 1816, in *Journals*, ed. Feldman and Scott-Kilvert, i. 112.

[29] David Marshall, *The Surprising Effects of Sympathy: Marivaux, Diderot, Rousseau, and Mary Shelley* (Chicago: University of Chicago Press, 1988), 187. Rousseau discusses the decision to 'abandon' his children in Books VII and VIII of the *Confessions* and the *Rêveries du promeneur solitaire*. Marshall points to the prominent part this incident plays in Mary Shelley's long and otherwise sympathetic biographical essay on Rousseau in the volume *Eminent Literary and Scientific Men of France* for Lardner's *Cabinet Cyclopedia* (1838–9). Though Mary Shelley wrote this article over twenty years after *Frankenstein* was published, as Marshall suggests, the language with which she reproaches Rousseau is 'remarkably similar to the reproaches that the monster makes to the parent who has abandoned and orphaned him' (p. 189, which also offers specific examples).

[30] Quoted in Marshall, *Surprising Effects of Sympathy*, 188.

a model for its eponymous hero, even by those who think his qualities eventually shift to Henry Clerval.[31] Shelley's idealism was as extreme as Godwin's: 'The word perfectibility,' writes a recent biographer, William St Clair, 'was seldom far from his lips. He longed for the day, he told his friends, when Man would live in accordance with Nature and with Reason and in consequence with Virtue.'[32] Percy Shelley's idealism, moreover, was 'philosophical'—that is, Platonic and Kantian—as well as political (he had been interested in Plato from his Eton years); the two types of idealism were linked, as in the 'Hymn to Intellectual Beauty', which is celebrated as a source both of earthly beauty and of freedom from slavery. In either political or philosophical forms, though, Mary Shelley mostly disapproved.

This disapproval, it has been argued, was lifelong. As early as the crude and unfinished 'A History of the Jews', an essay conjecturally dated between 1814 and 1816, 'glimmerings of . . . dissent'[33] from Radical idealism and perfectionism are discernible; in *Frankenstein* and the other early novels these glimmerings glow more brightly; in Mary's introduction to her 1839 edition of Percy's poems, they positively blaze. It is here, for example, that Mary disparages those of her husband's verses which are 'purely imaginative' as opposed to 'those which spring from the emotions of his heart'. Though the former cling to a 'subtler inner spirit', they do so at the expense of 'outward form'; that is, actual people and things.[34] Mary, on the other hand, seeks, as she puts it in a journal entry of 25 February 1822, speaking of her 'fellow creatures', to 'love that which is,—and not fix my affections on a fair form endued with imaginary attributes'.[35]

[31] See Muriel Spark, *Mary Shelley* (London: Constable, 1988), 145. The most interesting and exhaustive of the accounts of Victor's resemblance to Percy Shelley is found in Christopher Small, *Ariel Like a Harpy: Shelley, Mary and Frankenstein* (London: Victor Gollancz, 1972), 100–21.

[32] William St Clair, *The Godwins and the Shelleys* (London: Faber & Faber, 1989), 317.

[33] Blumberg, *Mary Shelley's Early Novels*, 29. Blumberg thinks Mary Shelley's questioning of 'optimism, idealism, and revolution' was present from the beginning of her writing life, though in the works which followed *Frankenstein* 'her criticisms become bolder and more confident' (p. 37).

[34] Mary Shelley, 'Preface by Mrs. Shelley to First Collected Edition 1839', in *The Complete Poetical Works of Percy Bysshe Shelley*, ed. Thomas Hutchinson (London: Oxford University Press, 1956), p. x.

[35] Entry of 25 Feb. 1822, *Journals*, ed. Feldman and Scott-Kilvert, 399.

As Percy suggests in his anonymous preface to the 1818 edition of *Frankenstein*, just such an ambition, paradoxically, underlies the novel's recourse to a story 'impossible as a physical fact': the story 'affords a point of view to the imagination for the delineating of the human passions more comprehensive and commanding than any which the ordinary relations of existing events can yield' (p. 6). Similarly, part of what is wrong with Victor's scientific ambitions is the way they oblige him to fix his attention 'upon every object the most insupportable to the delicacy of the human feelings' (p. 47).

What made Percy Shelley's idealism impossible for Mary Shelley were the unignorable realities of her experience, in particular the loss of children: a two-week-old daughter, Clara, in 1815, a year-old daughter, also Clara, in 1818, three-year-old William in 1819. It was not true, as Percy Shelley would have it, that 'all woe and pain' were within our control, a product of 'selfishness, or insensibility, or mistake', or that 'evil is not inherent in the system of creation, but an accident that might be expelled'.[36] Like Byron, as Ernest J. Lovell has argued, Mary Shelley sometimes opposed not only 'any ideas implying the perfectibility of man', but any lack of sympathy 'for such related ideas as a denial of predestination or of the positive existence of matter and of evil'.[37] The only way to maintain idealistic beliefs like these, Mary Shelley argued, was to close oneself off from the world. As she put it in a note to *Prometheus Unbound*, 'he sheltered himself from . . . disgusting and painful thoughts in the calm retreats of poetry, and built up a world of his own, with the more pleasure, since he hoped to induce some one or two to believe that the earth might become such'.[38] That the 'one or two' Mary Shelley refers to here were primarily the women Percy Shelley variously desired—Harriet Westbrook Shelley, Claire Clairmont, Emilia Viviani, Jane Williams, Mary Shelley herself—and the 'world of his own' one in which desire was to be unconstrained by such conventions as marriage, monogomy, or minority, gives ironic edge to the note.

[36] This is Mary Shelley's characterization, from a note in her edition of *The Poetical Works of Percy Bysshe Shelley*, 4 vols. (London: Edward Moxon, 1839), iii. 159.
[37] Ernest J. Lovell, 'Byron and Mary Shelley', *Keats–Shelley Journal*, 2 (19 Jan. 1953), 49.
[38] Mary Shelley (ed.), *Poetical Works of Percy Bysshe Shelley*, ii. 139.

Both Percy and Mary Shelley, though obviously to different degrees, suspected such 'idealism', even as they forwarded it. 'Alastor', for example, is as much about the dangers of idealism, of spurning actual or outward love and sympathy ('the spirit of sweet human love', line 203) in favour of a shadowy ideal, as it is about idealism's attractions; it is also, one could argue, about the inevitability of pain and loss. Though Percy Shelley continued to believe, in Mary Shelley's words, 'that mankind had only to will that there should be no evil, and there would be none', he also was prepared to admit evidence to the contrary.[39] This doubleness suggests that Percy may have been as drawn to Mary's scepticism as to what Claire Clairmont calls her 'great understanding and liking for the abstract subjects and high thoughts he delighted in'[40]; rather as Mary seems to have found Percy's ardour and idealism simultaneously dangerous and attractive, as reflected, for example, in the heroic as well as misguided character of Frankenstein's doomed defiance and persistence, his capacity to endure and suffer. Mary may never have been quite the fearless radical of Peacock's fictions— Anthelia in *Melincourt* (1817), Stella in *Nightmare Abbey* (1818)—but neither was she Trelawny's 'slave of convention'.[41] She simply insisted, as does *Frankenstein*, on the unignorable reality of the material world, the weight of which, as George Levine puts it, 'is a continuing comment on Victor's ambition, as the obscene flesh of the charnel house is the imaged irony of Victor's attempt to create life out of matter'.[42]

---

[39] From the preface to ibid. i., 126.

[40] Quoted in Sunstein, *Romance and Reality*, 72.

[41] See ibid. 104–6. For Trelawny's comment see *Letters of Edward John Trelawny*, ed. H. Buxton Forman (London: Oxford University Press, 1910), 225; see also the criticisms on pp. 229, 232, 234, 239–40, 259–60. Mary Shelley defended herself as follows. 'Some have a passion for reforming the world', she notes, in *Journals*, ed. Feldman and Scott-Kilvert, ii. 553–4, in an entry of 21 Oct. 1838, explaining 'my lukewarmness in the "Good Cause" '—'others do not cling to particular opinions. That my Parents and Shelley were of the former class, makes me respect it. . . . I earnestly desire the good and enlightenment of my fellow creatures—and see all in the present course tending to the same, and rejoice—but I am not for violent extremes . . . I have never written a word in disfavour of liberalism. . . . I believe that we are sent here to educate ourselves and that self-denial and disappointment and self-controul are a part of our education—that it is not by taking away all restraining law that our improvement is to be achieved.'

[42] George Levine, introduction, Levine and Knoepflmacher (eds.), *Endurance*, 6. Related discussion of Mary Shelley and 'reality' is found in Laurie Langbauer,

CHILDREN, WRITING, AND THE 'PROMETHEAN'
CHARACTER

The consequences of a Romantic or 'Promethean' outlook were, then, experienced first-hand by Mary Shelley, both as a daughter and a wife. They are also vividly imagined in her depictions of parenting and child-development in *Frankenstein*, a novel which can be seen as participating in contemporary debate about childhood and education, debate of obvious political moment (with the monster as 'Model Child', a related 'experiment' of the period). At the same time, they help to determine Mary Shelley's attitudes to writing and revision. In the 1831 introduction to *Frankenstein* the two themes are brought together when she refers to the novel as her 'hideous progeny' (p. 229), and declares as 'frightful' not just the creation, as in the novel's inaugurating dream, of 'the hideous phantasm of a man', but 'any human endeavour to mock the stupendous mechanism of the Creator of the world', including, as is clear from a subsequent reference to the phantasm's creator, that of the 'artist' (p. 228). Anne K. Mellor also points out that the period between the first letter Walton sends his sister, the letter which opens the novel, and the letter which ends it, is nine months, and that 'these nine months correspond almost exactly with Mary Shelley's third pregnancy', a pregnancy which itself mostly overlapped with the novel's composition.[43]

The death of Mary's first child, though, in 1815, was probably the crucial biographical experience underlying the novel, not only because of its effect on Mary herself, but because of Percy's behaviour during the whole episode, behaviour Mellor

'Swayed by Contraries: Mary Shelley and the Everyday', in Audrey A. Fisch, Anne K. Mellor, and Esther H. Schor (eds.), *The Other Mary Shelley: Beyond 'Frankenstein'* (New York: Oxford University Press, 1993), 185–203; for more general accounts of women and everyday experience, see Margaret Homans, *Bearing the Word: Language and Female Experience in Nineteenth-Century Women's Writing* (Chicago: University of Chicago Press, 1986), Dorothy E. Smith, *Everyday Life as Problematic: A Feminist Sociology* (Boston: Northeastern University Press, 1987), and Bettina Aptheker, *Tapestries of Life: Women's Work, Women's Consciousness, and the Meaning of Daily Experience* (Amherst, Mass.: University of Massachusetts Press, 1989).

[43] Mellor, *Mary Shelley*, 55.

characterizes as 'indifference'.[44] The evidence for this 'indifference' is found in the journal entries of the time, both those of Percy and of Mary (or 'Maie'). '[Maie] is in labour,' writes Percy in the entry for 22 February 1815, 'and, after very few addit[i]onal pains she is delivered of a female child—5 minutes afterwards Dr. Clarke comes. all is well. Maie perfectly well and at ease The child is not quite 7 months. The child not expected to live. S[helley] sits up with Maie. much agitated and exhausted.' The next day, Percy notes: 'the child unexpectedly alive, but still not expected to live'; and the day after, the 23rd, he writes of 'favorable symptoms in the child—we may indulge some hopes. . . . Dr. Clarke calls. confirms our hopes of the child.'[45] Such entries seem sensibly cautious or self-protective rather than unfeeling; by themselves they hardly constitute 'indifference'.

The entries that follow, from 26 February until the child's death on 6 March, are Mary's, and what immediately strikes one about them are her references to the child first as 'the baby', then as 'my baby': 28 February: 'I come down stairs—

---

[44] This behaviour is partly conjectured or inferred, and raises questions of biographical tact, questions eloquently voiced by Percy: 'I never will be a party in making my private affairs or those of others topics of general discussion. Who can know them but the actors? And if they have erred, or often when they have not erred, is there not pain enough to punish them?' (Percy Bysshe Shelley to Leigh Hunt, letter of (?) 20 Dec. 1820, *The Letters of Percy Bysshe Shelley*, ed. Frederick L. Jones, 2 vols. (Oxford: Clarendon Press, 1964), ii. 66). This was hardly Mary Shelley's view. For all her ladylike horror of 'improper' forwardness, Mary approved autobiography, self-reference in art, biographical speculation. Like Keats, she admired writers who explore the 'dark passages' of the human heart—that is, of their own hearts (Keats is thinking primarily of Wordsworth) (John Keats to John Hamilton Reynolds, 3 May 1818, in *The Letters of John Keats*, ed. Hyder Rollins, 2 vols. (Cambridge, Mass.: Harvard University Press, 1958), i. 281; Keats identifies Wordsworth as the modern poet for whom the human heart is 'the main region of his song'). Though, at times, 'the intrusion of self in a work of art' is to be deplored (as in Madame de Genlis's memoirs, which 'are one large capital *I* from beginning to end' (Mary Shelley to Jane Williams Hogg, 20 June 1828, *Letters*, ed. Bennett, ii. 48)), 'well-managed, there are few subjects . . . that excite stronger interest or elicit more beautiful lines'. The habit 'of self-analysation and display . . . has caused many men of genius to undertake works where the individual feeling of the author embues the whole subject with a peculiar hue. . . . Such persons turn to the human heart as the undiscovered country. They visit and revisit their own; endeavour to understand its workings, to fathom its depths, and to leave no lurking thought or disguised feeling.' Mary Shelley admires such persons, listing as favourites Burton, Sterne, Montaigne, Rousseau, Boswell, and her own parents. (In the essay 'Giovanni Villani', first printed in *The Liberal*, 4 (1823), repr. in *The Mary Shelley Reader*, ed. Bennett and Robinson, 331–2.)

[45] *Journals*, ed. Feldman and Scott-Kilvert, i. 65–6.

talk—nurse the baby and read Corinne [*Corinne; ou d'Italie*, by Madame de Staël, 1807] and work'; 1 March: 'Nurse the baby—read Corinne and work'; 2 March: 'A bustle of moving—read Corinne—I and my baby go about 3'; 3 March: 'Nurse my baby—talk and read Corinne—Hogg comes in the evening'; 4 March: 'Read talk and nurse'; 5 March: 'S and C[laire Clairmont] go to town—Hogg here all day—read Corinne and nurse my baby—in the evening talk—S finishes the Life of Chauser [by Godwin, published in 1803] H[ogg] goes at 11.'[46] From the beginning, these entries suggest, Mary was unable to maintain the emotional distance counselled by her doctor, a distance implied in Percy's references to 'the child'. At the same time, partly at Percy's bidding, her relations with Hogg were growing more intimate and complicated, as were Percy's with Claire Clairmont (at this time 'Clara' or 'Clary'). On 26 February, four days after the child's birth, Mary's journal entry reads as follows: 'Maie rises today—Hogg comes—talk—she goes to bed at 6. Hogg calls at the lodgeings we have taken—read Corinne S. and C. go to sleep—Hogg returns—talk with him till 1/2 11—he goes. S and C go down to tea—just settling to sleep when a knock comes at the door—it is Fanny [Imlay]—she came to see how we were—she stays talking till 1/2 3—and then leaves the room that S and M. may sleep. S. has a spasm.'[47]

It is difficult, with an entry like this, not to read between the lines. What is Mary's attitude to Hogg's constant presence, or to Percy's and Claire's gathering intimacy? Several journal pages from this period have been removed, but later entries provide clues. Two weeks after the entry of 26 February, on 11 March, Mary records the following despondent note: 'Talk about Clary's going away—nothing settled—I fear it is hopeless. She will not go to Skinner St [Godwin's home]—then our house is the only remaining place. . . . [W]hat is to be done[?]' The next morning, Mary pronounces herself 'happy': 'for Clary does not get up till 4'.[48] Mary's feelings about Hogg, however, are more puzzling. Hogg first met Mary in November 1814, and by 1 January 1815 had declared his love, a declaration sanctioned in part by Percy's theories. Mary responded in a letter of the same day, but in a manner neatly balanced between encouragement and

---

[46] Ibid. 67–8.   [47] Ibid. 66.   [48] Ibid. 69.

reserve: 'You love me you say—I wish I could return it with the passion you deserve—but you are very good to me and tell me that you are quite happy with the affection which from the bottom of my heart I feel for you—you are so generous so disinterested that no one can help loving you. But you know Hogg that we have known each other for so short a time and I did not think about love—so that I think that *that* also will come in time and then we shall be happier I do think than the angels who sing.'

Betty Bennett explains the ambivalences of this passage, and of the relation in general, as follows: 'Evidently she came to enjoy Hogg's attentions. Her strongest motivation in this experimental relationship, however, seems to have been to please Shelley by embodying his doctrine of love unrestrained by social conventions, and typically her expressions of affection for Hogg are overshadowed by her love for Shelley.' As for Percy's and Claire's relations, we know for certain that Percy was writing love poems to her, the 'Constania' lyrics of 1816. Whether they actually made love is less clear. Kenneth N. Cameron, 'reviewing the various analyses', concludes that they may well have been having an affair, but that if so it was short-lived.[49] Percy's physical complaints are also suggestive. By 1814 he was convinced he had contracted syphilis and was going to die, and in the winter of 1814 and the summer of 1815 he consulted William Lawrence, a surgeon and physician in Godwin's circle. Though this fear was unfounded, the spasms of pain he suffered seem to have been perfectly genuine, and may indeed have resulted, as he claimed, from earlier injury, but according to Thornton Leigh Hunt, 'they tended to occur at times when Shelley was under some mental strain'.[50] In a period, then, in which she was trying to nurse her dangerously premature first-born infant daughter to health (without, it should be added, much in the way of experienced help or advice), Mary had also to consider not only Percy's complaints, but the emotional entanglements he could be thought to have initiated.[51]

[49] See *Letters*, ed. Bennett, i. 6 for Mary's letter to Thomas Jefferson Hogg, also for Bennett's footnote summarizing their relations and Cameron's account of the relations of Claire and Percy.

[50] See *Journals*, ed. Feldman and Scott-Kilvert, i. 66 n.

[51] As Moers notes, 'there is nothing in the journal about domestic help or a nurse in attendance' ('Female Gothic', in Levine and Knoepflmacher (eds.), *Endurance*, 82).

The intensity with which Mary reacted to the infant's death is pathetically, protectively masked in the journal. Here is the famously laconic entry of Monday, 6 March: 'Find my baby dead—Send for Hogg—talk—a miserable day—in the evening read fall of the Jesuits [*Despotism; or, the Fall of the Jesuits*, by Isaac D'Israeli, published in 1811] H. sleeps here.' The extraordinary calm of this entry is partly explained by an entry written a week later, on 13 March: 'S[helley] H.[ogg] and C.[lary] go to town—stay at home net and think of my little dead baby—this is foolish I suppose yet whenever I am left alone to my own thoughts and do not read to divert them they always come back to the same point—that I was a mother and am so no longer.'[52] The prophylactic effects of reading, however, work only until sleep, and after another week, on 19 March, Mary dreams a dream almost as important to *Frankenstein* as the nightmare which was its immediate inspiration: 'Dream that my little baby came to life again—that it had only been cold and that we rubbed it by the fire and it lived—I awake and find no baby— I think about the little thing all day—not in good spirits— Shelley is very unwell.'[53]

Though it is impossible to know precisely how Mary Shelley connected the trauma of her baby's death with Percy's mysterious (needy?) symptoms and the tangled emotional relations he helped foster, the whole episode is bound to have raised questions about the 'Promethean' character, questions *Frankenstein* obviously anatomizes. 'The thoughtless rejection of family in the pursuit and perpetuation of universal perfectibility, deeply disturbed her,' a recent student of the early novels is convinced, 'and it is clear that she often resented PBS . . . for his refusal to be intellectually, artistically or spiritually compromised by a family's needs.'[54] That this refusal was unconsciously connected

---

[52] Entry of 13 Mar. 1815 in *Journals*, ed. Feldman and Scott-Kilvert, i. 69. Keats, too, provides evidence of the prophylactic effects of reading. According to Walter Jackson Bate, *John Keats* (New York: Oxford University Press, 1966), 27, 'the time at which Keats began to read so eagerly (during the last three terms he was at school, as Clarke [John Clarke, whose school it was] said) would start almost exactly after the death of his mother in March 1810. Unquestionably this final loss, coming after others, had much to do with his sustained commitment to study, to reading.'

[53] *Journals*, ed. Feldman and Scott-Kilvert, i. 70.

[54] Blumberg, *Mary Shelley's Early Novels*, 54.

in Mary Shelley's mind with the death of her children ('unintentionally', claims Marilyn Butler, Percy 'even contributed to the death of her second daughter, another Clara, in September 1818, by ordering Mary to travel across Italy with the sick child in the Italian summer heat'[55]) might well account for the name she gave to the monster's first victim, the child William, the name also of her infant son, who would die in 1818 at age 3.[56]

Such suspicions relate directly to authorial attitudes. Mary Shelley took authorship seriously. That it was impossible 'to dispose of my writings without being in England', she claims in a letter of *c.*2 July 1823 to Jane Williams, was her sole reason for leaving Italy after Percy Shelley's death.[57] The burden of her parents' literary legacy left her 'ever afraid of being proud of what I do not possess', yet determined to possess it.[58] Never, though, was Mary Shelley anything like as obsessive or perfectionist about her writing as, say, Wordsworth, especially at the beginning of her career. She may have taken authorship seriously, but she also found it difficult to think of herself as an author, and her early journals and letters barely mention composition (the journal entries are restricted to the matter-of-fact expressions 'write' or 'work'). Family affairs, the mundanities of child-rearing and travel in particular, take priority. She was also open about the defects of her writing, of her style in particular, as also about the writing's often unconscious origins.[59]

Which is not to say that authorship was for Mary Shelley a mere 'activity', as Byron claimed it to be for himself, or that she

[55] *Frankenstein*, ed. Butler, p. xiii.

[56] Mary Shelley may also have associated Percy Shelley with the death of their second daughter, Clara, whose health was endangered by a long carriage journey undertaken at Percy's urging—just the sort of carriage journey that had endangered the life of Percy Shelley's first daughter, Ianthe (See William Veeder, *Mary Shelley and Frankenstein: The Fate of Androgyny* (Chicago: University of Chicago Press, 1986), 13).

[57] Mary Shelley to Jane Williams, *c.*2 July 1823, in *Letters*, ed. Bennett, i. 343.

[58] See Sunstein, *Romance and Reality*, 34.

[59] As Wendy Lesser acutely notes, in the introduction to her Everyman edn. of *Frankenstein*, p. xvi, to write *Frankenstein* was for Mary Shelley 'an act of enormous hubris and a submission to forces beyond the author's control, "I busied myself *to think of a story*," she tells us in the preface; "I had *thought of a story*," she says after her crucial dream. But in between these two comments, in which her italics wilfully stress the element of will, Mary Shelley describes to us the dream origins of her story, the circumstances whereby her "imagination, unbidden, possessed and guided me"'.

ever shared her husband's stress on process over product, an outlook she saw as evasive. As Mellor puts it, 'even before Percy Shelley in his *Defence of Poetry* dismissed the composed poem as a "fading coal" of its originary inspiration, Mary Shelley understood that the Romantic affirmation of the creative process over its finite products could justify a profound moral irresponsibility on the part of the poet'; the poet, she believed, 'must take responsibility for his actions'.[60] Hence the place she was careful to find for revision in the composing process. 'I hope to finish the rough transcript this month,' she writes to Maria Gisborne of *Valperga,* 'I shall then give a month to correction and then I shall transcribe it—It has indeed been a child of mighty slow growth.'[61] The failure of responsibility to one's products—to their proper 'rearing' or 'correcting'—is of a piece for Mary Shelley with failures of responsibility towards one's family, the very failures figured in Victor Frankenstein's irresponsible engendering and abandonment of the monster, or in the irresponsibility of the real-life models on whom Frankenstein was based.

That Mary Shelley's sense of personal responsibility never led her to illusions of authorial autonomy is also a product of her sense of her writings as 'progeny'. In the introduction to the 1831 edition of *Frankenstein,* she recounts the circumstances out of which the novel grew, its communal inception. But she also, it is clear, wants to be acknowledged as the novel's ultimate author, insisting that she 'certainly did not owe the suggestion of one incident, nor scarcely of one train of feeling' to Percy Shelley (p. 229). When the first edition appeared in 1818, and Sir Walter Scott mistook Percy for its creator, she was quick to reveal herself as author, ostensibly to prevent Scott from 'continuing in the mistake of supposing Mr. Shelley guilty of a juvenile attempt of mine; to which—from it being written at an early age, I abstained from putting my name—and from respect to those persons from whom I bear it'.[62] This ambivalence is seen also in a letter to Hobhouse of 10 November 1824, in which Mary declares 'an irreversible objection to the seeing of my name in print', but also insists that 'the Preface to

[60] Mellor, *Mary Shelley,* 80.
[61] Mary Shelley to Maria Gisborne, 30 June 1821, in *Letters,* ed. Bennett, i. 203.
[62] Mary Shelley to Sir Walter Scott, 14 June 1818, ibid. 71.

Frankenstein proves that that story was conceived before Lord Byron's and Shelley's tour around the lake, and that [Monk] Lewis did not arrive in Geneva until some time after'.[63]

These contradictory attitudes derive, in part, from Mary Shelley's desire that her novel be seen as 'natural', 'healthy', despite its horrid subject-matter and its author's seeming 'unnaturalness' (her sex, her age, her unconventional upbringing, with its absence of the sort of 'gentle and feminine tutelage' that civilizes and restrains Walton). The novel's subject-matter left the anonymous reviewer of the March 1818 *Quarterly Review* 'in doubt whether the head or the heart of the author be the most diseased', a reaction that may in part have been politically motivated, a product of the novel's dedication to Godwin.[64] But Mary, too, was given to doubts about her naturalness, as the language of the 1831 introduction suggests, with its talk of the vision that helped inspire the novel having 'so possessed my mind, that a thrill of fear ran through me' (p. 228), a phrase which suggests the very galvanic spark or charge that brings the monster itself to life.

The desire to see her novel as 'natural', Ellen Moers suggests, connects with the pregnant Mary's anxieties about her capacity to have a healthy child.[65] It also connects, I believe, with the novel's depressing account of single parenting, even when the parent in question is as benevolent as Victor's father, a man who 'gradually relinquished many of his public employments, and devoted himself to the education of his children' (p. 28), or old Mr DeLacey.[66] Children—'progeny'—need fathers *and* mothers. When the monster comes to knowledge, chief among the lessons that impresses him most deeply is that of 'the birth and growth of children; how the father doated on the smiles of

[63] Mary Shelley to John Cam Hobhouse, 10 Nov. 1824, ibid. 455.

[64] See the introduction to Mary Shelley, *Frankenstein*, ed. Hindle, p. viii. The dedication was dropped in the 1831 edn.

[65] See Moers, 'Female Gothic', 79–87.

[66] Such kindly fathers are exceptions, to be contrasted with 'a series of forbidding fathers—the father whose "dying injunction" forbade Walton to embark on a sea-faring life; Henry Clerval's father, who insists that his son be a merchant rather than a poet; the "inexorable" Russian father who tries to force his daughter into a union she abhors; the treacherous Turkish father who uses Safie to obtain his freedom yet issues the "tyrannical mandate" that she betray Felix' (Knoepflmacher, 'Thoughts on the Betrayal of Daughters', in Levine and Knoepflmacher (eds.), *Endurance*, 104).

the infant, and the lively sallies of the older child; how all the life and cares of the mother were wrapt up in the precious charge' (p. 116); he also bitterly complains that 'no father had watched my infant days, no mother had blessed me with smiles and caresses' (p. 117). Percy Shelley's collaboration gives the book two 'parents', makes its engendering 'normal', freeing Mary Shelley and her literary offspring from the female author's taint of forwardness or abnormality, the sort of taint that causes her in the 1831 introduction to stress that it was Percy Shelley who 'urged me to develope the idea at greater length' (p. 222). 'Shelley and I talk about my story,' she notes in a journal entry of 21 August 1816—like parents chatting about children.[67] The manuscript offers several instances of collaborative interplay, of Mary, in effect, improving on Percy's additions, as when Percy's gothicizing 'I knew the vessel in which he was concealed and he escaped I know not how,' becomes Mary's 'I took my passage in the same ship but he escaped I know not how' (p. 200).[68]

Mary Shelley's subsequent work as editor and amanuensis reinforced her sense of authorship as collaborative. As we have seen, she was the most trusted of Byron's amanuenses. She began copying for him in 1818, transcribing 'Ode to Venice' and *Mazeppa*, and continued to do so until his death in 1824, providing fair copies for many important poems, including the final ten cantos of *Don Juan*. From the first, in the *Mazeppa* manuscript, Mary Shelley made minor alterations (mostly involving capitalization and punctuation); it is ironic to see her in 1818, while transcribing *Mazeppa*, 'clarifying' Byron's text precisely as Percy Shelley clarified *Frankenstein* two years earlier: eliminating imprecise end-of-line dashes, adding commas, full stops, more emphatic internal dashes. Byron 'evidently approved' fifty-four of these emendations.[69] He also approved

---

[67] Entry of 21 Aug. 1816, *Journals*, ed. Feldman and Scott-Kilvert, i. 130.

[68] The origins of the novel, moreover, ought not to be forgotten. The ghost story competition at the Villa Diodati, in Marilyn Butler's words, was 'genuinely collaborative in that the four stories or versions of stories we have (to include both those attributed to Polidori) represent variations on the same two themes. One is the punishment ironically but justly visited on the protagonist for his or her transgression, another the idea that the Eastern European or Near-Eastern figure of the vampire is especially the bearer of such a punishment' (*Frankenstein*, ed. Butler, p. xxiii).

[69] Blumberg, *Mary Shelley's Early Novels*, 206.

several more substantial revisions, though at this very early stage in their professional relation he rarely sanctioned changes in whole words. Later on, as Byron's confidence in her grew (thanks, perhaps, to what Jane Blumberg identifies as an 'audition' for the fair-copying of *Don Juan*, a 'vigilantly' proofed transcript of *Werner*, 1822),[70] so did the boldness of Mary Shelley's alterations. On occasion, Byron offered her alternative couplets to choose from, abiding by her decisions. He even authorized an unproofed transcript of Canto 16, the last completed canto, to be used as printer's copy. This easiness can only have reinforced the lessons of mutuality Mary Shelley both taught and learned in *Frankenstein* and its creation.

Nowhere is the professional trust between Byron and Mary Shelley more remarkable than over questions of sexual tact or delicacy, precisely the questions over which Byron felt the advice of Murray's Utican Senate untrustworthy. For example, though stoutly resisting Mary Shelley's repeated attempts to substitute 'heart' for 'breast' (as in Canto 6, stanzas 15, 66, and 86) Byron uncomplainingly accepted 'w—re' for 'Whore' (also in Canto 6, stanza 91), and willingly changed an unprintable personal joke in Canto 8 about 'being taken by the tail—a taking | Fatal to warriors and to women,' to Mary's more acceptable 'a taking | Fatal to bishops as to soldiers.' Here and elsewhere, Mary Shelley's alteration is not so much prudish as prudent. The allusion to sodomy is still obvious, but as Blumberg observes, is 'at least open to alternative interpretation [while] removing Byron personally from the fray'.[71] That the passage is not to Mary Shelley's taste is only secondarily the cause of its revision; more important is her sense that it would lose the poem readers. For unlike less notoriously 'conventional' friends and associates of Byron, including Teresa Guiccioli, who also acted as copyist, Mary Shelley admired the poem, even at its riskiest and most *risqué*; she wanted it to have an audience. 'I have nearly finished your *savage* Canto,' she writes to Byron on 21 October 1822 (of Canto 11), 'You will cause Milman to hang himself.... Your fashionable world is delightful'; 'these last Cantos', she tells Trelawny, in a letter of 2 April 1823, 'are unequalled in their strictures upon *life* and flashes of wit'; 'I

---

[70] Ibid. 209.   [71] Ibid. 214.

delight in your new style much more than in your former *glorious one*,' she announces to Byron of *The Deformed Transformed*, her first assignment after *Mazeppa*.[72] Similarly, when in 1830, while editing Trelawny's *Adventures of a Younger Son*, and trying to get it published, she advises him to cut certain potentially offensive passages, the market remains her prime motive. 'I beseech you', she writes him, on 27 December 1830, 'to let me deal with them as I would with Ld Byrons Don Juan—when I omitted all that hurt my taste—Without this yielding on your part I shall experience great difficulty in disposing of your work.'[73]

These experiences of collaborative authorship are anticipated in *Frankenstein* itself. When Frankenstein 'corrected and augmented' Walton's notes, he sought to give the narrative 'life and spirit'; without his help it might have been delivered to posterity in a 'mutilated' form (p. 207), a term which recalls Percy's addition of the word 'abortion' (p. 219) to describe the monster. But as the novel also suggests, it is not enough merely to 'normalize' the work's creation or birth; the infant or draft has also to be 'raised', a belief implicit in the novel's emphasis 'not upon what precedes birth, not upon birth itself, but upon what follows birth'[74]—most importantly, abandonment, the experience with which the novel's composition began (chapter 4 in the 1818 edition, chapter 5 in the edition of 1831). Once the

---

[72] Letters of Mary Shelley to Lord Byron, 21 Oct. 1822, John Edward Trelawny, 2 Apr. 1823, and Lord Byron, 16 Nov. 1822, in *Letters*, ed. Bennett, i. 283, 326, 288. Paul A. Cantor, in 'Mary Shelley and the Taming of the Byronic Hero: "Transformation" and *The Deformed Transformed*,' in Fisch, Mellor, and Schor (eds.), *The Other Mary Shelley*, 89, thinks Mary Shelley's short story 'Transformation', published in 1830 in *The Keepsake* annual, 'clearly constitutes a rewriting' of Byron's *The Deformed Transformed*.

[73] Mary Shelley to Edward John Trelawny, 27 Dec. 1830, *Letters*, ed. Bennett, ii. 120. William St Clair restores the expurgated passages in his edn. of Trelawny's *Adventures of a Younger Son* (London: Oxford University Press, 1974). The most notable of the missing episodes concerns a visit to a brothel in India. In addition to the collaborations with Trelawny and Byron, two other instances are worth mentioning: *The History of a Six Weeks' Tour*, which was published in 1817 by T. Hookham and the Olliers, could be considered a joint creation, since it contains a journal to which both Percy and Mary contributed, four descriptive letters (two by each), as well as 'Mont Blanc'; and Mary Shelley's own *Journals*, which, as Mary Jean Corbett points out in 'Reading Mary Shelley's *Journals*: Romantic Subjectivity and Feminist Criticism', in Fisch, Mellor, and Schor (eds.), *The Other Mary Shelley*, 78, was originally conceived as a 'co-production' with Percy.

[74] Moers, 'Female Gothic', 81.

first draft was completed, it could not just be abandoned (in the offhand manner Byron affected, a manner Mary Shelley may also have related to his treatment of actual children, in particular his and Claire Clairmont's daughter, Allegra); to revise her works was to treat them as she would have her children—any children—treated. The good parent, like the good author, neither abandons its offspring nor seeks wholly to control or shape them.

Hence, in part, Mary Shelley's behaviour in the final stages of the novel's publication. The corrected holograph manuscript (in the Abinger collection in the Bodleian) differs markedly from the printed text of 1818, but the fair copy from which the printers worked has never surfaced. Mary Shelley corrected proofs, but she also authorized Percy to do so; as Mellor has properly objected, the assumption of previous editors that Percy alone altered proofs is simply wrong.[75] Proofs were sent directly to Percy (partly to protect Mary's anonymity), who assured the publishers in a letter of 22 August 1817 that he'd been 'authorized' to amend 'any mere inaccuracies of language', and were returned to the publisher on 23 October, with a covering letter declaring that he'd 'paid considerable attention to the correction of such few instances of baldness of style as necessarily occur in the production of a very young writer'.[76] That Mary Shelley had indeed authorized such changes is clear from a note of 24 September 1817 accompanying her own corrections. 'In looking it over,' she writes to Percy, 'there appeared to me some abruptnesses which I have endeavoured to supply—but I am tired and not very clear headed so I give you carte blanche to make what alterations you please.'[77]

Mary Shelley did not abandon her novel when she granted Percy Shelley *carte blanche*, she merely bowed to what she saw as reality: she was exhausted from nursing a child and running a family, and Percy Shelley was a more accomplished stylist. On this last point she was unselfconsciously clear: unless carefully deliberated, she told Leigh Hunt, apropos the unauthorized printing of passages from a letter, her writing lacked

[75] Mellor, *Mary Shelley*, 66.
[76] Percy Shelley to Lackington, Allen, & Co., 22 Aug. and 23 Oct. 1817, in *Letters*, ed. Jones, i. 553, 565.
[77] Mary Shelley to Percy Shelley, 24 Sept. 1817, in *Letters*, ed. Bennett, i. 42.

'print-worthy dignity'; unedited, she 'cut a very foolish figure'.[78] This sensible recognition not only of self-limitation but of the role of external forces in literary creation, of contingency, is found also in her reactions to analogous non-literary dilemmas. When, for example, Godwin at last relented and broke his silence with Percy and Mary, he did so to caution Percy about his choice of estates; not, on the face of it, an especially disinterested or rational reason. 'All this is very odd and inconsistent,' comments Mary, 'but I never quarrel with inconsistency —folks must change their minds.'[79] This comment recalls Byron on contradiction, but its spirit is different; it aims neither to shock nor affront, is no incitement to despair or cynicism. It is simply forgiving or understanding.

Emily Sunstein, in her biography of Mary Shelley, connects such a temperament to genre. 'Her optimism', she writes, 'was tempered by modulated expectations and acceptance of an irreducible human condition. A natural novelist, she liked detail, complexities.'[80] Novels, moreover, especially in the early decades of the nineteenth century, had relevant class associations. 'Mary Shelley's rejection of the "me" and her embrace of non-originary authorship,' writes Carson, 'are signs of the anti-elitist, "popular" nature of her work.'[81] Such signs, of course, can also be read in conventional feminist as well as generic or class terms, as a refusal of 'patriarchal' notions of selfhood, in which, in Toril Moi's words, 'the self is the *sole author* of history and of the literary text. . . . God in relation to his world, the author in relation to his text.'[82]

The compositional consequences of Mary Shelley's temperament, whatever the terms one uses to explain it, are clear: she was able to produce drafts 'fast and with few strike-outs' (the initial text was apparently written 'nearly without emendation'),[83] conscious that they would have to be altered or edited—by

---

[78] Mary Shelley to Leigh Hunt, ibid. 53.

[79] Quoted in Sunstein, *Romance and Reality*, 94.   [80] Ibid. 113.

[81] Carson, 'Bringing the Author Forward: *Frankenstein* through Mary Shelley's Letters', 450.

[82] Toril Moi, *Textual/Sexual Politics: Feminist Literary Theory* (London: Methuen, 1985), 8.

[83] The quotation is from Sunstein, *Romance and Reality*, 127; the remark about emendation from E. B. Murray, 'Shelley's Contribution to Mary's *Frankenstein*', in *Keats–Shelley Memorial Bulletin*, 29 (1978), 51 n.

herself, but also by friends and advisers. Like Walton, she 'did not belong to that class of men who are offended by advice' (p. 23). This initial ease of composition was related to a more general tendency or principle: an unwillingness to sacrifice 'life' to 'art', in the manner of a Frankenstein. For example, though willing harshly to criticize her father in *Mathilda*, a thinly disguised autobiographical novella (but featuring a father's incestuous love for his daughter) written in the late summer of 1820, Mary Shelley also consulted him about publication; when Godwin inevitably objected, calling the work 'disgusting and detestable',[84] it never appeared. Similarly, when Mary sent a draft copy of *Valperga* to Godwin, Percy suspected, in a letter of 29 May 1822, that she'd be 'delighted to amend any thing that her father thought imperfect in it'.[85] He was right. Though Godwin confessed to Mary that he had 'taken great liberties with [the work?], and I am afraid your *amour propre* will be proportionately shocked',[86] Mary accepted these liberties calmly. It was Percy, the 'Promethean' poet, who would resist what Mary elsewhere calls her father's 'curtailments'.[87] Percy was particularly exercised about Mary's depiction of the 17-year-old prophetess Beatrice, whose speeches are sometimes openly blasphemous. If Godwin wants the character of Beatrice altered, he writes, '*I* should lament the deference which should be shown by the sacrifice of any portion of it to feelings or ideas which are but for a day.'[88]

Mary's antipathy to such high-mindedness is seen in her work on Percy's texts as well as in her own authorial practice. As editor, writes Betty Bennett, 'Mary Shelley became Shelley's collaborator, returning more than in kind the guidance he had given her when she wrote *Frankenstein* and other early works.'[89]

---

[84] Quoted in Elizabeth Nitchie, *Mary Shelley: Author of Frankenstein* (New Brunswick, NJ: Rutgers University Press, 1953), 214 n.

[85] Percy Shelley to Mary Jane Godwin, 29 May 1822, in *Letters*, ed. Jones, ii. 428.

[86] Feb. 1823, quoted in C. Kegan Paul, *William Godwin: Friends and Contemporaries*, 2 vols. (London: Henry S. King, 1876), ii. 277.

[87] Mary Shelley to Maria Gisborne, 3 May (6 May) 1823, in *Letters*, ed. Bennett, i. 336.

[88] Percy Shelley to Mary Jane Godwin, 29 May 1822, in *Letters*, ed. Jones, ii. 428.

[89] *Letters*, ed. Bennett, ii. p. xvii. Bennett's view is seconded by Susan J. Wolfson in 'Editorial Privilege: Mary Shelley and Percy Shelley's Audiences', in Fisch, Mellor, and Schor (eds.), *The Other Mary Shelley*, 49, in which Mary's editorial labours are said to amount at times to 'co-creation'.

Here, too, I would add, collaboration, the attempt to realize or fulfil or share her husband's original aims and interests, has been mistaken for imposition—just as in the case of Percy's work on *Frankenstein*. For example, after Mary Shelley's relations with Trelawny had begun to sour (perhaps because, as we have seen, she discouraged his attempts to write Percy Shelley's life), Trelawny took grave objection to her edition of Percy Shelley's poems, in particular to the omission of certain controversial passages in *Queen Mab* (as well as the dedication to Percy's first wife). Mary protested her innocence as follows: 'My motive for the omission was simply that when Clarke's edition appeared [a pirated version of 1821] Shelley rejoiced that it was omitted—and expressed great satisfaction thereon. It *could* be nothing to *me* but a matter of pleasure to publish it. My motive was the purest and simplest that ever activated any one. If convinced that I am in the wrong, it shall be restored in the next edition.'[90] The following day, in a journal entry, Mary repeats this explanation, but also offers a different motive for the omission, one that recalls her earlier warning about the indelicate passages in Trelawny's own writings: 'when I was told that certain portions would injure the copyright of all the volumes to the publisher, I yielded'.[91] This motive also recalls the explanation she gave to Leigh Hunt, in a letter of 6 October 1839, for the omission of the essay 'On the Devil and Devils' (?1819–21) from her edition of the collected *Essays, Letters from Abroad, Translations and Fragments by Percy Bysshe Shelley* (1840): that its inclusion would 'preclude a number of readers [of the volume as a whole] who else would snatch at it'.[92]

The tone of the journal entry about *Queen Mab*, though, is complicated. The offending verses were omitted 'to do him

[90] Mary Shelley to Thomas Jefferson Hogg, 11 Feb. 1839, in *Letters*, ed. Bennett, ii. 309. As Blumberg reminds us, that the poem 'was never intended for the general public was well known. PBS apparently told Shelley, when news of the pirated 1821 edition reached the couple in Italy, that he preferred the poem in its unauthorized form; without the dedication to Harriet and with some of the more shocking passages removed' (*Early Novels*, 165). There was a prudent or practical side to Mary Shelley's suppression in her edition. With the notes, *Queen Mab* was still liable to prosecution, although not likely to be prosecuted. When these notes were restored, in the next edition, a prosecution was brought simply to prove the liability.
[91] Entry of 12 Feb. 1839, in *Journals*, ed. Feldman and Scott-Kilvert, ii. 560.
[92] Mary Shelley to Leigh Hunt, 6 Oct. 1839, in *Letters*, ed. Bennett, ii. 326.

honour—What could it be to me?—There are other verses I should well like to obliterate for ever—but they will be printed—and any to her [Jane Williams, presumably] could in no way tend to my discomfort; or gratify one ungenerous feeling. They shall be restored.'[93] The sense of personal injury in this episode is palpable; these are verses, one feels, Mary Shelley would herself not have wanted printed had she been their author; restoring them in the one-volume second edition, also of 1839, like publishing the two 'Jane Williams' poems, 'The Invitation' and 'The Recollection', is thus both an act of principle ('I don't like Atheism,' she wrote to Leigh Hunt on 12 December 1838, 'yet I hate mutilation'[94]) and a crossing or thwarting of personal or temperamental preference. That Percy Shelley himself shared her reservations she means to prove by including in the second edition his letter of 22 June 1821 to *The Examiner* denying he ever intended to release the poem for the general public: 'not so much from literary vanity, as because I fear it is better fitted to injure than to serve the cause of freedom'[95]—which is much like the reason Mary settles on for its initial censoring.

In sum, though Mary Shelley's editing of her husband's writing was far from complete or error-free, as P. D. Fleck puts it, in reference to the 1824 *Posthumous Poems*, there is little evidence 'that she manipulated Shelley's texts in the light of a personal critical judgement of his thought'.[96] Her aim, on the contrary, was fidelity to the original work. It was Mary herself, for example, who first published Percy's reproachful dedication to her from 'The Witch of Atlas', a poem in which an ideal

[93] Entry of 12 Feb. 1839, in *Journals*, ed. Feldman and Scott-Kilvert, ii. 561.
[94] Mary Shelley to Leigh Hunt, 12 Dec. 1838, in *Letters*, ed. Bennett, ii. 304.
[95] Shelley, *Poetical Works*, ed. Mary Shelley, 40.
[96] P. D. Fleck, 'Mary Shelley's Notes to Shelley's Poems and *Frankenstein*', *Studies in Romanticism*, 6/4 (1967), 227–8. Charles H. Taylor, Jr., in 'The Errata Leaf to Shelley's *Posthumous Poems* and Some Surprising Relationships Between the Earliest Collected Editions', *PMLA*, 70 (June 1955), agrees: many of Mary Shelley's misreadings exist for no more sinister reason than that 'she failed to notice them' (p. 416). Similarly, *Letters*, ed. Bennett, ii. p. xvii, thinks Mary Shelley's 'editorial principles, stated or implied, stand up well even by modern standards'. For a contrary or critical modern view see Joseph Raben, 'Shelley's "Invocation to Misery": An Expanded Text', *Journal of English and German Philology*, 65 (1966), 65–74. As Blumberg points out, it is in her notes to Percy Shelley's *Essays, Letters from Abroad and Fragments* that Mary Shelley's praise not only 'becomes extravagant and her image of him as an ethereal being the most vivid', but that 'she highlights the "Christian" features of his work' (*Mary Shelley's Early Novels*, 181, 182).

creature or 'fair Shape' (line 325)—a sort of anti-monster—is created by 'strange act' from 'fire and snow' (line 321). Nor was publishing the dedication, in which Percy accuses Mary of being 'critic-bitten' (line 1), an act of self-abasement. As her notes to the poem make clear, Mary stood by her criticisms. She opposed what the dedication calls 'visionary rhyme' (line 8) only in part for market reasons: 'It was not only that I wished him to acquire popularity as redounding to his fame; but I believed he would retain a greater mastery over his own powers, and greater happiness in his mind, if public applause crowned his endeavours. The few stanzas that precede the poem were addressed to me on my representing these ideas to him. Even now I believe that I was in the right.'[97]

PERCY SHELLEY'S REVISIONS

At the heart of the controversy over Percy Shelley's revisions of *Frankenstein* lies a question of degree: when does advice or assistance become collaboration or co-authorship? James Rieger, in the influential introduction to his 1974 reprinting of the 1818 edition, claims that Percy Shelley was responsible for important general (that is, thematic and structural) features of the narrative. These include wording the contrasts between Victor's and Elizabeth's characters; singling out the Swiss republic for praise (in one of the novel's few overt political passages, an important locus for Marilyn Butler's sense that it is only with *Frankenstein* and *Melmoth the Wanderer* 'that an ideological hatred of oppression and value for the person can be read into a sustained English Gothic tale'[98]); providing the most powerful features of the novel's description of Mont Blanc; suggesting that Frankenstein travel to England to create a female companion for his monster; and supplying the sombre note on which the novel ends. He also credits Percy with more local narrative and thematic clarifications, especially the smoothing of transitions, the correction of misspellings, grammatical and factual mistakes, scientific or technical imprecisions ('laboratory'

---

[97] *Poetical Works*, ed. Mary Shelley, 278–9.
[98] Marilyn Butler, *Jane Austen and the War of Ideas* (Oxford: Clarendon Press, 1975), 50–1.

for 'workshop' (p. 162), 'instruments' for 'machines' (p. 46)), obvious implausibilities (for example, changing the duration of Frankenstein's pursuit of the monster at the North Pole from three months to three weeks (p. 204)), and awkward phrasing. Percy Shelley's assistance, he concludes, 'at every point in the book's manufacture was so extensive that one hardly knows whether to regard him as editor or minor collaborator' (p. xvii).

This was the view also of E. B. Murray, the first critic to look closely at Percy Shelley's revisions. To Murray, the revisions were 'original enough to suggest that at times his creative impulse added its own initiative to the novel's effect'.[99] Anne Mellor, in contrast, thinks Percy Shelley's revisions less extensive; she also thinks they damaged as well as improved the text.[100] Mellor rightly points out that Percy Shelley merely expanded rather than initiated both the contrast between Victor's and Elizabeth's characters and the description of Mont Blanc, a description which owes more to Mary Shelley's 1816 journal observations and letters to Fanny Imlay, subsequently published in 1817 in *History of a Six Weeks' Tour*, than to Percy Shelley's poem. As for the journey to England, Percy merely suggested that Victor rather than Alphonse propose the idea; the journey itself was Mary's invention.

The first objection Mellor raises to the actual character of the revisions is that 'by far the greatest number' substitute a formal, pedantic diction—'stilted, ornate, putatively Ciceronian'[101]—for Mary Shelley's looser and more natural language (e.g. 'conversed' for 'talked', 'augment' for 'add to', 'penury' for 'poverty'; and on the level of the phrase, 'a considerable period elapsed' for 'it was a long time', 'neither of us possessed preeminence over the other' for 'we were all equal', 'eyes . . . insensible to' for 'eyes . . . shut to', 'depositing the remains' for 'wrapping the rest'). When critics complain of the 'inflexibly public and oratorical nature of even [the novel's] most intimate passages',[102] it may well be Percy Shelley's work, or his influence, about which they are complaining. Mary's Frankenstein swears that he 'would not die until my adversary lay at my feet', Percy's accepted revision has him declaring that he would 'not relax

---

[99] Murray, 'Shelley's Contribution to Mary's *Frankenstein*', 67.
[100] Mellor, *Mary Shelley*, 58.   [101] Ibid. 60.
[102] George Levine, quoted ibid. 60.

the impending conflict until my own life, or that of my adversary, were extinguished' (p. 192). 'I do not wish to claim that Mary Shelley was a great prose stylist,' declares Mellor after an anthology of such passages, 'but only that her own prose, despite its tendency toward the abstract, sentimental, and even banal, is more direct and forceful than her husband's revisions.'[103]

But could it not be argued that Percy's style is appropriate? Characters like Frankenstein, Walton, even the monster (a student, after all, of Plutarch, Milton, and Goethe), are at least in part figures of Percy Shelley himself. Ought they not to speak like him? Though Percy Shelley may not have intended his alterations to make the novel's characters take on his voice—formal, cultured, 'Ciceronian'—they did, and Mary Shelley doubtless knew or sensed as much, approving. This point is hardest to make, of course, with respect to the monster, whose status as victim is somewhat obscured by Percy Shelley's more commanding and rhetorical idiom—the idiom, for example, of the final thirteen pages of the revised manuscript, in which the monster recounts his feelings after having murdered Clerval. The artless dashes, short sentences, and syntactic simplicity of the original present a significantly less sinister and culpable figure than that of the fair copy, with its complex and composed flourishes. Here is Mary's original text of the monster's confession:

When Clerval died I returned to Switzerland heart-broken and overcome—I pitied Frankenstein and his bitter sufferings—My pity amounted to horror—I abhorred myself—But when I saw that he again dared for happiness—that while he heaped wretchedness and despair on me he sought his own enjoyment in feelings and passions from the indulgence of which I was forever banned—I was again roused to indignation and revenge. I remembered my threat and resolved to execute it—Yet when she died Nay then I was not miserable—I cast off all feeling and all anguish. I rioted in the extent of my despair and being urged thus far—I resolved to finish my demoniacal design. And it is now ended—There is my last victim.

Here is Percy's edited and expanded version of the passage:

After the murder of Clerval, I returned to Switzerland, heartbroken and overcome. I pitied Frankenstein; my pity amounted to horror: I

---

[103] Ibid. 62.

abhorred myself. But when I discovered that he, the author at once of my existence and of its unspeakable torments, dared to hope for happiness; that while he accumulated despair and wretchedness upon me, he sought his own enjoyment in feelings and passions from the indulgence of which I was forever barred, then impotent envy and bitter indignation filled me with an insatiable thirst for vengeance. I recollected my threat and resolved that it should be accomplished. I knew that I was preparing for myself a deadly torture; but I was the slave, not the master of an impulse, which I detested, yet could not disobey. Yet when she died!—nay, then I was not miserable. I had cast off all feeling, subdued all anguish to riot in the excess of my despair. Evil thenceforth became my good. Urged thus far, I had no choice but to adapt my nature to an element which I had willingly chosen. The completion of my demoniacal design became an insatiable passion. And now it is ended; there is my last victim! (pp. 217–18)

I would agree that Mary Shelley's original makes the monster sound marginally more sympathetic than he does in Percy Shelley's version; the monster is, indeed, as others have argued, 'more frightening than we had imagined precisely because he does not stumble or speak in monosyllables'.[104] Percy Shelley himself, moreover, may have shared this view, since the passage is something of an exception, his alterations to the monster's story being less frequent than those to Walton's or Frankenstein's narratives.

That Mary Shelley herself went on, in 1823 and 1831, to further elevate the novel's idiom, suggests that she admired and emulated Percy Shelley's high or formal style—which is partly why she accepted his revisions in the first place.[105] When Percy Shelley's revisions seek to clarify, when he repeatedly excises

[104] George Levine, in the preface to *Endurance*, p. xiii.

[105] For an account of the differences between the 1818 and 1831 revisions see *Frankenstein*, ed. Rieger, 230–59. The larger narrative changes made in the 1831 edn. are three in number: the presentation of Elizabeth as unrelated to Frankenstein, the dissociation of Frankenstein's father from science, and the decision to have Frankenstein journey alone to Chamounix. Each of these changes can be seen as an improvement, as in David Ketterer's *Frankenstein's Creation: The Book, The Monster, and Human Reality*, English Studies Monograph Series, 16 (Victoria, BC: University of Victoria Press, 1979), 110. *Frankenstein*, ed. Marilyn Butler, on the other hand, sees the changes as more significant, especially those involving Frankenstein's character. In 1831 Frankenstein 'is partly absolved from blame for his early errors . . . yet also reproaches himself more than in the first version' (p. 199); also, his links with materialist science are played down, and he's given 'an explicitly religious consciousness' (p. 200).

the indefinite 'this', or replaces dashes with colons or semicolons, or substitutes a subordinating 'which' for a co-ordinating
'that', Johanna Smith accuses him of 'imposing his order on
[Mary Shelley's] ideas', of seeking 'to control her text'.[106] But
what grounds are there for positing Mary Shelley's disapproval,
for thinking clarification was for her 'imposition'? Though one
can always argue that she grew more conservative with age—
was a different person—her later revisions suggest quite the
opposite: their aim, after all, as she declares in the 1831 introduction, was to mend faults of language 'so bald as to interfere
with the interest of the narrative' (p. 229)—that is, to mend
unclarities.

A second and related objection to Percy Shelley's revisions,
aside from the claim that they make the novel more stilted, is
that they distort Mary Shelley's meaning, both inadvertently, as
in the sort of stylistic 'improvements' we have been examining,
and with conscious intent. Here is another example in which it
is claimed that Percy's revisions make the monster more hideous—more monstrous—than he was in Mary Shelley's draft.
When Frankenstein destroys the monster's 'bride', the monster
withdraws in the holograph 'with a howl of devilish despair',
to which Percy Shelley adds 'and revenge'. Mellor objects to
this addition on the grounds that Percy is 'blunting our sympathy for the forever forsaken creature and destroying the author's more perceptive understanding'.[107] 'Blunting' perhaps
(though it is Mary who calls him 'devilish'), but 'destroying'?
Moreover, is 'author' quite the right word here? Again, the
voice we are listening to is Frankenstein's. Should we not see
this revision, too, as appropriate to the narrative, as an expression of the narrator's—that is, Frankenstein's—point of view?
Besides, what of Mellor's subsequent claim that although 'Mary
Shelley saw the creature as potentially monstrous . . . she never
suggested that he was other than fully human'?[108] How is this
possible given the holograph's stress—much noted by Mellor—
on the 'inhuman', 'unnatural', 'unspeakable' character of the
monster's creation? Part of the novel's power derives from the
monster's being both human *and* monstrous. 'I have written a

---

[106] *Frankenstein*, ed. Smith, 273.
[107] Mellor, *Mary Shelley*, 62.   [108] Ibid. 63.

book', she tells Leigh Hunt, in a letter of 6 April 1819, 'in
<favour> of Polypheme'[109]—that is, depicting the essentially
monstrous as worthy of human sympathy. Percy understood
this dual perspective as clearly as Mary, which is why he was
also, as Mellor herself points out, responsible for revisions which
stress the monster's generosity, as in Felix's bewilderment at
finding the creature's gifts: 'to his perpetual astonishment, he
found his store always replenished by an invisible hand' (p.
108), a revision which makes the DeLaceys all the more culpable in their subsequent horrified rejection of the monster.

Then there's the effect Percy Shelley's revisions have on
Frankenstein himself. Mellor thinks these flatten his character.
For example, in the original, Mary Shelley allows Frankenstein
to justify his obsessive behaviour as follows: 'I wished, as it
were, to procrastinate all that related to my feelings of affection, until the great object of my affections was completed.'
Percy Shelley then rewrites the passage (presumably to excise
the repeated 'affection'): 'I wished, as it were, to procrastinate
all that related to my feelings of affection until the great object,
which swallowed up every habit of my nature, should be completed' (p. 50). Mellor thinks this revision unsubtle: it 'removes
Mary's powerful dramatic irony: Frankenstein will of course
feel no affection whatsoever for his creature. Moreover, Mary's
calculated repetition underlined the degree to which Frankenstein
had substituted work for love.'[110] The lost irony Mellor laments
here seems to me heavy-handed, not worth the awkwardness;
the 'calculated' (how can she know?) repetition of 'affection' is
hardly necessary to suggest that Frankenstein is sublimating. It
could even be argued that the revision makes the passage more
not less subtle, as well as smoother. So also with what Mellor
sees as the loss of complexity in a subsequent passage, in which
Frankenstein paces the streets of Ingolstadt the morning after
the creature 'awakens' and flees. In Mary's original draft,
Frankenstein describes himself as looking 'as if I sought the
wretch whom I feared every turning of the street would present to
my view', which Mellor praises for its psychological complexity,
since it discloses 'the contradiction inherent in Frankenstein's

[109] Mary Shelley to Leigh Hunt, 6 Apr. 1819, in *Letters*, ed. Bennett, i. 91.
[110] Mellor, *Mary Shelley*, 63.

project (his desire to create what he did not wish to have)'.[111] When Percy Shelley inserts 'avoid' after 'sought', producing 'as if I sought to avoid the wretch whom I feared' (p. 540), she claims, the complexity is lost. But examination of the manuscript in the Bodleian suggests that the complexity Mellor finds in the original is her own rather than Mary Shelley's. In the original, what Mary Shelley actually wrote was 'as if I ~~ough~~ sought to the wretch'—that is, the presence of 'to' in the original suggests that Mary Shelley herself intended 'avoid', but simply forgot, perhaps because the '~~ough~~ sought' correction threw her off.

Mellor also accuses Percy Shelley of softening as well as simplifying Victor's characterization, of portraying him as victim rather than perpetrator (thus anticipating 'the same story that Percy Shelley would tell in *Adonais* of both Keats and himself at the hands of the critics'[112]). For example, she thinks it egotistical of Victor to assume that the monster will follow him to England, sparing his family and friends. When Percy persuades Mary to introduce doubts ('I was agonized by the possibility that the reverse of this might happen' (p. 151)), Mellor calls the addition 'disastrous', since it undercuts the novel's 'otherwise consistent portrayal of Frankenstein as an egotist who perceives only his own feelings and dangers'.[113] Once again, this strikes me as an oversimplification, and the revision, if anything, an improvement. Victor is egotistical, but he's not consistently egotistical. In the two sentences that precede Percy Shelley's 'disastrous' intervention, Victor claims to be 'haunted' with a feeling 'which filled me with fear and agitation'. This feeling is 'that I should leave my friends unconscious of the existence of their enemy, and unprotected from his attacks, exasperated as he might be by my departure' (p. 151). Are these sentences not an expression of concern for others?

As for Victor's confidence that the monster will follow him: 'he had promised to follow me wherever I might go; and would he not accompany me to England?' (p. 151). This question is authored by Mary, and already implies doubt; Percy's addition merely makes it more explicit—even as it underlines the complexity or subtlety of Victor's character, his capacity to be

---

[111] Ibid.   [112] Ibid. 69.   [113] Ibid. 67.

alternately egotistical and selfless. Again, Mellor herself provides evidence of Percy's awareness that Victor was perpetrator as well as victim. When Mary has the monster tell Frankenstein, 'I am thy Adam,' it is Percy who alters 'am' to 'ought to be', just as he later has the monster distinguish between the pain caused by Frankenstein and those 'who owe me nothing' (p. 95). Moreover, several changes between the rough draft and the printed version, apparently made by Mary (no fair copies exist), serve to soften Frankenstein and harden the monster; and, of course, this is true also of several of the 1831 revisions, as in her alteration of 1818's 'How is this . . . I thought I had moved your compassion and yet you still refuse to bestow on me the only benefit that can soften my heart' to 'How is this? I must not be trifled with: And I demand an answer.'

In other words, the specific instances of 'imposition' adduced by Mellor are neither as alien nor as damaging as she claims. Nowhere is this clearer than in her account of the novel's final sentence. The original manuscript ends with Walton's last vision of the monster: 'I soon lost sight of him in the darkness and distance.' The fair copy in the Abinger collection ends with a revised version in Percy Shelley's hand: 'he was soon borne away by the waves and lost in darkness and distance' (p. 221). Mellor calls Percy's revision 'a defensive maneuver to ward off anxiety and assert final authorial control over his wife's subversive creation',[114] but 'lost in darkness and distance' is hardly more final or comforting than 'lost sight of . . . in the darkness and distance'. Mellor accuses Percy of 'flatly asserting' that the monster is 'lost in darkness and distance', but the phrase is hardly unambiguous. It is as likely to mean, or to be read as, 'lost to sight' as 'lost to existence'. Again, if anything, the revision is more open-ended than the original. What such instances suggest is that Percy Shelley ought to be treated seriously when he claims to have been 'united' in purpose with Mary Shelley, describing her 'excellencies' in terms that make him feel like 'an egoist expatiating upon his own perfections'.[115] Such an admission may sound like 'narcissism', as Johanna Smith puts it, but the revisions themselves bear it out.

None of which is to deny that Mary Shelley is likely to have

---

[114] Ibid. 68.   [115] Quoted in Spark, *Mary Shelley*, 21.

felt dependent on Percy Shelley or was insecure about her style;
it is only to maintain that his revisions of *Frankenstein* may
have posed less of a test or threat than Mellor thinks. Even in
the rare instances when Mary Shelley defies—ignores? omits?—
her husband's alterations, it is not always easy to see why. As
the monster peers into Frankenstein's laboratory in Scotland,
his creator thinks, in the words of the original draft, that the
creature's 'countenance expressed the utmost extent of malice
and barbarity', a sentence Percy alters as follows: 'his countenance appeared to express the utmost extent of malice and
treachery'. In the published version, Mary drops the added doubt
(though 'treachery', as opposed to 'barbarity', stays) (p. 164).
Mellor may be right in thinking this omission consistent with
'Mary's idea of how Frankenstein interprets faces and the general role of physiognomy in the novel',[116] but such an idea is
neither more subtle than the conception of Frankenstein's character implied in Percy's revision nor consistent with the overall
depiction of Frankenstein's character. Frankenstein, after all, is
elsewhere capable of doubt, and doubt is an obvious compo-
nent of his torment. Here, as elsewhere, what the Shelleys are
weighing are questions of emphasis. Victor is both victim and
perpetrator, in Mary's original draft and Percy's revisions.

Mellor is more persuasive when she discusses Percy Shelley's
additions of a political or ideological nature. Left to herself,
Mary Shelley was quite capable of describing Frankenstein's
experiments as an offence to God, or of referring to 'Christian
lovers', a phrase Percy changes to 'youthful lovers' (p. 120).
The monster's destruction, she writes, 'is a task enjoined by
heaven'. It is Percy, one suspects, who feels compelled to add
the secular alternative: 'the mechanical impulse of some power
of which I was unconscious' (p. 202) (though, again, this way
of speaking is perfectly consonant with Frankenstein's scientific
character). In some instances, Mary, or Mary and Percy, caught
such discordances, so that on 'third' thought, as opposed to
second, they were eliminated, as in two extended additions to
the rough draft in which Percy aims clearly personal satirical
barbs at the pettiness of Oxford customs and ceremonies. Less
obtrusive, but still startling, are Percy's interpolated attacks on

[116] Mellor, *Mary Shelley*, 64.

hierarchical privilege, in the comparison of Swiss with English and French institutions (p. 60), and on the 'slow torturing manner' of the legal profession (p. 83). In both instances, the narrative is disturbed; one senses the presence of an alien voice. Even here, though, there remain questions. The attack on hierarchical privilege reads as follows:

The republican institutions of our country have produced simpler and happier manners than those which prevail in the great monarchies that surround it. Hence there is less distinction between the several classes of its inhabitants; and the lower orders, being neither so poor nor so despised, their manners are more refined and moral. A servant in Geneva does not mean the same thing as a servant in France and England. (p. 60)

Though Percy interpolated this passage, it may well owe something to an earlier letter Mary wrote from Lake Geneva, one published prior to *Frankenstein* in the *History of a Six Weeks' Tour Through a Part of France, Switzerland, Germany, and Holland* (1817). 'There is more equality of classes here than in England', writes Mary in the letter. 'This occasions a greater freedom and refinement of manners among the lower orders than we meet with in our own country. I fancy the haughty English ladies are greatly disgusted with the consequences of republican institutions.'[117] In the light of a passage like this, who is to say that Percy's interpolation was an imposition? The revision may introduce a discordant voice, but this voice may well be Mary's. As Carson suggests, 'in this and other additions to *Frankenstein*, Percy Shelley may be writing as he thinks his wife would (or should) write. What better way of writing like Mary Shelley than elaborating upon a passage from one of her own letters?'[118] How appropriate, moreover, that Percy 'borrow' from Mary in a passage that is meant to have been written by a woman, Elizabeth Lavenza, in a letter to her brother. Here, as elsewhere, the novel's revision 'enacts' its themes of mutuality and interdependence. Writing becomes a genuinely social activity, limitation is equably acknowledged, authorship becomes a less fraught—some would say a more humane—activity.

[117] Mary Shelley to Fanny Imlay, 1 June 1816, *Letters*, ed. Bennett, i. 21.
[118] Carson, 'Bringing the Author Forward: *Frankenstein* through Mary Shelley's Letters', 449.

CHAPTER FIVE

JOHN TAYLOR AND
THE POEMS OF CLARE

NOWHERE in the writing of the English Romantic period do questions of imposition figure more prominently than in the revision of the poems of John Clare, the work mostly of Clare's publisher, John Taylor. The current consensus on these revisions, shared both by Clare's modern editors and a number of his most influential critics, is that they importantly alter the poems, domesticate, smooth, diminish them. Hence, for example, the decision of Eric Robinson and David Powell, the editors of *The Early Poems of John Clare*, an Oxford English Texts edition of 1989, not only to print manuscript over published versions, relegating subsequent alterations, including those of first printed editions, to the apparatus, but to arrange the entirety of Clare's output of 1804–22, 'a huge mass of material that was excluded from the original books',[1] under the headings of his published volumes. This arrangement obscures the distinction between published and unpublished works (including obviously unworked scraps and fragments), presumably on the grounds that selection, like revision, was mostly Taylor's province not Clare's. Hence also the decision of Robinson and Geoffrey Summerfield in 1964 to reprint for 'the general reader' a manuscript edition, wholly unpunctuated and with only 'minimal alterations', of *The Shepherd's Calendar* (1827), the most radically revised of his works, an edition corrected and updated

---

[1] *The Early Poems of John Clare 1804–1822*, ed. Eric Robinson and David Powell, 2 vols. (Oxford: Clarendon Press, 1989), i. p. xxvii. The Oxford English Texts ed. of Clare's poems was inaugurated with *The Later Poems of John Clare 1837–1864*, also ed. Robinson and Powell, and first published in 1984. Four volumes of the middle poems are forthcoming. Though this chapter takes issue with some of the larger editorial principles underlying Robinson and Powell's editions, it is, like all work on Clare, deeply indebted to their painstaking scholarship and passionate advocacy, as it is to that of other champions of 'raw' or unedited Clare, including R. K. R. Thornton and the late Geoffrey Summerfield.

by Robinson and Powell in 1993.[2] A comparable rationale underlies Kelsey Thornton and Anne Tibble's 1979 edition of *The Midsummer Cushion*, a volume Clare planned in 1832, advertised, and hoped to publish himself through private subscription.[3] For a variety of reasons, *The Midsummer Cushion* never appeared in print (until 1979, that is), though a number of its poems were included in *The Rural Muse* (1835), a volume edited and arranged for the press by Clare's benefactress, Mrs Emmerson, with the assistance of Taylor. This volume, too, has been re-edited from the original manuscript, again by Thornton (1982).

As these and other examples suggest, when it comes to recent editions of Clare's texts, the bias is obvious and unembarrassed: earliest is best. 'At long last', declares Andrew Motion, scholarship has established Clare's 'authentic texts'.[4] But what is the nature of the evidence that Clare would have preferred manuscript versions of his early poems—unpunctuated, misspelled, ungrammatical, metrically defective, irregularly rhymed, poorly structured, repetitive—to the versions printed in the first two collections, *Poems Descriptive of Rural Life and Scenery* (1820) and *The Village Minstrel* (1821), or even *The Shepherd's Calendar*? After Taylor's 'slashing' (his word) of *The Shepherd's Calendar*, Clare still praised him, in a draft preface of 10

---

[2] John Clare, *The Shepherd's Calendar*, ed. Eric Robinson, Geoffrey Summerfield, and David Powell, 2nd edn. (1964; repr. Oxford: Oxford University Press, 1993), p. xxiv.

[3] John Clare, *The Midsummer Cushion*, ed. Anne Tibble and R. K. R. Thornton (Ashington: Mid-Northumberland Arts Group with Carcanet Press, 1979). Even while Clare sought to publish *The Midsummer Cushion* by private subscription he was also offering it to Taylor: 'I sent a printed sheet to Mr. Taylor wishing him to aid me with a few subscribers & telling him he should publish the book if he chose,' he tells Henry Francis Cary in a letter of 20 Oct. 1832, in *The Letters of John Clare*, ed. Mark Storey (Oxford: Clarendon Press, 1985), 595, 'but I have not heard a syllable from him of either disapproval or commendment.' (In accordance with Storey's editorial procedures, I have left spaces in the letters where, he conjectures, 'a sentence might be supposed to have ended', p. xxxiii.) Barbara Strang, in 'John Clare's Language', an appendix to Thornton's ed. of *The Rural Muse* (Ashington: Mid-Northumberland Arts Group with Carcanet Press, 1982), 159, thinks *The Midsummer Cushion* 'may have been intended to house all the work he wished to keep rather than what he thought a publisher might be able to publish'.

[4] Andrew Motion, 'Watchful Heart: The Poetics and Politics of John Clare', review of Hugh Haughton, Adam Phillips, and Geoffrey Summerfield (eds.), *John Clare in Context* (Cambridge: Cambridge University Press, 1994), in *Times Literary Supplement*, 8 July 1994, p. 5.

September 1826, as 'an early literary friend who first ushered my Poems into notice and still corrects them for publication to his critical abilitys I owe a great portion of my success and surely such deeds should not pass without acknowledgments'.[5] These words Taylor then cut, along with two-thirds of the draft preface.

Clare may not have approved all Taylor's revisions, but he expected his poems to be revised, or did so until the onset of madness. Though he might rail against the tyranny of fashion and, with Keats in mind, 'the cold hearted butchers of annonymous Critics',[6] he remained keen, for several reasons, to meet public expectations. To begin with, literary success offered the possibility of escape from arduous and ill-paid manual farm labour.[7] When Clare eventually lost his audience, the result was a return to the fields (to support what by 1837 had become a family of seven, plus aged parents)—and collapse. Chief among his delusions after this collapse was a belief that he was Lord Byron: the most popular poet of the age.[8] The poems he intended to publish, he intended to publish for a wide audience: 'Ambitious prospects fired his little soul,' he writes in the autobiographical poem, 'The Village Minstrel', 'And fancy soared and sung, 'bove poverty's control' (stanza 3). Though, like Taylor himself, he was perfectly aware of his poems' distinctive (that is, 'incorrect') strengths, he sought to balance or combine these strengths with whatever he could gather ('steal', it sometimes felt) from tradition—that is, from the polite or literary culture. This balance, I shall argue, was vital to the construction not just of a poetical but a personal identity; without it, his sense of self literally shattered. 'At different times you know I'm different people,' Clare told an asylum visitor, 'that is the same

---

[5] Quoted by Eric Robinson and Geoffrey Summerfield, 'John Taylor's Editing of Clare's *The Shepherd's Calendar*', *Review of English Studies*, 14/56 (1963), 359.

[6] John Clare to John Taylor, 5 May 1821, in *Letters*, ed. Storey, 188.

[7] As Elisabeth Helsinger points out, in 'John Clare and the Place of the Peasant Poet', *Critical Inquiry*, 13 (Spring 1987), 522, 'Unlike Marx (or his English contemporaries, Ruskin and Morris), Clare never, even in his most utopian moments, imagines that physical labor might be happiness, the natural expression of human capacities.'

[8] There were other reasons for Clare's identification with Byron. He was also, as John Lucas puts it, in *John Clare* (Plymouth: Northcote House, 1994), 64, a recent volume in the British Council's 'Writers and Their Work' series, 'the successful lover of a socially superior woman'. Clare, in contrast, was thwarted in his love of Mary Joyce, in part for class reasons.

person with different names.'[9] To fail as a public poet was to fail to contain these 'people'—the people he wished to be— within a single identity; or as John Lucas puts it, Clare's poems struggle with forces 'as much within him as without'.[10] Once Clare turned poet, he was, famously, a man caught between worlds (at the very time enclosure, on the one hand, was squeezing his class and community, and the public demand for poetry, on the other, seemed to have evaporated). The best of the early poems bridge or balance these worlds, forging an identity— Coleridge's *ego contemplatus*—neither Helpston, the 'gloomy' Northamptonshire village Clare was born in and loved, nor literary London, could sustain.[11]

Taylor played a vital role in the forging of this identity—at Clare's behest. 'I have been trying songs', he writes to Taylor on 11 May 1820, '& want your judgement only either to stop me or to set me off at full gallop . . . the rod of critiscism in your hand has as much power over your poor sinful rhymer as the rod of Aaron in the Land of Egypt.'[12] Five months later, after Taylor approves one of Clare's pastorals, off the poet gallops: 'you have clapt a spur to old Peggy [Pegasus]'.[13] Similar

---

[9] Cited in J. W. and Anne Tibble, *John Clare: A Life* (London: Michael Joseph, 1972), 373. Clare's remarks had been made to G. F. De Wilde, editor of the *Northampton Mercury*. De Wilde sometimes met Clare in Northampton, which the asylum allowed him to visit.

[10] John Lucas, 'Clare's Politics', in Haughton, Phillips, and Summerfield (eds.), *John Clare in Context*, 150. Dr Matthew Allen, who treated Clare at High Beech Asylum, marvelled that 'the moment that he gets pen or pencil in hand he begins to write most beautiful poetic effusions. Yet he has never been able to maintain in conversation, nor even in writing prose, the appearance of sanity for two minutes or two lines together, and yet there is no indication whatever of insanity in his poetry' (quoted in Roy Porter, ' "All Madness for Writing": John Clare and the Asylum', ibid. 264).

[11] It is Clare himself who calls Helpston 'gloomy', in 'Sketches in the Life of John Clare', repr. in *John Clare's Autobiographical Writings*, ed. Eric Robinson (Oxford: Oxford University Press, 1983), 1. The desire to combine Helpston and all it meant with London and the literary world is poignantly voiced in a letter of 8 Feb. 1822 to John Taylor, in *Letters*, ed. Storey, 230: 'I wish I livd nearer you at least I wish London w[oud] creep within 20 miles of helpstone I don't wish helpstone to shift its station   I live here among the ignorant like a lost man in fact like one whom the rest seem careless of having anything to do with—they hardly dare talk in my company for fear I shoud mention them in my writings & I find more pleasure in wandering the fields then in musing among my silent neighbours who are insensible to every thing but toiling & talking of it & that to no purpose.'

[12] John Clare to John Taylor, 11 May 1820, in *Letters*, ed. Storey, 64.

[13] John Clare to John Taylor, 3 Oct. 1820, ibid. 99.

comments occur throughout the letters: 'The fact is if I cannot
hear from John Taylor now & then I cannot ryhme';[14] 'I think
your taste & mine had I education woud be as like "as pin to
pin" ';[15] 'You will see agen that I agree in almost every particular of your alterations.' This last quote, from a letter of 17
February 1821, is followed, with easy trust, by the noting of a
possible exception:

The 'Milton Hunt' on a second thought I am loth to leave out [of *The
Village Minstrel*] but I always disliked the 4 last lines   what say you
to this proposal—suppose we repeat the 4 last lines of the first verse
agen 'The bugle sounds away, away' &c &c after '& scampers from
his plough' & cut 'The muse &c &c' out   I think it woud make a
good hunting Song then & free me of being fond of the barberous
sport   what think you—the alusion to Milton is what I wish to preserve but do as you please.[16]

It is Clare here who speaks unselfconsciously of what 'we' should
do, and elsewhere he is no less open and trusting:

Stone rockd waggon &c will do better than I coud have alterd it had
I tryd at it a month so take that likewise—tis a good thought—I am
rather sorry to loose this 'Grey girded eve & rosey wreathed morn'
but a line too much will not do & *morn of rosey hue* being far from
bad—take that also—& get on as fast as you can—& dont be nice
on trifles   I shall not disagree about altering a word or so if wanted
as necessary & if time be precious . . . we must as you justly observe
have it as free from faults as possible—write agen when you want to
know anything.[17]

As quotes like these suggest, Taylor was seen for the most part
(references to rods and slavery notwithstanding, especially since
Aaron's rod blossoms as well as scourges) as a valued collaborator, 'a friend that coud bring me before the public in the best
manner'.[18] Though in later years, the easy trust between poet
and publisher breaks down, it does so, as we shall see, at least
as much because Clare imposes upon his collaborator as because Taylor's revisions impose upon Clare.
   Clare was not the only poet of the period whose writing was

---

[14] John Clare to John Taylor, 14 Dec. 1820, ibid. 114.
[15] John Clare to John Taylor, 10 June 1820, ibid. 74.
[16] John Clare to John Taylor, 17 Feb. 1821, ibid. 154.
[17] John Clare to John Taylor, 13 Feb. 1821, ibid. 152.
[18] John Clare to John Taylor, 4 May 1820, ibid. 58.

importantly revised by a publisher—whose autonomy, that is, was called into question (as it would have been in past eras by a patron) by what Jerome McGann calls 'institutional affiliations'.[19] Though his reliance on Taylor was extreme, this extremity throws into relief revisionary relations and pressures experienced by most writers, or at least most writers who seek publication. Clare and Taylor belonged to a generation in which the patron, though still a presence, was finally supplanted by the publisher; yet the publisher's role, the degree of authority he was meant to exercise, was unclear. Hence Clare's weird insistence upon *Taylor's* independence, as when, at the beginning of their relation, he cautions him not to 'let some folks spoil your judgment by approving pieces which you have rejected', even when those pieces are the poet's favourites.[20] Hence also Taylor's several attempts to identify or demarcate roles, as when he announces 'my province qualifies me to cut out but not to introduce anything';[21] or his frequent requests that Clare himself become more actively engaged, as in 'I wish you would revise these Lines in particular, & see if you can mend any of them. . . . I have been in general dissatisfied with my Corrections, & may possibly restore many of the passages as they stood in the original, so freely express your opinion of all of them.'[22] When revision goes well for Taylor: 'I fancy you are at my Elbow prompting every Thought when I am correcting, and in fact I merely hold the Pen—thus it is that what I do to the Proofs is so like what you would have done that when done it hits your Ideas exactly.'[23]

To see Taylor as a mere oppressor or exploiter, as in Andrew Motion's clever conflation 'enclosing lands, banishing nomadic wanderers, planting hedges and putting in punctuation',[24] is not

[19] 'Institutional affiliation' is a phrase from Jerome McGann's *A Critique of Modern Textual Criticism* (Chicago: University of Chicago Press, 1983), 43. For a survey and excellent annotated bibliography of studies of the 'collaboration' of English and American poets and novelists with their publishers see Jack Stillinger, *Multiple Authorship and the Myth of Solitary Genius* (New York: Oxford University Press, 1991).
[20] John Clare to John Taylor, 11 May 1820, in *Letters*, ed. Storey, 67.
[21] John Taylor to John Clare, 29 Sept. 1820, quoted ibid. 98 n.
[22] John Taylor to John Clare, 23 Jan. 1821, ibid. 145.
[23] John Taylor to John Clare, 26 Mar. 1821, ibid. 171.
[24] Motion, 'Watchful Heart', 6. Rhetorical enclosure is a common trope in Clare criticism. See also Lucas, 'Clare's Politics', 347: 'The hundred years between 1750 and 1850 is the century of dictionaries, of grammatical rules, and of the standardizing

only to misunderstand the relation of publisher to poet but to misrepresent the man. Almost from the first, Taylor was distressed by the authority Clare ceded him, as well as by the problems his manuscripts posed. 'Have I altered these for the better?' he would ask.[25] 'Are these to be omitted also?'[26] He pleaded with Clare to correct or 'finish' his works before submitting them, and he frequently complained about having to revise them. 'If I could have found any one who would [have] taken the Editing off my Hands,' he wrote to Clare on 29 August 1821, just prior to publication of *The Village Minstrel*, 'I would gladly have given them 100£.'[27] Nor was Taylor's relation with Clare exclusively 'institutional', or passively market-driven. As Tim Chilcott, Taylor's biographer, points out: 'By helping several authors [Clare included] by loans and gifts of money, by continuing to encourage their efforts after critical attack [or falling sales, as in Clare's case], he had directly tried to wrest from the reading public some of its power of collective patronage.'[28] As for challenging the power of critical orthodoxy, of the most influential and aesthetically narrow Tory reviews in particular, this was precisely Taylor's aim in purchasing the *London Magazine* in 1821, the principal liberal rival to *Blackwood's Magazine* and the *Quarterly Review*.

The argument for unrevised versions rests not only on Romantic notions of poetic autonomy, of the poet as solitary genius—an ideal as central to the 'textual primitivism' of Clare's modern editors as to the fashion for 'uneducated' or 'peasant' poets in Clare's age—but on a no less Romantic undervaluing of secondary processes, including what the Coleridge chapter

of pronunciation. As I have elsewhere remarked this is, in short, the period when the language is being enclosed. Small wonder, then, that Taylor should have wished to revise Clare in order to bring him within the enclosed areas of official or orthodox English.'

[25] John Taylor to John Clare, 11 Feb. 1821, quoted in Tim Chilcott, *A Publisher and His Circle* (London: Routledge & Kegan Paul, 1972), 97. According to Johanne Clare, *John Clare and the Bounds of Circumstance* (Kingston: McGill-Queen's University Press, 1987), 118, 'only Tim Chilcott has argued that within the pressures of his time and place Taylor acted responsibly, tactfully, and in Clare's best interests', an argument, Johanne Clare continues, 'with which I find myself in complete agreement'.

[26] John Taylor to John Clare, 6 Jan. 1821, in *Letters*, ed. Storey, 135.

[27] John Taylor to John Clare, 29 Aug. 1821, quoted in Chilcott, *A Publisher and His Circle*, 97.   [28] Ibid. 209.

termed 'nomination', the decision to identify one's writing as finished, as a work. 'The poem, like all human utterances,' McGann reminds us, 'is a social act which locates a complex of related human ideas and attitudes. Unlike non-aesthetic utterance, however, poetry's social evaluations are offered to the reader *under the sign of completion.*' Completion or nomination, though, can take different forms. The author's intentions or purposes are variously codified, for example in 'choice of time, place, and form of publication—or none of the above, by which I mean his decision *not* to publish at all, or to circulate in manuscript, or to print privately'.[29] Unpublished versions of poems Clare chose to publish can hardly be more 'authentic' (as poems, that is) than published versions, provided Clare's choice to publish was free. Whether it was or not—to the extent that any choice can be—is a more complicated question than many of Clare's modern critics and editors admit. Though there are clear instances of censorship in the revision of Clare's poems, Clare was no merely passive victim, and Taylor no brute.[30] It is not the case, the chapter will argue, that unrevised or manuscript versions are the versions Clare would have wanted published.

CLARE AS REVISER

Clare was frank about his problems with revision. 'I always wrote my poems in great haste and generally finishd them at

[29] Jerome McGann, 'Keats and the Historical Method in Literary Criticism', in *The Beauty of Inflections: Literary Investigations in Historical Method and Theory* (Oxford: Clarendon Press, 1985), 21–3.
[30] Even when Clare seems most passive, when he offers no comment on Taylor's revisions, for example, that hardly means he is uninvolved. In Nov. 1820, Clare saw an advertisement for his second collection, *The Village Minstrel*, announcing that it was in press (it wasn't, the advertisement was intended merely to keep Clare's name in print). Clare immediately fired off a troubled letter to Hessey, complaining that he hadn't been sent proofs: 'I feel dissatisfied with Taylors proceedings & tho I alow his judgment to be correct in such matters yet he must know without my seeing the proofs he will not posses the universal taste to please me always. . . . nothing is more satisfying to an author then the perusal of his writings as they slowly proceed from the press to see that all pleases him.' Even, then, in the afterglow of the success of *Poems Descriptive*, Clare insists on approving or acceding to Taylor's alterations; insists, that is, on the collaborative nature of the revision process—as does Taylor, who neither here nor at any other time withheld proofs. See John Clare to James Hessey, 28 Nov. 1820, in *Letters*, ed. Storey, 107–8.

once, wether long or short,' he records in an autobiographical fragment (itself unaltered by Clare's modern editors, though reprinted in a volume intended for general readers), 'for if I did not they generaly were left unfinishd what corrections I made I always made them & never coud do any thing with them after wards'.[31] This claim (something of an exaggeration, the manuscripts reveal) is only in part an expression of principle, fashion, temperament; lack of education also plays its part. Clare's parents had little schooling: his mother was illiterate and his father only barely literate, though he could recite over a hundred ballads by heart. By the time he was 10, Clare's formal education was pretty much over, and he joined his father in casual farm labour, 'threshing in winter, tending, birdscaring and weeding in spring and summer'.[32] In 'Sketches in the Life of John Clare', a partial and unfinished autobiography drafted in 1821, Clare claims to have attended school up to the age of 11 or 12, though only for three months per year. At the age of 13, thanks to a young Helpston weaver who introduced him to James Thomson's *The Seasons*, he developed a passionate interest in poetry—in writing as well as reading it.[33] This was the extent of his early literary training.

As a consequence, a variety of elementary forms of polish or 'finish', obvious aspects of revision, were largely unavailable to Clare: he could not, for example, be relied upon to correct spelling, punctuation, or grammatical solecisms.[34] For all the

[31] *Autobiographical Writings*, ed. Robinson, 86. Sometimes the reluctance to revise seems a matter of principle, a thoroughly Romantic faith in spontaneity: e.g. in a letter of mid-1819 to Isaiah Knowles Holland, in *Letters*, ed. Storey, 12: ' "The Jewel of all" "To an April Daisy" & "The Winds" are the Productions of a Moment & as such are always the best in my Opinion.' Even in revision, spontaneous judgement is favoured by Clare. 'When I come to see your second thought admisions into the Vols [of *The Village Minstrel*] of what you first rejected,' Clare writes to Taylor, c.15 Mar. 1821, ibid. 166, 'I shall certainly see no improvement—as you tell me you often take them at last—I always consider your first omisions & alterations the most happy.' At other times, failure to revise seems to derive from a defensive laziness, as when Clare complains again to Holland in a subsequent mid-1819 letter, ibid. 13, that he 'would have corrected ['The Fate of Amy'] but repet[it]ions are irksome & tireing & I could not set my self to it'.
[32] Hugh Haughton and Adam Phillips, 'Introduction: Relocating John Clare', in Haughton, Phillips, and Summerfield (eds.), *Clare in Context*, 2.
[33] See *Autobiographical Writings*, ed. Robinson, 1–16.
[34] 'You make me laugh when you tell me to try to spell better,' Clare writes Markham E. Sherwill, 13 May 1820, in *Letters*, ed. Storey, 55–56: 'had you saw my first writings you might have hinted it then but I thought I was a fel hand at it now.'

bold variety of his poetical experimentation, formal irregularity or roughness, including off or false rhymes, is a frequent occurrence in his verse; yet even the most conservative of his reviewers —those, for example, who hammered Keats for his versification —make little fuss. Here was a poet, after all, who 'never saw a book on grammar before I was 20 or knew anything what ever of the proper construction of sentences'—handicaps Taylor was careful to emphasize in his introduction to *Poems Descriptive of Rural Life and Scenery*.[35] To criticize the finish of such poems, in the words of an unsigned notice of March 1820 in the *Monthly Magazine*, 'would be trying them by a poetical law from which they ought to be exempt'.[36]

Clare's struggles with grammar often infuriated him, as in the following exchange with Taylor concerning a problematic stanza in 'The Approach of Spring', a poem that first appeared in March 1822 in the *London Magazine* and then in *The Shepherd's Calendar*—in both cases minus the offending stanza. The stanza in question reads as follows:

> And, fairest Daughter of the year,
> Thrice welcome here anew;
> Tho' gentle Storms tis thine to fear
> The roughest blast has blew.

'I cannot mend this Verse, pray help me out with it,' announces Taylor in a letter of 18 February 1822. '*Blew* ought to be *Blown*.'[37] Clare's frustrated response is to call the stanza 'a develish puzzle I may alter but I cannot mend grammer in learning is like Tyranny in government—confound the bitch Ill never be her slave & have a vast good mind not to alter the verse in question—by g-d Ive tried an hour & cannot do a syllable so do your best or let it pass.' Clare then offers an alternative version, which he rightly declares 'd——d lame' (it ends, 'Tho gentle storms 'tis thine to fear | The worst has bade adieu'), and Taylor, no less rightly, ignores it. Here and elsewhere, Clare's exasperation never quite modulates into genuine defiance or revolt; defective grammar is no matter of principle

[35] *Autobiographical Writings*, ed. Robinson, 90–1. Taylor's introduction to *Poems Descriptive* is reprinted in Mark Storey (ed.), *Clare: The Critical Heritage* (London: Routledge & Kegan Paul, 1973), 43–54.   [36] Ibid.
[37] John Taylor to John Clare, 18 Feb. 1822, in *Letters*, ed. Storey, 231 n.

for him, like post-structuralist defiance of 'the tyranny of clarity'.[38]

[38] John Clare to John Taylor, 21 Feb. 1822, ibid. 231. See also Clare to Eliza Emmerson, 21 Dec. 1829, ibid. 491: 'I am gennerally understood tho I do not use that awkard squad of pointings called commas colons semicolons &c & for the very reason that altho they are drilled <daily> hourly daily & weekly by every boarding school Miss who pretends to gossip in correspondence they do not know their proper exercise for they even set gramarians at loggerheads & no one can assign them their proper places for give each a sentence to point & both shall differ—point it differently.' A comparable sense of the false pretensions of grammar as a system, and the exaggerated claims made for correctness (i.e. that without it one could not be understood), is found in the autobiographical 'Sketches': 'stumbling on a remark that a person who knew nothing of grammer was not capable of writing a letter nor even a bill of parcels, I was quite in the suds, seeing that I had gone on thus far without learning the first rudiments of doing it properly for I had hardly hard the name of grammer while at school—but as I had an itch for trying at every thing I got hold of I determ[i]ned to try grammer, and for that purpose, by the advice of a friend, bought the "Universal Spelling Book" as the most easy assistant for my starting out, but finding a jumble of words classd under this name and that name and this such a figure of speech and that another hard worded figure I turned from further notice of it in instant disgust for as I knew I coud talk to be understood I thought by the same method my writing might be made out as easy and as proper, so in the teeth of grammer I pursued my literary journey as warm as usual' (*Autobiographical Writings*, ed. Robinson, 15).

In a note in praise of William Cobbett's popular grammar, entitled *A Grammar of the English Language in a Series of Letters Intended for the Use of Schools and of Young Persons in general: but, more especially for the Use of Soldiers, Sailors, Apprentices, and Plough-boys* (London, 1819), Clare again opposes over-systematization. Grammatical scrupulosity is oppressive as well as useless and a distraction, he argues: 'it will only serve to puzzle and mislead to awe and intimidate instead of aiding and encouraging . . . therefore it pays nothing for the study. . . . A man who learns enough of grammer to write sufficiently plain so as to be understood by others as well as to understand his own consceptions himself and trys out the way to make his consceptions correct thinkings rather than the correct placing of particles and stops and other trifling with which every writer on grammar seems to be at loggerheads about with each other—such an attainment will get the possessor an enlightened and liberal mind and if he attain not with this broad principle an excellence in composition the niceties of intricate Lectures on grammer with its utmost perfection will not attain it for him' (repr. in Eric Robinson and David Powell (eds.), *John Clare*, in the Oxford Authors series (Oxford: Oxford University Press, 1984), 481. The mixture here of common sense and wounded defensiveness is characteristic, as is the stress on comprehensibility. Were someone—Taylor, for instance—to justify grammar and punctuation on grounds of increased clarity, Clare would not object.

According to Johanne Clare, *John Clare and the Bounds of Circumstance*, 120, 'because Clare's refusal [to learn correct grammatical forms] was expressed in military and political metaphors (punctuation as a drill-master, grammar as tyranny), it is inviting to suppose that his grammatical errors represented a gesture of solidarity with the uneducated, disenfranchised, working class and an act of resistance to the grammatical standards and cultural hegemony of the "genteel race." But the wilfulness of Clare's refusal was the wilfulness not of principle but of

Distortion alone can make an exchange like this 'imposition'; but this is what it has become. Here is how Tom Paulin reconstructs the exchange in an essay entitled 'John Clare in Babylon' (1992), itself a reworked *TLS* review of 1986 (of Mark Storey's edition of Clare's *Letters*): 'Taylor edits, shapes and sometimes rewrites Clare's poems, sends them back, and Clare replies, "your verse is a develish puzzle I may alter but I cannot mend grammer in learning is like Tyranny in government".'[39] Paulin's essay offers no indication that 'your verse' in the original context means 'that verse of mine you single out'. The reader is left with the false impression that Taylor has rewritten the verse, and that Clare's exasperation is with editorial meddling, as opposed to grammatical complication. Presumably, Paulin would justify his procedures on the grounds that elsewhere Taylor edits, shapes, and rewrites, and that Clare had been known to protest; or that Taylor is, after all, 'interfering', by alerting Clare to a grammatical solecism ('the blast has blew'). But Clare's protests, as it happens, were less frequent than most critics suggest, as were Taylor's impositions. Moreover, would Paulin have preferred Taylor not to interfere? Would Taylor have been doing Clare a favour by publishing 'the blast has blew'?

Lack of education only partly explains Clare's inability or disinclination to revise. Clare's initial impulse to write derived

indifference. He intended nothing by his grammatical errors. He simply made them because he had not bothered to follow the sort of regimen in grammatical self-improvement which Cobbett had advised.' For a recent and detailed expression of the contrary (and majority) view see James McKusick, 'John Clare and the Tyranny of Grammar', *Studies in Romanticism*, 33 (Summer 1994), 262–3: 'Far from being ignorant of grammar and spelling, Clare possessed a fairly good knowledge of the standard authorities and could conform to their prescribed usage when it suited him. Despite his knowledge of these authorities, however, his poetic language actually became *less* conventional over the course of his career, while he became more stubbornly resistant to the attempts of Taylor and others to correct his poems. . . . Ultimately . . . he rejected the prevailing linguistic norm, with its emphasis upon the standards of written language, in favor of a more radical tradition of linguistic theory that advocated the expressive potential of local vernacular speech.' That Clare could be 'correct' if he wanted to, and was familiar with important and rival grammatical and lexical guides and theories, McKusick's essay makes clear; that his grammatical mistakes and misspellings were political, an expression of conscious resistance, as opposed to what Johanne Clare calls 'indifference' (also fatigue, growing anxiety, unsettledness) is not clear at all.

[39] Tom Paulin, 'John Clare in Babylon', in *Minotaur: Poetry and the Nation State* (London: Faber & Faber, 1992), 53.

'from down right pleasure in giving vent to my feelings. . . . I pursued pleasure in many paths & never found her so happily as when I sung imaganery songs to the woodland solitudes & winds of autumn.' At first these 'songs' were little more than inarticulate murmurings or exclamations of feeling. As Clare explains in 'The Dawnings of Genius', a poem from the first collection, the uneducated poet

> . . . feels enraptur'd though he knows not why;
> And hums and mutters o'er his joys in vain,
> And dwells on something which he can't explain.
> The bursts of thought, with which his soul's perplex'd,
> Are bred one moment, and are gone the next;
> Yet still the heart will kindling sparks retain,
> And thoughts will rise, and Fancy strive again.

Clare struggled to put such thoughts in writing in order 'to understand them myself', and thus preserve them, a process he found 'long & pleasing painful'. For almost ten years, the only audience for his poems was his parents. Getting the poems published, he claimed, somewhat disingenuously, was an 'accident'; when they were noticed by the critics, he was 'astonished'.[40] Like Byron, then, Clare liked to think of writing as expression or process rather than communication or product. That *he* should take pleasure from what he had written was Clare's first imperative; initially, the outside audience, even the immediate Helpston audience, was an afterthought. Though he subsequently longed for public acclaim, his initial habits of composition were inward-looking. 'No matter how the world approved,' he later declared, in 'The Progress of Rhyme' (or 'Ryhme', as his modern editors insist), an autobiographical poem from the unpublished *Midsummer Cushion*, 'Twas nature listened I that loved | No matter how the lyre was strung | From my own heart the music sprung' (ll. 207–9).[41]

---

[40] See *Autobiographical Writings*, ed. Robinson, 85. In 1814 Clare began preserving his poems in a notebook purchased at Market Deeping. In 1817 he set out to find an audience for his poems, drawing up and having printed a proposal for publishing them by subscription. It is this proposal, partially repr. in Storey (ed.), *Critical Heritage*, 30, which Edward Drury, the Stamford bookseller, saw and drew to his cousin John Taylor's attention in 1818.

[41] See John Clare, *The Midsummer Cushion*, ed. Tibble and Thornton, 228. Inconveniently, neither Tibble and Thornton's edn. of *The Midsummer Cushion* nor Thornton's edn. of *The Rural Muse* have line numbers. The poem is printed, with line numbers, in Robinson and Powell (eds.), *John Clare*, 158.

Clare's 'nature', like his experience of rural life in general, not only lay outside literature ('the world', in 'The Progress of Rhyme'), with its pastoral and other traditions, but could be thought of as threatened by it; as it could also be thought of as threatened by more elementary conventions of written discourse. That Clare himself sometimes feared a falsifying normalization or finish, for example, in addition to the falsifications of pastoral tradition, can be seen in his struggles with punctuation: the earliest attempts to revise or polish manuscripts sometimes involved manic overpunctuation; in later years Clare barely punctuated at all, in prose or verse. To some modern editors, this later indifference signals maturity and confidence,[42] recognition of the constitutive role of his writing's 'irregularity', of the odd-sounding need, voiced in 1832, 'to stand upon my own bottom as a poet without any apology as to want of education or any thing else'.[43] But it could also signal gathering isolation, a retreat to mere expression, to another, more damaging mania.[44]

The shift away from punctuation was accompanied by what could be seen as a comparably regressive deterioration in handwriting. Part of Taylor's reluctance to get to work on the poems of *The Shepherd's Calendar* derives from the sheer difficulty of deciphering Clare's hand. As early as 1823, Taylor's partner James Hessey complained to Clare that he would enjoy his poems much more 'if you would bestow a little more pains on the writing, the mechanical operation of writing I mean'.[45] By 1826, Taylor himself was thoroughly exasperated:

Look at the Vol. of MS. Poems which I now send you, and show it where you will, & let any of your Friends say whether they can even read it.—I can find *no one* here who can perform the Task besides

[42] *Early Poems*, ed. Robinson and Powell, i. p. xxiii.

[43] John Clare to Eliza Emmerson, 13 Nov. 1832, in *Letters*, ed. Storey, 604. See also an earlier letter of 20 Oct. 1832 to Henry Francis Cary, ibid. 594: 'I wished to be judged of by the book itself [*The Midsummer Cushion*] without any appeals to want of education lowness of origin or any other foil that officiousness chuses to encumber my path with.'

[44] See James McKusick's suggestion, in 'Beyond the Visionary Company: John Clare's Resistance to Romanticism', in Haughton, Phillips, and Summerfield (eds.), *Clare in Context*, 229, that 'as Clare and Taylor developed a good working relationship, Clare ceased to attempt to punctuate his poems and eventually relegated all responsibility for accidentals to Taylor'.

[45] James Hessey to John Clare, 13 Oct. 1823, Egerton 2246, fo. 245ᵛ; the manuscript in question is Peterborough MS A30. The relevant portion of Hessey's letter is repr. in Storey (ed.), *Critical Heritage*, 194.

myself. Copying it therefore is a Farce for not three words in a line on the average are put down right, & the number omitted, by those whom I have got to transcribe it, are so great, that it is easier for me at once to sit down & write it fairly out myself.[46]

What the gathering obscurity of Clare's handwriting may recall is a central theme in his life and work: fear of exposure, precisely the fear, it has been argued, that lies at the heart of Clare's loathing of enclosure. When Clare first began writing, he tried to conceal his authorship not only from his employers, whose time he, as it were, 'stole', but from friends and parents as well, pretending, by what Hugh Haughton and Adam Phillips call 'a strategy of inverse plagiarism',[47] that his poetry was copied 'out of a borrowed book and that it was not my own'.[48] Once he began publishing, the fact that only Taylor could decipher his manuscripts meant the poems were temporarily safe from public view (just as he hoped they would be in the asylum years, when he sometimes wrote in private shorthand); no one would see them until they had been thoroughly, protectively tidied, in the process muting, through Taylor's participation, the transgressive associations writing always had for Clare, associations inevitable in a writer of Clare's •background.[49] Taylor, wrote Clare in 1820, 'is a kind of screne between me and the world—a sort of hiding place for me in the hour of danger'.[50] This hour, metaphorically, is the moment the writer must expose himself or herself to the world.

LANGUAGE

Chief among the charges against Taylor is 'his failure to appreciate the nuances of Clare's use of dialect'.[51] By substituting literary for provincial terms, Taylor robs Clare of a crucial

---

[46] John Taylor to John Clare, 28 Jan. 1826, in *Letters*, ed. Storey, 357.

[47] Haughton and Phillips, 'Introduction: Relocating John Clare', 3. For Clare's sense of stealing from his employers see Phillips, 'The Exposure of John Clare', in Haughton, Phillips, and Summerfield (eds.), *Clare in Context*, 182.

[48] *Autobiographical Writings*, ed. Robinson, 12.

[49] For the connection between writing and transgression see John Goodridge and Kelsey Thornton, 'John Clare: The Trespasser', in Haughton, Phillips, and Summerfield, *Clare in Context*, 130–47.

[50] John Clare to James Hessey, 29 June 1820, in *Letters*, ed. Storey, 78.

[51] Robinson and Summerfield, 'Taylor's Editing of Clare', 360.

strength. In fact, though, Taylor was perfectly aware of this strength, and took pains to defend it. 'Some of his friends object, in my opinion most unreasonably, to his choice of words,' writes Taylor, in 'A Visit to John Clare', published in the November 1821 edition of the *London Magazine*:

one wishes that he would *thresh* and not *thump* the corn, another does not like his eliding the first syllable of some of his words. . . . But in reality, Clare is highly commendable for not *affecting* a language, and it is a proof of the originality of his genius. . . . In poetry, especially, you may estimate the originality of the thoughts by that of the language; but this is a canon to which our approved critics will not subscribe; they allow of no phrase which has not received the sanction of authority, no expression for which, in the sense used, you cannot plead a precedent.[52]

The question of 'precedent' raises in turn one of metropolitan bias, a question Taylor addresses directly, both here and in his introduction to the first collection. Though 'new' or unfamiliar, he writes in the introduction, 'a very great number' of Clare's words

are, in fact, some of the oldest in our language: many of them are extant in the work of our earliest authors; and a still greater number float on the popular voice, preserved only by tradition . . . many of them [are] as well-sounding and significant, as any that are sanctioned by the press. In the midland counties they are readily understood without a glossary.[53]

Words such as 'arrivance', 'pismire', and 'puddock', as Barbara Strang has pointed out, are found in Shakespeare as well as Clare's Northamptonshire; 'rime' and 'hurd' 'had earlier been literary and by Clare's time were dialectal'.[54] Taylor's policy for the first collection, accordingly, was to print the poems 'with the usual corrections only of orthography and grammar, in such instances as allowed of its being done without changing the words: the proofs were then revised by CLARE, and a few

---

[52] The *London Magazine* article is repr. in Storey (ed.), *Critical Heritage*, 161. Among the 'friends' who objected to Clare's choice of words was Charles Lamb, writing to Clare on 31 Aug. 1822, to inform him that 'in poetry slang of every kind is to be avoided. There is a rustic Cockneyism as little pleasing as ours of London' (repr. ibid. 175).   [53] Ibid. 48.
[54] Barbara Strang, 'John Clare's Language', app. 1 of *The Rural Muse*, ed. R. K. R. Thornton, 165.

alterations were made at his desire. The original MSS. may be seen at Messrs. Taylor and Hessey's.' He also included a brief glossary of dialect words 'not found in Johnson's Dictionary'.[55] These are not the procedures of a high-handed, unfeeling editor.

Taylor respected other aspects of Clare's individuality aside from his use of regionalisms. He writes with admirable sympathy and understanding of the strengths of Clare's irregular grammar as well: 'in this respect CLARE's deficiencies are the cause of many beauties—for though he must, of course, innovate, that he may succeed in his purpose, yet he does it according to that rational mode of procedure, by which all languages have been formed and perfected'. When Clare uses verbs as substantives ('Dark and darker *glooms* the sky') or adjectives as verbs ('Spring's pencil *pinks* thee in thy flushy stain'), comments Taylor, 'he has done no more than the man who first employed *crimson* as a verb: and as we had no word that would in such brief compass supply so clearly the sense of this, he was justified no doubt in taking it'. Even when Clare's irregularities serve no immediately discernible purpose, they rarely 'give any real embarrassment to the reader'. When Clare renders the proverbial 'Autumn of Life', as 'Autumn's Life', in the line 'Just so 'twill fare with me in Autumn's Life', 'who can doubt the sense'?[56] When a word or construction might cause embarrassment, though, it is quietly, tactfully altered: 'In the next line I would say *boundless* as you propose, and "Immensity" is a fitter and more legitimate Word than "Stupendity".'[57]

Taylor, then, was no slave to correctness; he valued clarity. He was a classicist (self-taught) and widely read, but he rarely confused learning with poetical power. 'Education never *made* a Poet', he writes Clare in 1821, 'though it may help a Man much who is one. I wish we had fewer of these fellows who dress themselves up as the Sons of Apollo, and by the dint of Words and the Repetition of certain Greek and Latin Lines, gain possession of the Poet's Fame to the Exclusion of the rightful Heir.'[58] Taylor's sonnet 'On Simplicity' begins with similar sentiments:

---

[55] Storey (ed.), *Critical Heritage*, 53, 48.   [56] Ibid. 47.

[57] John Taylor to John Clare, 26 Mar. 1821, in *Letters*, ed. Storey 171.

[58] John Taylor to John Clare, 26 Mar. 1821, ibid. 172. See also Taylor to Clare, 1 Jan. 1821, ibid. 130: 'If he [Clare] has a soul of native Fancies, Let him study

> Simplicity is strength; whether display'd
> In Language, or by the creative aid
>   Of Colour, or when Sounds melodious run
>   Their changes.

This sonnet, though mostly unremarkable, ends with a fine performative anti-flourish:

> List the Lyre of earliest Times, or how the Winds inspire
> One only String;—and think how deadly ran
> These words in David's Ear 'Thou art the Man'.

The concluding phrase, spoken by the prophet Nathan, reveals David's guilt to him, writes Chilcott, 'in four words of monosyllabic directness, without concessive clauses or the slightest modification of a complete accusation'.[59]

Taylor's handling of punctuation—his punctuating at all, in fact—has been as frequently and unfairly criticized as his supposed insensitivity to dialect. Taylor punctuates Clare's poems for ease of reading, not out of unconscious political or class-based hostility, an accusation derived in part from an analogy with enclosure—that is, the conflation of rhetoric and land economy. When Clare describes the unbounded character of pre-enclosure landscapes, the absence of punctuation in unrevised versions yields obvious advantages, as in the opening of the manuscript version of 'The Mores', as reprinted by Robinson and Powell in the Oxford Authors *Clare*:

> Far spread the moorey ground a level scene
> Bespread with rush and one eternal green
> That never felt the rage of blundering plough
> Though centurys wreathed springs blossoms on its brow
> Still meeting plains that stretched them far away   5
> In uncheckt shadows of green brown and grey
> Unbounded freedom ruled the wandering scene
> Nor fence of ownership crept in between
> To hide the prospect of the following eye

to express what it dictates in that Language it will bring with it; then he will write like himself & no one else: if he has not that innate Poesy he may write clever Poems like many others who are called Poets, but he will have no just claim to the Title.'

[59] Chilcott, *A Publisher and His Circle*, 88. Chilcott reprints Taylor's sonnet on the same page.

Its only bondage was the circling sky   10
One mighty flat undwarfed by bush and tree
Spread its faint shadow of immensity
And lost itself which seemed to eke its bounds
In the blue mist the orisons edge surrounds.

The temporary confusions occasioned here by lack of punctuation hardly outweigh performative benefits, as in, for example,
the absence of a full-stop at the end of line 6, or a semicolon
at the end of line 7, or a comma after 'itself' in line 13—all of
which, along with grammatical and other corrections, are to be
found in a revised and retitled version in J. W. and Anne Tibble's
1965 Everyman *Selected Poems*.[60] Clare might still prefer a
revised version to one without punctuation, but the unpunctuated or manuscript version neatly complements, or enacts, the
unbounded, fenceless, self-obliterating qualities the lines in
question mean to evoke.[61]

Elsewhere, lack of punctuation is harder to defend. Consider
the following minor but representative instance from 'The Nightingale's Nest', in Kelsey Thornton's primitivist edition of *The
Rural Muse*: 'How curious is the nest no other bird | Uses such
loose materials or weaves | Their dwellings in such spots.' The
absence of punctuation after 'nest' in the first line is momentarily

---

[60] For the manuscript version of 'The Mores' see Robinson and Powell (eds.),
John Clare, 167. The edited version by J. W. and Anne Tibble, entitled 'Enclosure',
is repr. in their Everyman ed. *John Clare: Selected Poems* (London: Dent, 1965),
114, which is itself a selection based on the texts of *The Poems of John Clare*, ed.
J. W. Tibble, 2 vols. (London: Dent, 1935), an edition Johanne Clare, in *John Clare
and the Bounds of Circumstance*, 196, pronounces 'not quite as poisonously unreliable as has been supposed'.

[61] Lack of punctuation is performative in other ways as well. When Clare describes 'The stepping stones that stride the meadow streams', in a sonnet entitled
'Stepping Stones', from *The Midsummer Cushion*, ed. Tibble and Thornton, absence of punctuation neatly enacts the precariousnesss with which 'the traveller
with a wary pace' attempts the crossing (p. 414); when the unbounded energies of
a storm are being described, as e.g. in 'November', in *The Shepherd's Calendar* (ll.
73–81 in the MS version, p. 90 in the published or 1827 version), disorder or
mobility is what one wants. As Timothy Brownlaw puts it: 'To compare the published version of 1827, "improved" by John Taylor, with [the] 1964 version, edited
from manuscripts by Robinson and Summerfield, is to compare a set piece prepared
for an Academy exhibition in contrast to an original sketch; more presentable,
perhaps, but less inspired' (*John Clare and Picturesque Landscape* (Oxford:
Clarendon Press, 1983) 92). Obviously, if Clare never punctuates his poems there
are bound to be moments—like these—in which readerly uncertainty yields performative benefits.

distracting, more so than in the three cases singled out from the opening lines of 'The Mores'. Is such distraction fruitful, appropriate, necessary, a desired consequence, as in 'The Mores', of what Hugh Haughton calls Clare's 'open field' poetics?[62] Are we to imagine Clare himself intended any enhancing or performative doubt about the pause after 'nest'? In this instance, as in many others (Strang seems to me perverse to claim that syntactic ambiguities 'are rarer in Clare than in most orthodox poets'[63]), one doubts it, as one also doubts the superiority of 'Their' to a grammatical 'Its' in the third line, 'dwellings' notwithstanding. Clare, here, is not considering his audience: *he* knows when to pause; *he* isn't troubled by lack of agreement. The published or 1835 version reads 'How curious is the nest! no other bird | Uses such loose materials, or weaves | Its dwelling in such spots.' What is lost here except one's awareness of Clare as 'peasant' poet, the very identity his supporters accuse Taylor of exploiting? The revision is a straightforward and representative improvement.

In other instances, grammatical irregularity and lack of punctuation produce more serious—that is, more than merely distracting—ambiguities. Consider the opening lines of 'The Maple Tree', a late sonnet:

> The Maple with its tassel flowers of green
> That turns to red a stag horn shaped seed
> Just spreading out its scallopped leaves is seen
> Of yellowish hue yet beautifully green

Douglas Chambers calls this sonnet 'more complex than anything in Keats', and points to several fine effects in subsequent lines. But the complexity of the opening lines seems to me indistinguishable from confusion. Chambers argues that ' "Just spreading out . . . is seen" has the gerundive ambiguity for which Keats's "darkling I listen" is more famous, and . . . serves to unify blossom, fruit and leaf in a metamorphic image that confuses the order of the seasons in order to present the wholeness of the

---

[62] Hugh Haughton, 'Progress and Rhyme: "The Nightingale's Nest" and Romantic Poetry', in Haughton, Phillips, and Summerfield (eds.), *Clare in Context*, 52.
[63] The statement only makes sense if Strang rules out ambiguities produced by lack of punctuation; Clare's syntax is otherwise, of course, a good deal simpler than that of most poets. See Strang, 'John Clare's Language', 161.

tree.'[64] Perhaps, but Clare's more characteristic complexity is tonal, the objects and processes he describes are rarely puzzling and uncertain in this way, at least in the poems of his sanity. Here and elsewhere in manuscript poems, the difficulty one encounters may be unintentional or inadvertent, of a sort Clare was perfectly prepared—sought—to have drawn to his attention for revision, usually by Taylor. Nowhere in his writings does Clare champion indirection or ambiguity, as does, say, Blake, when he asserts that 'that which can be made explicit to the Idiot is not worth my care'.[65] On the contrary, Clare favours simplicity or 'naturalness'.

This bias explains why, as he recalls in the 1821 autobiographical 'Sketches', Clare so valued the responses of his unlettered parents to his poems: 'their remarks was very useful to me . . . some verse they woud desire me to repeat again as they said they coud not understand them here I discoverd obscurity from common sense and always benefited by making it as much like the latter as I coud, for I thought if they coud not understand me my taste shoud be wrong founded and not agreeable to nature'.[66] Presumably, the premium Clare places in this passage on comprehensibility would have applied also if his parents were literate—and thus encountered his poems, as do today's readers, without punctuation, the print equivalent of vocal 'pointing'. As Keats comments to his brother and sister-in-law, 'writing has this disadvan[ta]ge of speaking, one cannot write a wink or a nod, or a purse of the Lips, or a *smile—O law!* One can[not] put one's finger to one's nose, or yerk ye in the ribs, or lay hold of your button in writing.'[67] The modern taste for 'difficulty', in other words, which partly explains the fashion for uncorrected or manuscript versions, was no taste of Clare's.

---

[64] Douglas Chambers, ' "A Love for Every Simple Weed": Clare, Botany and the Poetic Language of Lost Eden', in Haughton, Phillips, and Summerfield (eds.), *Clare in Context*, 252, 253. 'The Maple Tree' is printed in *Later Poems*, ed. Robinson and Powell, ii. 1025.

[65] William Blake to Dr J. Trusler, 25 Aug. 1799, in *The Letters of William Blake*, ed. Geoffrey Keynes (London: Rupert Hart-Davis, 1956), 35.

[66] *Autobiographical Writings*, ed. Robinson, 12.

[67] John Keats to George and Georgiana Keats, 20 Sept. 1819, in *The Letters of John Keats 1814–1821*, ed. Hyder Rollins, 2 vols. (Cambridge, Mass.: Harvard University Press, 1958), ii. 205.

The question of Taylor's role in the promotion of Clare as 'peasant' is worth considering in this context. 'He was having trouble keeping Clare to his role,' writes Lucas of Taylor's relations with Clare in 1821.

He insisted that Clare's projected title for the volume [*Ways of a Village*] be changed to *The Village Minstrel*. This gave off the necessary aroma. The echo of Beattie's *The Minstrel*, that sentimental tale of the inspired bard, reinforced Clare's place in the tradition of the native genius to which reviewers and admiring readers had, with the help of Taylor's revisions, assigned him.[68]

This is unfair. Clare's original idea, enthusiastically seconded by Taylor, was, indeed, to write a volume of poems entitled 'Ways of a Village' (sometimes 'Week in a Village'). One of its poems, 'The Peasant Boy' (Clare's title), so impressed Taylor that it made him 'alter my Mind about the Title: we must put this poem first and call it I think The Village Minstrel; and the title will then run The Village Minstrel, & other Poems, By JC. &c.'[69]

Taylor's first act of 'exploitation', then, was to prefer 'The Village Minstrel' as a title to 'The Peasant Boy', not on the face of it an especially radical change; his second was, in his enthusiasm, to suggest it as a title for the whole volume. In fact, though ('we must' notwithstanding), Taylor was thoroughly aware of his proposed title's derivative and diminishing associations, of its 'aroma', worrying over them and soliciting alternatives from Clare. When Clare suggests 'Village Minstrelsy' as an alternative, retaining 'The Village Minstrel' for 'The Peasant Boy', Taylor comments:

'Village Minstrelsy' is not free from the same Charge which comes against the other Titles. It is too like 'English Minstrelsy'—a Compilation of Walter Scott's which did not sell, & that is another bad sign. I have preferred your old Title The Peasant Boy after duly Considering all Circumstances.—For some time I thought favourably of 'The Village Minstrel'—and also 'The Village Muse' but unless you recommend either of them I cannot trust to adopting either.[70]

---

[68] John Lucas, 'Revising Clare', in Robert Brinkley and Keith Hanley (eds.), *Romantic Revisions* (Cambridge: Cambridge University Press, 1992) 345.
[69] John Taylor to John Clare, 6 Jan. 1821, in *Letters*, ed. Storey, 135.
[70] John Taylor to John Clare, 10 Feb. 1821, ibid. 148.

This sort of uncertainty persists, right up to the final decision, an exhausted reversion to 'The Village Minstrel'. 'Insistence' is hardly the word to describe it. Nor is there any question of Taylor's having trouble 'keeping Clare in his role as peasant poet', a role Clare, if anything, was more anxious to advertise than Taylor. 'I have had my dose of "Village Minstrelsy",' is how Clare responds to Taylor's titular suggestions: 'would not sell is plenty to abandon anything of that nature so I am content but "Minstrel Villager" & "Village Muse" are very poor & very bad—the "Peasant Boy" is but middling while your "Village Minstrel" still sticks in my memory as best of all'.[71] It was Clare himself, in other words, not Taylor, who finally settled on the work's title.

Taylor's revision of Clare's spelling has also been controversial. Some of what we take to be Clare's misspellings are perfectly proper by eighteenth-century standards (Barbara Strang points to 'extasy' as a common example). Others belong to what Strang calls 'private spelling conventions, perfectly regular and correct in their place, but quite different from, and more archaic than, those used in print'. The example she points to is 'tho' for 'though'. A third category may be intended to alert readers to the desired pronunciation of words that can be vocalized differently, such as 'hawthorn' | 'awthorn' or 'hopeless' | 'hopless'. The most frequent defence of Clare's eccentric spellings,

[71] John Clare to John Taylor, 13 Feb. 1821, ibid. 151. That Clare himself was at this time anxious to advertise his peasant status is clear from the notebook he set aside for the 'Ways of a Village' project. This notebook, now in the Pierpont Morgan library (MA 1320), contains a mock title-page reading 'Village Scenes and Subjects on rural Occupations. By John Clare the Northamptonshire Peasant Author of "Poems on life and Senery" & "Rural Poems & Songs" Helpstone August 21 1820' (quoted in *Cottage Tales*, ed. Eric Robinson, David Powell, and P. M. S. Dawson (Ashington: Mid-Northumberland Arts Group with Carcanet Press, 1993), p. xxi). That Clare was also prepared to go to extremes in displaying his humility is seen in the following draft dedication to the second edition of *Poems Descriptive*, from a letter to Taylor of 22 Feb. 1820, in *Letters*, ed. Storey, 32. The dedication was wisely spiked by Taylor: 'Sympathy drops her tear expressive of their [the R. Hon. Earl Fitzwilliams and the R. Hon. Lord Viscount Milton] goodness in secret & it is sweet   she offers up her silent prayers to heaven where the Being resides who warms the rich & powerful to help up & be a prop to the weak & needy who directs the wise that are in the broad <road> way of fame to turn an eye to the dark cold corner of Obscurity where merit creeps his lonly way & dwindles in darkness like the lowley blossom coverd & hid in the long ramping grass of the [?repining] spring & may that heavenly benefactor from whom all good deeds origionate requite them for their kind notice of distress in as worthy & deserving returns is the sincere wish of their thankful & lowly servant.   John Clare'

though, is that of their enriching multiplicity. Thus, in *The Rural Muse*, when 'enamoured' becomes 'enarmoured', it does so in contexts 'in which the image of *armour* is also appropriate, since they refer explicitly to metallic sheen as well as love: "the gold locks of the enarmoured sun", "the bright enarmoured sunshine", the "wind enarmoured" aspen as its leaves, when blown, "Turn up their silver lining to the sun" '.[72]

What, though, of a host of less felicitous or explicable examples? 'Pissmire', for example, in 'Remembrances', also from *The Rural Muse*. What enhancing suggestion operates here? Or consider the opening lines of the unrevised version of one of Clare's most famous poems, 'Mouse's Nest':

> I found a ball of grass among the hay
> And proged it as I passed and went away
> And when I looked I fancied somthing stirred
> And turned agen and hoped to catch the bird

What is gained here by retaining Clare's misspelled 'somthing', 'agen', and 'proged' (for 'progged')? None of these cases fit Strang's categories, except, perhaps, for the stem-vowel-shortened 'somthing', though, again, what purpose is being served—especially since for the most part Clare 'does not put pressure on the reader to realise the poems in any particular accent, as Barnes, or even the Spenser of the September eclogue does'?[73] Clare, moreover, could and did spell these words conventionally; 'again' even appears later in this very sonnet, in line 11. The prime effect of such misspelling is to draw attention away from the poem itself to its provenance, to the poet as peasant.

Implicit in the systematic rejection or reversal of Taylor's revisions, it sometimes seems, is a vision of Clare's unedited writing as an originally pure or 'natural' linguistic landscape. For Paulin, 'the restored texts of the poems embody an alternative social idea. With their lack of punctuation, freedom from standard spelling and charged demotic ripples, they become a form of Nation Language that rejects the polished urbanity of Official Standard.'[74] From the beginning, though, Clare's

---

[72] Strang, 'John Clare's Language', 161–2.   [73] Ibid. 162.

[74] Tom Paulin (ed.), *The Faber Book of Vernacular Verse* (London: Faber & Faber, 1990), p. xix. Elizabeth Helsinger, in 'Clare and the Place of the Peasant Poet', 510, likens this view of Clare's language to 'what Frederic Jameson terms "strong" political art, that is, "authentic cultural creation ... dependent for its existence on authentic collective life, on the vitality of the 'organic' social group" '.

language was mixed: demotic *and* urbane. Clare made use of the language of Helpston in his poetry, but he was no dialect poet, no Burns.[75] 'I think vulgar names to the flowers best', he famously tells Hessey in a letter of 18 October 1820, '<as> but I know no others',[76] a qualification less frequently cited, and one unlikely to be true, since as Douglas Chambers points out, Clare also claimed to have bought as a child a secondhand copy of James Lee's *Botany*, 'the classic popular version of Linnaeus's nomenclature'.[77] In other words, though 'bindweed' may predominate in Clare's poetry, 'convolvulus', too, has its place, its uses.

Consider, in this regard, the language of the following unrevised lines, again from 'The Nightingale's Nest':

> Sing on sweet bird may no worse hap befall
> Thy visions then the fear that now decieves
> We will not plunder music of its dower
> Nor turn this spot of happiness to thrall
> For melody seems hid in every flower   .
> That blossoms near thy home—these harebells all
> Seem bowing with the beautiful in song
> And gaping cuckoo with its spotted leaves
> Seems blushing of the singing it has heard.

Haughton describes these lines as Clare's 'stateliest Romantic Elizabethan cadences', and rightly invokes Keats's 'Thou wast not born for death, immortal bird'.[78] What such examples recall, as James McKusick puts it, is that Clare's unrevised or 'natural' writing is already a 'curious hybrid, mixing the earthy immediacy of regional dialect with the more abstract and paraphrastic lexicon of standard eighteenth-century [and Romantic and Elizabethan] diction.'[79] Hence, typically, the following description of the 'old mouse' Clare's 'proging' makes bolt from 'The Mouse's Nest':

---

[75] Stephen Wade, 'John Clare's Use of Dialect', *Contemporary Review*, 223 (July–Dec. 1973), 82, likens Clare's use of dialect to that of Scott in the Waverley novels: 'The passages of dialogue in Gaelic-English in Scott are surely fair examples to use as a comparison with Clare; the amount of dialogue used by both writers is about the same in relation to their work as a whole.'

[76] John Clare to James Hessey, 18 Oct. 1820, in *Letters*, ed. Storey, 107.

[77] Chambers, '"A Love for Every Simple Weed"', 239.

[78] Haughton, 'Progress and Rhyme', 67, 66.

[79] McKusick, 'Beyond the Visionary Company', 225.

> With all her young ones hanging at her teats
> She looked so odd and so grotesque to me
> I ran and wondered what the thing could be

'Grotesque', here, is startling, right, and literary or educated, unlikely to be a staple of Paulin's conjectured 'Nation Language', with its unspecified but obviously levelling 'social idea'. The surrounding simplicity gives the word its power, as with other unexpected words in Clare's manuscripts: 'ebon', 'freaked', 'graven', 'houseless', 'raiment'.[80] The poem's language, in other words, artfully interweaves or balances realms of discourse. For Motion and others this hybrid quality reflects Clare's 'anxiety about his audience—an anxiety shared and exacerbated by Taylor'.[81] But it might also reflect simple love of language, a poet's perfectly 'natural' instincts of imitation, the sort that also inspired Clare's bold, unanxious experiments with stanza form and metre. When Clare writes of trespassing 'on parnass plain', for example, the mark of trespass (the irregular 'parnass') is as likely to be a literary allusion or 'theft' as a misspelling; 'parnass' (as opposed to 'Parnassus'), Strang tells us, comes from Spenser, one of Clare's models. Similarly, when critics chide Clare for alternately employing '-eth' and '-s' endings for third person singular indicative verbs (as in 'doth' and 'has'), the inconsistency is as likely to derive from reading (it is found in Shakespeare, for example) as inadvertancy.[82]

The most puzzling feature of Taylor's corrections or revisions is their seeming inconsistency. 'The very grain of Clare's language was smoothed and planed away,' complain Robinson and Summerfield of Taylor's word substitutions in *The Shepherd's Calendar*. They then list ten examples, including 'plunge' for 'douse', 'scratching' for 'scratting', 'saunters' for 'sawns'.[83]

---

[80] See Strang, 'John Clare's Language', 163–4.

[81] Motion, 'Watchful Heart', 5.

[82] Strang, 'John Clare's Language', 163–5.

[83] Robinson and Summerfield, 'Taylor's Editing of Clare', 367. They say also: 'Almost all of Clare's "provincialisms" were replaced by words acceptable to London literary taste' (from *Clare: Selected Poems and Prose*, ed. Robinson and Summerfield (London: Oxford University Press, 1966), 23). According to Barrell, in *The Idea of Landscape and the Sense of Place 1730–1840: An Approach to the Poetry of John Clare* (Cambridge: Cambridge University Press, 1972), 125, in a judgement clearly drawn from Robinson and Summerfield, 'by the time *The Shepherd's Calendar* was being prepared for publication, Taylor had come to find Clare's dialect as obnoxious as Lamb had found it'.

Several of these examples, though, suggests Chilcott, are misreadings; moreover, Robinson and Summerfield leave unmentioned dozens of comparably non-standard words Taylor retained. Chilcott lists fourty-four examples from the 1827 title poem alone, including 'crizzling', 'sliveth', 'stulps', and 'croodling'.[84] Why retain these words and not others? Because Taylor was seeking balance or catholicity not 'purity', a search that had been Clare's as well: hence the retention of some but not all provincialisms, though individual choices remain puzzling.

The common goal of a balanced or mixed style partly explains the relative absence of complaint from Clare. It also helps to explain why Clare sticks with Taylor, even when Taylor's omissions and corrections seem most cavalier. When Taylor's neglect tempts Clare to seek publication elsewhere, the result is disastrous: 'I am obliged to trust the judgment of others who mangle & spoil them [his poems],' Clare informs Taylor on 19 December 1825, 'the Ballad that I wrote to the "Souvenir" [a literary annual] is so polished & altered that I did not scarcely know it was my own'[85]—unlike, presumably, the poems Taylor revised for him, including *The Shepherd's Calendar*. 'I hope when you talk of an assistant to help you,' writes Clare a week later, 'you dont mean to trust it to anothers judgement in passing it thro the press.'[86] In other words, Clare not only needed Taylor but actively solicited Taylor's help, thought of him as tolerant or restrained in revision, even in 1825.

Only rarely does Clare protest the excision of 'dialect', and even then without heat. It is Taylor's modern critics who generate the heat. 'He was prepared (for the sake of speedier publication) to defer to Taylor,' writes Douglas Chambers, 'but there are times when he was obdurate. "You cross'd *"gulsh'd"*, he wrote to Taylor, "I think the word expressive but doubt it's

---

[84] Chilcott, *A Publisher and His Circle*, 108–9. So many such words were retained in the volume, in fact, that the absence of a glossary occasioned complaint. 'There was nothing, perhaps, which more provoked our spleen than the want of a glossary,' writes an anonymous reviewer in the June 1827 edition of the *London Weekly Review*, 'for without such an assistance, how could we perceive the fitness and beauty of such words as—*crizzling—sliveth—whinneys—greening—tootles—croodling—hings—progged—spindling—siling—struttles*—&c.' (quoted in Storey (ed.), *Critical Heritage*, 206–7).

[85] John Clare to John Taylor, 19 Dec. 1825, in *Letters*, ed. Storey, 351.

[86] John Clare to John Taylor, 27 Dec. 1825, ibid. 355.

a provincialism[.] it means tearing or thrusting up with great force." [87] What Clare then adds, in words Chambers omits, is 'take it or leave it as you please', which hardly suggests obduracy. Chambers also detects 'more than a little sense of impatience' in the following explanation of the word 'Woodseers':

'Woodseers' is inscets which I daresay you know very well wether it be the proper name I dont know tis what we call them & that you know is sufficient for us—they lie in little white notts of spittle on the backs of leaves & flowers how they come I dont know but they are always seen plentiful in moist weather—& are one of the shepherds weather glasses when the head of the insect is seen turnd upward it is said to token fine weather when downward on the contrary wet may be expected.

Whether Clare is impatient here is hard to tell. The sentences immediately preceding the quote, though, are revealing:

I shall write little this time as theres little necessity for it you will see I approve of most of your alterations as usual—No 5 you left out in the letter so I could not say [Taylor's proof corrections were numbered consecutively] but be what it will do as you woud with my approval the Poem you wish to omit I agree too & think it right as there is plenty to pick out of the 2 verses in the Ramble your reasons for omitting them is convinced me of my mistake in thinking them good so omit them & welcome—you know I urge nothing—I only suggest—& if you dont select them with the same judgment as you woud was they your own productions you do your self an injury by being cramp'd with opinions was I to know that was the case I woud suggest no more your taste is preferable to any I have witnessd & on that I rely—mines not worth twopence—& critics is too severe for me—a man of feeling that looks on faults with indulgence & never willfuly passes by a blossom he may chance to find on his journey is a man to my mind & such a one (no flattery mind from me) I reckon John Taylor—'Woodseers' is insects which I daresay you know very well . . . [88]

Clare's praise sounds genuine, particularly when he calls Taylor a 'man of feeling', contrasting him with 'too severe' critics. The ensuing account of the 'woodseer', which might well be read as easy and confident as opposed to impatient, is richly particular;

[87] Chambers, '"A Love for Every Simple Weed"', 247. The Clare quote is from a letter to Taylor of 20 Mar. 1821, in *Letters*, ed. Storey, 168.

[88] John Clare to John Taylor, 8 Mar. 1821, ibid. 162-3.

so much so that Taylor includes it verbatim—properly punctuated, spelled, and initialled ('J.C.')—in the glossary of *The
Village Minstrel*. Though Taylor's tastes may have grown more
conventional or timid after 1821, Clare himself, as we have
seen, was changing, becoming increasingly cavalier about audience needs (leaving them wholly to Taylor), while still desper-
ately seeking public recognition. One extreme may well have
called forth another, banishing this early, easy collegiality.

SELECTION, CENSORSHIP, AND THE MARKET

Taylor's much-criticized 'slashings' involve whole poems—the
revision of a volume, as it were—as well as parts of poems. But
these, too, are often perfectly defensible. Clare was astonish-
ingly, worryingly prolific. As his early supporter, Octavius
Gilchrist, wrote James Hessey, Taylor's partner, Clare could
not 'pass five minutes without jingling his poetic bells'.[89] 'When
I am in the fit', Clare himself announces, 'I write as much in
one week as woud knock ye up a fair size Vol.'[90] Everything he
wrote ('the whole of my rubbish which I have scribbled lately',
as one note reads),[91] he then sent to Taylor, ceding authorial
autonomy—the initial choice of a volume's contents—from the
start. For the first collection, for example, Taylor was sent more
than twice as many poems as any publisher could afford to
print; for *The Village Minstrel*, even a two-volume format (some
420 pages) required omissions. As for *The Shepherd's Calendar*, warned Taylor, 'I have been reckoning the number of Lines
and Pages which the present Plan of our new Volume gives us
and I find that we shall have about twice as much matter as we
require [440 pages, he estimates]. . . . I am as you see at a loss
what to do, but let me have your opinion.'[92] When critics express

---

[89] Octavius Gilchrist to James Hessey, 23 Apr. 1820, quoted in Chilcott, *A
Publisher and His Circle*, 97. Gilchrist may have got 'jingling' from Clare himself,
as in the following complaint to Edward Drury, 20 Dec. 1819 (in *Letters*, ed.
Storey, 22), about the constraints of the sonnet: "Tis not a 14 lines Son: I cannot
be confined wi'in its narrow bounds Especialy when the Gingling fit attacks me
most warmly.'
[90] John Clare to John Taylor, 20 May 1820, in *Letters*, ed. Storey, 70.
[91] John Clare to John Taylor, 1822–3?, ibid. 253.
[92] John Taylor to John Clare, 15 June 1825, ibid. 331.

outrage that Taylor and Hessey 'lay out the poems according to the dictates of acceptable literary conventions; and lines, stanzas and, on occasions, entire poems are dropped,'[93] they neglect to mention circumstances like these. Nor are they fair to Taylor, as we shall see, in their accounts of the censoring of already published editions.

Cost was an obvious consideration in Taylor's omissions, but not the only one. As the editors of the *Early Poems* themselves admit, 'proper literary discrimination required also that the young poet should be presented in the best light possible and only his best work seen.' But in whose best light? Clare's? Taylor's? That of the public? While Taylor was assembling and editing Clare's first volume, the poet's new wife was 'well advanced in pregnancy before her marriage'.[94] Taylor's decision to exclude poems which, for example, question her fidelity, or detail Clare's philanderings, or his continuing devotion to Mary Joyce, his first love, hardly amounts to imposition or censorship. Even if in Clare's world such matters were less than shameful, or at least more openly discussed, in the world to which the poems were directed, they were not. Was Taylor wrong to assume that Clare would have wished to avoid embarrassing or humiliating his wife—or himself—in the eyes of this larger world? From the moment his poems were taken up by the Stamford bookseller Edward Drury, who eventually brought them to his cousin Taylor's attention, Clare feared public ridicule. 'If I knew such things I dissaprove of shoud appear in print after my death,' he writes to Drury in late 1819, 'it would be the greatest torture possible.'[95] 'I dreaded laughter more than blame,' he writes of his earliest authorial ambitions in 'The Progress of Rhyme', 'And dare not sing aloud for shame' (ll. 279–80).[96]

More problematic is the omission of 'vulgarity' of a less personalized character, as in such titles as 'The Crafty Maid' or 'Love Epistles between Richard and Kate', neither of which

---

[93] Lucas, 'Revising Clare', 343.
[94] *Early Poems*, ed. Robinson and Powell, i. p. x.
[95] John Clare to Edward Drury, late 1819, in *Letters*, ed. Storey, 14.
[96] The lines are quoted from Robinson and Powell (eds.), *John Clare*, 159. The Tibbles, in their Everyman *Selected Poems*, 127, alter the second line to 'I dared not sing aloud for shame,' which straightens out the tenses but has no authorial approval, since the poem never passed beyond the manuscript stage.

Taylor allowed in the first collection, or the bowdlerization and eventual suppression of titles he originally admitted, such as 'Dolly's Mistake'. Only a very few such poems, of which there are a number, appear in the early volumes, or the early editions of the early volumes, and Clare's modern editors are obviously right to say these volumes therefore misrepresent the totality of the early work. The same is true of omissions of a political and religious nature, as well as those that outlaw flagrant grammatical or lexicographic irregularity. 'If a poem was too unorthodox in its sentiments, its language, or its punctuation and grammar, its chances of survival into print were very limited,' comment Robinson and Powell.[97] Taylor himself, though, as we shall see, often neither approved nor initiated these censorings.

The omission of poems from less controversial popular genres is easier to accept, though no less distorting. The editors themselves characterize the omitted 'patriotic songs about Nelson and Wellington, ballads of lovers parted by the war, invocations to the king to right the wrongs of the people, poems about battles and shipwrecks', as 'about as good as such things usually are . . . some would pass if set to music'.[98] Unfortunately, no such criticisms excuse the omission of most of the narrative poems planned for *The Shepherd's Calendar*. These poems or tales, partly modelled on the verse stories of Wordsworth and Bloomfield, partly on the ballads and songs Clare grew up with in Helpston (and later collected and transcribed, in the 1820s), were originally to accompany descriptive poems, one for each month. Their claims were rightly pressed by Clare, and are easier to credit, even, than those Robinson and Summerfield press for the original 'July', which Taylor also rejected, professing to find Clare's draft almost wholly without merit. As we shall see, Taylor was under enormous pressure when cutting *The Shepherd's Calendar*, and these and other judgements are uncharacteristically intemperate; still, it remains the case that some sort of radical surgery was needed to produce a volume of saleable length.

The reasons for Taylor's political and moral revisions or censorings, and Clare's willingness to accept them, are complicated. Taylor himself, as his biographers are at pains to point

---

[97] *Early Poems*, ed. Robinson and Powell, i. p. xi.   [98] Ibid. p. xvi.

out, was neither prudish nor reactionary. Nor was he as metropolitan or establishment a figure as is sometimes suggested. He was born in 1781, the son of a Lincolnshire bookseller, printer, and auctioneer; his father was prosperous, though not prosperous enough to send his son to university. Taylor apprenticed with his father; moved to London in 1803 at age 22; began work at James Lackington (the eventual publisher of *Frankenstein*), where he met his future partner, James Hessey; and moved on to a rival firm, Vernor and Hood, in 1804, where he seems to have got on excellently with his boss, Thomas Hood, father of the poet. At Vernor and Hood Taylor helped to publish the best-selling Robert Bloomfield, one of Clare's heroes and a precursor 'peasant poet'. Taylor and Hessey set up in partnership in Fleet Street as publishers and booksellers in 1806. In 1816, with a fall in the price of paper and a resumption of trade across the channel, book sales in Britain, especially of poetry and novels, boomed, and Taylor became, in Chilcott's words, an 'active seeker-out of new talent'.[99] Taylor and Hessey greatly expanded the publishing side of their business, signing a number of new writers, including John Keats, to whose work they had been introduced by another of their authors, John Hamilton Reynolds.

Like most publishers, Taylor cared about profit. The house survived (its finances were always precarious) by publishing religious and moral books, in particular the conduct books of Mrs Ann Taylor and Miss Jane Taylor. These books—*Maternal Solicitude for a Daughter's Best Interests* (1813), *Practical Hints to Young Females* (1815), *Display, a Tale for Young People* (1815)—were best sellers, but they were not the firm's priority. In Chilcott's words: 'the house would consider enduring talent first, and the balance-sheet afterwards'.[100] Hence its policy on novels. 'Miss Edgeworth's New Novel is enclosed,' Taylor writes to Hessey in 1814, 'Johnsons printed 3000 and could deliver only half what were subscribed for—When shall we pick up a

[99] Chilcott, *A Publisher and His Circle*, 21. For a detailed account of the role of paper prices and other material factors on the sale of poetry see Lee Erikson, 'The Poets' Corner: The Impact of Technological Changes in Printing on English Poetry, 1800–1850', *English Literary History*, 52 (1985), 893–911; for paper prices in particular, 894, 902.

[100] Chilcott, *A Publisher and His Circle*, 68.

Miss Edgeworth?'[101] They never did, but then neither did they publish lesser novelists. Taylor and Hessey published only two novels in its entire history, despite huge demand, ample opportunity, and the success of the two it did publish.

Taylor also took on writers with poor sales records (Keats, for example, whose *Endymion* he published in 1818, the very year the firm's final profit was calculated at £2); or those embroiled in sales-inhibiting controversy (Hazlitt, at war with Gifford's *Quarterly* and *Blackwood's Magazine*). Charles and James Ollier, the publishers of Shelley's early poems and of Keats's first volume, *Poems* (1817), were only too happy to rid themselves of Keats, a commercial flop: 'We regret that your brother ever requested us to publish his book,' responded James Ollier to an ill-judged enquiry about contracts from George Keats: 'by far the greater number of persons who have purchased it from us have found fault with it in such plain terms that we have in many cases offered to take the book back rather than be annoyed with the ridicule which has, time after time, been showered upon it.'[102] Yet Taylor not only took Keats on as an author, but loaned him money, offering support in exchange for first refusal on all future works—because he was convinced of Keats's genius. Though Taylor hoped to make money from his authors, Clare included, as such behaviour suggests, he was hardly exploitative, nor was he craven in the face of market pressures.

Some pressures, though, could not be ignored. Chief among Clare's censors was his most important patron, Lord Radstock, second son of the third Earl Waldegrave, a retired admiral, friend of Nelson, ex-Naval Governor of Newfoundland, prominent Evangelical, and leading light of the Society for the Suppression of Vice and Immorality. In 1819 Radstock arranged a subscription list among wealthy and titled friends to afford Clare a steady yearly income. When Radstock took exception to lines from Clare's first collection attacking wealth and station (the lines in question come from 'Helpstone' and 'Dawnings of Genius'), he did so with brutal directness, threatening to denounce the poet publicly. According to Mrs Emmerson, Lord

---

[101] John Taylor to James Hessey, 18 Jan. 1814, quoted ibid. 22.
[102] Quoted in Walter Jackson Bate, *John Keats* (New York: Oxford University Press, 1966), 150–1.

Radstock asked her to 'tell Clare if he still has a recollection of what I have done, and am still doing for him, he must give me unquestionable *proofs* of being that Man I would have him to be—he must *expunge—expunge!*'[103] Clare was much annoyed, but capitulated; Taylor at first resisted ('I am inclined to remain obstinate, and if any Objection is made to my judgement for so doing I am willing to abide the Consequences'[104]), but then reluctantly acceded. In Chilcott's words, 'he remained convinced of the needlessness of the omissions for the reasons Radstock had given, but since "so decided a Set" was clearly to be made against Clare if they were not, "let them be expunged and welcome. . . . When the Follies of the Day are passed with all the Fears they have engendered we can restore the Poems according to the Earlier Editions."'[105] Here, certainly, is an unproblematic instance for modern editors: the omitted lines (which were not cut until the fourth edition) should be restored.

Similarly, when Radstock objected to stanzas 107 and 108 of 'The Village Minstrel' (at the time still titled 'The Peasant Boy'), Taylor again tried to resist:

Lord R. has put his Mark 'This is radical Slang' against 2 of the best stanzas, viz. 107 'There once were Lanes &c' & 108 'O England, boasted Land of Liberty'—Are these to be omitted also?—If so, others will be offensive next, & your Poem will be like the Man who had 2 Wives.—for I shall pluck out all the white Hairs.[106]

Taylor seems almost to be egging Clare on, steeling him to defy his patron. Again, though, both men capitulated. Here, too, is an obvious instance of censorship; the original lines ought to be restored. That Clare went on to write relatively few poems of explicit political content or purpose, and tried to publish even fewer, is hardly a mystery.

Lord Radstock's interference eventually forced a confrontation. Taylor wrote him a letter of steely abruptness, and Clare had to take sides.[107] That the side Clare took was Taylor's was

[103] Eliza Emmerson to John Clare, 11 May 1820, quoted in Chilcott, *A Publisher and His Circle*, 93.
[104] John Taylor to John Clare, 6 June 1820, in *Letters*, ed. Storey, 69 n.
[105] Chilcott, *A Publisher and His Circle*, 93. Taylor's letter to Clare, which Chilcott quotes, is from 27 Sept. 1820.
[106] John Taylor to John Clare, 6 Jan. 1821, ibid. 135.
[107] Taylor recounts the episode to Clare, quoting from his steely letter to Radstock of 11 Dec. 1820, in a letter of 16 Dec. 1820, in *Letters*, ed. Storey, pp. 117–19.

as much an expression of personal loyalty, friendship, and ideological compatibility (that is, relative compatibility) as of commercial calculation. Publishers, with their access to the market or reading public, mattered more than patrons, though patrons were still powerful (which is, in part, why Clare was quick to mollify Radstock and Mrs Emmerson[108]); but there were other reasons for favouring Taylor, and he and Radstock are unfairly bracketed. In terms of the most notorious of the early political censorings, it is Radstock not Taylor who bears responsibility. Moreover, the letters provide many instances of easy, amiable collaboration.

Nor is Taylor wholly responsible for the early censoring of sexual material. Consider, for example, the frequently cited omission of 'Dolly's Mistake' and 'My Mary' from the 1820 third edition of *Poems Descriptive*, an omission to which Clare objected strenuously and wittily:

I have seen the third Edition & am cursed mad about it   the judgment of T[aylor] is a button hole lower in my opinion—it is good—but too subject to be tainted by medlars *false delicasy* damn it I hate it beyond every thing . . . what in the name of delicasy doth poor Dolly say to incur such malice as to have her artless lamentations shut out—they blush to read what they go nightly to balls for & love to practice   alas false delicasy—I fear thou art worse than dolly   say nothing to T.—he is left to do as he likes you know—and if we controul him he will give us up—but I think I shall soon be qualified to be my own editor—pride once rooted grows very fast you percieve . . . I think to please all & offend all we shoud put out 215 pages of blank leaves and call it 'Clare in fashion'.[109]

Two points are worth noting here: Clare admits he has left Taylor 'to do as he likes', and he knows Taylor holds a trump card, the threat to 'give us up', which, of course, is only a trump card if one believes, as Clare seems to, that no one else would publish him.

Chilcott thinks this belief correct: 'John Murray, whom the

---

[108] From the first, Clare knew how to please his 'betters'. His earliest letter to a patron, in this case Revd Isaiah Knowles Holland, 'written early 1819?', conjectures *Letters*, ed. Storey, 4, thanks Holland for 'his *Condesension & notice*', and refers to himself as 'a *Clown* who as yet *Slumbers* in *Obscurity* and perhaps whose *merits* deserves no better *Fate*'.

[109] John Clare to James Hessey, 10? July 1820, ibid. 83.

poet met during his visit to London in 1822, might praise his work; but could he, or Constable or Blanchard or any of the more renowned publishers, ever have devoted the amount of time and patience that Taylor had?'[110] When, moreover, Murray eventually does publish a work by an author of Clare's 'station', *Attempts in Verse by John Jones, An Old Servant with Some Account of the Writer, Written by Himself and an Introductory Essay by Robt. Southey, Esq., Poet Laureate* (1831), the condescension the volume shows towards Jones makes Taylor's treatment of Clare seem all the more exemplary. Why promote Jones's poems, wonders Southey in the introductory essay? Because 'there were many, I thought, who would be pleased at seeing how much intellectual enjoyment had been attained in humbler life, and in very unfavourable circumstances; and that this exercise of the mind, instead of rendering the individual discontented with his station, had conduced greatly to his happiness, and if it had not made him a good man, had contributed to keep him so'.[111] Nothing remotely as patronizing is to be found in Taylor's several introductions to Clare's poems or in any of his correspondence.

Why, though, did Clare not approach a less prestigious or established firm? Or try publishing the book himself by subscription, as he later tried with *The Midsummer Cushion*? Why not even withhold the edition from publication, as a matter of principle? These were Clare's options, and his decision not to take them recalls the conventional nature of his aspirations as well as his straitened circumstances, his desire for mainstream success, public acclaim, money to support his family.[112] In

---

[110] Chilcott, *A Publisher and His Circle*, 127. Erikson, in 'Technological Changes in Printing', 905, points out how few options Clare had among 'publishers of poetry in the century of any note', listing only Archibald Constable and Longman as alternatives to Taylor and Hessey and Murray for the mid-1820s.

[111] John Jones, *Attempts in Verse by John Jones*, etc., 2nd edn. (1831; London: John Murray, 1834), 11–12. Clare read Southey's introductory essay and was deeply offended by it: 'Mr Southey seems to hold uneducated poets in very little estimation & talks about the march of mind in a sneering way—as to eduction it aids very little in bringing forth that which is poetry—& if a mans humble situation in life is to be the toleration for people to praise him I should say such admiration is worth but little' (John Clare to John Taylor, 7 Mar. 1831, in *Letters*, ed. Storey, 538).

[112] As Elizabeth Helsinger, in 'Clare and the Place of the Peasant Poet', 532 n. points out, the expectation of Clare's friends and patrons 'that he could combine poetry with agricultural labor [was] bitterly unrealistic—especially during a period

September 1820, he writes to Gilchrist of a potential rival, another provincial poet: 'I was rather jealous but am now very cool'd by satisfaction there is but 5 lines that strikes me a little four of which I suspect are Crabbs.'[113] This is the voice of literary ambition, of the 'reviews', about which Clare was 'forever anxious';[114] the image of Clare as incapable of, or above, professional calculation is sentimental, Romantic, 'pastoral'. As for 'poor Dolly', what she says is not the problem; the problem is the simple fact of her 'mistake', especially when treated so lightly. The subject of a young girl's seduction is simply too 'indelicate' for the 'primpt up misses' Clare disparages in the letter about Taylor's taste—at least according to the parents and guardians who kept pressuring Taylor for cuts.

Hessey's response to Clare, in a letter of 11 July 1820, defends Taylor:

he perceived that objections were continually made to them [the cancelled 'indelicacies'] & that the sale of the Volume would eventually be materially injured & therefore he determined on leaving them out. Whether it be true or false delicacy which raises the objection to these pieces it is perhaps hardly worth while to enquire. If we are satisfied that in the Society which we frequent certain subjects must not even be alluded to, we must either conform to the rules of that Society or quit it. An author in like manner is expected to concede something to the tone of moral feeling of the Age in which he lives, and if he expects or wishes his works to be popular, to afford amusement or convey instruction, he must avoid such subjects as are sure to excite a Prejudice against him & prevent his works from being generally read.[115]

The acceptability of this defence, which we will again encounter in discussion of Keats, depends importantly on how one interprets the 'tone of moral feeling of the Age'. As Chilcott insists, the

of falling wages and scarce employment in the fields. Clare was not able to make himself either economically independent by his pen, or—for social and psychological as well as economic reasons—to write poetry as an amateur while he lived the life of a laborer.'

[113] John Clare to Octavius Gilchrist, 26 Sept. 1820, in *Letters*, ed. Storey, 96. See also Clare's worry of Apr. 1819, to Edward Drury, ibid. 8: 'A Poet at Exton is Started up   your Information wether good or bad as soon as possible   Wether he puts on the Spectackles of Books become an Imitator or writes from Nature in Original—Inform me.'

[114] According to Storey, in 'Clare and the Critics', in Haughton, Phillips, and Summerfield (eds.), *Clare in Context*, 28.

[115] James Hessey to John Clare, 11 July 1820, quoted in Chilcott, *A Publisher and His Circle*, 111–12.

need to propitiate this tone was no paranoid illusion: 'Leigh Hunt had been attacked for his "crude, vague, ineffectual, and sour Jacobinism", Shelley for his atheism, Hazlitt for his immorality, Keats for an imagination "better adapted to the stews". It was impossible that any publisher should completely ignore such attacks or the inflexible moral attitudes which lay behind them,'[116] particularly when the writer in question was a 'peasant'.[117] Yet Taylor's resistance to Radstock and Mrs Emmerson, and his reluctant and belated censoring of radical and 'indelicate' passages in the first collection, suggest that his inclinations were to resist public pressure, to respond only when 'objections were continually made' and sales endangered. This is not to say that Taylor shared Clare's sense of what was proper, as modern readers mostly do ('Jinny-burnt-arse', for example, Clare's wonderful phrase for marsh gas in 'The Village Minstrel' becomes 'Jack-a-lantern' in Taylor's revision, with no prompting from Lord Radstock). It is only to say that Radstock was responsible for the most egregious censorings, and that Taylor was no Radstock. Clare makes no objection to Hessey's letter defending Taylor; less than a week after his angry complaint he asks Hessey to 'give my love to my old chuckey Taylor, when you write him tell him I am all anxiety to hear from him agen'.[118]

When Clare himself faced up to 'the tone of moral feeling of the Age', as opposed to leaving it to others, he and Taylor collaborated happily, with Taylor even, at times, sounding more daring than Clare. In a letter of 17 February 1821, Clare proudly offers the following alteration of a potentially offensive stanza from 'The Village Minstrel', one about which Taylor had expressed concern:

I have got the verse from Stamford & alterd it I think just such as you can wish no better to be done—at least all indelicacy is lost or the delicate will be damd puzzld to attribute that to it—here it is

[116] Ibid. 112.

[117] As Lucas suggests, in 'Clare's Politics', 161, 'peasant poets were not allowed to voice truths appropriate (if at all) to poets in very different social circumstances'. Lucas makes similar suggestions in the chapter on Clare in *England and Englishness: Ideas of Nationhood in English Poetry 1688–1900* (London: Chatto & Windus, 1990); in 'Revising Clare', in Brinkley and Hanley (eds.), *Romantic Revisions;* and in *John Clare* (Plymouth: Northcote House, 1994).

[118] John Clare to James Hessey, 16 July 1820, in *Letters*, ed. Storey, 81.

> Along the road were coupl'd maid & swain
> & dick from dolly now for gifts did sue
> Hed gen her ribbons & he deemd again
> Some kind return as nothing but his due
> & he told things as ploughmen rarely knew
> Bout breaking hearts & pains—a mighty spell
> Her sunday clo'hs might damage wi the dew
> She quite forgot them while he talkd so well
> & listnd to his tales till darkness round em fell

I am pleasd with it by throwing such disguise over it to think how it will wrock [wrack] the prudes to find fault   there is something in it but theyll know not were to get at it—tis quite delicate now.

Taylor, meanwhile, offered a rewrite of his own, one neither as artful nor as delicate:

> Some homeward-bound were coupled, maid & swain
> And Dick from Dolly now for gifts did sue;
> He'd given her Ribbons, and he deem'd again
> Some kind return as nothing but his due;
> And he told things that ploughmen little knew,
> Of bleeding hearts & pains—she seiz'd the spell,
> And tho' at first she murmur'd 'bout the dew
> Spoiling her Sunday-Gown—he talk'd so well
> She yielded up at last to what no Words dare tell.—[119]

In the end, Clare and Taylor put the two versions together. The first six lines, with their relatively unimportant 'corrections' ('given' for 'gen', '*that* ploughmen little knew' for '*as* ploughmen rarely knew', 'bleeding' for 'breaking', plus punctuation) were from Taylor's revised version; the last three, spelling excepted, were Clare's, both parties recognizing the sly appeal of Clare's closing indirection. In later years, for a variety of reasons, Taylor alone was left to negotiate such difficulties.

CLARE'S SAMENESS

Behind many of Taylor's selections, or omissions, lay an anxiety that also affected his excisions within poems. From the

[119] John Clare to John Taylor, 17 Feb. 1821 and John Taylor to John Clare, 17 Feb. 1821, ibid. 156–8.

start, Taylor encouraged Clare to vary his poetry, both from poem to poem and within poems, particularly longer poems—for reasons applicable to all writers. 'In Authorship you will find,' he writes on the eve of the first volume's publication, '*if* you succeed now, that greater things will be expected from the next work, and so on successively. . . . Bloomfield lost what I fear he will never recover, by failing in his last Work, the Banks of the Wye.' Hessey seconds this caution in a letter to Edward Drury of 2 August 1820: 'Clare you know has a reputation to *support* and what he publishes in future must not only not be inferior, it should be beyond his former Efforts, Selection and Caution are therefore quite requisite.' Clare, though, was in full flow after the success of the first volume, and Taylor had to beg him 'to be more patient in the attempt to write, whatever you may do with Respect to reading. Your best pieces are those which you were the longest Time over, and to succeed in others you must not hurry.'[120] Critical reaction to the second volume supports this view, and Chilcott partly attributes the volume's reduced sales to Clare's inability to heed Taylor's advice,[121] a failure Clare himself came to recognize, as when he pronounced the work's sixty sonnets 'poor stuff' or criticized the title poem, wishing he had withheld it 'a little more for revision'.[122]

Taylor's modern critics characterize his advice about variation and finish as pernicious and insensitive, as though the publisher were blind to, or undervalued, Clare's strengths. Partly this is a matter of revaluing supposed weaknesses. A letter of 1826, in which Taylor, ill and overworked, voices reservations about *The Shepherd's Calendar*, is frequently cited:

I have often remarked that your Poetry is much the best when you are not describing common things, and if you would raise your Views generally, & speak of the Appearances of Nature each Month more philosophically (if I may so say) or with more Excitement, you would greatly improve these little poems. . . . they have too much of the language of common everyday Description;—faithful I grant they are, but

[120] John Taylor to John Clare, 30 Nov. 1819, James Hessey to Edward Drury, 2 Aug. 1820, and John Taylor to John Clare, 13 Jan. 1820, all quoted in Chilcott, *A Publisher and His Circle*, 97.　　　　　　　　　　　　　[121] Ibid. 98.
[122] Quoted in *John Clare: Selected Poems and Prose*, ed. Robinson and Summerfield, 114–15.

that is not all—'What in me is low, Raise & Refine' is the way in which you should conceive them as addressing you.[123]

Though Taylor grants the merit of Clare's descriptive passages here, he wants more. Nor was he alone in doing so; the complaint is familiar and persistent, though in recent years much scorned. Keats, for example, admired Clare's first volume but also felt, according to Taylor, that his 'Images from Nature are too much introduced without being called for by a particular Sentiment. . . . the Description overlaid and stifled that which ought to be the prevailing Idea.'[124] What Taylor and Keats want, according to Taylor's modern critics, is for Clare to be a more conventional poet, to 'place', in the loco-descriptive tradition of Thomson and Wordsworth, the poem's many local felicities—'fine isolated verisimilitudes', as it were, of common or everyday life—and so elevate them, framing his world in a way John Barrell and others have taught us to see as class specific, and thus a potential betrayal.[125]

I view Taylor's anxieties in a less 'ideological' light. Consider, for example, the original 'July' of *The Shepherd's Calendar*, as 'rescued' by Robinson, Summerfield, and Powell. Though packed with riches, it also lacks dramatic or logical shaping, though it gathers to an evening repose. The result is wearing, especially without punctuation, making the poem, in words Haughton and Phillips apply to the 'rescued' or 'raw' version as a whole, 'less accessible to the general reader. Less *readable* in fact,' a defect they term 'an unfortunate side-effect'.[126] The poem's virtues are 'little', then, not so much because its concerns are everyday or commonplace—or levelling, so that, as the *Monthly*

---

[123] John Taylor to John Clare, 4 Mar. 1826, as excerpted in *Letters*, ed. Storey, 363 n. The sentence beginning 'What in me is low . . .' is omitted in *Letters*, ed. Storey, but printed in Robinson and Summerfield, 'Taylor's Editing of Clare', 364.

[124] John Taylor to John Clare, 29 Sept. 1820, excerpted ibid. 99 n.

[125] Barrell, *The Idea of Landscape*, 138, characterizes Clare's relation to landscape as follows: 'Clare's pleasure is not in the idea of the design, and the active control he has over the landscape, but in the multiplicity and particularity of images in the landscape, which he cannot control and before which he is passive—they approach his sight, his eye does not roam out over them, ordering and placing them.' When Clare attempts to write in the controlling Thomson tradition, the prospect tradition, he does so 'without any of the experience Thomson had, and his readers had, of mobility, and of the ability to compare one landscape and another that their mobility allowed them' (ibid. 143).

[126] Haughton and Phillips, 'Introduction: Relocating John Clare', 20.

Review puts it, 'there is no *aristocracy of beauty*, but the stag and the hog, the weed and the flower, find an equal place in his verse'[127]—as because they are local, specific: one effect, then another effect, then another, a quality Clare's modern readers often see as a virtue, a way of registering, in Seamus Heaney's words, 'the inexorable one-thing-after-anotherness of the world'.[128] Hessey makes a similar objection in a letter of 3 November 1824: Clare, he complains, once again describes 'the Morning & the Noon & the Evening & the Summer & the Winter, & the Sheep & Cattle & Poultry & Pigs & Milking Maid & Foddering Boys . . . the world will now expect something more than these; let them come in incidentally, but they must be subordinate to higher objects'.[129]

By 'higher objects', here, Hessey does not mean—not necessarily, that is—explicitly philosophical or cultivated objects, just as Taylor's 'little' does not necessarily mean 'common' (though 'What in me is low, Raise & Refine,' I admit, suggests otherwise). Consider, for example, the only passage of the 'July' manuscript Taylor thought worth preserving, a 16-line section beginning as follows:

---

[127] From an unsigned review of *Poems Descriptive* in the Mar. 1820 *Monthly Review*, reprinted in Storey (ed.), *Critical Heritage*, 75. See also Lucas, *John Clare*, 52: 'To quote from [*The Shepherd's Calendar*] is practically impossible, without at least quoting at length, precisely because Clare refuses to reject or scorn, and because he won't select, either—that is, won't rank or make a hierarchy of customs, flora and fauna. The teeming hierarchy of his lines democratizes all it gathers up.'

[128] Heaney, 'John Clare: A Bi-centenary Lecture', in Haughton, Phillips, and Summerfield (eds.), *John Clare in Context*, 137. See also *The Rural Muse*, ed. Thornton, 19: 'The poems in this volume well illustrate Clare's usual process of ordered accretion, even in the odes which look back to the tradition of Gray and Collins. The elements of his poems are not ranked in value any more than on the whole clauses are subordinated to each other—the "so often commencing with 'and'" which disturbed Taylor is an inherent part of Clare's inclusiveness of affection. Stanzas are not ranked either, even poems are not ranked, their major link being the connecting and creating mind of the poet, fixing things in a verse eternity where fluid language catches the changing world and allows it to be continually recreated in the mind of the reader.' Lucas, *John Clare*, 7, makes a comparably shrewd point about Clare's rhymes: 'for Clare rhyme is nearly always a "marker", a way of signifying a line ending rather than offering the chance of exploiting the possibilities of reversal or surprise—or any of those many devices that belong to rhyme in a print culture'.

[129] James Hessey to John Clare, 3 Nov. 1824, excerpted in Storey, (ed.) *Critical Heritage*, 195.

> Noon gathers wi its blistering breath
> Around and day dyes still as death
> The breeze is stopt the lazy bough
> Hath not a leaf that dances now   290
> The totter grass upon the hill
> And spiders threads is hanging still
> The feathers dropt from moorhens wing
> Upon the waters surface clings
> As steadfast and as heavy seem
> As stones beneath them in the stream
> Hawkweed and groundsels fairey downs
> Unruffld keep their seeding crowns
> And in the oven heated air
> Not one light thing is floating there   300
> Save that to the earnest eye
> The restless heat swims twittering bye

This passage is neither especially elevated nor reflective, but its familiar materials are organized in such a way as to make them 'subordinate to higher objects'. What distinguishes the passage, argues Chilcott, is 'a firm centre of tone and idea which sustains and synthesizes the various descriptive touches. The blistering heat of a noonday in summer is at the centre of Clare's imagination; and all incidental detail derives from it, and relates back to it, as parts to a whole.'[130] Here and elsewhere, Clare's distinctive particularity, the unique closeness of his vision, coexists with larger controlling or structuring purposes; the two need not be, as is sometimes implied, mutually exclusive.

A similar desire to bring shape to the entire collection, in addition to its constituent poems, underlies Hessey's early suggestion, in a letter of October 1823, that Clare focus on 'human interest—a Story or a more particular delineation of character',[131] or Taylor's subsequent plan for the pairing of descriptive and narrative works. Again, it is not so much that Taylor disparaged description, or 'had pushed the verse tales in preference to the descriptive verse', as that he wanted both.[132] It ought to

---

[130] Chilcott, *A Publisher and His Circle*, 119.
[131] James Hessey to John Clare, 13 Oct. 1823, ibid. 194.
[132] John Clare, *Cottage Tales*, ed. Eric Robinson, David Powell, and P. M. S. Dawson (Ashington: Mid-Northumberland Arts Group and Carcanet Press, 1993), p. xxxii. The editors do admit, however, that 'Taylor had in fact located what was to be a continuing problem for Clare: that of discovering a framework within

be possible to want both—to acknowledge a potentially limit-ing repetitiveness or lack of variety in Clare's verse, and a related atomizing tendency (the typical Clare sonnet, according to Heaney, is 'seven couplets wound up like clockwork and then set free to spin merrily through their foreclosed mo-tions')[133]—without being labelled shallow, unfeeling, or 'Cock-ney', an epithet Robinson, Powell, and Dawson apply to Taylor, almost in the spirit of *Blackwood's Magazine*.[134] Robinson and Summerfield defame Taylor's taste as 'essentially artificial', like that of Mrs Emmerson or the reading public she, and later Clare himself, catered for in annuals and keepsakes. 'He wanted everything blown up,' they declare, 'he wanted significant state-ment pushed into poetry.'[135] On the contrary, like another of his authors, John Keats, Taylor deplored poetical 'obtrusive-ness'; if anything, simplicity, as we have seen, was his ideal.

Chilcott's account of Taylor's radical restructuring of the ending of 'February' shows how the publisher's active interven-tions could be improving. The lines in question, as at the ends of other months, are meant to settle the poem into a repose of sorts, in this case a return, after thaw, to winter, a time when 'all is sad and dumb again' (stanza 16). In Clare's original ending, 'the fluidity and calm which the words express is not altogether reflected in the structure of the lines which tends to be episodic'.[136] The wintry return is disrupted by scenes of activity, just as earlier stanzas of busy release during the thaw nestle cheek by jowl with quieter—more wintry—ones. Taylor's revision simply gathers together the reflective stanzas, so the

which his talents could be deployed to best effect. Taylor shows some perceptive-ness in his realization that such a framework was more likely to be in the nature of a compendium, built up of and comprising a variety of elements, rather than a single monolithic work.'

[133] Heaney, 'John Clare: A Bi-centenary Lecture', 132. See also Elizabeth Helsinger, 'Clare and the Place of the Peasant Poet', 516, on Clare's heroic couplets in 'The Mores', which 'mimic the unenclosed landscapes the poem celebrates: he almost always observes the boundary of the line (marked by rhyme and coinciden-tal with syntactical breaks) but rarely counterpoints these strictly regular pauses with any internal ones. No fences divide his lines into smaller parcels. The result, to an ear trained on Pope—or any of the masters of blank verse—is a certain monotony, an absence of tension between metrical and syntactic patterns.'

[134] See John Clare, *Cottage Tales*, ed. Robinson, Powell, and Dawson, p. xli.

[135] John Clare, *The Shepherd's Calendar*, ed. Robinson, Summerfield, and Powell, pp. vii–ix.   [136] Chilcott, *A Publisher and His Circle*, 113.

poem's action or story, of winter's return, is more easily discerned, giving it a smoother and more shapely movement.

One of the stanzas Taylor moves, the eleventh in Clare's original twenty-stanza version, is itself shaped in a way analogous to the larger restructuring. In the original, the stanza in question follows a stanza describing sauntering gossips and tales of love and is followed in turn by a stanza describing busy sparrows, wrens, and 'dancing gnats'. The stanza reads as follows:

> A calm of pleasure listens round
> And almost whispers winter bye
> While fancy dreams of summer sounds
> And quiet rapture fills the eye
> The sun beams on the hedges lye
> The south wind murmurs summer soft
> And maids hang out white cloaths to dry
> Around the eldern skirted croft

In the revision, Taylor removes this stanza from its busy context and places it towards the end of the poem (fourteenth out of the published edition's sixteen stanzas), just after the last of the poem's happily active pre-thaw descriptive stanzas. He then reverses the order of the lines so that the stanza moves from activity to reflection, by way of introducing two concluding stanzas of wintry activity.

XIII

> The mavis thrush with wild delight,
>   Upon the orchard's dripping tree,
> Mutters, to see the day so bright,
>   Fragments of young Hope's poesy:
> And oft Dame stops her buzzing wheel
>   To hear the robin's note once more,
> Who tootles while he pecks his meal
>   From sweet-briar hips beside the door.

XIV

> The sunbeams on the hedges lie,
>   The south wind murmurs summer soft;
> The maids hang out white clothes to dry
>   Around the elder-skirted croft:

A calm of pleasure listens round,
    And almost whispers Winter by;
While Fancy dreams of Summer's sound,
    And quiet rapture fills the eye.

xv

Thus Nature of the Spring will dream
    While south winds thaw; but soon again
Frost breathes upon the stiff'ning stream,
    And numbs it into ice: the plain
Soon wears its mourning garb of white;
    And icicles, that fret at noon,
Will eke their icy tails at night
    Beneath the chilly stars and moon.

In Clare's original, the quietly evocative return in this last stanza
('Thus Nature of the Spring will dream') is preceded by a stanza
of energetic activity:

The hedgehog from its hollow root
Sees the wood moss clear of snow
And hunts each hedge for fallen fruit
Crab hip and winter bitten sloe
And oft when checkd by sudden fears
As shepherd dog his haunt espies
He rolls up in a ball of spears
And all his barking rage defies

When one then gets 'Thus Nature of the Spring will dream', the
result is puzzling. Is the 'dreaming' metaphorical, as if to say,
'all this activity—dogs barking, hedgehogs hunting—is a sort of
dream of spring'? Perhaps, but Taylor's revision gives 'Thus
dreaming' a local referent: the immediately preceding lines 'While
Fancy dreams of Summer's sound, | And quiet rapture fills the
eye.' The revision makes better sense as well as improving the
flow of the poem. Here, as elsewhere, Clare's letters reveal no
disquiet over Taylor's reshaping.

As for the omissions, they too, it can be argued, improve the
flow of the poem, though one is hard-pressed to say why the
four stanzas omitted were more expendable than others. Out
go the sauntering gossips; the sparrows, wrens, and 'dancing
gnats'; the cackling hens, cocks and jackdaws; even the hive
bees 'fancying winter oer | And dreaming in their combs of

spring'. There is much to admire in the omitted material; but had Clare added, say, another twenty stanzas, there would be much to admire in those as well. As Taylor explains in a note about an earlier poem, 'Solitude', what is cut is not necessarily deficient. Although he liked the poem, 'from an Apprehension that it contains rather too much minute Description I feel desirous of cutting out a Couplet here & there.—The difficulty is the greater in parting with them, as they are generally excellent in their Way.'[137] That Clare himself acknowledged the force of such arguments is clear from the letters: 'you rogue you, the pruning hook has been over me agen I see in the vols but vain as I am of my abilities I must own your loppings off have bravely amended them the "Rural Evening" & "Cress gatherer" are now as compleat as any thing in the Vols'.[138] The necessity for 'pruning' in a long poem such as *The Shepherd's Calendar* is even greater, since, as Chilcott puts it, 'the absence of any underlying pressure or synthesizing force results at times in an impression of structural haphazardness. There are too many stanzas which may be shifted from their context to another without any loss of meaning or effort.'[139] Taylor's revisions thus focus on what the manuscripts often lack—balance, shape, proportion, 'feeling', which is also to say, the needs of the reader.

THE SHEPHERD'S CALENDAR

So important are Taylor's revisions of *The Shepherd's Calendar* to his tarnished reputation, that they deserve a moment's more attention. There is no question that at times Taylor is simply culpable, ignoring or overriding Clare's obvious intentions. In the political sphere, for example, he omits the last four lines of 'June':

---

[137] John Taylor to John Clare, 16 Mar. 1820, excerpted in *Letters*, ed. Storey, 38 n.
[138] John Clare to John Taylor, 10 July 1821, ibid. 204.
[139] Ibid. 115–16. As Thomas De Quincey, another of Taylor's authors and an admirer of Clare's verse, puts it in a related comment: 'The description is often true even to a botanical eye; and in that, perhaps, lies the chief defect . . . in searching after this too earnestly, the feeling is sometimes too much neglected' (*The Collected Writings of Thomas De Quincey*, ed. David Masson, 14 vols. (Edinburgh: Adam and Charles Black, 1896–7), iii. 144–5).

As proud distinction makes a wider space
Between the genteel and the vulgar race
Then must they fade as pride oer custom showers
Its blighting mildew on her feeble flowers   (ll. 165–8)

The ending of 'May', which talks of the 'faded smiles' of a landscape in which 'enclosure has its birth | [And] spreads a mildew oer her mirth' (ll. 459–60), is cut by 100 lines. Taylor also cuts references to 'tyrant justice' ('October', l. 46), as well as the following lines protesting enclosure and the sufferings of the poor from 'The Sorrows of Love', one of the four narrative poems retained from Clare's original manuscripts: 'Ere vile enclosure took away the moor | & farmers built a workhouse for the poor' (ll. 173–4).

Other instances of censorship involve sex or the body, as when Taylor excises both the 'hot swain' 'stript in his shirt' and his sweetheart 'in her unpind gown', 'wi heaving breast' ('August', ll. 109, 110, 117); or when he cuts from 'May' the 'smell smocks [lechers] that from view retires | Mong rustling leaves and bowing briars' (ll. 131–2). Presumably the omission of the image of fairies crowded in a cupboard 'thick as mites in rotten cheese', derives from a related squeamishness. Such instances, argue Robinson and Powell, obscure Clare's true pastoral tradition: rough, loose-limbed, that of Chaucer's 'Reeve's Tale', Herrick's 'The Horkey', Gay's 'The Shepherd's Week'.[140] Their effect is like that produced by the excision of provincialisms, the correction of spelling, punctuation, and grammar. Such tidying, argue Taylor's critics, robs the verse 'of much of the particularity and locality of language that are among the poet's greatest strengths'.[141] Though Chilcott points to several 'retained lines which qualify the argument',[142] including one describing a milkmaid's 'swelling bosom loosely veiled' ('July', l. 152), there is no question that the manuscript versions are more robust or 'indelicate'.

These political and sexual excisions derive, as we have seen, from years of pressure, on Taylor as well as Clare, pressure which threatened Clare's poetical fortunes, as he knew full well.

---

[140] John Clare, *The Shepherd's Calendar*, ed. Robinson, Summerfield, and Powell, p. xviii.   [141] Ibid. p. xxii.
[142] Chilcott, *A Publisher and His Circle*, 110.

That still Clare sent Taylor 'offensive' material after their battles over *Poems Descriptive* and *The Village Minstrel*—that is,
their battles against Clare's censors—was in this instance less a
sign of exasperation or defiance than of debility: the letters of
this period betray growing impatience and anger but little evidence of incipient revolt; on the contrary, Clare's relations with
Radstock were comparatively cordial (partly because of Taylor's
inattention). For the first half of 1824, Clare was both physi-
cally and mentally unwell; in fact, throughout the period 1823–
5 he suffered spells of prolonged and severe illness. He also, of
course, had serious money worries. 'The volume had clearly
been sent to Taylor,' write Robinson and Summerfield, in explanation of other aspects of its peculiarity, 'when Clare was
distracted or overwhelmed by troubles, and he was certainly
experiencing difficulty in seeing any job through to a satisfac-
tory conclusion.'[143] 'I have sent this rough book,' Clare writes
to Taylor, 'tis all I have got of the Calendar here & if I should
get better you may send me it back to finish if not you must
make the best of it.'[144] Taylor cannot have been pleased.

The more maddening the manuscript the more radical and
intemperate the excisions. 'July' gets such harsh treatment because, as the editors point out, it is such a mess:

not only did it run to over 500 lines, but to add insult to injury it
suddenly turned into another poem. After about 500 lines, Clare seems
to have realised that he was, in effect, writing another poem, more
particularly concerned with the evening, and so he interpolated a
further title, *A Village Evening*, and the remainder of the poem which
had started as *July* is to be seen as prepatory draft of *A Village
Evening* which is found as an independent poem in MS. 37 (Peterborough). *July*, then, in the MS. 9 version is clearly an unfinished poem.[145]

An unfinished poem of 714 lines. Robinson and Summerfield
downplay the effect of this sort of confusion and excess, stress-
ing instead Taylor's gathering 'failure of sympathy' with Clare's
writing, part of a larger disillusion with poetry in general. They
point to Taylor's revision of a draft of 'January' from much

---

[143] Robinson and Summerfield, 'Taylor and Clare', 362.
[144] Clare's note to Taylor is found on p. 73 of MS 9 [Peterborough]; it is quoted
ibid. 362.   [145] Ibid.

cleaner manuscripts, manuscripts Clare himself corrected and transcribed. Taylor reduced the draft 'to a mere torso'.[146]

The details of this revision, though, as supplied by Robinson and Summerfield themselves, are hardly conclusive. The draft in question presents 'January' as two poems, 'A Winter's Day' and 'A Cottage Evening'. Their combined length (557 lines) is thus almost as exceptional or anomalous as that of the original version of 'July', given the lengths of the other descriptive poems. Taylor cut 'A Winter's Day' from 222 lines to 92, but he cut relatively little from 'A Cottage Evening'. The resulting 1827 'January' retains approximately 70 per cent of the original two-poem version. In the case of 'July', in contrast, Taylor threw Clare's draft out completely, and Clare immediately submitted an alternative version of 163 lines. Moreover, as Robinson and Summerfield themselves admit, in general 'the poems for which Taylor used MS 9 fared much worse'.[147] In other words, though Taylor cut clean as well as messy manuscripts, sometimes radically, he cut messy manuscripts more. The state of the manuscript bears some relation to the severity of the revision. This is not to deny Taylor's understandable reluctance to continue publishing poetry at a loss, an important ingredient in his conjectured lack of sympathy.[148] It is simply to point out that Clare's manuscripts, even when clean, asked rather a lot of a publisher, in terms both of time and of creative responsibility. Taylor felt overburdened by them, taken advantage of (though Clare's more profound difficulties muted complaint), especially as he had '*no one* who can perform the Task but myself'.

---

[146] Ibid. 364. For the causes of Taylor's larger disillusion, as a publisher, with poetry, see Erikson, 'Technological Changes in Printing', 897–8: 'Despite an increase of twenty-three percent in the number of titles appearing annually between 1815 and 1828 (1121 as compared to 1377) and another thirty percent increase in titles between 1828 and 1832 (1377 as compared to an estimated 1789), by 1830 almost all publishers refused to publish poetry. John Murray refused all manuscripts of poetry after Byron's death in 1826; Longman said "nobody wants poetry now," and encouraged authors to write cookbooks instead of volumes of verse; John Taylor wrote to John Clare in 1830 saying that his firm "was no longer a publisher of poetry"; and Smith, Elder told Clare in the same year that they would publish poetry only at the author's risk.... The answer [to this anti-poetry bias] lies in the great technological revolution that occurred in printing and the effects it had upon publishing and the reading public.'

[147] Ibid. 365.

[148] On 3 Aug. 1827, Taylor wrote to Clare that 'the Time has passed away in which Poetry will answer' (see *Letters*, ed. Storey, 394 n.).

But Clare's manuscripts were not alone in causing Taylor problems at this period. The years 1822–6, those of the ill-starred gestation of *The Shepherd's Calendar*, were the most difficult of Taylor's career, in large part because of overwork. Taylor had sole responsibility for the publishing side of Taylor and Hessey (Hessey ran the retail or bookselling side of the firm); he had occasional advisers in the early years, including Thomas Hood, the lawyer Richard Woodhouse, and John Hamilton Reynolds, but never once in the firm's history could he afford an assistant, a secretary, or a reader. If he was dilatory in his dealings with Clare, he was hardly idle. As mentioned earlier, in 1821, partly as a means of protecting and promoting their authors, Taylor and Hessey took over the *London Magazine*, and from 1821–4 Taylor was its editor. These jobs were too much for one man; as Clare himself warned Taylor, 'if you dont give somthing up you will dye without joking—why the devil cant you sit in your chamber with as much indolent pomposity as the Albermarle bookseller [Murray] does'.[149] But Taylor couldn't, and as a result his health deteriorated (he was incapacitated by illness in the early summer of 1822, in March and Autumn of 1823, in Autumn 1824, in August 1825), his work suffered, with a consequent deterioration of his relations with writers (who were sometimes edited without consultation, or not paid with sufficient dispatch), and the firm's losses began to mount. 'The house', writes Chilcott, 'had lost on Carlyle, on Landor, and Lamb, and probably on Hazlitt also. The *London Magazine* had left them with a deficit of £500 a year. With perhaps the single exception of Ann and Jane Taylor, they had failed to discover a best-selling author.'[150] It was only after 1827, in fact, when Taylor began publishing textbooks and books of political science, that the firm began to make a profit.

Clare first broached the idea of *The Shepherd's Calendar* in August 1822, just after Taylor's first illness; two years later Taylor had in his possession the majority of the poems for the collection. When Harry Stoe Van Dyk, a friend of Lord Radstock and Mrs Emmerson, volunteered to transcribe Clare's chaotic manuscripts, Taylor willingly agreed. But Van Dyk was distracted

[149] John Clare to John Taylor, 3 Sept. 1821, ibid. 213.
[150] Chilcott, *A Publisher and His Circle*, 178.

by business in the West Indies, and when, finally, he did attend
to the job, he took it upon himself to edit—cutting and adding
material—as well as to transcribe the poems.[151] Clare's understandable irritation led to a frosty exchange of letters with
Taylor, who seems to have put *The Shepherd's Calendar* out of
mind once Van Dyk volunteered his services; when Taylor offered
to back out of the project in a frequently quoted letter of 28
January 1826, one which figures in earlier discussion of Clare's
handwriting, Clare calmed down, and both sides apologized.

Taylor's letter of 28 January 1826 makes clear both his continuing admiration for Clare and the grounds of his impatience;
it also importantly complicates the questions both of imposition and of the role of 'institutional affiliation' in the revision
process. Taylor begins by announcing that he has sent Clare the
money he asked for in a letter of 24 January. He then claims
not to be upset 'at your pressing me for payment of this or any
other Money which may be coming to you'.[152] What bothers—
'hurts'—him is Clare's accusation of 'Promise-breaking &c
... for not getting faster forward with the Poems'. In the
letter of the 24th, Clare likens these 'promises' to 'lawsuits in
Chancery tho I dont say that you feel that they are so—so
keenly as I do because you have so many things in town to
attract you[r] attention while mine has nothing but one point
to look at every day till the same repetitions make me half mad
with disappointments'. Clare pronounces himself 'all anxiety
about the book', fancies 'it will never come out at all', and
concludes from the delays 'that promises & performances are
not near neighbours by a wide difference'.[153] These last complaints are typical of the letters from 1821–5. Taylor was Clare's
only hope, Clare felt, yet Taylor never wrote. 'My dear Taylor,'
begins a letter of 9 July 1823, 'It perhaps woud have been more
appropriate to have said "Sir" considering the long silence
between us.'[154] 'I have just nothing to do,' begins another, '&

[151] Ibid. 104.
[152] Clare came eventually to exonerate Taylor from all accusations of financial
misdealing or intrigue, rightly identifying Taylor's cousin, John Drury, as the problem.
As Clare writes to Mrs Emmerson, in a letter of 13 Nov. 1832, in *Letters*, ed. Storey,
605: 'I am very sorry that Taylor should be brought into the matter for I am sure
he is utterly above such things & like myself a man of business only by necessity.'
[153] John Clare to John Taylor, 24 Jan. 1826, in *Letters*, ed. Storey, 355–6.
[154] John Clare to John Taylor, 9 July 1823, ibid. 276.

to pass time away I scribble this with not a single thought to begin with nor one perhaps worth reading ere I get [to the] end—I wait impatient for the end of the month to see the dream in print ['Superstition's Dream: A Poem', *London Magazine*, February 1822].'[155] 'I do not wish to hurt the feelings of any one nor do I wish they shoud hurt mine,' Clare writes to Hessey, to whom he turned increasingly in these years, 'but when delay is carried into a system its cause must grow a substitute for a worse name—I will go on no further but I will ask you to give a moments reflection to my situation & see how you woud like it yourself'.[156]

Taylor gathers together Clare's several accusations from the letter of 24 January and responds toughly:

I have desired to serve you in this Matter as I did at first, from no Hope or Expectation of Gain, but with a single Wish to your individual Interest: & if all were known that has been done in the business by Hessey & myself, & in what Manner we have been recompensed for our Trouble, our greatest Enemies would not think we had profited too much by the Speculation.

This Ollier-like thrust is followed by an offer to relinquish publication rights; Clare is free to find another publisher if he wishes. As for the delay, though previously 'I have submitted, & apologized, & taken Blame to myself', the 'frankness' of Clare's last letter 'has relieved me from my irksome Situation'. The present delay, he insists, is principally Clare's fault, a product not only of the state of the manuscripts but of the poems themselves. 'The Poems are not only slovenly written but as slovenly *composed*, & to make good Poems out of some of them is a greater Difficulty than I ever had to engage with in your former Works,—while in others it is a complete Impossibility.'

The pressure of Clare's needs and demands, especially those occasioned by his inability or unwillingness to revise, has taken its toll. Taylor can no longer, given his increased workload and the gathering disorder of the manuscripts, take on such authorial responsibility:

[155] John Clare to John Taylor, 24 Jan. 1822, ibid. 224.
[156] John Clare to James Hessey, 17 Apr. 1825, ibid. 326.

You have more time than I have. You have far more Talent, indeed no other Person can mend or make some of your Poems but yourself.—I have gone as well as I can to the End of June.—here I stop, & must stop.—A Desire to Save you Trouble is now out of the Question—I have done all I can.

Here as elsewhere, Taylor sees himself as burdened by the authority Clare cedes him.

You can write better when you choose, & therefore I beg & hope you will—not a better hand only, but better poetry. . . . I cannot make a Volume fit to be seen out of such Materials as this Poem on July: & I should be loth to incur the Blame, when I have troubled myself so as I never was perplexed before, of having ruined your Reputation by my injudicious Editing.

The letter ends with Taylor reiterating a sense of grievance. Clare is still his 'Friend'; he will continue to do all he can, 'in Reason', to help him; but now Taylor must look to his own needs: 'I cannot submit to have charges brought against me of which I know myself innocent without repelling them, especially when there exists no good Ground for my sacrificing my own Peace of Mind to save yours from a little useful Interruption.'[157]

Before he receives an answer to this letter, Taylor writes again, obviously uneasy. The letter of the 28th, he admits, was written 'under a Feeling of some Irritation, at seeing how freely I was censured for the Delay of the Work'. It galls him to be taken to task about a project which 'had I done what any other man would under such Circumstances I should have declined having any Concern with', especially since he only undertook the project because of 'your ill Health and my sincere Wish to be of service to you'. How can Clare accuse him of wilful delay when

even my own Interest would have been a Sufficient Spur to me to do all I could, for it is not a very politic Thing for me to have laid in the paper & have to pay near 80£ for it a year at least before the Work can be published—to say nothing of the Loss of my own Time.

It is no longer possible, Taylor declares, to 'complete the Undertaking' while 'keeping my Regrets to myself'. Clare himself

<hr>

[157] John Taylor to John Clare, 28 Jan. 1826, ibid. 356–8.

must 'put your own Shoulder to the Wheel or the Work will never come out'.

After a temperate beginning, Taylor's sense of grievance, only in part a product of defensiveness, resurfaces. Clare has been selfish, self-absorbed:

> there should be some Delicacy observed towards even me—& because I wish to do all I can toward the Correcting & preparing your Poems for the Press it does not follow as a Matter of course that I can take them in any Condition & still make them fit to be seen.—I feel I must confess a little sore at having had more imposed upon me than it was possible for me to perform.[158]

This plea deserves some credit. That Clare's circumstances were altogether more perilous than Taylor's does not mean Taylor's own difficulties were insignificant. Taylor was in trouble, and Clare's anxieties increased that trouble, in part by producing difficult or rushed manuscripts. Taylor *was* dilatory, but he was ridiculously overworked. Hence the feeling of being 'imposed upon'. Clare, he felt, had upset a collaborative balance. This is why, just as Clare urged Taylor's independence early in their relation, so now Taylor urges Clare's independence, insisting that he 'send me for my Judgement Poems as good as *you* can write in a Hand any *other* Person can read'. Such poems 'I will cheerfully undertake to edit'.

Clare's response to the letter of the 28th is sober and collected. He is 'disappointed at hearing that you are not able to get on with the poems'. He mentions two poems in manuscript that might be used in place of the rejected 'July'. He defends 'July', saying he thought it 'one of the best [poems] I had written or I shoud not have sent it'.[159] What he does not do is respond to Taylor's counter-accusations, except implicitly—in the dignified collectedness of his tone. He puts aside the agitation of his earlier letter of the 24th, and addresses Taylor as an equal. He neither fawns nor fulminates. Later, he even admits that careful recopying leads to drastic revision: 'for if a first copy co[n]sists of a 100 lines its second corrections gennerally dwindle down to half the number & I heartily wish I had done so at first'.[160]

---

[158] John Taylor to John Clare, 2 Feb. 1826, ibid. 360–1.
[159] John Clare to John Taylor, 1 Feb. 1826, ibid. 358–9.
[160] John Clare to John Taylor, 18 Mar. 1826, ibid. 367.

What follows is salutary and affecting: just as Taylor's intemperate outburst brings Clare back to a sense of his responsibilities, so Clare's response brings forth a more conciliatory note from Taylor. Both men have been at fault, and both now acknowledge the necessity of collaboration. Clare's modern editors and critics have been too quick to condemn this collaboration as forced and to demonize Taylor. Taylor's revisions were rarely callous or cavalier; moreover, Clare himself not only acceded to—sanctioned—them, but sought them out. Poets who want their poems published need publishers; the publisher's job is to mediate between poet and audience, negotiating in revision sometimes incompatible needs and tastes. That Taylor took this job seriously and performed it responsibly has for too long been obscured by Romantic ideology, by primitivist bias against secondary and social processes of creation in particular.

CHAPTER SIX

KEATS, THE CRITICS, AND THE PUBLIC

THOUGH determined to be 'among the English Poets', a great and lasting writer worthy of 'the Temple of Fame' or 'the laurel wreath on high suspended',[1] John Keats also needed immediate recognition, to be 'successful and respected' as well as great.[2] In early 1818, soon after the publication of his first collection, *Poems* (1817), Keats determined to 'overwhelm' himself in poetry ('Sleep and Poetry', 1. 96);[3] hence in part the attraction of epic. 'In Endymion', he writes to Hessey, 'I leaped headlong into the sea,' a total immersion which was also 'a test, a trial of my Powers of Imagination'.[4] But this trial had, if not quite to pay its way, then to promise work that would; Keats had already declared to his guardian, Richard Abbey, his intention to 'gain his living' by poetry;[5] he was in no position to ignore

[1] John Keats to George and Georgiana Keats, 14 Oct. 1818, and to Benjamin Bailey, 8 Oct. 1817, in *The Letters of John Keats 1814–1821*, ed. Hyder Rollins, 2 vols. (Cambridge, Mass.: Harvard University Press, 1958), i. 394, 170; henceforth cited as *Letters*, ed. Rollins. Among Keats's poems which reflect on lasting fame, often distinguishing it from contemporary neglect or censure, are 'Oh Chatterton! how very sad thy fate', 'To my Brother George', 'Sleep and Poetry', 'Great spirits now on earth are sojourning', and 'Bards of passion and of Mirth'.

[2] Jack Stillinger, 'Keats and His Helpers: The Multiple Authorship of *Isabella*', ch. 2 of *Multiple Authorship and the Myth of Solitary Genius* (New York: Oxford University Press, 1991), 46.

[3] All quotations from Keats's poetry are taken from *The Poems of John Keats*, ed. Jack Stillinger (Cambridge, Mass.: Harvard University Press, 1978); henceforth cited as *Poems*.

[4] John Keats to James Hessey, 8 Oct. 1817, in *Letters*, ed. Rollins, i. 169.

[5] See Hyder Rollins (ed.), *The Keats Circle: Letters and Papers 1816–1878*, 2 vols. (1948; Cambridge, Mass.: Harvard University Press, 1965), i. 307–8; henceforth cited as Rollins (ed.), *KC*. Keats had passed his examinations at Guy's Hospital, and was not without ways of making a living. As W. J. Bate puts it, in *John Keats* (New York: Oxford University Press, 1966), 113: 'Every discerning acquaintance [Keats] ever had stresses his common sense; he was only too aware of the problem of making a living. He was still going to the hospital two weeks after he had taken the copy of his first volume to Abbey. It was May before he finally abandoned work as a dresser; and by then he was immersed in his long struggle with *Endymion*. . . . Even so, for the next three years, he kept entertaining at least

his audience, an audience that was in the process of being turned against him by critical opinion, which he understandably professed to despise. The Olliers, publishers of the first collection, had, as we have seen, abandoned him, principally because of poor sales. Of the many wounding moments in John Gibson Lockhart's notorious *Blackwood's Magazine* review of *Endymion* (1818), the most alarming may well have been Lockhart's 'small prophecy that his bookseller will not a second time venture £50 upon any thing he can write'.[6] That bookseller was the firm of Taylor and Hessey, which, together with a circle of early advisers including John Hamilton Reynolds and Richard Woodhouse, set out in editing Keats's poems—demurring, questioning, suggesting alternatives, clarifying and correcting—to put him right with the critics, or at least to deflect their hostility.

Once again, then, revision derives in part from external sources, is a 'collaborative' enterprise involving not only friends and publishers, as in the cases of *Frankenstein* and Clare's published volumes, but the public itself, in opinions partly formed and reflected by critics.[7] In the case of Taylor's revisions of Clare's poems, public tastes and interests (poetical, moral, political) were largely anticipated, often in the light of Taylor's experiences with Keats. The revisions we shall be looking at in this final chapter, those to *Endymion* and *Lamia, Isabella, the*

---

the possibility of setting up practice.' John Barnard, in *John Keats* (Cambridge: Cambridge University Press, 1987), 7–8, 11–13, argues for the reasonableness (the hope was not, that is, impossible) of Keats's aspiring to support himself as a poet and/or man of letters.

[6] G. M. Matthews (ed.), *Keats: The Critical Heritage* (London: Routledge & Kegan Paul, 1971), 109; henceforth cited as Matthews (ed.), *CH*.

[7] The relationship of the critics or reviewers in the major periodicals of the early nineteenth century to the larger reading public is summarized by Jon P. Klancher, in *The Making of English Reading Audiences, 1790–1832* (Madison: University of Wisconsin Press, 1987), 50: 'The most significant journals gathered audiences of five to fifteen thousand readers each: the *Edinburgh Review* (1802), the *Examiner* (1808), the *Quarterly Review* (1809), the *New Monthly Magazine* (1814), *Blackwood's Edinburgh Magazine* (1817), the *London Magazine* (1830), the *Metropolitan* (1831). Their total readership could only be guessed at, but Francis Jeffrey's estimate still stands: some twenty thousand among what he called "fashionable or public life": upper civil servants and clergy, the richer merchants and manufacturers, the gentry, and the professionals, all earning more than eight hundred pounds a year. Much more selectively, the journals also reached into the "middling classes" of some two hundred thousand teachers, lesser clergy and civil servants, and shopkeepers, each earning three hundred pounds or less per year.'

Eve of St Agnes and Other Poems (1820), respond directly to specific criticisms, those levelled at *Poems*, and then *Endymion* itself. Here, too, I shall argue, the poet's relation to revision has been misrepresented. Though no writer of the period revised so infrequently ('manuscript after manuscript shows him getting *most* of the words right the first time', comments Stillinger[8]), or had more 'Romantic' views about authorial autonomy or the composing process, Keats both participated in, and largely (though, on occasion, reluctantly) approved, the attempts of Woodhouse, Taylor, and others to propitiate public censure. 'It is a sorry thing for me', he concludes to Taylor on 27 February 1818, after approving Taylor's revisions to *Endymion*, 'that any one should have to overcome Prejudices in reading my Verses.'[9]

EARLY VIEWS

Keats's first collection, *Poems*, initially received a decent press. Of the six reviews to appear in 1817, three were by friends (Reynolds in *The Champion*, George Felton Mathew in *The European Magazine*, Leigh Hunt in *The Examiner*), while those from anonymous independent authors (in *The Monthly Magazine*, *The Eclectic Review*, and Constable's *Edinburgh Magazine*) were also positive. Negative reaction only set in after the publication of *Endymion*, in April 1818, initiated in September by *Blackwood's* infamous attack on Keats as a member of 'the Cockney School of Poetry', an attack which also disparaged *Poems*.[10] This hatchet-job was the work of John Gibson Lockhart, perhaps with help from John Wilson. Also in September, John Wilson Croker's unsigned attack on *Endymion* in the other major Tory periodical of the day, *The Quarterly Review*, was even more damaging, in part because of its comparatively judicious air. From this point onwards critical commentary on Keats was *parti pris*: 'his friends thought he was a genius; his friends'

---

[8] Jack Stillinger, 'Keats's Extempore Effusions and The Question of Intentionality', in Robert Brinkley and Keith Hanley (eds.), *Romantic Revisions* (Cambridge: Cambridge University Press, 1992), 309.

[9] John Keats to John Taylor, 27 Feb. 1818, in *Letters*, ed. Rollins, i. 238.

[10] Both the *Blackwood's* and *Quarterly Review* attacks appeared in Sept. 1818, although in the Aug. and Apr. issues, respectively.

political enemies represented him as a charlatan or a foolish boy, "Johnny Keats", whose head had been turned by the company he kept'.[11]

This company was seen as politically and socially suspect, principally because Leigh Hunt, editor of the radical *Examiner*, stood at its centre. Hunt had been imprisoned from 1813 to 1815 for an article attacking the Prince Regent, and his political stance in the *Examiner*, which he edited from 1808 to 1821, was consistently liberal or reformist. 'Of the author of this small volume we know nothing more,' begins the October 1817 *Edinburgh Magazine* review of *Poems*, 'than that he is said to be a very young man, and a particular friend of the Messrs Hunt, the editors of the *Examiner*, and of Mr. Hazlitt'.[12] Hunt's championing of Keats was early and consistent (despite *Blackwood's* and Benjamin Haydon's attempts to suggest otherwise). He was the first person to publish one of Keats's poems, printing the sonnet 'O Solitude' in the *Examiner* on 5 May 1816; he introduced Keats to Shelley, Hazlitt, Haydon, and other literary and artistic figures; and he also attempted to prepare the way for *Poems* by praising Keats in a notice of 1 December 1816 entitled 'Young Poets', which also printed Keats's second published poem, 'On First Looking into Chapman's Homer'. It was this notice that identified Keats, Shelley, and Reynolds with 'a new school of poetry rising of late, which promises to extinguish the French one that has prevailed among us since the time of Charles the 2nd'.[13] 'Such a prediction,' Reynolds later commented, in defence of *Endymion*, 'was a fine, but dangerous compliment, to Mr. Keats: it exposed him instantly to the malice of the *Quarterly Review*'.

[11] Matthews (ed.), *CH* 1. Lewis M. Schwartz, in 'Keats's Critical Reception in Newspapers of His Day', *Keats–Shelley Journal*, 21–2 (1972/3), 186–7, argues for the importance of daily and weekly newspapers, as opposed to the major monthly or quarterly periodicals, in shaping the reception of Keats's poems: 'Were it not for the steady stream of favorable material in newspapers between 1818 and 1820,' Schwartz concludes, 'Jeffrey, who was cautious enough to wait two years in any case, might never have come to Keats's defense in the *Edinburgh*. By 1820, Keats's reputation, the views of Byron, Hazlitt, and Shelley notwithstanding, had survived the Tory assault on *Endymion*, and mainly as a result of a vast body of favorable newspaper material which has received only slight notice by scholars of the period' —perhaps because it figures so marginally in the correspondence of Keats and his advisers.
[12] Matthews (ed.), *CH* 71.   [13] Ibid. 41–2.

It also inspired the first of Lockhart's attacks on 'the Cockney School', to be followed eventually, in the fourth attack, by one on Keats himself.[14]

Keats licenses the identification with Hunt, not only in the dedicatory sonnet which opens *Poems* ('To Leigh Hunt, Esq.') and the motto to the next poem in the volume, 'I Stood Tip-toe upon a little hill', a motto taken from Hunt's *The Story of Rimini* (1816), but from the volume's concluding poem, 'Sleep and Poetry' ('an ominous title', comments Byron[15]), which contains the following caricature of the old or 'French' school ('Pope's school', according to Reynolds[16]), addressed to the 'dismal soul'd' (1. 187):

> But ye were dead
> To things ye knew not of,—were closely wed
> To musty laws lined out with wretched rule
> And compass vile: so that ye taught a school
> Of dolts to smooth, inlay, and clip, and fit,
> Till, like the certain wands of Jacob's wit,
> Their verses tallied. Easy was the task:
> A thousand handicraftsmen wore the mask
> Of Poesy. Ill-fated, impious race!
> That blasphemed the bright Lyrist to his face,
> And did not know it,—no, they went about,
> Holding a poor, decrepit standard out
> Marked with most flimsy mottos, and in large
> The name of one Boileau! (ll. 193–206)

The imprudence of this attack (Hunt thought it merely 'irreverend'[17]) was compounded by extravagant praise of Keats by his friends. Reynolds, in his review of 9 March 1817 in the *Champion*, thought Keats 'likely to make a great addition to those who would overthrow that artificial taste which French criticism has long planted amongst us. At a time when nothing is talked of but the power and passion of Lord Byron, and the playful and elegant fancy of Moore, and the correctness of

---

[14] Ibid. 118. For the first use of the term see 'Z' (Lockhart's pseudonym), 'On the Cockney School of Poetry. No. I', in the Oct. 1817 issue of *Blackwood's Magazine*, reprinted in Donald H. Reiman (ed.), *The Romantics Reviewed: Contemporary Reviews of British Romantic Writers*, Pt. C, 2 vols. (New York: Garland Publishing, 1972), i. 47–51.

[15] Matthews (ed.), *CH* 129.   [16] Ibid. 48.   [17] Ibid. 62.

Rogers, and the sublimity and pathos of Campbell (these terms we should conceive are ready composed in the Edinburgh Review-shop) a young man starts suddenly before us, with a genius that is likely to eclipse them all.'[18] This is the sort of talk that leads critics such as the anonymous author of a notice in the *Eclectic Review*, an ultimately favourable notice, to talk of Keats being 'flattered'[19] into premature publication. It is also the sort of talk that earned Keats influential enemies.

The principle objections to Keats's verse are clear from the earliest notices, even those by friends. Keats is charged with 'looseness' and 'extravagance' (or 'luxuriousness'). 'His natural freedom of versification, at times passes to an absolute faultiness of measure,' comments Reynolds. He should 'abstain from the use of compound epithets as much as possible', presumably because they are extravagant, making his descriptions 'overwrought'.[20] Mathew, in much the most stringent of the puffing pieces, censures both 'the slovenly independence of his versification' and a more general 'foppery and affectation',[21] qualities he specifically associates with Hunt. Hunt himself worries about extravagance, although without associating it with his own work. Keats notices everything 'too indiscriminately and without an eye to natural proportion and effect'; his verse suffers from 'superabundance of detail'.[22] Hunt also thinks the versification loose, lacking 'due consideration of . . . principles'.[23] Though Keats means to challenge a prevailing correctness, he must beware 'the fault on the opposite side . . . mere roughnesses and discords for their own sake',[24] blemishes which produce poetry the *Edinburgh Magazine* characterizes as 'straggling and uneven, without the lengthened flow of blank verse, or the pointed connection of couplets'.[25] This looseness extends also to rhyme, as in 'favours' and 'behaviours', 'put on' and 'Chatterton',

---

[18] Ibid. 45.   [19] Ibid. 69.

[20] From Reynolds's unsigned *Champion* review of 9 Mar. 1817, ibid. 49. For a contemporary enumeration of the 'luxuriant' or 'overwrought' in Keats see Andrew Bennett, *Keats, Narrative and Audience: The Posthumous Life of Writing* (Cambridge: Cambridge University Press, 1994), 1: 'What may most fundamentally be identified as the "character" of Keats's poetry involves the uncontainable intensities of an inundation of figures, such as oxymoron, enjambment, neologism, and an adjectival distortion and syntactical dislocation, by which "thought"—the ideational or "thetic"—is apparently subsumed within the suffocating sensuousness of "language".'   [21] Matthews (ed.), *CH* 51, 53.

[22] Ibid. 58.   [23] Ibid. 57.   [24] Ibid. 59.   [25] Ibid. 72

'burrs' and 'sepulchres', examples of 'facetious' rhyming picked out for censure by the *Eclectic Review*.[26]

Behind the accusations of looseness and luxuriance lay qualities the term 'Cockney' would bring to the foreground, qualities the early reviews only hinted at. In the unsigned *Edinburgh Magazine* review, Keats is associated with the 'school' of Hunt and Hazlitt, and then advised to cast off its 'uncleannesses'. These uncleannesses, as Jerome J. McGann puts it, are 'not merely the erotic subjects in Keats's poetry but Keats's peculiarly mannered treatment of sexual images and subjects'.[27] Only by casting off such defects will Keats attain 'manly singleness of heart, or feminine simplicity and constancy of affection'. Poetical identity, in the writings of Hunt and his school, it is implied, is somehow inauthentic—assumed, factitious, duplicitous. The 'truest strain of poetry' expresses 'natural' passion, does not preen and parade; it is 'content with the glory of stimulating, rather than of oppressing, the sluggishness of ordinary conceptions'.[28] Hunt's school, in contrast, tries too hard, is overdressed, 'too full of conceits and sparking points, ever to excite anything more than a cold approbation at the long-run'.[29] Its lack of 'soundness' is figured in the looseness of its versification, an educational deficiency dressed up as principle.

TAYLOR AND *ENDYMION*

Taylor's revisions of *Endymion*, affecting some 130 to 140 lines, concentrate on objections of this sort, as Keats knew they would. Though at one point, in 1816, Taylor and Hessey considered publishing both a new volume of Hunt's poems and, in association with R. Triphook, a second edition of *The Story of Rimini*, by the time the firm decided to publish Keats, commercial

---

[26] Ibid. 68–9.

[27] Jerome J. McGann, 'Keats and the Historical Method in Literary Criticism', in *The Beauty of Inflections: Literary Investigations in Historical Method and Theory* (Oxford: Clarendon Press, 1985), 29. For the *Edinburgh Magazine* accusation of 'uncleanness' see Matthews (ed.), *CH* 72. See, also, Lockhart's complaint against Hunt in the second of the 'Cockney School' attacks, in which he condemns *The Story of Rimini* not so much for its incestuous subject-matter as for the poem's treatment of that subject-matter: 'It would fain be the genteel comedy of incest' (Reiman (ed.), *Romantics Reviewed*, i. 56).

[28] Matthews (ed.), *CH* 73.   [29] Ibid. 72.

considerations (and misunderstandings) had made them wary. Reynolds was right, association with Hunt meant instant enmity from the *Quarterly Review* (circulation 12,000, readership 'fifty times ten thousand'[30]), whose editor, William Gifford, had, in John Scott's words, 'long been at war' with Hunt, a fact 'known to every one in the least acquainted with the literary gossip of the day'.[31] Taylor thus sought and received an assurance from Keats 'that the poet was not likely to repeat such indiscretions as the dedication to Leigh Hunt in any later work'.[32] It is one of the great ironies of the prominence given to Hunt in the September 1818 attacks on *Endymion* that they occurred months after Keats had consciously sought to distance himself from Hunt's poetical influence.

Keats finished the draft of *Endymion* on 28 November 1817, seven and a half months after he'd begun the poem in mid-April. He then took a month off to 'racket' about London and visit friends, before settling down to revise and copy the manuscript, a process which took him three months.[33] The best known of these revisions—communicated to Taylor by letter, after completion of the fair copy—throws light on Keats's attitudes both to Taylor and to revision in general. Keats has been brooding over a passage late in Book 1, a discussion of happiness:

> Wherein lies happiness? In that which becks
> Our ready minds to blending pleasureable:
> And that delight is the most treasureable
> That makes the richest Alchymy. Behold
> The clear Religion of Heaven!

'This appears to me the very contrary of blessed', writes Keats to Taylor on 30 January 1818. He then offers the following well-known alternative:

> Wherein lies happiness? In that which becks
> Our ready minds to fellowship divine,
> A fellowship with essence; till we shine,
> Full alchemiz'd, and free of space. Behold
> The clear religion of heaven! (1. 777–81)

[30] Ibid. 8. [31] Ibid. 115.
[32] For Taylor's letter, to his father, see Robert Gittings, *John Keats* (London: Heinemann, 1968), 193.
[33] John Keats to John Taylor, 10 Jan. 1818, in *Letters*, ed. Rollins, i. 202.

'You must indulge me by putting this in,' writes Keats, 'for setting aside the badness of the other, such a preface is necessary to the Subject. The whole thing must I think have appeared to you, who are a consequitive Man, as a thing almost of mere words—but I assure you that when I wrote it, it was a regular stepping of the Imagination towards a Truth.'[34]

Keats's revision perfectly meets the objections voiced by the reviewers of *Poems* (1817). To begin with, it jettisons the jaunty or 'facetious' rhyme of 'pleasureable' and 'treasureable', which undermines, in a fashion characteristic of Hunt (accused by Keats, in his growing disillusion, of 'making fine things petty'[35]), the seriousness of the thought, which Keats calls a 'Truth'. The thought itself, meanwhile, is made less vague; or rather, its vagueness is invested with a Wordsworthian solemnity or weight. What seemed merely redundant in the first version—that 'blending pleasureable' which is, unsurprisingly, a 'delight', and also 'most treasurable', because 'the richest Alchymy'—not only becomes more muscular and plain in revision (recalling the *Edinburgh Magazine* on the need for 'manly singleness' and 'female simplicity'), but sounds 'consequitive' or logical (rather than metaphorical or appositional). What is happiness? It is 'fellowship divine'. What is fellowship divine? It is 'fellowship with essence' (a characteristically Wordsworthian 'clarification'). What is the result of fellowship with essence? That we 'shine | Full alchemiz'd, and free of space.' The revision creates an impression of philosophical deliberation, of dignity, solidity, 'soundness', qualities Keats associates with the 'consequitive' Taylor.

Taylor's suggested revisions work in comparable ways, and are no less committed to original or authorial intentions. 'I assure you that when I wrote it,' Keats insists of the unrevised passage, 'it was a regular stepping of the Imagination towards a Truth.' In other words, though Keats may have changed his views or grown more reflective in the period between the passage's original composition and the revision, the new lines clarify rather than change, are no work of new self. Similarly, when Taylor suggests emendations, at least for *Endymion*, he does so

---

[34] John Keats to John Taylor, 30 Jan. 1818, ibid. 218.
[35] John Keats to George and Georgiana Keats, 17 Dec. 1818, ibid. ii. 11.

uncontroversially, in the capacity of facilitating editor. That Keats felt this to be so is seen not only in his praise ('Your alteration strikes me as being a great improvement—the page looks much better'[36]) but in his attitude to proofs. Though he read proofs of Book 1 of *Endymion*, those for subsequent books seem to have been left to Taylor and Charles Cowden Clarke, son of the headmaster of Keats's old school, and a longstanding friend and literary guide. Later, Keats apologized for this dereliction, in ways that not only recall Clare but implicitly question Romantic attitudes. 'I did very wrong to leave you to all the trouble of Endymion—but I could not help it then—another time I shall be more bent to all sort of troubles and disagreeables—Young Men for some time have an idea that such a thing as happiness is to be had and therefore are extremely impatient under any unpleasant restraining.'[37] In future, Keats implies, he will be more 'mature'; which is to say, he will attend to secondary as well as primary processes.

The history of Taylor's part in the revision of *Endymion* is easily told. Keats delivered the poem to Taylor a book at a time from 20 January 1818 to 21 March 1818, and Taylor made a number of suggestions on the revised fair copy.[38] Books 1 and 2 were printed by Taylor before he'd seen 3 and 4, and Keats was reading proofs of Book 1 by late February, while still revising Book 3. Taylor's enthusiasm for Book 1, which led him to suggest that the poem as a whole be published in quarto (if Haydon would draw a frontispiece), was not matched by his reactions to Book 2, with its troublingly lush description of the hero's love for Cynthia. Though Taylor brackets or queries a number of extravagances, for the most part his suggested revisions, here and elsewhere, were confined to formal matters—awkwardnesses or irregularities ('looseness') of metre, rhyme, grammar.

[36] John Keats to John Taylor, 27 Feb. 1818, ibid. i. 238.
[37] John Keats to John Taylor, 24 Apr. 1818, ibid. 270.
[38] The first draft, which Reynolds claims to have read and marked, is lost, though we know something of it from Woodhouse's elaborate notation of Keats's emendations and excisions in Books 2–4, revisions amounting to what Stillinger estimates to be 660 lines or 'between one-fifth and one-fourth of the total in these books' (*Poems*, ed. Stillinger, 574). Books 2–4 were last seen in 1847 (there is no record of the draft of Book 1), when John Hamilton Reynolds lent the manuscript to Richard Monckton Milnes, Keats's first biographer (see Rollins (ed.), *KC* ii. 227). Woodhouse's transcription of variants in the first draft makes no mention of Reynolds as a reviser.

That Taylor's revisions were suggestions rather than impositions is everywhere apparent, not least in the fact that there
were many more of them for Book 1, which seems to have been
revised jointly by poet and publisher, than for Books 2–4, which
we have no evidence Keats saw.[39] The same is true of proof
revisions. Margaret Ketchum Powell identifies only twenty-four
changes Taylor made in the 3058 lines of proof for Books 2–
4, which Keats did not see (being away at Teignmouth, as
Taylor knew he would be), of which seven may be printer's
errors (the remainder were again mostly stylistic, regularizing
metre, clarifying grammar, supplying missing rhymes, deleting
a poor one, that of 'nonny' and 'honey', in 4. 702–3). When
poet and publisher worked together in revision, their relations
were easy and flexible. For example, in lines 137–8 of the fair
copy of Book 1, on the recto side of the manuscript (the side
on which the draft is mostly transcribed), Keats introduces a
procession of 'young damsels', dancing and singing, 'Each with
a handy wicker over-brimmed | With April's tender younglings.'[40]
On the verso, opposite the first of these lines, Taylor offers two
alternatives: 'Each brought a little wicker over-brimmed' and
'Each bringing a white wicker over-brimmed', presumably because 'handy' (from the original 'Each with a handy wicker')
struck him as precious or banal. In the event, Keats rejected
both alternatives, producing instead a revised version of his
own: 'Each having a white wicker over-brimmed' (paraphrased
by Woodhouse as 'a white wicker [*basket*] full of the first *fruits*
of April'[41]), which hardly betters Taylor's suggestions (especially 'Each brought a little wicker'), but eliminates 'handy'.

[39] Margaret Ketchum Powell, in 'Keats and His Editor: The Manuscript of
Endymion', *The Library*, 6 (1984), 145–6, identifies 'four revisions made interlin-
early in ink, all occurring within a portion of the poem 160 lines long' as potentially unauthorized revisions by Taylor. But she then concludes against this possibility,
arguing that 'the pattern of the rest of his work on the manuscript of Book 1 is
one of editorial suggestion, not independent revision.'

[40] *Keats: The Complete Poems*, ed. Miriam Allott (London: Longman, 1970),
146, identifies the cancelled fair copy version of this line as 'Each with a heavy
wicker over-brimmed', in which 'heavy' hardly suits dancing damsels and 'tender
younglings'.

[41] See John Keats, *Endymion (1818): A Facsimile of Richard Woodhouse's
Annotated Copy in the Berg Collection*, ed. Jack Stillinger (New York: Garland
Publishing, 1985), 39. This is vol. iii of the four volumes devoted to Keats in the
Garland series, Manuscripts of the Younger Romantics. Donald H. Reiman is the
general editor of the series.

Elsewhere, when Taylor's suggestions are more obvious improvements, Keats simply accepts them, as when 'to tint her pretty cheek' (1. 368) becomes 'to tint her pallid cheek', or when incorrect verb forms are queried, usually because Keats has forgotten to match second-person verb endings with second-person subjects. At other times, Keats overrides Taylor's offerings, as when 'bob', in the original, is prefered to Taylor's 'push' or 'raise', in 'Ionian shoals | Of dolphins bob their noses through the brine' (1. 310–11);[42] or three lines later when marine associations are retained (illogically, since the poem is back on land), as 'fair living forms *swam* heavenly | To tunes forgotten', rather than 'mov'd' to them, as in Taylor's suggested revision.

When Taylor calls Keats's attention to grammatical solecisms or potential inconsistencies, illogicalities, or unclarities he gets a better hearing than when he offers 'improvements' or conventional alternatives (as in, say, the expansion of contractions, which Keats at one point strenuously resisted, calling retention of the abbreviated forms 'done 't' or 'is 't' 'of great consequence'[43]). His suggestions are also more likely to be accepted when they concern formal verse properties, as when a line has too few or too many feet. Thus: 'So wingedly: when we amalgamate with' (1. 813), becomes, after Taylor's several pencilled false starts, 'So wingedly: when we combine therewith', a proper pentameter.[44] Taylor's revisions of rhyme were also often welcomed. For example, when Keats rhymes 'vase' and 'stars' in 'From his right hand there swung a milk white vase | Of mingled wine, out sparkling like the stars' (1. 153–4), Taylor suggests a verso alternative: 'From his right hand there swung a vase milk-white | Of mingled wine, out sparkling generous light'. This is no triumph (especially the fatuous 'out sparkling generous light'), but it eliminates the original false or slant rhyme,

[42] That Keats considered and rejected Taylor's suggestions is confirmed by Woodhouse, in a note in a book of transcripts, quoted by Jack Stillinger, *The Texts of Keats's Poems* (Cambridge, Mass.: Harvard University Press, 1974), 148: 'the words raise, push, were suggested to the Author: but he insisted on retaining *bob*'.

[43] John Keats to John Taylor, 24 Apr. 1818, in *Letters*, ed. Rollins, i. 273.

[44] Since it is unclear whether Keats saw Taylor's suggested emendations to Book 3, we cannot blame him for the absence in the 1818 published version of Taylor's pencilled revision of l. 665—from the awkward 'Against that hell-borne Circe. The crew had gone' to 'Against that hell-borne Circe. All had gone', which works metrically.

which is presumably why Keats accepts it. Other rhymes Taylor seems to have questioned were 'vile' and 'toil' (2. 146–7) and 'lute' and 'to't' (2. 164–5), neither of which Keats changed. Such formal or stylistic blemishes are precisely the sort of thing Keats's critics deride.

More problematic is Taylor's uneasiness with Keats's physicality, to some modern critics a particular Keatsian virtue. This is not just a matter of revising obvious 'indelicacies', as in the prudish 'whiter still | Than Leda's love' (1. 157–8), which Taylor offered in place of 'white | As Leda's bosom', a revision Keats may well have adopted for metrical reasons (since it emends the weak ending of the original 'Wild thyme and valley-lilies white as Leda's'). More often the physicality in question is only obscurely indelicate, recalling Clare's 'mites in rotten cheese'. Consider, for example, Taylor's suggested omission of the following metaphorical extravagance:

> . . . a shallow dream forever breeding
> Tempestuous Weather in that very Soul
> That should be twice content, twice smooth, twice whole,
> As is a double Peach   (1. 723)

These lines, which Taylor brackets in pencil, Keats subsequently deletes in ink. Elsewhere, though, Keats resists, as in the retention of 'His snorting four' (1. 552), which Taylor also bracketed in pencil. The difficulty with such instances is that frequently they are both striking ('His snorting four' is a case in point) and risky, because suggestive or sensuous—often in a way reminiscent of Hunt. 'A double Peach', for example, like many of the physicalities Taylor questions, is 'overripe', faintly ludicrous— as is the word 'puff', which occurs a few lines later in the fair copy, in 'when Zephyr bids | A little puff to creep between the fans | Of careless butterflies' (1. 763–5). Taylor offers 'breath' as an alternative to 'puff', and Keats eventually settles on 'breeze'. A comparable excess may prompt Taylor's suggested substitution of 'daisies' for 'bud-stars' in 'lushest blue-bell bed, | Handfuls of bud-stars' (1. 631–2), which Keats approved, just as it more clearly prompted the substitution of 'sigh'd' for 'died' in 'I sigh'd | To faint once more by looking on my bliss' (1. 651–2), a rhetorical extravagance along the lines of 'maddest Kisses', 'hot eyeballs . . . burnt and sear'd' (both in a passage omitted from the fair copy at 1. 897) and 'By the moist languor of thy breathing face' (2. 757), which became 'By the most soft completion of thy face'. Each of these excesses Taylor queried, as he did other lines in the overheated exchange between Endymion and Cynthia in Book 2, including the following lament:

Endymion! dearest! Ah, unhappy me!
His soul will 'scape us—O felicity!
How he does love me! His poor temples beat
To the very tunes of love—how sweet, sweet, sweet.   (2. 761–5)

Taylor bracketed the last two of these lines in pencil, but they stayed in, as did other queried passages. As for Huntian diction—affectedly 'poetical' or quaint—Taylor again does what he can. 'Pight', for example, in 'The silver lakes | Pight among western cloudiness' (l. 740–1), which Keats then revises to 'Pight amid western cloudiness,' is happily altered to 'Pictur'd' in Taylor's revision. In these and other instances Taylor, responsibly, has his eye on the critics; Keats, though, frequently resists, sometimes, one feels, shrewdly, out of a proper appreciation, in the words of a recent commentator, of the 'energies of solecism',[45] at other times, as we shall see, callowly or defensively, out of pride or 'Romantic' prejudice. In retrospect, though, his overall approval was clear: 'the book pleased me very much,' he writes to Taylor, 'it is very free from faults; and although there are one or two words I should wish replaced, I see in many places an improvement greatly to the purpose.'[46]

THE REJECTED PREFACE TO *ENDYMION*

After completing the fair copy of *Endymion*, Keats wrote a preface to the poem which he sent to Taylor and Hessey on 21 March 1818.[47] This preface neatly exemplifies the young poet's

[45] Bennett, *Keats, Narrative and Audience*, 1. See also p. 4: 'Poetry, especially the poetry of Keats, is grounded in solecism because of its distortions of and within language. For poetry, the decorum of grammar is violated, conventions are disrupted, language itself is "tortured"; words must be stretched, misplaced, collided incongruously with other words, dissected into etymology, fragmented into paronomasia, semantically voided, and then bombarded with meaning.'

[46] John Keats to John Taylor, 24 Apr. 1818, in *Letters*, ed. Rollins, i. 270–1.

[47] The original preface is repr. in *Poems*, ed. Stillinger, 738–9, the source of subsequent quotation.

ambivalences and anxieties about his audience. Keats begins by
calling the very idea of a preface for the poem 'a sort of imper-
tinent bow to strangers who care nothing about it', a remark
which recalls the pathetic valedictory ('I always made an awkward bow') of his last letter.[48] He then adverts to the critical
response to *Poems*, 'read by some dozen of my friends, who
lik'd it; and some dozen whom I was unaquainted with, who
did not', a summary which misrepresents the volume's generally favourable reception. The new work, he continues in the
same vein, should 'rather be consider'd as an endeavour than a
thing accomplish'd: a poor prologue to what, if I live, I humbly
hope to do. In duty to the Public I should have kept it back for
a year or two, knowing it to be so faulty: but I really cannot
do so' (for unspecified reasons). At which point, Keats antici-
pates a variety of criticisms drawn from the reception of *Poems*:
to the 'lovers of Simplicity' he apologizes 'for touching the spell
of Loveliness that hung about Endymion' (hardly an apology at
all); to factionalists he professes neutrality, declaring obscurely
'that I have not any particular affection for any particular phrase,
word or letter in the whole affair. I have written to please
myself and in hopes to please others, and for a love of fame;
if I neither please myself, nor others nor get fame, of what
consequence is Phraseology?'; to champions of 'correctness' he
warns that his poem is 'not exactly in chime', and professes to
be braced for critical heavy weather ('a London drizzle or a
scotch Mist'), even while 'facetiously' pre-empting it, in a manner Reynolds woundingly identifies as Huntian.

Reynolds's allusion to Hunt comes in a letter Taylor seems to
have solicited from him, one in which Reynolds apparently also
calls the preface 'affected'. We know this, and that Taylor initially disapproved, through Keats's reply of 9 April 1818, in a
letter of hurt defiance:

Since you all agree that the thing is bad, it must be so—though I am
not aware there is anything like Hunt in it, (and if there is, it is my
natural way, and I have something in common with Hunt) look it over
again and examine into the motives, the seeds from which any one
sentence sprung—I have not the slightest feel of humility towards the

---

[48] For the 'awkward bow' see John Keats to Charles Brown, 30 Nov. 1820, in
Letters, ed. Rollins, ii. 360.

Public—or to anything in existence,—but the eternal Being, the Principle of Beauty,—and the Memory of great Men—When I am writing for myself for the mere sake of the Moment's enjoyment, perhaps nature has its course with me—but a Preface is written to the Public; a thing I cannot help looking upon as an Enemy, and which I cannot address without feelings of Hostility—If I write a Preface in a supple or subdued style, it will not be in character with me as a public speaker—I would be subdued before my friends, and thank them for subduing me—but among Multitudes of Men—I have no feeling of stooping, I hate the idea of humility to them—I never wrote one single Line of Poetry with the least Shadow of public thought.[49]

The tone of this passage derives in part from youthful defensiveness (as when Keats refuses to defer not just to 'the Public' but 'to anything in existence') and in part from Romantic views about 'great Men', poets as superior and thus alienated beings, the sorts of views Keats may have found in Wordsworth's 'Essay, Supplementary to the Preface' (1815), with its distinction between the 'factitious influence' of a transitory and superficial 'Public', on the one hand, and that of the 'People's' somehow more lasting judgement, 'which the Deity inspires', on the other.[50] Its illogicality—though indifferent to public opinion, Keats cannot address the Public 'without feelings of Hostility'—also betrays defensiveness. The trouble with the preface is not so much 'affectation', as Reynolds claims, nor what Keats calls 'an undersong of disrespect to the Public' (by which he means public opinion or literary fashion, the product of a 'thousand jabberers about Pictures and Books . . . swarms of Porcupines with their Quills erect "like lime-twigs set to catch my Winged Book" '[51]), as fear of criticism.

[49] John Keats to J. H. Reynolds, 9 Apr. 1818, ibid. i. 266–7.
[50] William Wordsworth, 'Essay, Supplementary to the Preface' (1815), in *The Prose Works of William Wordsworth*, ed. W. J. B. Owen and Jane Smyser, 3 vols. (Oxford: Clarendon Press, 1974), iii. 84. For an almost identical distinction between 'Public' and 'People', see Keats to Benjamin Haydon, 22 Dec. 1818, in *Letters*, ed. Rollins, i. 415: 'I never expect to get anything by my Books: and moreover I wish to avoid publishing—I admire Human Nature but I do not like *Men*—I should like to compose things honourable to Man—but not fingerable over by *Men*.' For the poet as Romantic outsider see Keats to Sarah Jeffrey, 9 June 1819, ibid. ii. 115: 'one of the great reasons that the english have produced the finest writers in the world; is, that the English world has ill-treated them during their lives and foster'd them after their deaths'.
[51] John Keats to J. H. Reynolds, 9 Apr. 1818, ibid. i. 267.

This fear Keats openly alludes to the next day, 10 April, in a letter to Reynolds, which includes a much shorter, and in W. J. Bate's words, more 'manly' Preface—that is, a preface of 'manly singleness', without the first version's defensive face-tiousness. For a while, Keats tells Reynolds, he contemplated no preface at all: 'however, don't you think this had better go?—O, let it—one should not be too timid—of committing faults.'[52] 'Timidity', though, is precisely what the revised preface inadvertently reveals, prompting Croker's cruel 'confession', in his attack in the *Quarterly*, 'that we should have abstained from inflicting upon him any of the tortures of the *"fierce hell"* of criticism, which terrify his imagination, if he had not begged to be spared in order that he might write more'.[53] Comments like these lead Keats, in his darker moments, to question the point of publication at all, 'writing poems and hanging them up to be flyblown on the Reviewshambles'.[54]

Yet the revised version did improve matters, was better 'without those thing[s] you have left out', as Keats subsequently acknowledged to Taylor.[55] As Tim Chilcott puts it: 'by rewriting the preface in a quieter tone and by omitting the more barbed of the darts he had thrown at the public, Keats did not change his ground. He merely made it appear more reasonable'[56]—though not reasonable enough, it must be admitted, to deter enemies. What is best about the new preface—is most 'single' and 'manly' about it—ironically, is its acknowledgement of doubleness (an irony characteristic of the mature poems, the Odes and 'Lamia' in particular):

The imagination of a boy is healthy, and the mature imagination of a man is healthy; but there is a space of life between, in which the soul is in a ferment, the character undecided, the way of life uncertain, the ambition thick-sighted: thence proceeds mawkishness, and all the thousand bitters which those men I speak of ['men who are competent to

---

[52] John Keats to J. H. Reynolds, 10 Apr. 1818, ibid. 269.
[53] Matthews (ed.), *CH* 112.
[54] John Keats to George and Georgiana Keats, 3(?) Mar. 1819, in *Letters*, ed. Rollins, ii. 70.
[55] John Keats to John Taylor, 24 Apr. 1818, ibid. i. 272.
[56] Tim Chilcott, *A Publisher and His Circle* (London: Routledge & Kegan Paul, 1972), 30–1. As Bennett points out, though, in *Keats, Narrative and Audience*, 43, so self-critical is the second preface that it 'virtually amounts to a request to his audience not to read it'.

look, and who do look with a zealous eye, to the honour of English literature'] must necessarily taste in going over the following pages.

I hope I have not in too late a day touched the beautiful mythology of Greece, and dulled its brightness; for I wish to try once more, before I bid it farewel.

The manner here is simple, straightforward, single, sound; it is everything Taylor could have wanted. Though problems of tone remain in two earlier paragraphs, here at least the new preface strikes the right—safe—note, while also reflecting intelligently on its inauthenticity; which is to say, on the endemic self-consciousness or doubleness of adolescence (the period between boyhood and 'mature imagination'), and its dangers.[57] Just such a mixture, as we shall see, not only characterizes the best of his writings but is often produced by secondary or revisionary processes.

ENDYMION AND THE CRITICS

The first and wittiest of the critical drubbings *Endymion* suffered (there were nine major reviews altogether, three by friends, three mixed, three famously hostile) appeared in the *British Critic* of June 1818, in an unsigned notice that began by declaring of the poem that 'if Mr. Leigh Hunt had never written, we believe we might have pronounced it to be *sui generis* without fear of contradiction'.[58] The reviewer's technique is plot summary, generously larded with incriminating quotation. For example:

One day after the priest of Patmos had sung a song to Pan . . . a shout arises among the multitude, just as 'when Ionian shoals of dolphins *bob* their noses through the brine,' (1. 310.) In consequence of this noise, and 'Niobe's caressing tongue,' which 'lay a lost thing upon her paly lip' (1. 340) Endymion goes to sleep among some 'pouting zephyr-sighs,' where, while his sister sits 'guarding his forehead with her round elbow,' he lies 'aye, e'en as dead still as a marble man, frozen

---

[57] The most obvious of these problems is the suggestion that nobody should read the poem, since 'the two first books, and indeed the two last, I feel sensible are not of such completion as to warrant their passing the press'. This admission, Keats continues, 'is not written with the least atom of purpose to forestall criticisms, of course'.   [58] Matthews (ed.), *CH* 91.

in that old tale Arabian,' (1. 405.) After sleeping this 'magic sleep, O comfortable bird!' for a 'triple hour,' he 'opens his eyelids with a healthier brain.'[59]

And so on, interspersed with flurries of more concentrated Keatsian self-incrimination: ' "Honey-feels," "honey-whispers," which come "refreshfully," "obscure and hot hells," "secreter caves," "sigh-warm kisses and combing hands which travelling cloy and tremble through labyrinthine hair." ' At one point, Endymion stands ' "on the pebble-head of doubt," and runs "into the fearful deep to hide his head from the clear moon, (not very wise when he is in pursuit of her,) the trees, and coming madness;" from this he passes into "a vast antre," where he "seeth" (and this rhymes to "beneath,") many things, "which misery most drowningly doth sing." '[60] The impression such quotation creates is both that the poem wasn't edited ('a real friend of the author would have dissuaded him from an immediate publication,' writes Scott, in a comment that may well have affected Taylor's subsequent caution with Clare[61]) and that Hunt, as opposed to Shakespeare, was its 'presider'.[62] The review ends by alluding to the preface, where the author declares 'that though he is something between man and boy, he means by and by to be plotting and fitting himself for verses fit to live', an aspiration so manifestly absurd, the review implies, as to require no comment. All the reviewer adds of the poem, in a cuttingly understated concluding sentence, is 'that it is all written in rhyme, and, for the most part, (when there are syllables enough) in the heroic couplet'.[63]

One other feature of this review deserves notice. When its author turns 'from unmeaning absurdity into the gross slang of voluptuousness', a slang wielded 'with as much skill as the worthy prototype whom he has selected' (i.e. Hunt), quotation again does the trick. 'Under the semblance of "slippery blisses, twinkling eyes, soft completion of faces, and smooth excess of

---

[59] Ibid. 92.   [60] Ibid. 93.   [61] Ibid. 116.

[62] See John Keats to Benjamin Haydon, 10 May 1817, in *Letters*, ed. Rollins, i. 141–2: 'I remember your saying that you had notions of a good genius presiding over you—I have of late had the same thought, for things which [I] do half at Random are afterwards confirmed by my judgment in a dozen features of Propriety—Is it too daring to Fancy Shakespeare this Presider?'

[63] Matthews (ed.), *CH* 96.

hands"', writes the reviewer, Keats 'would palm upon the unsuspicious and the innocent imaginations better adapted to the stews.'[64] He then quotes the very lines of Cynthia's lament —'How he does love me! His poor temples beat | To the very tune of love—how sweet, sweet, sweet' (2. 764–5)—Taylor encouraged Keats to cut (just as, previously, the offending 'bob', preferred to Taylor's 'push' or 'raise', is singled out for censure). This is a line of attack Taylor and his advisers had feared. In terms of 'genius', writes Benjamin Bailey,

> I know Keats is defensible, let him be abused as he may. And I hope they may attack him in this point. But the quarter I *fear*, & cannot defend, is the *moral* part of it. There are two great blotches in it in this respect. The first must offend *every* one of proper feelings; and indelicacy is not to be borne. . . . The second fault I allude to I think we have noticed—The approaching inclination it has to that abominable principle of *Shelley's*—that *Sensual Love* is the principle of *things*. . . . If he be attacked on these points, & on the *first* he assuredly will, he is *not* defensible.[65]

The intensity of the attack, though, is what the Keats circle failed to anticipate, an intensity produced in part by the fusion, in the minds of Keats's enemies, of sexual and social transgressions, what Marjorie Levinson calls 'the self-fashioning gestures of the petty bourgeoisie'.[66] To this fusion we will return.

That there is much ('the *moral* part' aside) to deplore or regret in *Endymion*—what even the poem's defender John Scott calls 'many, very many passages indicating haste and carelessness'[67]—the *British Critic* amusingly (and for the most part fairly) establishes; the review is worth recalling when subsequent sneering tempts one to inflate the poem's worth. What Lockhart's *Blackwood's* review, the most vicious of the three, makes clear is the social or class origins of this sneering. Lockhart's review begins with the celebrity of Robert Burns and Joanna Baillie, which 'has had the melancholy effect of turning the heads of we know not how many farm-servants and unmarried ladies; our very footmen compose tragedies, and there

---

[64] Ibid. 94.
[65] Benjamin Bailey to John Taylor, 29 Aug. 1818, in Rollins (ed.), *KC* i. 34–5.
[66] Marjorie Levinson, *Keats's Life of Allegory: The Origins of a Style* (Oxford: Basil Blackwell, 1988), 4.   [67] Matthews (ed.), *CH* 116.

is scarcely a superannuated governess in the island that does not leave a roll of lyrics behind her in her band-box'. It ends by snidely alluding to Keats's training as a surgeon and apothecary: 'so back to the shop Mr. John, back to "plasters, pills, and ointment boxes" '.[68]

As in the *British Critic* review, Hunt's influence is invoked early and often, most cruelly in the reference to the two poets' physical stature: 'Mr. Hunt is a small poet, but he is a clever man. Mr. Keats is a still smaller poet, and he is only a boy of pretty abilities, which he has done every thing in his power to spoil.'[69] Early on, the review deplores the sonnet 'Great spirits now on earth are sojourning', on the grounds that Keats

> classes together WORDSWORTH, HUNT, and HAYDON, as the three greatest spirits of the age, and that he alludes to himself, and some others of the rising brood of Cockneys, as likely to attain hereafter an equally honourable elevation. Wordsworth and Hunt! what a juxtaposition! The purest, the loftiest, and, we do not fear to say it, the most classical of living English poets, joined together in the same compliment with the meanest, the filthiest, and the most vulgar of Cockney poetasters.[70]

Lockhart, only a year older than Keats, had graduated from Balliol College, Oxford, in 1813, and later studied law, and he prided himself on his classical education. The Cockney School, he declares, is made up of 'uneducated and flimsy striplings' who know neither the Greek tragedians nor Homer (except 'from Chapman'). The result in the case of *Endymion* is absurd anachronism: 'not a Greek shepherd, loved by a Grecian goddess ... merely a young Cockney rhymster'; 'costume' (to notice a mere 'trifle') violated 'in every page'; the Greek gods depicted 'as might be expected from persons of their education', that is, with only 'a vague idea that the Greeks were a most tasteful people, and that no mythology can be as finely adapted for the purposes of poetry as theirs'. In short, the Cockneys write like

---

[68] Ibid. 97–8, 100. Though Keats was no footman or farm labourer, his father was in trade (owned a stables); he himself was apprenticed as surgeon and apothecary (neither among the more affluent professions); he had never been to university; and he was born in London, in Finsbury. In short, he was a Cockney, a 'city spark' (ibid.). For a shrewd account of Keats's class position and that of Hunt's circle see Barnard, *Keats*, 1–14.

[69] Matthews (ed.), *CH* 104.   [70] Ibid. 99.

they dress, in borrowed robes, which they wear incorrectly.[71] Their 'loose, nerveless versification', for example, is a weak parody of 'English heroic rhyme'; their actual rhymes—Lockhart singles out 'higher' and 'Thalia', 'soft ear' and 'Lady Cytherea', from *Poems*—are marred by ignorance and incompetence.[72]

John Wilson Croker's shorter attack in the *Quarterly* is marginally less snobbish, or less directly snobbish. It begins with the admission that its author couldn't get past Book 1, which he also claims not to have understood. Keats, he grants, 'has powers of language, rays of fancy, and gleams of genius . . . but he is unhappily a disciple of the new school of what has been somewhere called Cockney poetry; which may be defined to consist of the most incongruous ideas in the most uncouth language'. Hunt, the 'hierophant' of this school, 'generally had a meaning'; his 'copyist', a 'simple neophyte',[73] is 'more unintelligible, almost as rugged, twice as diffuse, and ten times more tiresome and absurd than his prototype'. For Croker, the point of connection between 'unintelligibility' and 'Cockneyism' is lack of substance or soundness, something unearned or illegitimate, mere dressing. Because Keats's writing, as his revised preface protests, has no axe to grind, 'advance[s] no dogmas', 'his nonsense therefore is quite gratuitous; he writes for its own sake'.[74]

This criticism recalls a September 1817 review of *Poems* by Josiah Conder in the *Eclectic Review*, in which Conder asks rhetorically: 'What should we think of a person's professedly sitting down to write prose, or to read prose composition, without reference to any subject, or to the quality of the thoughts, without any definite object but the amusement afforded by the euphonous collocation of sentences?'[75] Keats's poems, both Conder and Croker contend, are content-free, an objection Croker extends to their formal as well as thematic features. Keats's rhymes in *Endymion*, for example, are criticized not so much because they are vulgar or incorrect, as because they undermine thought, or take its place:

[71] Ibid. 101, 103. See, also, Lockhart's attack on the vulgarity of Hunt's *The Story of Rimini*, in 'On the Cockney School of Poetry. No. I,' in Reiman (ed.), *Romantics Reviewed*, i. 50: 'One feels the same disgust at the idea of opening Rimini, that impresses itself on the mind of a man of fashion, when he is invited to enter, for a second time, the gilded drawing-room of a little mincing boarding-school mistress, who would fain have an *At Home* in her house.'
[72] Ibid. 104.   [73] Ibid. 111, 114.   [74] Ibid. 111.   [75] Ibid. 64.

He seems to us to write a line at random, and then he follows not the thought excited by this line, but that suggested by the *rhyme* with which it concludes. . . . He wanders from one subject to another, from the association, not of ideas but of sounds, and the work is composed of hemistichs which, it is quite evident, have forced themselves upon the author by the mere force of the catchwords on which they turn.[76]

Though Croker concludes by rehearsing standard objections to the poem's Huntian diction and grammar, its central criticism concerns the absence of meaning, which neatly dovetails into attacks on 'Cockney' flash and pretension.

It also, as Levinson argues, dovetails into attacks on the poetry's 'indelicacy'. The charge of meaninglessness is of a piece with the charge that Keats's poetry reduces to mere words. This is also the charge underlying its 'artificiality'. 'By the stylistic contradictions of his verse', writes Levinson, 'Keats produces a literature which is aggressively *literary* and therefore not just "not literature" but, in effect, *anti*-literature: a parody.' Or elsewhere:

In Keats's poetry, the diverse cultural languages which we call the Tradition are both the means and the *manner* of representation, both object and subject. The 'self' upon which the verse reflects is, precisely, 'not self': a fetishized, random collection of canonical signatures. One can see that this bad imitation of that earnest Romantic exercise, self-reflection, was, in effect, a burlesque.

Hence Byron's disdain: 'You know my opinion of *that second-hand* school of poetry'; hence also his association of Keats's poetry with masturbation, another, as it were, second-hand activity—mere activity, without issue—as in 'the *outstretched* poesy of this miserable Self-polluter of the human mind', 'a sort of mental masturbation . . . viciously soliciting his own ideas into a state', 'the *Onanism* of Poetry'.[77] The poetry's eroticism, like the excesses of its language, suggests rootlessness, mobility, a socially threatening profligacy.[78]

---

[76] Ibid. 112.

[77] Levinson, *Keats's Life of Allegory*, 5, 16. For the quotations from Byron see Matthews (ed.), *CH* 131, and *Byron's Letters and Journals*, ed. Leslie A. Marchand, 12 vols. (Cambridge, Mass.: Harvard University Press, 1973–82), ii. 217.

[78] The precise nature of the threat is complicated. According to Kim Wheatley, in 'The *Blackwood's* Attacks on Leigh Hunt', *Nineteenth Century Literature*, 6, 'writers for *Blackwood's* flatter their commercial and professional readers by apparently

KEATS'S RESPONSE

At first it looks as though Keats will be equal to such attacks. Aileen Ward thinks his initial reaction 'was to withdraw—like Shakespeare's snail shrinking back "into his shelly cave with pain"—into a kind of aesthetic isolation, in which the creation of the poem itself becomes the sole locus of value'.[79] The instinct to withdraw, though, is habitually countered or qualified by self-consciousness and doubts about the sufficiency of Beauty, in both the letters and the poems. 'Praise or blame has but a momentary effect on the man whose love of beauty in the abstract makes him a severe critic of his own Works,' Keats writes to Hessey on 8 October 1818, in a frequently cited letter:

My own domestic criticism has given me pain without comparison beyond what Blackwood or the <Edinburgh> Quarterly could possibly inflict. . . . J.S. [John Scott] is perfectly right in regard to the slipshod Endymion. That it is so is no fault of mine.—No!—though it may sound a little paradoxical. It is as good as I had power to make it— by myself—Had I been nervous about its being a perfect piece, & with that view asked advice, & trembled over every page, it would not have been written; for it is not in my nature to fumble—I will write independently.—I have written independently *without Judgment*—I may write independently & *with Judgment* hereafter. . . . In Endymion, I leaped headlong into the Sea, and thereby have become better

casting them as the defenders of aristocratic values, high culture, established religion, and national morality. Opposed to social and moral stability are reformers like Hunt, whose newspaper, the *Examiner*, is included by [Jon P.] Klancher among the "middle-class" periodicals, but whom the Tory reviewers associate with a large, highly susceptible lower-class readership.' Klancher, in *The Making of English Reading Audiences, 1790–1832*, 48, sees periodicals like *Blackwood's* and the *Quarterly*, 'beginning to recognize what Coleridge already knew: the middle-class audience must be redirected to become fully conscious of its hegemonic power'. To the extent that Keats, Hunt, Hazlitt and the other 'Cockneys' were identified, however inaccurately (according to Klancher), with 'a highly susceptible lower-class readership', they were seen by men such as Lockhart as a threat to middle-class hegemony. There may also have been an element of self-hatred in *Blackwood's* vituperation. Klancher detects 'a strong stylistic tendency in this most influential of middle-class journals to experiment with turning the form of a discourse into a layer of its content, forcing the sentence to signify more than it can possibly say' (pp. 54–5)—thus resulting in a style one might almost call Keatsian.

[79] Aileen Ward, ' "That Last Infirmity of Noble Mind": Keats and the Idea of Fame', in Hermione de Almeida (ed.), *Critical Essays on John Keats* (Boston: G. K. Hall, 1990), 19.

acquainted with the Soundings, the quicksands, & the rocks, than if I had \<stayed\> stayed upon the green shore, and piped a silly pipe, and took tea & comfortable advice.[80]

Self-sufficiency, here, is hardly the same as withdrawal. By not taking 'comfortable advice', for example, Keats means not taking the advice to write something less ambitious, to 'withdraw' from epic. Earlier in the passage, 'advice' (in 'asked advice, & trembled over every page') means advice about particulars, the sort that helps make a poem 'perfect'. In either sense, though, the result would have inhibited and isolated; had he worried about the wisdom of each step he was taking the poem would not have been written, as surely as if he'd taken tea and allowed himself to be dissuaded from epic. But writing is only half the story. Keats's silence on the topic of publication is telling: an implicit admission that the poem would not have been a poem, would not have been finished—and thus its creator no poet— had it been left in a drawer or never reached an audience. As for the future, to write 'with Judgment' means no longer to publish 'slipshod' work, the sort that contains, as John Scott puts it, 'many, very many passages indicating haste and carelessness'. That *Endymion* is slipshod is a shame, but also 'no fault of mine', since 'it is as good as I had power to make it— by myself'. This assertion sounds pretty straightforwardly Romantic until the next sentence makes clear that the poem *had* to be written this way, since otherwise, presumably, the enormity of the task would have overwhelmed Keats. Hessey and Taylor should have taken comfort from this letter: the time for vulnerably rash or 'headlong' writing, Keats was admitting, was over; the audience would be attended to.

A comparable doubleness—professions of self-sufficiency oddly yoked with audience concern—is expressed later in the month in a letter of 27 October 1818 to Woodhouse:

I am ambitious of doing the world some good: if I should be spared that may be the work of maturer years—in the interval I will assay to reach to as high a summit in Poetry as the nerve bestowed upon me will suffer. The faint conceptions I have of Poems to come brings the blood frequently into my forehead—All I hope is that I may not lose all interest in human affairs—that the solitary indifference I feel for

[80] John Keats to J. A. Hessey, 8 Oct. 1818, in *Letters*, ed. Rollins, i. 373–4.

applause even from the finest Spirits, will not blunt any acuteness of vision I may have. I do not think it will—I feel assured I should write from the mere yearning and fondness I have for the Beautiful even if my night's labours should be burnt every morning and no eye ever shine upon them.[81]

Here is the same mixture of defensive bravado (he would write even if his works were never to be seen) and good sense, the suspicion that complete indifference to audience could harm his work, 'blunt any acuteness of vision I may have'. Such a view recalls the centrality of the audience or reader in several of Keats's best-known critical pronouncements. Keats, famously, has no time for poetry that is didactic or bullying, which 'if we do not agree, seems to put its hand in its breeches pocket'.[82] The poetry Keats approves works in partnership with the audience. According to another well-known letter of February 1818 to Taylor, in which Keats lists his aesthetic 'Axioms', poetry 'should strike the Reader as a wording of his own highest thoughts, and appear almost a Remembrance'.[83] Even when most tempted to withdraw from public exposure, then, because most recently wounded, a sense of the audience remains; just as the professed loss of 'all interest in human affairs' coexists with the desire to do the world some good.

The relative composure of these early letters was hard to sustain. In a heated letter of 19 February 1819, for example, Keats characterizes the influence of critics as wholly pernicious. Though he has 'no doubt of success in a course of years if I persevere ... the Reviews have enervated and made indolent mens minds—few think for themselves—These Reviews too are getting more and more powerful and especially the Quarterly— They are like a superstition which the more it prostrates the Crowd and the longer it continues the more powerful it becomes just in proportion to their increasing weakness'.[84] At the

---

[81] John Keats to Richard Woodhouse, 27 Oct. 1818, ibid. i. 387–8.
[82] John Keats to John Hamilton Reynolds, 3 Feb. 1818, ibid. 224.
[83] John Keats to John Taylor, 27 Feb. 1818, ibid. 238.
[84] John Keats to George and Georgiana Keats, 18 Feb. 1819, ibid. ii. 65. For a comparable view of the power of the reviews see Coleridge, *Biographia Literaria*, ed. James Engell and W. Jackson Bate (Princeton: Princeton University Press, 1983), ii. 59: 'Poets and Philsophers, rendered diffident by their very number, addressed themselves to "*learned* readers"; then, aimed to conciliate the graces of "the *candid* reader"; till, the critic still rising as the author sunk, the amateurs of literature

very least, the extremity of the attacks on *Endymion* should have put readers on their guard: 'but no they are like the spectators at the Westminster cock-pit—they like the battle and do not care who wins or who looses'.[85] Here as elsewhere, Keats refuses Woodhouse's comforting distinction between 'men of sense' and ' "Dandy" readers, male & female, who love to be spared the trouble of judging for themselves'.[86] 'Men of sense' may exist, but Dandies predominate—and make or break careers. Though Keats could satisfy them, he won't: 'I feel every confidence that if I choose I may be a popular writer,' he declares to Taylor in a letter of 23 August 1819, written, suggestively, seven days after Peterloo, 'that I will never be; but for all that I will get a livelihood.'[87]

What follows in the letter of the 23rd is an all-out 'rhodomontade' (*sic*), with Keats likening public favour to 'the love of a woman—they are both a cloying treacle to the wings of independence', calling critics 'the commonplace crowd of the little-famous'. Beneath this bombast, though, lies a pervasive irony or self-consciousness; Keats knows he is ranting, knows 'this is not wise—I am not a wise man'. 'I have of late been indulging my spleen', he tells Taylor, 'by composing a preface *at* them:

collectively were erected into a municipality of judges, and addressed as THE TOWN! And now finally, all men being supposed able to read, and all readers able to judge, the multitudinous PUBLIC, shaped into personal unity by the magic of abstraction, sits nominal despot on the throne of criticism. But, alas! as in other despotisms, it but echoes the decision of its invisible ministers, whose intellectual claims to the guardianship of the muses seem, for the greater part, analogous to the physical qualifications which adapt their oriental brethren for the superintendence of the Harem.'

[85] John Keats to George and Georgiana Keats, 19 Feb. 1819, *Letters*, ed. Rollins, ii. 65.

[86] Richard Woodhouse to John Keats, 21 Oct. 1818, in Rollins (ed.), *KC* i. 46.

[87] Aileen Ward, in ' "That Last Infirmity of Noble Mind": Keats and the Idea of Fame', 24, attributes a softening of Keats's attitude to the public to Peterloo: '*The Fall of Hyperion* explores, among other things, the nature of the imaginitive community between the poet and the ordinary man. For this theme to emerge, however, something was required to bridge the abyss which had opened up between Keats and his imagined readers in the latter part of 1818, some recovery of his earlier faith in his audience—not in the Public but in the countervailing force of the People, or what Keats had called his "fellows." The events of the summer and fall of 1819—the Manchester Massacre and Henry Hunt's triumphal entry into London in September, which Keats witnessed—seem to have effected this change. . . . "I am certain any thing really fine will in these days be felt," Keats wrote to Haydon a few weeks later. "I have no doubt that if I had written Othello I should have been cheered by as good a Mob as Hunt." ' See John Keats to Benjamin Haydon, 3 Oct. 1819, in *Letters*, ed. Rollins, ii. 219.

after all resolving never to write a preface at all. "There are so many verses," would I have said to them, "give me so much means to buy pleasure with as a relief to my hours of labour." ' This passage is an obvious fantasy, as Keats admits (its easy 'egotism' is also a sign of trust in Taylor, recalling Clare's comparable trust). 'Pardon me for hammering instead of writing,' Keats concludes, clearly distinguishing between unconsidered indulgence—composition 'without Judgment'— and 'writing'. Once again, then, though clearly heated, Keats continues to acknowledge both public responsibilities and the role of secondary, implicitly revisionary, processes. His 'Pride and egotism' is controlled, reserved for letters; it is for the most part (we shall be looking at exceptions) a species of what the psychoanalysts call 'regression in the service of the ego', a regression that 'will enable me to write finer things than any thing else will'.[88]

Which is not to say that Keats misrepresents the superficiality of the public. As Woodhouse reminds Taylor, no one wants Keats 'to minister to the depraved taste of the age'. 'Is he wrong to be dissatisfied with the Prospect of a mere "seat on the Bench of a myriad-aristocracy in Letters" ', asks Woodhouse, 'or to keep aloof from them and their works,—or to dislike the favour of such a "public", as bepraises the Crabbes and the Barretts, and the Codruses of the day?'[89] Clearly not, as long as the distinction between dislike and disapproval, on the one hand, and dismissal or outright defiance, on the other, is observed. The 'attempt to crush me' by the *Quarterly* was, indeed, 'a mere matter of the moment';[90] Keats was right, in several senses, to elevate his sights, take the long view. Though the interaction or collaboration of poet and audience, as expressed, for instance, in the opening lines of 'The Fall of Hyperion', is definitional (that 'poesy alone can tell her dreams' is what distinguishes poet from dreamer, fanatic, or savage[91]), it is also

---

[88] John Keats to John Taylor, 23 Aug. 1819, ibid. 144.
[89] Richard Woodhouse to John Taylor, 31 Aug. 1819, in Rollins (ed.), *KC* i. 82.
[90] John Keats to George and Georgiana Keats, 14 Oct. 1818, *Letters*, ed. Rollins, i. 394.
[91] Though the distinctions forwarded in the opening lines of 'The Fall of Hyperion' are confusing and, in the light of the whole poem, contradictory, what I have called the 'definitional' role of the audience is clear. As Bennett puts it, in *Keats, Narrative and Audience*, 153, the poem 'asserts most fundamentally . . . a social function for

transformative, of audience as well as poet. The poet takes on the sufferings of the audience, 'the miseries of the world', in a purgatorial ascent, one involving self-loss; he does so, though, in order to mend the audience, to pour out 'a balm upon the world' (1. 201), being 'a humanist, a physician to all men' (1. 190). In other words, care for the audience need not mean capitulation to the audience, talk of 'balm' (as opposed to the dreamer's 'vexing', 1. 202) notwithstanding.[92] The poet's job is to humanize and make well, which precludes pandering as surely as it does withdrawal. For all their hurt pride and anger, this is the position the post-*Endymion* letters work towards, a position confirmed, as we shall see, in the revision of subsequent poems.

REVISING FOR THE 1820 COLLECTION

That Keats and his advisers mean to pay attention to the audience is clear not only from Woodhouse's careful 'Notes on the Critiques on *Endymion* in the *Quarterly Review* and *Blackwood's Edinburgh Magazine*' of October 1818,[93] but from the first work Keats undertakes after the attacks, the revision of 'Isabella' and the composition of 'Hyperion'. While revising *Endymion* in February 1818, Keats devised with Reynolds a plan for a volume of versified stories based on the *Decameron*. The only such story Keats attempted (the project was quickly abandoned) was 'Isabella; or, the Pot of Basil', the first six stanzas of which were composed that February, though the poem was not finished until April 1818.[94] Keats revised the draft in the summer,[95] after *Endymion* appeared but before the

poetry, an acknowledgement of the pragmatic, public nature of poetic discourse and, at the same time, a recognition of the fundamental importance of the relationship between poet and audience: if the audience judges well, then the poem exists as a poem, if they judge against it, the dream is a "fanatic's"'.

[92] See also 'Sleep and Poetry', which enjoins us not to 'forget the great end | Of poesy, that it should be a friend | To sooth the cares, and lift the thoughts of man' (ll. 245–7).   [93] See Rollins (ed.), *KC* i. 44–5.

[94] Reynolds also completed only one story, 'The Garden of Florence', also published separately, in *The Garden of Florence* (London: Taylor & Hessey, 1821). Keats completed the poem in Teignmouth, where he was nursing his brother Tom, instead of reading proofs of Books 2–4 of *Endymion*.

[95] 'In passages for which the draft text is available,' writes Stillinger (in *Poems*, 604), 'the fair copy shows revisions from the draft in heading (the draft has none) and the wording of some fifty lines.'

negative reviews, and from this revised version Woodhouse made three transcripts, the last of which served as printer's copy for the text published in the 1820 collection. These transcripts were produced after the September 1818 reviews, as were the suggestions Reynolds offered in October 1818, upon reading Keats's fair copy. The poem was altered in direct response to Keats's critics, and the resulting 1820 text constitutes, for Jack Stillinger and others, a paradigmatic instance of creative collaboration. What its evolution, like that of the 1820 volume as a whole, discloses, according to Stillinger, is 'a rather attractive overall picture of Keats, Woodhouse, Taylor, Reynolds, and Brown all pulling together to make Keats's lines presentable to the public'.[96]

This desire to produce 'presentable' lines could also be said to underlie the poem's very inception, the idea of the *Decameron* project itself. The idea for the project seems to have originated with Hazlitt, in a lecture 'On Dryden and Pope', delivered on 3 February 1818 and subsequently published in *Lectures on the English Poets* (1818). 'I should think', Hazlitt remarks parenthetically, 'that a modern translation of some of the other serious tales in Boccaccio and Chaucer, as that of Isabella . . . if executed with taste and spirit, could not fail to succeed in the present day.'[97] Keats may claim to 'hate a Mawkish Popularity' (in the course of defending the imprudent draft preface to *Endymion*), but as Kurt Heinzelman argues, 'if "mawkish" means capturing an audience by capitalizing on its sentimentality, on the popular sense of what will "succeed," then this is perilously close to the kind of success Hazlitt was projecting for a translator of *Isabella*'.[98]

Keats's eventual reluctance to publish 'Isabella' was also audience-oriented. The poem, he insists to Woodhouse, is

[96] Jack Stillinger, 'Keats's Extempore Effusions and the Question of Intentionality', 316. The paradigmatic status of 'Isabella' is conferred on the poem in ch. 2 of Stillinger's *Multiple Authorship*, 25–49, which reworks much of the material in 'Keats's Extempore Effusions'.

[97] William Hazlitt, 'On Dryden and Pope', in *The Collected Works of William Hazlitt*, ed. A. R. Waller and Arnold Glover (London: J. M. Dent, 1902–6), v. 82. For a modern scholarly corroboration of Hazlitt's view that versified tales from Boccaccio would be popular in Keats's age see Herbert Wright, *Boccaccio in England from Chaucer to Tennyson* (London: Athlone Press, 1957), 331–478, cited by Bennett, *Keats, Narrative and Audience*, 203.

[98] Kurt Heinzelman, 'Self-Interest and the Politics of Composition in Keats's *Isabella*', *English Literary History*, 55 (1988), 168.

too smokeable—I can get it smoak'd at the Carpenters shaving chimney much more cheaply—There is too much inexperience of live [life], and simplicity of knowledge in it—which might do very well after one's death—but not while one is alive. There are very few would look to the reality. I intend to use more finesse with the Public. It is possible to write fine things which cannot be laugh'd at in any way. Isabella is what I should call were I a reviewer 'A weak-sided Poem' with an amusing sober-sadness about it. Not that I do not think Reynolds and you are quite right about it—it is enough for me. But this will not do to be public—If I may so say, in my dramatic capacity I enter fully into the feeling; but in Propria Persona I should be apt to quiz it myself.[99]

What Keats is determined to avoid by witholding 'Isabella' is the sort of criticism visited upon *Endymion*. He will in future write with judgement, be a 'whole' person (which is partly what 'in Propria Persona' means), something presumably impossible when one's 'dramatic capacity' allows one to 'enter fully into the feeling'. Though in posterity readers may look past the poem's vulnerabilities to its 'reality', Keats wants more than posthumous fame. Woodhouse may like the poem (as did Taylor, Reynolds, and Lamb), but Woodhouse is not 'the Public', which Keats rightly feels he cannot trust. The phrase 'were I a reviewer', comments Bate, 'is now equivalent, to Keats, to saying if one were deliberately trying to find weak spots'.[100] This fear of the critics has been suggested also as the origin not only of the poem's themes—of secrecy, safety, social stigma, market pressure ('the institutionalized capitalism described in *Isabella*', Heinzelman notes, 'is foreign to Boccaccio's Italy'[101])—but of its *ottava rima* stanza form as well, a form which, according to Andrew Bennett, 'applies inward pressure on the language—an enclosing delimitation of linguistic invention and narrative dilation. In this way, the lax, flowing expansiveness of *Endymion* becomes far more taut . . . each stanza demands a separate "theme" and a separate, minimal dilation on that theme.'[102]

---

[99] John Keats to Richard Woodhouse, 22 Sept. 1819, in *Letters*, ed. Rollins, ii. 174.   [100] Bate, *Keats*, 314.
    [101] Heinzelman, 'Self-Interest in Keats's *Isabella*', 162.
    [102] Bennett, *Keats, Narrative and Audience*, 83. Both Heinzelman and Bennett also suggest that Keats's uneasy allusions to his source ('There is no other crime, no mad assail | To make old prose in modern rhyme more sweet', ll. 155–6, and 'O for the gentlenes of old Romance, | The simple plaining of a minstrel's song!

The collaborative revision of 'Isabella' begins before Wood-house's transcriptions, when Reynolds reads the fair copy in October. Reynolds's response was communicated in a letter of 14 October 1818, after he'd read the *Blackwood's* and *Quarterly* attacks. He praises the poem for its 'completeness' and its 'simplicity and quiet pathos', qualities Keats's verse had been criticized for lacking; he says it should be published; and he calls it 'a full answer to all the ignorant malevolence of cold lying Scotchmen and stupid Englishmen'. But he also warns Keats to 'look it over with that eye to the *littlenesses* which the world are so fond of excepting to'. The letter offers no actual revisions, but alludes to a previously queried word ('with that word altered which I mentioned, I see nothing that can be cavilled at'); its warning about littlenesses, though, may well account for five single-word revisions Keats made above the line in the fair copy.[103] Three of these interlineations suggest the sort of vigilance Reynolds advises: the change from 'sigh' to 'noise' in 'His continual voice was pleasanter | To her, than noise of trees or hidden rill' (ll. 13–14); 'Sick and wane' for 'Pale and wan' (l. 213), which avoids repetition, another 'excess' singled out for mockery by the critics; and 'olive trees' for 'forest trees' (l. 168), the revision Stillinger thinks Reynolds specifically prompts, which avoids redundancy.[104]

When Keats hands the fair copy over for transcription to Woodhouse early in 1819 editorial vigilance increases. Wood-house was literary and legal adviser to Taylor and Hessey, and an early and passionate supporter of Keats. 'Whatever People <say they> regret that they could not do for Shakespeare or Chatterton, because he did not live in their time,' Woodhouse writes to Taylor, 'that I would embody into a rational principle,

| Fair reader, at the old tale take a glance, | For here, in truth, it doth not well belong | To speak:—O turn thee to the very tale', ll. 387–91) betray ambivalence about commercial motives: 'the more Keats apologizes to Boccaccio, the more he links himself implicitly to the brothers' venturing capitalism' (Heinzelman, 'Self-Interest in Keats's *Isabella*', 175); 'Boccaccio's language is plainer, his story ... unencumbered by a sophisticated rhetoric which for the modern poet mediates the tragic tale, and so easily converts pathos into sentimentality' (Bennett, *Keats, Narrative and Audience*, 89), a conversion which marks Cockney excess, the mark of the new class.

[103] J. H. Reynolds to John Keats, 14 Oct. 1818, in *Letters*, ed. Rollins, i. 376–7.
[104] For Stillinger's conjecture see *Multiple Authorship*, 29.

and (with due regard to certain expediencies) do for Keats'.[105] In addition to offering financial support, as in this instance, Woodhouse set out to copy as many of Keats's manuscripts and letters as he could find, recording 'dates, variant readings, circumstances of composition, and add[ing] notes concerning sources and similarities in other poets'.[106] The alterations resulting from these transcriptions—of spelling, punctuation, capitalization, and other 'accidentals'—were inevitable; as Stillinger points out, the system of shorthand Woodhouse employed for the first transcript, the transcript upon which the other two were based, 'preserves most of the consonants of the words that are being recorded but very little else'. Keats, though, seems to have welcomed the consequent alterations, counting on them to improve—to correct—his poems, treating them, rather than his own holographs, as 'the principal finished versions of the poems before publication'.[107]

In the case of 'Isabella', Woodhouse made three sorts of revisions: he introduced 'substantive changes in half a dozen lines of his shorthand transcript'; he 'marked words, lines, and stanzas in Keats's fair copy' and in subsequent transcripts; and he 'penciled suggested revisions for several passages on the opposite (that is, facing) versos of Keats's leaves', as well as in subsequent transcripts. These alterations and suggestions Keats saw and pondered, sometimes himself adding further alterations; then Taylor reviewed Woodhouse's final transcript, 'clarifying some of the revisions, arbitrating between Keats's and Woodhouse's phrasings, and occasionally entering other revisions of his own'.[108] Woodhouse and Taylor initiated the revision of sixty lines, Keats of half a dozen. Stillinger's detailed account of the nature and character of these revisions, from which I have been quoting, leads him to conclude that all three men concentrated on precisely the stylistic features—versification and rhyme; the literal meaning of words; correctness of grammar, of punctuation, of literary and mythological allusion; clarity, coherence, and logic; repetition and redundancy—singled out for attention by the reviewers.

---

[105] Richard Woodhouse to John Keats, 31 Aug. 1819, in *Letters*, ed. Rollins, ii. 151.   [106] Stillinger, *The Texts of Keats's Poems*, 27.
[107] Stillinger, *Multiple Authorship*, 28.
[108] Ibid. 29.

The most concentrated and telling of the examples of collaborative revision Stillinger analyses concerns a fair copy stanza
beginning at line 57 and introduced by a couplet spoken by
Isabella:

> 'Lorenzo, I would clip my ringlet hair
> To make thee laugh again and debonair!'
> 'Then should I be,' said he 'full deified;
>   And yet I would not have it, clip it not;
> For Lady I do love it where 'tis tied
>   About the Neck I dote on; and that spot
> That anxious dimple it doth take a pride
>   To play about—Aye Lady I have got
> Its shadow in my heart and ev'ry sweet
>   Its Mistress owns there summed all complete.'

Woodhouse's repeated querying, crossing out, and rewriting of
this passage resulted eventually in the radical reconception of
the initial couplet and the complete disappearance of the stanza
it introduced. That the impetus for these changes was commercial is clear from Stillinger's astute summary of the passage's
potential difficulties:

From a conservative reader's point of view, there are plenty of problems concerning style, sense, and tone in these lines, and the *Endymion*
reviewers, as Woodhouse knew, would have had a field day in making
fun of them. The problems begin with Isabella's silly notion that she
could please Lorenzo by cropping her hair, and continue with the non-
parallelism of verb and adjective in 'laugh . . . and debonair,' the extravagance of Lorenzo's reaction (he would be 'full deified'), the
misleading suggestion that Isabella wears her hair tied around her
neck, the potentially embarrassing physicality (and questionable location) of Isabella's 'anxious dimple,' the overly decorative personifica-
tions of both hair and dimple (the former 'take[s] a pride' in its play,
the latter is 'anxious'), the ploddiness of the expression 'have got,' and
the vagueness and obscurity of 'shadow' and 'ev'ry sweet' (and what
it means to 'sum' such things) at the end.[109]

The closeness of this catalogue of problems to the incriminating
plot summaries of the *British Critic* review is obvious. Though
it is unclear how many stages of revision—of which there were
several, as Stillinger shows—Keats saw, that he clearly approved

---

[109] Ibid. 35.

the final product helps account for the poem's subsequent inclusion in the 1820 volume.

Questions of inclusion figure also in the second of Keats's extended poetical projects immediately following the *Endymion* reviews: the writing of 'Hyperion'. Here, too, the influence of the critics is obvious. 'Hyperion' was begun in the closing months of 1818, though Keats's hopes for the poem were elaborated some nine months before he actually began writing, in a letter of 23 January 1818 to Haydon. These hopes reflect the criticisms of *Poems* and anticipate those for *Endymion*. 'Hyperion' will afford Keats the opportunity to treat his subject 'in a more naked and grecian Manner' than that employed for *Endymion*, by which he means, in part, more simply, without Huntian or other forms of decoration. Since 'the march of passion and endeavour' in the poem (its plot) 'will be undeviating', as opposed to Keats's earlier digressive or overly-descriptive narratives, no one will complain of its lacking 'manly singleness', a quality produced also by the character of its hero, Apollo. Endymion, 'being mortal [was] led on, like Buonaparte, by circumstance; whereas the Apollo in Hyperion being a fore-seeing God will shape his actions like one'.[110]

Though the poem was begun at the end of 1818, Keats seems to have had trouble with it throughout the winter of 1818–19, putting it aside temporarily. He picked it up again in the spring, abandoning it a second time in April 1819, when Woodhouse borrowed and copied it. (Three months later, towards the end of July, Keats made a third attempt at the story, which became 'The Fall of Hyperion', itself abandoned two months later.[111]) Woodhouse's transcript was recopied by two of his clerks, he himself then checked this second transcript over, and eventually it was used as printer's copy for the 1820 collection. Keats disapproved the decision to print the incomplete poem, and there is no evidence that he saw either of the transcripts. However, the existence of a number of changes between the second transcript and the printed version, changes which restore readings from the draft text, leads Stillinger to conclude that Keats eventually became involved in the revision process, not only

---

[110] John Keats to Benjamin Haydon, 23 Jan. 1818, in *Letters*, ed. Rollins, ii. 207.
[111] See *Poems*, ed. Stillinger, 670–1.

adding late alterations but approving 'the various other changes as well'.[112] That there were relatively few such changes, at least substantive ones, is a sign of how rigorously (and constrictingly, as he himself later complained) Keats set out to expunge 'weak-sidedness'.

One such change, involving an egregious lapse just before the poem is abandoned, deserves a moment's notice. When 'wild commotions' shake Apollo in Keats's original draft, they make him flush

> Into a hue more roseate than sweet pain
> Gives to a ravish'd Nymph when her warm tears
> Gush luscious with no sob.

This is the language of *Endymion*, especially the unfortunate 'Gush luscious',[113] and though Woodhouse begins by inter-lineating more restrained alternatives in the draft, eventually, in the second transcript, he pencils out the lines completely. Though any number of reasons have been advanced for the poem's abandonment, the marked reversion here and elsewhere in Book 3 to the mannered eroticism or sensuality of Keats's earlier style—'disturbingly' reminiscent of *Endymion*, according to Bate[114]—is telling. The study of Milton which preceded and may have inspired 'Hyperion' produced exactly the 'manly vigour' (Bailey's phrase) Keats and his critics sought, but at a price: 'Miltonic verse', Keats comes to believe, in words applied to both 'Hyperion' and 'The Fall of Hyperion', 'cannot be written but in artful or rather artist's humour'; the beauty of 'Hyperion' is a 'false beauty proceeding from art, and one // to the true voice of feeling'.[115] That Taylor and Woodhouse were

---

[112] Ibid. 640.

[113] As Miriam Allott points out, in her Longman edn. of *The Complete Poems*, 440, Keats's only other use of the word 'luscious' occurs in *Endymion* 2. 942.

[114] Bate, *Keats*, 403. That the earlier, 'weak-sided' style is still detectable at the end of the poem was conceded by Leigh Hunt himself: at the end of 'Hyperion' he complains of 'something too effeminate and human in the way Apollo received the exaltation which his wisdom is giving him. He weeps and wonders somewhat too fondly.' This quotation, from the *Indicator*, 2 (9 Aug. 1820), 352, is quoted by Susan J. Wolfson, in 'Feminizing Keats', in de Almeida (ed.), *Critical Essays on John Keats*, 319.

[115] For 'manly vigour' see Benjamin Bailey to R. M. Milnes, 7 May 1849, in *KC* ii. 283. For Keats's reasons for abandoning both 'Hyperion' and 'The Fall of Hyperion' see his letter to Reynolds, 21 Sept. 1819, in *Letters*, ed. Rollins, ii. 167:

right to print the poem and give it pride of place (it closed the 1820 volume), though, if only for commercial reasons, is clear: no work in the collection received more praise, even Byron approved. Though Keats objected both to the initial decision to print the fragment and to the reason Taylor gives in the advertisement for the poem's abandonment (that the reception given to *Endymion* 'discouraged the author from proceeding', a reason Keats calls 'a lie'[116]), the end result can hardly have been displeasing: here, surely, were 'presentable' lines.

REACTION: 'THE EVE OF ST AGNES'

Some part of Keats's ambivalence towards his audience— including his reluctance to revise to meet its needs and tastes— derives from issues of gender, issues already hinted at not only in phrases like 'manly singleness' and 'manly vigour' but in the association of public favour with 'the love of a woman'. Neither of Keats's first two volumes sold. *Poems* (1817) 'was hardly

'I have given up Hyperion—there were too many Miltonic inversions in it—Miltonic verse cannot be written but in artful or rather artist's humour. I wish to give myself up to other sensations. English ought to be kept up. It may be interesting to you to pick out some lines from Hyperion and put a mark X to the false beauty proceeding from art, and one // to the true voice of feeling.' See also the same day's journal letter to George and Georgiana Keats, ibid. 212: 'I have but lately stood on my guard against Milton. Life to him would be death to me. Miltonic verse cannot be written but i[n] the vein of art—I wish to devote myself to another sensation.'

    Jonathan Bate, in 'Keats's Two *Hyperions* and the Problem of Milton', in Brinkley and Hanley (eds.), *Romantic Revisions*, 326, questions the conventional account of Milton's oppressive influence on the original 'Hyperion': Keats 'nowhere talks of the oppressive Miltonic influence as the reason for his first abandonment. The chronology is as follows: Keats gives up the first version, starts the second, then re-reads *Paradise Lost* and is struck by its beauties, and finally gives up the second version because of its persistent Miltonics. If Keats did give up the first version because he was unhappy with its poetic diction, the problem was perhaps not so much the Miltonics as a certain return to Endymionese, to luxuriant imagery at the expense of narrative focus, in the third book.' Perhaps, but might this return not have been symptomatic, itself a product of, or reaction to, oppressive influence?

[116] For the printed advertisement, written by Taylor, see *Complete Poems*, ed. Allott, 764. Woodhouse wrote a preliminary draft, printed in Rollins (ed.), *KC* i. 115–16. For Keats's disapproval, registered at the end of the advertisement, in a copy of the 1820 collection presented to his Hampstead neighbour, Burridge Davenport, see Amy Lowell, *John Keats*, 2 vols. (Boston: Houghton Mifflin, 1925), ii. 424: 'This is none of my doing—I was ill at the time. This is a lie.'

subscribed at all, except for Keats's immediate friends',[117] and *Endymion* fared little better. According to G. M. Matthews, speaking of *Endymion*, 'the *Quarterly* did undoubtedly kill off any chance of serious interest. Six months after publication, Hessey was reporting the sale of single copies, as if even this marked an upturn of trade.'[118] On 19 February 1819, while at work on 'The Eve of St Agnes', Keats admitted to his brother and sister-in-law that *Endymion* 'has not at all succeeded'.[119] These failures were associated not only with the critics, but with a reading public Keats came increasingly to identify with women. The result was contradiction or conflict, 'a gordian complication of feelings':[120] Keats needed women in order to achieve immediate success and thus support himself as a poet; yet many of the qualities for which his poems were ridiculed by the critics were implicitly female or 'unmanly'.

The revisionary history of 'The Eve of St Agnes' plays out this tension or contradiction. Keats began the poem in January 1819, perhaps in reaction to 'Hyperion', with which he was then struggling. 'Hyperion', as we have seen, was both 'manly' and 'presentable', and would go down well with the critics, but Keats felt it lacked 'the true voice of feeling', a voice he associated with both women and sales. The idea for the poem came from a woman, Mrs Isabella Jones, and from the first Keats associated it with the reader-friendly 'Isabella; or, the Pot of Basil'. In a letter of 14 August 1819 to Bailey he mentions having 'written two tales, one from Boccaccio call'd the Pot of Basil; and another call'd St Agnes' Eve on a popular superstition'.[121] When discussing the 'weak-sidedness' of 'Isabella', in a previously quoted letter of 22 September 1819, written shortly after revising 'The Eve of St Agnes', Keats professes to find 'no objection of this kind to Lamia—A Good deal to St Agnes Eve—only not so glaring'.[122] Earlier, in an entry of 14 February

---

[117] Gittings, *Keats*, 179.   [118] Matthews (ed.), *CH* 8.

[119] John Keats to George and Georgiana Keats, 19 Feb. 1819, in *Letters*, ed. Rollins, ii. 65. Almost two years later, Taylor and Hessey write to George Keats of *Endymion* that 'we are still minus £110 by "Endymion"'. In the end, the poem was remaindered.

[120] John Keats to Benjamin Bailey, 18 July 1818, ibid. i. 342.

[121] John Keats to Benjamin Bailey, 14 Aug. 1819, ibid. ii. 139.

[122] John Keats to Richard Woodhouse, 22 Sept. 1819, ibid. 174. Keats informs Taylor of being 'occupied in revising St Agnes Eve' in a letter of 5 Sept. 1819, ibid. 157.

1819 from a journal letter to his brother and sister-in-law, he
lists recent works: 'the Pot of Basil, St Agnes eve, and if I
should have finished it a little thing call'd the "eve of St Mark"
you see what fine mother Radcliff names I have'.[123] The reference to Ann Radcliffe suggests that market considerations are
on Keats's mind, especially since it comes immediately after
mention of Byron's recent successes, as with Canto 4 of *Childe
Harolde* (4,000 copies sold, £25,000 profit), successes as importantly indebted to women readers as the successes of Mrs
Radcliffe. 'Because of changing patterns of work and leisure,
women (whose schooling led them to prefer novels or narrative
verse) had been replacing the elite group of classically educated
men as the chief consumers of literature,' writes Margaret
Homans.[124] Keats means to cater to these women, but is uneasy
about doing so, as the protectively or defensively ironic reference to 'mother' Radcliffe suggests.

This unease has personal as well as literary origins. Most
critics associate 'The Eve of St Agnes' with Keats's developing
relationship with Fanny Brawne, whose reading tastes ran to
Byron and Gothic horror (as a schoolgirl, she confesses, she
was 'half wild' for Byron's poetry).[125] 'When Keats vies with

[123] John Keats to George and Georgiana Keats, 14 Feb. 1819, ibid. 62.

[124] Margaret Homans, 'Keats Reading Women, Women Reading Keats', *Studies
in Romanticism*, 29 (1990), 346. Wolfson, 'Feminizing Keats', 321, points out that
the Olliers had tried to capitalize on what they assumed were the attractions of
Keats's first volume to women readers by advertising it in *The British Lady's
Magazine*. She also quotes the epigraph for an article in the 1821 *Pocket Magazine*
which predicts of Keats's poems that 'Albion's maidens . . . Will cherish thy sweet
songs,' while the article itself characterizes the themes of these songs as 'peculiarly
formed for the endearments of love and the gentle solaces of friendship'. Lee
Erikson, 'The Poet's Corner: The Impact of Technological Changes in Printing on
English Poetry, 1800–1850', *English Literary History*, 52 (1985), 899, argues for
audience stratification by class and gender: 'The literary Annuals, in particular,
revealed that the readership of poetry had become increasingly young and female
and that this new market could be successfully segmented from the old with a new
format and packaging. The Annuals effectively divided poetry into one kind for a
limited audience made up largely of artistic gentlemen and scholars and another for
a much larger audience composed primarily of women and children. New poets and
their publishers felt the shifting taste of the expanding readership first.' For a more
general theoretical account of the role of women in the literary marketplace see
Sonia Hofkosh, 'The Writer's Ravishment: Women and the Romantic Author—The
Example of Byron', in Anne K. Mellor (ed.), *Romanticism and Feminism*
(Bloomington, Ind.: Indiana University Press, 1988), 93–114.

[125] See Bate, *Keats*, 427–9; also Beth Lau, 'Keats and Byron', in de Almeida (ed.),
Critical Essays on John Keats. Lau is the source of the 'half wild' citation, told to
Keats's sister (p. 212).

Byron for Fanny's attention,' comments Homans, 'it is not only for her, but also for the female readers that Fanny represents,' readers who 'at least in Keats's view identify sexual with literary attraction'.[126] Hence Keats's persistent jealousy of Byron, his need to 'trounce' him.[127] Keats resents his commercially prudent, self-imposed task of wooing women readers, sometimes with a lover's intensity. He also retains worries about the critics. When the audience is conceived of as female, catering to it, as Keats was partly doing in 'The Eve of St Agnes', opens him again to wounding accusations of weakness, effeminacy, lack of power—even as it confirms wounding class associations. Class, though, is a complicated matter in this instance: on the one hand, women's tastes are conceived of as inferior, women in general associated with subordination, as in such sub-definitions of 'Cockney' (from the *OED*) as 'a squeamish or effeminate fellow. . . . Sometimes applied to a squeamish, over-nice, wanton, or affected woman,' or 'a derisive appellation for a townsman, as the type of effeminacy in contrast to the hardier inhabitants of the country'; on the other hand, the specific women who bought and read books of poetry, and made poetical careers, were Keats's social superiors, and thus resented.[128] The reasons for wishing to defy as well as attract such an audience, then, were multiple and conflicting.

Keats's gesture of defiance comes at the end of the summer of 1819. On 12 September Keats breakfasts with Woodhouse and tells him of several alterations he has made in a second or fair copy manuscript of the poem, now lost. These proposed alterations alarm Woodhouse who writes to Taylor at Retford, where Taylor was convalescing from a recent illness. Woodhouse's letter of 19, 20 September details Keats's mood as well as specific revisions. Keats is all business, wishing to publish

---

[126] Homans, 'Keats Reading Women', 358.

[127] John Keats to George and Georgiana Keats, 15 Apr. 1819, in *Letters*, ed. Rollins, ii. 84.

[128] For these and other quotations from *OED* see Wolfson, 'Feminizing Keats', 319. For the aristocratic character of the book-buying public, male as well as female, see Erikson, 'Technological Changes in Printing', 896: 'In a country of eleven million people lacking many of our modern forms of instruction or entertainment, a book in great demand sold ten to twenty thousand copies in 1810. Almost all books were read and bought by the wealthy, even though book clubs and circulating libraries in the late eighteenth and early nineteenth centuries were bringing books to the middle classes—that is, to the rest of the upper ten percent of the population.'

'The Eve of St Agnes' and 'Lamia' *'immediately'*; 'Isabella', though, goes unmentioned, and when pressed by Woodhouse, Keats pronounces it 'mawkish'. This judgement Woodhouse sees as temporary, a natural result of Keats's current 'more sober & <ab> unpassionate' mood, a mood detectable also in the first few revisions Woodhouse describes:

He had the Eve of St. A copied fair: He has made trifling alterations, inserting an additional stanza early in the poem to make the *legend* more intelligible, and correspondent with what afterwards takes place, particularly with respect to the supper & the playing on the Lute.— he retains the name of Porphyro—has altered the last 3 lines to leave on the reader a sense of pettish disgust, by bringing Old Angela in (only) dead stiff & ugly.—He says he likes that the poem should leave off with this Change of Sentiment—it was what he aimed at, & was glad to find from my objections to it that he had succeeded.—I apprehend he had a fancy for trying his hand at an attempt to play with his reader, & fling him off at last—I sho[d] have thought, he affected the 'Don Juan' style of mingling up sentiment & sneering: but he had just before asked Hessey if he co[d] procure him a sight of that work, as he had not met with it, and if the E. of St A. had not in all probability been altered before his Lordship had thus flown in the face of the public.[129]

What these initial revisions betray is a writer determined to counter or moderate the poem's prevailing 'true voice of feeling'. An early stanza is introduced (after stanza 6 of the printed version) to make the bedroom banquet more 'intelligible' or logical, no mere dreaming luxuriance. The happy-ever-after ending of the original is darkened or steeled by the closing reference to Angela 'dead stiff & ugly', an alteration Woodhouse percipiently associates with late Byron. Late Byron, the Byron of *Don Juan* and the comic poems, set out, in Woodhouse's phrase, to 'fling off' the mostly female readers who had made him so successful, 'mingling sentiment and sneering'. This is the aim also of the masculine hardness Keats, who feels similarly compromised and defiant, means to inject into his poem, a hardness which is in one sense anti-commercial (because anti-female), but in another reviewer-driven; just as Byron's late style combined defiance of female taste with implicit deference

[129] Richard Woodhouse to John Taylor, 19 Sept. 1819, in *Letters*, ed. Rollins, ii. 162–3.

to the critics, to their complaints of commercially motivated sameness or repetition in particular.

Keats, though, goes further, in a revision which occasioned his only important conflict with Taylor and Woodhouse. Woodhouse's letter continues:

There was another alteration, which I abused for 'a full hour by the *Temple* clock.' You know if a thing has a decent side, I generally look no further—as the poem was orig^y written, *we* innocent ones (ladies & myself) might very well have supposed that Porphyro, when acquainted with Madeline's love for him, and when 'he arose, Etherial flush^d &c &c (turn to it) set himself at once to persuade her to go off with him, & succeeded & went over the 'Dartmoor black' (now changed for some other place) to be married, in right honest chaste & sober wise. But, as it is now altered, as soon as M. has confessed her love, P. <instead> winds by degrees his arm round her, presses breast to breast, and acts all the acts of a bonâ fide husband, while she fancies she is only playing the part of a Wife in a dream. This alteration is of about 3 stanzas; and tho' there are no<t> improper expressions but all is left to inference, and tho' profanely speaking, the Interest on the reader's imagination is greatly heightened, yet I do apprehend it will render the poem unfit for ladies, & indeed scarcely to be mentioned to them among the 'things that are.'—He says he does not want ladies to read his poetry; that he writes for men—& that if in the former poem there was an opening for doubt what took place, it was his fault for not writing clearly & comprehensibly—that he sh^d despise a man who would be such an eunuch in sentiment as to leave a <Girl> maid, with that Character about her, in such a situation: & sho^d despise himself to write about it &c &c &c—and all this sort of Keats-like rhodomontade.

Leaving aside for a moment the question of whether Woodhouse is right about the commercial impact of this revision, even about its greater explicitness, Keats's motives are clear.[130] He will be

---

[130] The revised version is printed in *Poems*, ed. Stillinger, 314:

> See, while she speaks his arms encroaching slow,
> Have zoned her, heart to heart,—loud, loud the dark winds blow!
>
> For on the midnight came a tempest fell;
> More sooth, for that his quick rejoinder flows
> Into her burning ear: and still the spell
> Unbroken guards her in serene repose.
> With her mild dreams he mingled, as a rose
> Marrieth its odour to a violet.
> Still, still she dreams, louder the frost wind blows.

manly: will write for men, will ravish women (the revision is an assault, leaving no room for innocence or false supposition), will be no 'eunuch', the sort who would leave a willing maid untouched. The identification with Porphyro is telling: both (so it might seem to Keats) abject themselves to women ('Thou art my heaven, and I thine eremite,' delares Porphyro at 1. 277), while also using calculation (Porphyro's 'strategem', 1. 139), and both boldly ravish. The 'heaven' or 'paradise' Madeline represents is, among other things, a commercial paradise, a success of Byronic proportions; that Keats is deeply conflicted about this success contributes to the ambivalences of the poem, of its attitudes to Madeline and Porphyro in particular.[131]

Woodhouse's displeasure with this revision was tempered with realism (as when he admits that 'profanely speaking' the reader's interest is heightened or when, like Mary Shelley revising Byron, he counsels reticence, leaving things 'to inference'); his displeasure, though, was immediately and angrily seconded by Taylor, and again, as in moments of intemperance with Clare, mitigating circumstances intervene. Taylor was unwell, recuperating 200 miles from London. The firm had lost money on *Endymion*, 'well over £150' to date, yet Keats was pressing Taylor to publish a new collection.[132] Less than a month earlier, on 23 August, Taylor had received the most vituperative of Keats's anti-audience diatribes, in which the poet dismissively compares 'the favour of the public with the love of a woman'. Chilcott summarizes 'the position as Taylor saw it', given these and other factors:

If, as Keats claimed, he did not want women to read his poetry, then he had immediately cut away a half at least of his potential public; and for Taylor, the folly of such an attitude as far as sales and public recognition were concerned must have been obvious. From the past

To Bennett, *Keats, Narrative and Audience*, 112, 'the question of whether the revisions make the sexuality of "St Agnes" more explicit is debatable (indeed, Woodhouse's reading seems to be highly questionable)'.

[131] Stillinger, in the title essay of *The Hoodwinking of Madeline and Other Essays on Keats's Poems* (Urbana Ill.: University of Illinois Press, 1971), 67–93, most clearly anatomizes the complexities and ambivalences of Keats's attitudes to the lovers.

[132] See Chilcott, *A Publisher and His Circle*, 40. Keats urged publication of a new collection on 11 Sept. 1819, according to Woodhouse's letter to Taylor of 19 Sept. (in *Letters*, ed. Rollins, ii. 162).

experience of the house, both Hessey and he had seen numerous examples of the immense influence that the female reading public wielded over the sales of new books. . . . Only a year previously, the *British Critic* had obsessively lashed the supposed sexual impurity of *Endymion*. If so much capital had been made from so little provocation, how much greater might be the attack against the far clearer case of sexual licence that Woodhouse had indicated?[133]

Taylor's response, relayed to Woodhouse in a letter of 25 September, is tough and impatient, cutting straight to Keats's ambivalence about the public. The proposed revisions are 'the most stupid piece of Folly I can conceive':

He does not bear the ill opinion of the World calmly, & yet he will not allow it to form a good Opinion of him & his Writings. He repented of this conduct when Endymion was published as much as a Man can repent, who shews by the accidental Expression of Disappointment, Mortification & Disgust that he has met with a Result different from that which he had anticipated—Yet he will again challenge the same Neglect or Censure, & again (I pledge my Discernment on it) be vexed at the Reception he has prepared for himself. This Vaporing is as far from sound Fortitude, as the conduct itself in the Instances before us, is devoid of good Feeling & good Sense.[134]

Here, again, Keats's manhood is called into question: he lacks 'sound Fortitude'; he is unable to 'bear the ill opinion of the World calmly'; his behaviour is inconsistent, illogical—that is, childish, womanly (later in the letter Taylor calls it 'silly'). 'Had he known truly what the Society and what the Suffrages of Women are worth,' continues Taylor, a man of 38, with several serious romantic attachments behind him, 'he would never have thought of depriving himself of them'; which is partly to say, this boy of 24 knows nothing of women, is not yet a man.[135] Being a man, for Taylor, means facing up to the facts of the audience and the value of women—that is, knowing what women 'are worth' in several senses.

[133] Chilcott, *A Publisher and His Circle*, 41.
[134] John Taylor to Richard Woodhouse, 25 Sept. 1819, in Rollins (ed.), *KC* i. 96.
[135] Gittings, *Keats*, 180, describes Taylor as 'social, attractive to women . . . the consultant and ally of friends and relatives in love, both male and female, and . . . soon reckoned "so old a practitioner" that his advice and help was sought in the most complicated affairs'. Gittings thinks Taylor may have had an affair with Isabella Jones, whom Keats had met in Hastings in Jan. 1817, though Chilcott, *A Publisher and His Circle*, 39, thinks he merely 'tried and failed' to have an affair.

Taylor then issues an ultimatum: 'if he will not so far concede to my Wishes as to leave the passage as it originally stood,
I must be content to admire his Poems with some other im-
print'.[136] To this ultimatum Keats accedes, a fact we know from
a note Woodhouse appends to his own (as opposed to his
clerks') transcript of Keats's fair copy, opposite the beginning
of the poem: 'This Copy was taken from K's original M.S. He
afterwards altered it for publication, & added some stanzas &
omitted others. His alterations are noticed here. The Published
Copy differs from both in a few particulars. K. left it to his
Publishers to adopt which they pleased, & to revise the whole.'[137]
The printed version restores the original, less explicit, if more
impassioned, consummation at lines 314–22, omits the stanza
clarifying the legend and thus the banquet, which was to appear after line 54 (in part, no doubt, because of its sensual
extravagance, including the ironic sexuality of Madeline's waking 'warm in the virgin morn, no weeping Magdalen'[138]), and
tones down several impious exclamations—'Mercy' for Angela's
'Jesu' at line 98, 'Away' and then 'Go, go' (the printed version)
for 'O Christ' at line 143. (The rest of the forty or so substantive differences between the lost fair copy and the printed version

---

[136] John Taylor to Richard Woodhouse, 25 Sept. 1819, in *Letters*, ed. Rollins,
ii. 182–3.
[137] *Poems*, ed. Stillinger, 626. That Keats did not see the poem between the time
he handed Woodhouse the fair copy and the time he read proofs is also suggested
by a letter of 11(?) June 1820 to Taylor, in *Letters*, ed. Rollins, ii. 294–5.
[138] The omitted stanza is quoted in *Poems*, ed. Stillinger, 301:

> 'Twas said her future lord would there appear
> Offering, as sacrifice—all in the dream—
> Delicious food, even to her lips brought near,
> Viands, and wine, and fruit, and sugar'd cream,
> To touch her palate with the fine extreme
> Of relish: then soft music heard, and then
> More pleasures follow'd in dizzy stream
> Palpable almost: then to wake again
> Warm in the virgin morn, no weeping Magdalen.

Levinson, *Keats's Life of Allegory*, 114, sees innuendo, in addition to explicitness,
in the revised consummation scene: 'In the revised version . . . Keats prefaces the
aroma marriage with these lines: "More sooth[,] for that his quick rejoinder flows
I Into her burning ear . . ." The wink wink nod nod character of this erotic report
("re-joined her"; a "quick", "sooth[ing]" "flow" into a hot portal) might remind
us of some parts of *Don Juan*, particularly the Donna Julia and Lady Adeline
episodes.'

are Keats's doing or were approved by him.[139]) In all extant versions both Angela and the Beadsmen, as opposed to Angela alone, are 'brought in' at the poem's conclusion 'to leave on the reader a sense of pettish disgust', which leads Stillinger to conjecture 'that Woodhouse simply misunderstood the revised version here (he had heard Keats recite it when he wrote to Taylor, but had not yet actually read it)'.[140] So this revision, at least, was allowed to stand, perhaps because its satire, of a piece with the writings to follow ('Lamia', 'The Cap and Bells'), is comparatively non-assaultive—a 'flinging off' not a ravishment. Taylor, Hessey, and Woodhouse were no more in tune with satire than they were with blasphemy or overt sexuality, but sales would not be affected—half the audience would not be lost.

IDENTITY

Keats's ambivalent feelings about readers and critics return us, via questions of gender, to the problem of personal identity with which this book began. The 'manly' defiance inspiring the revisions to 'The Eve of St Agnes' was also an assertion of authorial autonomy, in respect at least to audience and advisers, if not reviewers. Talk of self-sufficiency, of not needing female readers, recalls the very features of the 'wordsworthian or egotistical sublime'[141] Keats had earlier disparaged, as in 'we hate poetry that has a palpable design upon us—and if we do not agree, seems to put its hand in its breeches pocket'. Keats puts his hand in his breeches pocket, acts like Wordsworth, with the 'Eve of St Agnes' revisions; he also 'cuts a figure', like Byron[142] (that is, individuates himself as well as puts on airs),

[139] As Stillinger, *Texts*, 214, points out, the alterations were made in proofs, which we know Keats read, and in at least two places Keats requested that Taylor restore fair copy readings (see John Keats to John Taylor, 11[?] June 1820, in *Letters*, ed. Rollins, ii. 294–5). That Keats dined with Taylor on 15 Nov. 1819 and then wrote him a friendly letter ('My dear Taylor') on 17 Nov. 1819, ibid. ii. 234–45, suggests that, as with comparable difficulties in Taylor's relations with Clare, the disagreement quickly passed.

[140] *Poems*, ed. Stillinger, 631.

[141] John Keats to Richard Woodhouse, 27 Oct. 1818, in *Letters*, ed. Rollins, i. 387.

[142] John Keats to George and Georgiana Keats, 19 Feb. 1819, ibid. ii. 67.

'flinging off' constricting commercial considerations. This active—or reactive—gesture of autonomy reflects an important shift in Keats's view of the artist: poetical power for 'late' Keats is no longer figured in passivity or receptivity and creative dissolution, but in hardened and coherent individuality or subjectivity, the very self-possession and autonomy Wordsworth and Coleridge labour to express in revision—and Byron expresses despite himself, even when subversively or deconstructively revising.

When 'late' Keats writes of poetical power, in the letters of 1819, as opposed to those of 1818 in which the theory of 'negative capability' is evolved, the poet is seen as both active and male: 'I know not why poetry and I have been so distant lately,' Keats muses in a journal-letter entry of 13 March 1819, 'I must make some advances soon or she will cut me entirely.' Earlier, 'reaching after' things—a form of 'making advances'—is seen as the very opposite of creative power; an 'irritable reaching after fact and reason'[143] leads to blockage and deficiency. 'Let us open our leaves like a flower and be passive and receptive,' writes Keats to Reynolds on 19 February 1818, 'budding patiently under the eye of Apollo and taking hints from eve[r]ly noble insect that favors us with a visit.'[144] Personal identity, in contrast, is associated in the letters of 1818 with activity or agency, is seen both as male and as anti-poetical, as one would expect from a poet bereft of 'natural' moorings (familial, financial, class), and only just out of adolescence, that time, as Keats puts it in the preface to *Endymion*, 'in which the soul is in ferment, the character undecided'. To 'early' Keats, the 'poetical Character' is 'not itself—it has no self—it is everything and nothing—It has no character'; though 'Men of Power' have 'a proper self', 'Men of Genius' are 'camelions', 'have not any individuality, any determined Character'.[145] 'By abrupt contrast,' notes Homans, 'in April 1819 the term "identity" has become a wholly favorable one'[146]—in, for example, the well-known

[143] From the 'negative capability' letter, John Keats to George and Tom Keats, 27(?) Dec. 1817, ibid. i. 193.
[144] John Keats to J. H. Reynolds, 19 Feb. 1818, ibid. 232.
[145] John Keats to Richard Woodhouse, 27 Oct. 1818, and to Benjamin Bailey, 22 Nov. 1817, ibid. 386–7, 184.
[146] Homans, 'Keats Reading Women', 353.

'vale of Soul-making' letter, in which human beings 'are not Souls till they acquire identities, till each one is personally itself'.[147] Homans quotes two other related passages from the letters: 'My own being which I know to be,' Keats writes to Reynolds on 24 August 1819, the day after the most extreme of his anti-audience diatribes, 'becomes of more consequence to me than the crowds of shadows in the Shape of Man and women that inhabit a kingdom. The soul is a world of itself and has enough to do in its own home'; and a year later, to Shelley, he announces that the artist 'must have "self-concentration," selfishness perhaps. . . . My Imagination is a Monastry and I am its Monk'.[148] To these quotations one might add Keats's assertion to Bailey, in a letter of 14 August 1819, that 'a fine writer is the most genuine Being in the World'.[149]

This new valuing of self or personal identity leads Keats to revalue conscious or secondary processes of creation, what he elsewhere calls writing '*with Judgment*'. 'The following Poem', Keats announces of the 'Ode to Psyche', in a letter of 30 April 1819, 'is the first and the only one with which I have taken even moderate pains—I have for the most part dash'd of[f] my lines in a hurry—This I have done leisurely—I think it reads the more richly for it and will I hope encourage me to write other thing[s] in even a more peacable and healthy spirit.'[150] At the same period (late April or early May), in the sonnet beginning 'If by dull rhymes our English must be chain'd,' he declares himself in search of

> Sandals more interwoven and complete
> To fit the naked foot of Poesy;
> Let us inspect the lyre, and weigh the stress

[147] John Keats to George and Georgiana Keats, 21 Apr. 1819, in *Letters*, ed. Rollins, ii. 102.

[148] John Keats to J. H. Reynolds, 24 Aug. 1819, and John Keats to Percy Bysshe Shelley, 16 Aug. 1820, ibid. 246, 323.

[149] John Keats to Benjamin Bailey, 14 Aug. 1819, ibid. 139.

[150] John Keats to George and Georgiana Keats, 30 Apr. 1819, ibid. 105–6. This statement is, of course, an exaggeration; the new attitude to secondary processes it describes is also, some would argue, misdated. To W. J. Bate, in *The Stylistic Development of Keats* (1924; London: Routledge & Kegan Paul, 1958), 141: 'Keats's stylistic achievement from the time of the writing of *Hyperion*, in the autumn of 1818, until the completion of the odes of May 1819, is in the direction of inevitability of phrase and enrichment of imagery and euphony, and at the same time of discipline and restraint.'

> Of every chord, and see what may be gain'd
> By ear industrious, and attention meet;
> Misers of sound and syllable, no less
> Than Midas of his coinage.

Even in the single most famous and 'Romantic' account we have of Keats's working habits, recollected by Woodhouse in an incomplete and heavily corrected manuscript from the summer of 1820, secondary processes figure prominently. Woodhouse's awkward self-cancellings in the recollection neatly counterpoint Keats's fluency:

[Keats] has repeatedly said in convers[ation] that he never sits down to write, <until> unless he is full of ideas—and then thoughts come about him in troops, as tho' soliciting to be acc[epte]d & he selects— one of his Maxims is that if P[oetry]. does not come naturally, it had better not come at all. the moment he feels any dearth he discontinues writing & waits for a happier moment. <He writes on> he is generally more troubled by a redundancy <of images> than by poverty of images, & he culls what appears to him at the time the best.— He never corrects, unless perhaps a word here or there . . . shd occur<s> to him as preferable to an expression he has already used—He is impatient of correcting, & says he would rather burn the piece in question & write ano[the]r or something else—'My judgement, (he says,) is as active when I am actually writing as my imagin[atio]n. . . . And shall I afterwards, when my imagination is idle, & the heat in which I wrote, has <cooled, sit> gone off, sit down coldly to criticise when in Poss[essi]on of only one faculty, what I have written, when almost inspired.'[151]

The creative process described here is by no means exclusively primary. The poem is not simply given to Keats, it is 'selected' from among 'troops' of thoughts; the poet is a maker (he 'selects') rather than a mage or seer. What has to come 'naturally' then, at least according to this passage, is not poetry, but the material from which poetry is 'culled', and the faculty which does the culling, the 'judgement', is *as active* (my italics) in the composition process as the imagination. Of course, that this process takes place, for the most part, in Keats's mind rather than on paper, with uncanny speed and decisiveness, is pretty remarkable—pretty 'Romantic'—but it does take place; poetical composition is better thought of as an activity than a visitation.

---

[151] Rollins (ed.), *KC* i. 128–9.

Though the passage expresses impatience with correction, reducing it to a matter of 'a word here or there', it is hardly incompatible with the sorts of stylistic second thoughts, Keats's own as well as those he pondered from his advisers, everywhere apparent in the 1820 collection.

That these second thoughts involve questions of commercial and critical reception is a judgement suggested not only by the creation and revision of 'Isabella', 'Hyperion', and 'The Eve of St Agnes', but by the 1820 collection as a whole, at least according to McGann and Levinson. To McGann, the 1820 volume 'was constructed with a profoundly self-conscious attitude towards the climate of literary opinion which prevailed at the time'.[152] To Levinson, the collection was

above all, a volume designed *not to offend*. . . . Keats conceived the danger in terms of stylistic unself-consciousness: a literature that wears its heart on its sleeve. . . . *1820* was to be 'good' in the sense of 'wise' rather than 'innocent.' It was to be 'good,' moreover, in a literary sense and in the manner of Byron: an urbane, ironic, large-minded, manly unexceptionability—not 'natural' feeling but a sophisticated and well-managed representation of feeling.[153]

Taylor, Woodhouse, and Keats's other advisers helped fashion this unexceptionability, though Byronic urbanity seems to have been Keats's idea alone.[154] Once impeding political associations had been severed, or at least muted, along with a related indelicacy, the advisers focused exclusively on 'style', which is to say, on the creation of a poetic voice that was both correct and controlled—stable, sound, single, no longer the expression of a poet whose 'relation to the object world was too ragged . . . too charged with desire'.[155]

---

[152] McGann, 'Keats and Historical Method', 52.

[153] Levinson, *Keats's Allegory of Life*, 115–16.

[154] For evidence of Keats's growing interest in Byron after the 'Eve of St Agnes' revisions see Lau, 'Keats and Byron', 215–17.

[155] Ibid. 231. McGann, in 'Keats and Historical Method', 52, foregrounds the muting of political associations: 'The key fact in the pre-publication history of the 1820 poems is the insistence by Keats's publishers that the book not contain anything that would provoke the reviewers to attack (they were especially concerned about charges of indecency and political radicalism). . . . The two poems published in Leigh Hunt's *Indicator* ['La Belle Dame sans Merci' and the sonnet 'As Hermes once to his feathers light'] did not find a place in the 1820 volume, and the reason for this is that Keats did not want to give the reviewers any occasion for linking Keats's new work with the politically sensitive name of Leigh Hunt.' Yet

Hence the calculated doubleness of the poems of Keats's maturity, from 'The Eve of St Agnes' onwards, a doubleness especially marked in 'Lamia' and the Odes, and one different in kind from that complained of by the reviewers of *Endymion* and *Poems* (1817). Hence also the high finish or 'craftsmanship' of the later poems. The revision of 'Lamia' provides a case in point. It begins when Taylor responds coolly to a fifty-nine-line sample of the poem (crossed in a letter of 5 September 1819), eighteen lines of which Keats cuts, altering other lines substantially.[156] The dropped lines, beginning after 2. 162 in the original, describe a belching, farting Glutton. Subsequent alterations focus almost exclusively on metrical and other particulars. The poem was polished by some fifty or so alterations, at least eight devoted to the proper pronunciation of Greek names and words (including 'Lamia' itself), a particular anxiety of Woodhouse and Taylor given Lockhart's criticisms of *Endymion*.[157] Nor was Keats uninvolved in these alterations. Consider, for example, the revision of the following couplet from the fair copy: 'She fled into that valley they must pass | Who go from Corinth out to Cencreas' (1. 173–4). When Keats was informed, no doubt by Woodhouse, of the false quantity these lines give to the Greek name 'Cencreas', he substituted the following alternative in the proofs: 'She fled into that valley they must skirt | Who go from Corinth out to Cenchrea's port.' This reconciles proper pronunciation with scansion, but at the expense of rhyme ('skirt' | 'port'), and Woodhouse, 'realizing

the advisers were not at all as thorough as McGann implies. 'Isabella', for example, was seen by Keats's defender, John Scott, in a review of the 1820 volume in the Sept. 1820 edn. of the *London Magazine* as a particular lapse in judgement. In Theodore Redpath's summary, from *The Young Romantics and Critical Opinion, 1807–1824* (London: Harrap, 1973), 114–15, the poem's tirades against Isabella's brothers as 'money-bags', 'Baalites of pelf', and 'ledger-men', 'were, in Scott's view, "no better than extravagant school-boy vituperation of trade and traders; just as if lovers did not trade,—and that, often in stolen goods—or had in general any higher object than a barter of enjoyment!" "Ledger-men" were not to be despised. Lamb's essay on the South-Sea House in *The London Magazine*'s last number was an "elegant reproof" of "such short-sighted views of character; such idle hostilities against the realities of life."'

¹⁵⁶ John Keats to John Taylor, 5 Sept. 1819, in *Letters*, ed. Rollins, ii. 157–9.
¹⁵⁷ Woodhouse makes sure, e.g., that, metrically, 'Phoebean', in 1. 78, is allowed all three syllables, or 'Lamia' itself, in 1. 272 and 1. 371, is reduced to two. See, also, in the textual apparatus to Stillinger's edn. of the *Poems*, 1. 115, 133, 173–4, 176, 225.

the rhyme would never pass the critics',[158] produced a third version, that of the eventual 1820 reading: 'She fled into that valley they pass o'er | Who go to Corinth from Cenchreas' shore,' which is at least formally unobjectionable.

Or consider Taylor's role in the last-minute improvement of the following late passage from the fair copy (beginning at 2. 291) describing the confrontation of Lamia and Apollonius:

> 'Fool!' said the sophist in an under-tone
> Gruff with contempt; which a death-nighing moan
> From Lycius answer'd, as he sank supine
> Upon the couch where Lamia's beauties pine.
> 'Fool! Fool!' repeated he, while his eyes still
> Relented not, nor mov'd; 'from every ill
> That youth might suffer have I shielded thee
> Up to this very hour, and shall I see
> Thee married to a Serpent? Pray you Mark,
> Corinthians! A serpent, plain and stark!'

Gittings is good on what Taylor might have disapproved of here (though not on why Woodhouse was unperturbed): 'There was the false rhyme of "supine" and "pine", the awkward run-on of "see Thee", the rhetorical repetition of "Serpent", and the odd "stark", a weak rhyme for "Mark" and liable to be misconstrued as "naked".'[159] Taylor brought these stylistic weaknesses to Keats's attention in his office in Fleet Street on 5 June 1820, and Keats immediately took up a piece of paper (as it happens, the back of a letter from Clare) and rewrote the 'supine' | 'pine' couplet to read 'From Lycius answer'd, as heartstuck and lost | He sank supine beside the aching ghost', which is the version printed in the 1820 volume. Taylor, meanwhile, made several attempts to revise the 'stark' | 'Mark' couplet in proof, offering 'Thee married to a Serpent? Mark the Cheat, | Corinthians! a Serpent, I repeat' and then 'That youth must suffer have I shielded thee | And married to a Serpent shalt thou be!' When the passage was brought to Woodhouse's attention, he defended 'stark', citing comparable usages in Spenser and Shelley; in the end, though, a new version was found, compressing the last four lines of the original into 'Of life have I preserved thee to this day, | And shall I see thee made a Serpent's

---

[158] Gittings, *Keats*, 574.   [159] Ibid. 575–6.

prey?'—which eliminates both 'stark' and the offending rhyme with 'Mark'.[160] Revisions like these produce a poem 'presentable' enough to head the 1820 volume.[161]

The style or voice these revisions helped produce did not, obviously, come 'naturally', but then nor were secondary processes alone the source of Keats's power. This power, as a number of recent critics have suggested, often derives from what lies outside attentiveness or control—from what would be considered 'bad' about the poems in the eyes, equally, of Wordsworth's contemporary admirers (Lockhart, for example) and of mainstream 'Romanticists'.[162] Such a suggestion, of course, can itself

[160] Gittings summarizes the virtues of the printed version as follows: 'The added compression and dramatic tension, the heightening of suspense by delaying the word "serpent" are happy results of Taylor's intervention. The final result is so unlike the neat poetic platitudes of either Taylor or Woodhouse that Keats clearly roused himself to a fresh and successful act of composition' (see ibid. 576). Both Gittings and Allott (*The Complete Poems*, 648) imply that the alternatives to the 'stark'/'Mark' couplet Stillinger identifies as Taylor's (in *Poems*, 668) were in fact Woodhouse's. Allott cites W. A. Coles, 'The Proof Sheets of Keats's "Lamia"', *Harvard Library Bulletin*, 8 (1954), 118–19, in corroboration.

[161] Keats was taking a risk opening the new volume with a poem in heroic couplets, the form of *Endymion*. But the couplets of 'Lamia' are much more controlled. As Bate puts it, in *The Stylistic Development of Keats*, 171: 'He wished greater emphasis and greater integrity of both line and couplet: he consequently adopted patterns of stress and pause absent in his early couplets, but common in the Augustan coupleteers; he abolished the feminine rhyme, avoided such vices of the Huntian couplet as concluding the line with an adjective or a preposition, and turned from the run-on to a more closed form of the couplet; and, to secure variety, confined himself largely to such traditional neo-classical devices as the triplet, the Alexandrine, and the initially inverted foot.'

[162] For the most influential of recent accounts of the sources of what Levinson, *Keats's Life of Allegory*, 5, sees as Keats's greatness—'not its capacious, virile, humane authenticity but its subversion of those authoritarian values'—see John Bayley, 'Keats and Reality', *Proceedings of the British Academy* (1962), and Christopher Ricks, *Keats and Embarrassment* (Oxford: Clarendon Press, 1974). Levinson identifies an opposing—older, more established and influential—tradition, the tradition that locates Keats's greatness in the poems of his maturity, the Odes in particular, as spearheaded by Helen Vendler, *The Odes of John Keats* (Cambridge, Mass.: Harvard University Press, 1983), with whom she associates earlier critics such as Bate, Douglas Bush, in *John Keats* (New York: Macmillan, 1966), David Perkins, *The Quest for Permanence: The Symbolism of Wordsworth, Shelley, and Keats* (Cambridge, Mass.: Harvard University Press, 1959), and Earl Wasserman, *The Finer Tone: Keats's Major Poems* (Baltimore: Johns Hopkins University Press, 1983). This tradition emphasizes gathering control and craftsmanship, what Barbara Everett, in 'Somebody Reading', a review of Vendler's book on the Odes, in the *London Review of Books*, 6 (1984), 11, calls 'consciousness triumphant', and is centrally related to the organicist values of New Critical and what I have called 'Romanticist' critics, as in, for example, Cleath Brooks's *The Well-Wrought Urn*:

tip into Romanticism, implicitly undervaluing secondary or revisionary powers, as in the various forms of textual primitivism we have encountered in this book. Keats revised his poems, or approved and collaborated in the revising process, in order to be a poet, which is not merely to say in order to support himself as a poet, but to create a discrete self or 'soul', and thus become an agent or maker. The impetus to revise was not simply external or imposed, a product of reader and critic, friend and publisher, the concerns of Part 2 of this book; it involved internal factors as well, in particular changing conceptions of personal identity such as are examined in Part 1. Revision, as ever, was multiply motivated. What studying such revision reveals is the inadequacy or incompleteness of the Romantic view: none of the writers discussed in this book fits the stereotype most of them helped construct. The spontaneous, extemporizing, otherworldly, autonomous author, the Romantic author, is a fiction much in need of revision—even, finally, in the case of Keats.

Studies in the Structure of Poetry (New York: Harcourt, Brace, 1947), with its aesthetic of controlled doubleness, or M. H. Abrams's privileging of the ode form in 'Structure and Style in the Greater Romantic Lyric', in Frederick W. Hilles and Harold Bloom (eds.), *From Sensibility to Romanticism: Essays Presented to Frederick A. Pottle* (New York: Oxford University Press, 1965), 527–60.

APPENDIX

PERSONAL IDENTITY IN EIGHTEENTH-CENTURY THOUGHT

The eighteenth-century philosophical debate about personal identity was inaugurated in Britain in the second or 1694 edition of the *Essay Concerning Human Understanding* (1690). In chapter 27 of book 2 of this edition, Locke takes aim at the traditional account of personal identity as immaterial substance, an account neatly summarized by the Roman philosopher Boethius, an influential link between classical and medieval belief. 'A person', Boethius declares in the *Treatise against Eutyches and Nestorius* (512), 'is the individual substance of a rational nature,' a view characterized by Locke's antagonist, John Clendon, writing in 1710, as 'Authentick, and in Effect held ever since.'[1] 'Individual substance', argue the traditionalists, is immaterial, indivisible, and immortal. Although allied to body, and issuing in characteristic deeds, it alone guarantees continuing identity or ontological permanence; in Locke's words, 'the *Identity* of Soul alone makes the same Man'.[2] This is a view Descartes could be said to share, for all the epistemic novelty of his system, being certain, as he puts it in a well-known formulation of the 'cogito' from the *Discourse on Method* (1637), that the self is a single, rational 'substance whose whole essence or nature is . . . to think'.[3]

---

[1] For Boethius see *The Theological Tractates*, trans. H. F. Stewart and E. K. Rand (London: Loeb Classical Library, 1918), 92; for John Clendon see *Tractatus Philosophico-Theologicus de Persona. Or, a Treatise of the Word Person* (London, 1710), 94, as quoted in Christopher Fox, *Locke and the Scriblerians: Identity and Consciousness in Early Eighteenth-Century Britain* (Berkeley: University of California Press, 1988), 15.

[2] John Locke, *An Essay Concerning Human Understanding*, ed. P. H. Nidditch (Oxford: Clarendon Press, 1975), 332. Subsequent page references to this edition are given in parentheses in the text.

[3] Here is the full passage from *Discourse on Method*, in which Descartes describes the workings of the *cogito*. He begins with the intention 'to pretend that all the things that ever entered my mind were no more true than the illusions of my dreams. But immediately I noticed that while I was trying thus to think everything false, it was necessary that I, who was thinking this, was something. And observing that this truth *I am thinking, therefore I exist* was so firm and sure that all the most extravagant suppositions of the sceptics were incapable of shaking it, I decided that

Locke agrees with Descartes and the traditionalists in respect to the inadequacy of matter or body as a determinant of personal identity. 'In the state of living Creatures, their Identity depends not on a Mass of the same particles,' he writes, 'for in them the variation of great parcels of Matter alters not the Identity' (p. 330). But Locke also finds 'Soul', Boethius's 'individual substance of a rational nature', Descartes's 'cogito', inadequate, since 'if the *Identity* of Soul alone makes the same Man, and there be nothing in the Nature of Matter, why [may] the same individual Spirit . . . not be united to different Bodies' (p. 332), including, as in transmigration, the bodies of beasts, an obvious absurdity? 'Those who place thinking in an immaterial Substance only', continues Locke, 'must shew why personal Identity cannot be preserved in the change of immaterial Substances' (p. 337), something they fail to do. For Locke, personal identity is a matter neither of an immaterial soul nor of a material body, but of consciousness, a term he seems to have coined.[4] Consciousness is 'inseparable from thinking, and as it seems to me essential to it: It being impossible for any one to perceive, without perceiving, that he does perceive' (p. 335). Consciousness ensures that 'every one is to himself, that which he calls *self* . . . and thereby distinguishes himself from all other thinking things, in this alone consists *personal Identity, i.e.* the sameness of a rational Being: And as far as this consciousness can be extended backwards to any past Action or Thought, so far reaches the Identity of that *Person*; it is the same *self* now as it was then; and 'tis by the same *self* with

---

I could accept it without scruple as the first principle of the philosophy I was seeking.
Next I examined attentively what I was. I saw that while I could pretend that I had no body and that there was no world and no place for me to be in, I could not for all that pretend I did not exist. I saw on the contrary that from the mere fact that I thought of doubting the truth of other things, it followed quite evidently and certainly that I existed; whereas if I had merely ceased thinking . . . I should have had no reason to believe that I existed. From this I knew I was a substance whose whole essence or nature is . . . to think.' (*Philosophical Writings*, trans. John Cottingham, Robert Stoothoff, and Duguld Murdoch, 2 vols. (Cambridge: Cambridge University Press, 1985), i. 127.) For a related account of the *cogito* as immaterial substance see Descartes's 1640 letter to Petrus Colvius, whom he thanks 'for drawing attention to the passage of St Augustine relevant to my *I am thinking, therefore I exist*', a passage he uses 'to show that this I which is thinking is an immaterial substance with no bodily element' (*Descartes's Philosophical Letters*, trans. Anthony Kenny (Oxford: Oxford University Press, 1970), 83).

[4] See Fox, *Locke and the Scriblerians*, 12: 'Outside of several minor uses of the word itself, the earliest written use of the word *consciousness* in the language is by John Locke. And in the sense of the "totality of the impressions, thoughts, and feelings, which make up a person's conscious being," Locke *is* the first. The *OED*, significantly, cites the earliest written occurrence of *consciousness* in this sense as book 2, chapter 27 of the *Essay concerning Human Understanding*.'

this present one that now reflects on it, that that Action was done' (p. 335).

It was Locke's hope that his theories would affirm, or more firmly establish, the self as the ground of ethical life. 'In this *personal Identity*', he claims of his conception of the self as consciousness, 'is founded all the Right and Justice of Reward and Punishment' (p. 341). Such a view of the self's moral importance accords with traditional or Christian belief, which depends, as Amélie Rorty puts it, on the 'idea of a person as a unified center of choice and action, the unit of legal and theological responsibility. If judgement summarizes a life, as it does in the Christian drama, then that life must have a unified location.'[5] Locke's opponents, though, immediately accused him of destabilizing both the self and morality. For Locke's theory raises the possibility that the same man or woman could be different persons at different times, that 'if the same *Socrates* waking and sleeping do not partake of the same *consciousness*, *Socrates* waking and sleeping is not the same Person'. Moreover, 'to punish *Socrates* waking for what sleeping *Socrates* thought, and waking *Socrates* was never conscious of, would be no more of Right than to punish one Twin for what his Brother Twin did' (p. 342). Locke offers other puzzles in chapter 27 (several involving body transportation, as in Parfit), to reinforce this person/man distinction, and with it a sense of the unreliability of deeds or acts as an index of self; he also recalls 'our way of speaking in *English*, when we say such an one *is not himself*, or is *besides himself*; in which Phrases it is insinuated, as if those who now, or, at least, first used them, thought, that *self* was changed, the *self* same Person was no longer in that Man' (pp. 342–3).

Such puzzles and problems had an immediate and lasting appeal to philosophers and other thinkers, though in a way exactly the reverse · of Locke's intention. Personal identity, and with it ethical accountability, was thrown into question. The self, according to another of Locke's opponents, Joseph Butler, in 'Of Personal Identity' (1736), became 'not a permanent, but a transient thing'.[6] 'My good friend,' Sterne writes in *Tristram Shandy* (1760), 'as sure as I am I—and you are you—And who are you? said he.—Don't puzzle me, said I.'[7] Sterne is alluding here to a debate of long standing (sixty-six years by 1760), involving writers as diverse as Stillingfleet, Shaftesbury, Butler,

---

[5] Amélie Oskenberg Rorty, 'A Literary Postcript: Characters, Persons, Selves, Individuals', in Rorty (ed.), *The Identities of Persons* (Berkeley: University of California Press, 1976), 309.

[6] Quoted in Fox, *Locke and the Scriblerians*, 17.

[7] Laurence Sterne, *Tristram Shandy*, ed. James A. Work (New York: Odyssey Press, 1940), 525.

Mandeville, Prior, Watts, the 'Scriblerians' (Pope, Swift, and Arbuthnot, poking fun at the pamphlet warriors Anthony Collins, on the Locke side, and Samuel Clarke, a traditionalist), Berkeley, and Hume.[8]

Hume's intervention in the debate, principally in section 6 of Book 1 of *A Treatise of Human Nature* (1739–40), deserves attention, for it was decisively destabilizing. It begins, in section 6 itself, by attacking Locke, since by 1740, as Hume says in an appendix, 'most philosophers seem inclin'd to think, that personal identity *arises* from consciousness'.[9] This attack is rooted in a larger scepticism, the subject of earlier sections, and differs entirely from that of the traditionalists. 'When I enter most intimately into what I call *myself*,' Hume confesses, 'I always stumble on some particular perception or other, of heat or cold, light or shade, love or hatred, pain or pleasure. I never can catch *myself* at any time without a perception, and never can observe any thing but the perception' (p. 252). The self is thus 'a bundle or collection of different perceptions, which succeed each other with an inconceivable rapidity, and are in a perpetual flux and movement ... nor is there any single power of the soul, which remains unalterably the same, perhaps for one moment' (pp. 252–3). The mind,

[8] See e.g. Edward Stillingfleet, *The Bishop of Worcester's Answer to Mr John Locke's Second Letter, Wherein his Notion of Ideas Is Prov'd to be Inconsistent with itself And with the Articles of the Christian Faith* (1698); Samuel Clarke, *A Third Defence of An Argument Made Use of in a Letter to Mr Dodwell* (1706) and Anthony Collins's *An Answer to Mr Clarke's Third Defence* (1708), key documents in the wearyingly comprehensive Clarke–Collins controversy; Anthony, Earl of Shaftesbury, *Characteristics of Men, Manners, Opinions, Times* (1711, rev. edn. 1713); George Berkeley, *Three Dialogues Between Hylas and Philonous* (1713) and *Alciphron: Or, The Minute Philosopher* (1732); Matthew Prior, *A Dialogue Between Mr John Lock and Seigneu de Montaigne* (1721); Bernard Mandeville, *A Treatise of the Hypochondriack and Hysteric Passions* (1730); Isaac Watts, *Philosophical Essays* (1733); Joseph Butler, 'Of Personal Identity' (1736). All these works (and many others) are discussed by Fox, in *Locke and the Scriblerians*, as is their parodying by the 'Scriblerus Club'. This 'club', formed in 1713, undertook, in the *Memoirs of Martinus Scriblerus* (printed in 1741, in the second edition of Pope's prose works), to ridicule false tastes in learning. Its original members were Swift, Pope, Gay, John Arbuthnot, Thomas Parnell, Francis Atterbury, and the Lord High Treasurer, the Earl of Oxford, though the *Memoirs* themselves seem to have been mostly, if not exclusively, the work of Arbuthnot. The *Memoirs* take the form of a pseudobiography, that of the learned scholar Martinus Scriblerus. Post-Lockean debate about consciousness and identity is ridiculed in chapter 7, which mocks the Lockean critique of the substantial self, chapter 12, which directly parodies the Clarke–Collins dispute, and chapters 14 and 15, which offer especially ludicrous 'thought experiments' or identity puzzles, in the manner of Locke's prince/cobbler or Parfit's Teletransporter examples.

[9] David Hume, *A Treatise of Human Nature*, ed. L. A. Selby-Bigge, rev. P. H. Nidditch (Oxford: Clarendon Press, 1978), 635. Subsequent references to this edition in parentheses in the text.

Hume continues, is like a theatre, in which successive perceptions 'pass, re-pass, glide away', though even this analogy is misleading, since 'the successive perceptions only . . . constitute the mind' (p. 253). As for our almost universal propensity 'to ascribe an identity to these successive perceptions, and to suppose ourselves possessed of an invariable and uninterrupted existence' (p. 253), this is a product of simple error or confusion, a 'mistake' (p. 254). We invent the supposed connections that identify objects through a process of association; 'we feign the continu'd existence of the perceptions of our senses, to remove the interruption; and run into the notion of a *soul*, and *self*, and *substance*, to disguise the variation' (p. 255).

It is the imagination that does the feigning. Identity 'is nothing really belonging to these different perceptions, and uniting them together; but is merely a quality, which we attribute to them, because of the union of their ideas in the imagination, when we reflect upon them' (p. 260). The role of memory in this process is crucial and constitutive: 'memory not only discovers the identity, but also contributes to its production' (p. 261). And later: 'Had we no memory, we never shou'd have any notion of causation, nor consequently of that chain of causes and effects, which constitute our self or person' (pp. 261–2)—that is, our imagined or fabricated sense of self or person. Though Hume shares with others a sense of the persuasive power of memory, its 'superior force and vivacity' (p. 87), memory can no more prove the existence of self than can the imagination.

Hume's stress on the constitutive role of imagination and memory was revalued in the later eighteenth and early nineteenth centuries, though its sceptical origins live on in writers such as Sterne, Friedrich Schlegel, and Byron.[10] Through the influence of David Hartley, the train of co-ordinating or connecting associations was traced and elaborated into a system that ultimately confirmed Christian morality and belief.[11] So, too, in German philosophy, the intuitive powers Hume

[10] See Anne K. Mellor, *English Romantic Irony* (Cambridge, Mass.: Harvard University Press, 1980), for a discussion of Friedrich Schlegel and Byron, but also Keats, Carlyle, Coleridge, and other subsequent writers identified with an irony very like, if not directly indebted to, Humean scepticism.

[11] See David Hartley, *Observations on Man, His Frame, His Duty, and His Expectations* (1749), facsimile and intro. Theodore L. Huguelet, 2 vols. (Gainsville, Fla.: Scholars' Facsimiles and Reprints, 1966), i. 82–3, where the process of association is said to spiritualize 'sensible Pleasures and Pains' into 'intellectual' ones, thus 'reduc[ing] the State of those who have eaten of the Tree of Knowledge of Good and Evil, back again to a paradisiacal one'. Later, after dutifully warning against the dangers of the imagination in the associative process, Hartley again goes on to commend both the process itself and the imagination, as leading men and women 'to the Knowledge of many important Truths relating to themselves, the external World, and its Author' (ii. 244).

stigmatized as feigning, fanciful, unphilosophical, became, for example in Kant's synthesis, agents of 'transcendental apperception', an a priori unity of consciousness available especially in epiphanal or sublime moments.[12] Thus, just as Locke's intended defence of the self proved destabilizing, so Hume's assault proved oddly restorative: personal identity gradually regained its authority for writers and thinkers, though with a new and undismayed stress on its alternately hidden or synthetic character, its character as something created or uncovered.

Consider, for example, the following passage from Boswell's *London Journal*, from an entry of 13 May 1763. Boswell has just returned from a discussion of philosophy ('We talked of Helvetius, Voltaire, Rousseau, Hume'). He is pleased with himself, describing his part in the discussion as 'rational and composed, yet lively and entertaining':

Could I but fix myself in such a character and preserve it uniformly, I should be uniformly happy. I hope to do so and to attain a constancy and dignity without which I can never be satisfied, as I have these ideas strong and pride myself in thinking that my natural character is that of dignity. My friend Temple is very good in consoling me by saying that I may be such a man, and that people will say, 'Mr. Boswell is quite altered from the dissipated, inconstant fellow that he was. He is now a reserved, grave sort of a man. But indeed that was his real character; and he only deviated into these eccentric paths for a while.' Well, then, let me see if I have resolution enough to bring that about.[13]

At work here in Boswell's self-portrait is a complex of attitudes familiar from eighteenth-century debate. There is the traditionalist's faith in a given 'real character', though the drama of the passage, as of the *Journal* generally, lies in this character's uncertain nature: as uniformly dignified or 'constant', or uniformly inconstant (and thus perilously close to Hume's 'perpetual flux and movement'). There is

[12] For an account of Kant's revaluing of intuitive powers see James Engell, *The Creative Imagination: Enlightenment to Romanticism* (Cambridge, Mass.: Harvard University Press, 1981), 128–39. For the relation of 'transcendental apperception' to the sublime see 'Analytic of the Sublime' (1790), in *Kant's Critique of Aesthetic Judgement*, trans. J. C. Meredith (Oxford: Clarendon Press, 1911). 'Transcendental apperception' is defined in the *Critique of Pure Reason* (1781, rev. edn. 1787), in J. N. Findlay's translation, in *Kant and the Transcendental Object: A Hermeneutic Study* (Oxford: Clarendon Press, 1981), 144: 'There could be no states of knowledge in us, and no connection and unity among the same, without this unity of consciousness which precedes all data of intuition, and in relation to which all representation of objects is alone possible. To this pure, original, unchangeable consciousness I give the name of Transcendental Apperception' (I find Findlay's translation clearer than that of Norman Kemp Smith, *Kant's Critique of Pure Reason* (New York: St Martin's Press, 1968), 170).
[13] James Boswell, *Boswell's London Journal 1762–1763*, ed. Frederick A. Pottle (London: William Heinemann, 1950), 257–8.

Locke's stress on consciousness as definitional; Boswell's 'ideas strong', which are ideas of himself, outweigh past dissipation or actual deeds. There is the self not as given but as a fabrication, something 'to bring . . . about', as Boswell puts it, a process Romantically valorized, as in the heroic resolve of the last sentence. Then there's the larger matter of autobiography per se. The *London Journal* belongs to a late eighteenth-century flowering of autobiography, a genre whose 'underlying obsession and final achievement', like that of the novel, it has been suggested, is 'selfhood and consistent identity'.[14] 'As a lady adjusts her dress before a mirror,' writes Boswell in the *Life of Johnson* (1791), 'a man adjusts his character by looking at his journal.'[15] This sense of the self as something made plays a significant part in the writing and revision of Boswell's age, as of that of the early nineteenth century.[16]

[14] Patricia Spacks, *Imagining a Self: Autobiography and Novel in Eighteenth-Century England* (Cambridge, Mass.: Harvard University Press, 1976), 315. The novel achieves its goal of unified selfhood or individuality 'by sheer illusion-making', autobiography does so 'through collaboration with experienced actuality' (ibid.).

[15] Entry for 31 Mar. 1778 in James Boswell, *Life of Samuel Johnson*, ed. G. B. Hill, rev. edn. L. F. Powell, 6 vols. (Oxford: Clarendon Press, 1934), iii. 228.

[16] For the most wide-ranging of accounts of the theme of the self in nineteenth- and twentieth-century British literature, including its relation to the theories of Locke and Hume, and to the psychoanalytic literature of identity (from Freud, through ego psychology, to Erik Erikson), see Robert Langbaum, *The Mysteries of Identity: A Theme in Modern Literature* (New York: Oxford University Press, 1977), especially 1–47. See also John N. Morris, *Versions of the Self: Studies in English Autobiography from John Bunyan to John Stuart Mill* (New York: Basic Books, 1966), Stephen D. Cox, *'The Stranger Within Thee': Concepts of the Self in Late Eighteenth-Century Literature* (Pittsburgh: University of Pittsburgh Press, 1980), J. O. Lyons, *The Invention of the Self* (Carbondale, Ill.: Southern Illinois University Press, 1978), Andrew M. Cooper, *Doubt and Identity in Romantic Poetry* (New Haven: Yale University Press, 1988), and Frederick Garber, *Self, Text, and Romantic Irony: The Example of Byron* (Princeton: Princeton University Press, 1988).

BIBLIOGRAPHY

ABRAMS, M. H., *The Mirror and the Lamp: Romantic Theory and the Critical Tradition* (New York: Oxford University Press, 1953).
—— *Natural Supernaturalism: Tradition and Revolution in Romantic Literature* (New York: W. W. Norton, 1971).
APTHEKER, BETTINA, *Tapestries of Life: Women's Work, Women's Consciousness, and the Meaning of Daily Experience* (Amherst, Mass.: University of Massachusetts Press, 1989).
ARAC, JONATHAN, 'Bounding Lines: *The Prelude* and Critical Revision', *Boundary* 2, 7/3 (Spring 1979), 31–48.
—— *Critical Genealogies: Historical Situations for Postmodern Literary Studies* (New York: Columbia University Press, 1987).
AUDEN, W. H., *The Collected Poetry of W. H. Auden* (New York: Random House, 1945).
—— *Collected Shorter Poems 1927–1957* (London: Faber & Faber, 1966).
—— *The Dyer's Hand and Other Essays* (London: Faber & Faber, 1963).
BALDICK, CHRIS, *In Frankenstein's Shadow: Myth, Monstrosity, and Nineteenth-Century Writing* (Oxford: Clarendon Press, 1987).
BARNARD, JOHN, *John Keats* (Cambridge: Cambridge University Press, 1987).
BARRELL, JOHN, *The Idea of Landscape and the Sense of Place, 1730–1840: An Approach to the Poetry of John Clare* (Cambridge: Cambridge University Press, 1972).
—— *The Dark Side of the Landscape: The Rural Poor in English Painting 1730–1840* (Cambridge: Cambridge University Press, 1980).
—— *Poetry, Language and Politics* (Manchester: Manchester University Press, 1988).
—— *The Infection of Thomas De Quincey* (New Haven: Yale University Press, 1991).
BARTHES, ROLAND, 'The Death of the Author', in *Image—Music—Text*, ed. Stephen Heath (New York: Hill & Wang, 1977).
BATE, JONATHAN, 'Keats's Two *Hyperion*s and the Problem of Milton', in Robert Brinkley and Keith Hanley (eds.), *Romantic Revisions* (Cambridge: Cambridge University Press, 1992).
—— *Romantic Ecology* (London: Routledge & Kegan Paul, 1992).

BATE, WALTER JACKSON, *The Stylistic Development of Keats* (1924; London: Routledge & Kegan Paul, 1958).

—— *John Keats* (New York: Oxford University Press, 1966).

—— *Coleridge* (New York: Macmillan, 1968).

BAYLEY, JOHN, 'Keats and Reality', in *Proceedings of the British Academy* (1962).

BAXTER, EDMUND, *De Quincey's Art of Autobiography* (Edinburgh: Edinburgh University Press, 1990).

BEER, JOHN, *Coleridge's Poetic Intelligence* (London: Macmillan, 1977).

BENNETT, ANDREW, *Keats, Narrative and Audience: The Posthumous Life of Writing* (Cambridge: Cambridge University Press, 1994).

BEWELL, ALAN J., 'The Political Implications of Keats's Classicist Aesthetics', *Studies in Romanticism*, 25 (Summer 1986), 220–9.

BLAKE, WILLIAM, *The Letters of William Blake*, ed. Geoffrey Keynes (London: Rupert Hart-Davis, 1956).

—— *The Poetry and Prose of William Blake*, ed. David V. Erdman (Garden City, NY: Doubleday, 1970).

BLUMBERG, JANE, *Mary Shelley's Early Novels: 'This Child of Imagination and Misery'* (London: Macmillan, 1993).

BOETHIUS, *The Theological Tractates*, trans. H. F. Stewart and E. K. Rand (London: Loeb Classical Library, 1918).

BOSWELL, JAMES, *Life of Samuel Johnson*, ed. G. B. Hill, rev. edn. L. F. Powell, 6 vols. (Oxford: Clarendon Press, 1934).

—— *Boswell's London Journal 1762–1763*, ed. Frederick A. Pottle (London: William Heinemann, 1950).

BOWERS, FREDSON, 'Some Principles for Scholarly Editions of Nineteenth-Century American Authors', in O. M. Brack and Warner Barnes (eds.), *Bibliography and Textual Criticism* (Chicago: University of Chicago Press, 1969).

BRIGGS, ASA, 'Middle-Class Consciousness in English Politics', *Past and Present*, 9 (Apr. 1956), 65–74.

—— 'The Language of "Class" in Early Nineteenth-Century England', in M. W. Flinn and T. C. Smout (eds.), *Essays on Social History* (Oxford: Clarendon Press, 1974).

BRINKLEY, ROBERT, and HANLEY, KEITH (eds.), *Romantic Revisions* (Cambridge: Cambridge University Press, 1992).

BROOKS, CLEANTH, *The Well-Wrought Urn: Studies in the Structure of Poetry* (New York: Harcourt, Brace, 1947).

BROWN, HUNTINGTON, 'The Gloss to the Ancient Mariner', *Modern Language Quarterly*, 6 (1945), 319–24.

BROWNLAW, TIMOTHY, *John Clare and Picturesque Landscape* (Oxford: Clarendon Press, 1983).

BUSH, DOUGLAS, *John Keats* (New York: Macmillan, 1966).

BUTLER, MARIA HOGAN, 'An Examination of Byron's Revision of *Manfred*, Act III', *Studies in Philology*, 7/4 (Oct. 1963), 627–36.

BUTLER, MARILYN, *Jane Austen and the War of Ideas* (Oxford: Clarendon Press, 1975).

—— *Romantics, Rebels and Reactionaries: English Literature and Its Background 1760–1830* (Oxford: Oxford University Press, 1981).

—— 'One Man in His Time', review of Jerome J. McGann, *Don Juan in Context*, *Essays in Criticism*, 28/1 (Jan. 1978), 52–60.

—— (ed.), *Burke, Paine, Godwin and the Revolution Controversy* (Cambridge: Cambridge University Press, 1984).

BYGRAVE, STEPHEN, *Coleridge and the Self: Romantic Egoism* (London: Macmillan, 1986).

BYRON, GEORGE GORDON, LORD, *Byron's 'Don Juan': A Variorum Edition*, ed. T. J. Steffan and W. W. Pratt, 4 vols. (Austin, Tex.: University of Texas Press, 1957).

—— *Byron's Letters and Journals*, ed. Leslie A. Marchand, 12 vols. (Cambridge, Mass.: Harvard University Press, 1973–82).

—— *Lord Byron: The Complete Poetical Works*, ed. Jerome J. McGann, 7 vols. (Oxford: Clarendon Press, 1980–93).

—— *Byron*, ed. Jerome J. McGann (Oxford: Oxford University Press, 1986).

CAFARELLI, ANNETTE WHEELER, *Prose in the Age of Poets: Romanticism and Biographical Narrative from Johnson to De Quincey* (Philadelphia: University of Pennsylvania Press, 1990).

CANTOR, PAUL, *Creator and Creation: Myth-Making and English Romanticism* (Cambridge: Cambridge University Press, 1984).

—— 'Mary Shelley and the Taming of the Byronic Hero: "Transformation" and *The Deformed Transformed*', in Audrey A. Fisch, Anne K. Mellor, and Esther H. Schor (eds.), *The Other Mary Shelley: Beyond 'Frankenstein'* (New York: Oxford University Press, 1993).

CARPENTER, HUMPHREY, *W. H. Auden: A Biography* (London: George Allen & Unwin, 1981).

CARSON, JAMES P., 'Bringing the Author Forward: *Frankenstein* Through Mary Shelley's Letters', *Criticism*, 30/4 (Fall 1988), 431–53.

CHAMBERS, DOUGLAS, ' "A Love for Every Simple Weed": Clare, Botany and the Poetic Language of Lost Eden', in Hugh Haughton, Adam Phillips, and Geoffrey Summerfield (eds.), *John Clare in Context* (Cambridge: Cambridge University Press, 1994).

CHANDLER, JAMES, *Wordsworth's Second Nature: A Study of the Poetry and Politics* (Chicago: University of Chicago Press, 1984).

—— 'Wordsworth after Waterloo', in *The Age of Wordsworth*, ed. Kenneth R. Johnston and Gene W. Ruoff (New Brunswick, NJ: Rutgers University Press, 1987).

CHILCOTT, TIM, *A Publisher and His Circle: The Life and Work of John Taylor, Keats's Publisher* (London: Routledge & Kegan Paul, 1972).

—— *A Real World and a Doubting Mind: A Critical Study of the Poetry of John Clare* (Pickering: Hull University Press, 1985).

CHRISTENSEN, JEROME, *Coleridge's Blessed Machine of Language* (Ithaca, NY: Cornell University Press, 1981).

—— 'Byron's Career: The Speculative Stage', *English Literary History*, 52/1 (Spring 1985), 59–84.

—— 'Byron: Class, Sexuality, and the Poet', in Elaine Scarry (ed.), *Literature and the Body: Essays on Populations and Persons* (Baltimore: Johns Hopkins University Press, 1988).

—— 'Theorizing Byron's Practice: The Performance of Lordship and the Poet's Career', *Studies in Romanticism*, 27/4 (Winter 1988), 477–90.

—— 'Perversion, Parody, and Cultural Hegemony: Lord Byron's Oriental Tales', *The South Atlantic Quarterly*, 88/3 (Summer 1989), 569–603.

CLARE, JOHANNE, *John Clare and the Bounds of Circumstance* (Kingston: McGill-Queen's University Press, 1987).

CLARE, JOHN, *Poems Descriptive of Rural Life and Scenery* (London: Taylor & Hessey, 1820).

—— *The Village Minstrel and Other Poems*, 2 vols. (London: Taylor & Hessey, 1821).

—— *The Shepherd's Calendar; with Village Stories, and Other Poems* (London: John Taylor, 1827).

—— *The Rural Muse, Poems* (London: Whittaker & Co., 1835).

—— *The Poems of John Clare*, ed. J. W. Tibble, 2 vols. (London: Dent, 1935).

—— *The Shepherd's Calendar*, ed. Eric Robinson, Geoffrey Summerfield, and David Powell (1964; repr. Oxford: Oxford University Press, 1993).

—— *John Clare: Selected Poems*, ed. J. W. Tibble and Anne Tibble (London: Dent, 1965).

—— *Clare: Selected Poems and Prose*, ed. Eric Robinson and Geoffrey Summerfield (London: Oxford University Press, 1966).

—— *The Midsummer Cushion*, ed. Anne Tibble and R. K. R. Thornton (Ashington: Mid-Northumberland Arts Group with Carcanet Press, 1979).

—— *The Rural Muse*, ed. R. K. R. Thornton (Ashington: Mid-Northumberland Arts Group with Carcanet Press, 1982).

—— *John Clare's Autobiographical Writings*, ed. Eric Robinson (Oxford: Oxford University Press, 1983).

—— *The Parish*, ed. Eric Robinson (Harmondsworth: Penguin, 1983).

CLARE, JOHN, *John Clare*, ed. Eric Robinson and David Powell (Oxford: Oxford University Press, 1984).
—— *The Later Poems of John Clare 1837–1864*, ed. Eric Robinson and David Powell, 2 vols. (Oxford: Clarendon Press, 1984).
—— *The Letters of John Clare*, ed. Mark Storey (Oxford: Oxford University Press, 1985).
—— *The Early Poems of John Clare 1804–1822*, ed. Eric Robinson and David Powell, 2 vols. (Oxford: Clarendon Press, 1989).
—— *Cottage Tales*, ed. Eric Robinson, David Powell, and P. M. S. Dawson (Ashington: Mid-Northumberland Arts Group with Carcanet Press, 1993).
CLARK, TIMOTHY, *Embodying Revolution: The Figure of the Poet in Shelley* (Oxford: Clarendon Press, 1989).
COHEN, PHILIP, 'Narrative and Persuasion in *The Ruined Cottage*', *Journal of Narrative Technique*, 8 (1978), 185–99.
COLERIDGE, SAMUEL TAYLOR, *Poetical Works*, ed. E. H. Coleridge (1912; rpt. Oxford: Oxford University Press, 1969).
—— *Collected Letters of Samuel Taylor Coleridge*, ed. E. L. Griggs, 6 vols. (Oxford: Clarendon Press, 1956–71).
—— *The Notebooks of Samuel Taylor Coleridge*, ed. Kathleen Coburn, 3 vols. (Princeton: Princeton University Press, 1957–73).
—— *The Friend*, ed. Barbara E. Rooke, 2 vols. (Princeton: Princeton University Press, 1969).
—— *Coleridge's Verse: A Selection*, ed. William Empson and David Pirie (New York: Schocken Books, 1972).
—— *Biographia Literaria*, ed. James Engell and W. Jackson Bate, 2 vols. (Princeton: Princeton University Press, 1983).
—— *Samuel Taylor Coleridge*, ed. H. J. Jackson (Oxford: Oxford University Press, 1985).
—— *Coleridge's 'Dejection': The Earliest Manuscripts and the Earliest Printings*, ed. Stephen Maxfield Parrish (Ithaca, NY: Cornell University Press, 1988).
—— *Table Talk*, ed. Carl Woodring, 2 vols. (Princeton: Princeton University Press, 1990).
—— *Poems*, ed. John Beer (London: Everyman Library, J. M. Dent, 1993).
COLES, W. A., 'The Proof Sheets of Keats's "Lamia"', *Harvard Library Bulletin*, 8 (1954), 118–19.
COOPER, ANDREW M., *Doubt and Identity in Romantic Poetry* (New Haven: Yale University Press, 1988).
CORBETT, MARY JEAN, *Representing Femininity: Middle-Class Subjectivity in Victorian and Edwardian Women's Autobiographies* (New York: Oxford University Press, 1992).

CORBETT, MARY JEAN, 'Reading Mary Shelley's *Journals*: Romantic Subjectivity and Feminist Criticism', in Audrey A. Fisch, Anne K. Mellor, and Esther H. Schor (eds.), *The Other Mary Shelley: Beyond 'Frankenstein'* (New York: Oxford University Press, 1993).

COX, STEPHEN D., *'The Stranger Within Thee': Concepts of the Self in Late Eighteenth-Century Literature* (Pittsburgh: University of Pittsburgh Press, 1980).

CRICK, BERNARD, *George Orwell: A Life* (London: Secker & Warburg, 1980).

CURTIS, JARED E., *Wordsworth's Experiments with Tradition: The Lyric Poems of 1802* (Ithaca, NY: Cornell University Press, 1971).

DE ALMEIDA, HERMIONE (ed.), *Critical Essays on John Keats* (Boston: G. K. Hall, 1990).

DE MAN, PAUL, *Blindness and Insight: Essays in the Rhetoric of Contemporary Criticism* (Minneapolis: University of Minnesota Press, 1983).

DE QUINCEY, THOMAS, *Selections Grave and Gay, from Writings, Published and Unpublished, of Thomas De Quincey, Revised and Arranged by Himself*, 14 vols. (Edinburgh: James Hogg, 1853–60).

—— *The Collected Writings of Thomas De Quincey*, ed. David Masson, 14 vols. (Edinburgh: Adam and Charles Black, 1896–7).

—— *A Diary of Thomas De Quincey, 1803*, ed. Horace A. Eaton (London: Noel Douglas, 1927).

—— *Confessions of an English Opium Eater*, ed. Althea Hayter (Harmondsworth: Penguin, 1971).

DESCARTES, RENÉ, *Descartes' Philosophical Letters*, trans. Anthony Kenny (Oxford: Oxford University Press, 1970).

—— *Philosophical Writings*, trans. John Cottingham, Robert Stoothoff, and Duguld Murdoch, 2 vols. (Cambridge: Cambridge University Press, 1985).

DONAHUE, MARY J., 'Tennyson's "Hail, Briton!" and "Tithon" in the Heath Manuscript', *PMLA* 64 (1949), 400–16.

DYCK, SARAH, 'Perspective in "The Rime of the Ancient Mariner"', *Studies in English Literature*, 13 (1973), 591–604.

EBBATSON, J. R., 'Coleridge and the Rights of Man', *Studies in Romanticism*, 11 (1972), 171–206.

EILENBERG, SUSAN, *Strange Power of Speech: Wordsworth, Coleridge and Literary Possession* (Oxford: Oxford University Press, 1992).

ENGELL, JAMES, *The Creative Imagination: Enlightenment to Romanticism* (Cambridge, Mass.: Harvard University Press, 1981).

ERIKSON, LEE, 'The Poet's Corner: The Impact of Technological Changes in Printing on English Poetry, 1800–1850', *English Literary History*, 52 (1985), 893–911.

FALCONER, GRAHAM, 'Genetic Criticism', *Comparative Literature*, 45 (Winter 1993), 1–21.

FERGUSON, FRANCES, 'Coleridge and the Deluded Reader: "The Rime of the Ancient Mariner"', *Georgia Review* (1977), 617–35.

—— 'On the Numbers of Romanticisms', *English Literary History*, 58 (1991), 471–98.

FINDLAY, J. N., *Kant and the Transcendental Object: A Hermeneutic Study* (Oxford: Clarendon Press, 1981).

FISCH, AUDREY A., MELLOR, ANNE K., and SCHOR, ESTHER H. (eds.), *The Other Mary Shelley: Beyond 'Frankenstein'* (New York: Oxford University Press, 1993).

FLECK, P. D., 'Mary Shelley's Notes to Shelley's Poems and *Frankenstein*', *Studies in Romanticism*, 6/4 (1967), 226–54.

FOUCAULT, MICHEL, 'The Discourse on Language', in *The Archaeology of Knowledge and the Discourse on Language*, trans. A. M. Sheridan Smith (New York: Pantheon, 1972).

—— 'What Is an Author?', tr. Josue V. Harari, in Harari (ed.), *Textual Strategies: Perspectives in Post-Structuralist Criticism* (Ithaca, NY: Cornell University Press, 1979).

FOX, CHRISTOPHER, *Locke and the Scriblerians: Identity and Consciousness in Early Eighteenth-Century Britain* (Berkeley: University of California Press, 1988).

FRAISTAT, NEIL, *The Poem and the Book: Interpreting Collections of Romantic Poetry* (Chapel Hill, NC: University of North Carolina Press, 1985).

FRUMAN, NORMAN, 'Review Essay: Aids to Reflection on the New *Biographia*', *Studies in Romanticism*, 24 (Spring 1985), 141–73.

—— 'Creative Process and Concealment in Coleridge's Poetry', in Robert Brinkley and Keith Hanley (eds.), *Romantic Revisions* (Cambridge: Cambridge University Press, 1992).

FRYE, NORTHROP, *Fables of Identity: Studies in Poetic Mythology* (New York: Harcourt, Brace, & World, 1963).

GALLAGHER, CATHERINE, 'George Eliot and *Daniel Deronda*: The Prostitute and the Jewish Question', in Ruth Bernard Yeazell (ed.), *Sex, Politics, and Science in the Nineteenth-Century Novel* (Baltimore: Johns Hopkins University Press, 1986).

GALPERIN, WILLIAM, *Revision and Authority in Wordsworth: The Interpretation of a Career* (Philadelphia: University of Pennsylvania Press, 1989).

GARBER, FREDERICK, *The Autonomy of the Self from Richardson to Huysmans* (Princeton: Princeton University Press, 1982).

—— *Self, Text, and Romantic Irony: The Example of Byron* (Princeton: Princeton University Press, 1988).

GILL, STEPHEN, 'Wordsworth's Poems: The Question of Text', *Review of English Studies*, 34 (May 1983), 172–90.

—— '"Affinities Preserved": Poetic Self-Reference in Wordsworth', *Studies in Romanticism*, 24/4 (Winter 1985), 531–49.

—— *William Wordsworth: A Life* (Oxford: Clarendon Press, 1989).

—— *William Wordsworth: 'The Prelude'* (Cambridge: Cambridge University Press, 1991).

GITTINGS, ROBERT, *John Keats* (London: Heinemann, 1968).

GLOVER, JONATHAN, *I: The Philosophy and Psychology of Personal Identity* (Harmondsworth: Penguin Books, 1988).

GODWIN, WILLIAM, *Enquiry Concerning Political Justice*, ed. Isaac Kramnick (Harmondsworth: Penguin Books, 1976).

GOODRIDGE, JOHN, and THORNTON, KELSEY, 'John Clare: The Trespasser', in Hugh Haughton, Adam Phillips, and Geoffrey Summerfield (eds.), *John Clare in Context* (Cambridge: Cambridge University Press, 1994).

GREETHAM, D. C., 'Textual and Literary Theory: Redrawing the Matrix', *Studies in Bibliography*, 42 (1989), 1–13.

GREG, W. W., 'The Rationale of Copy-Text', *Studies in Bibliography*, 3 (1950–1), 19–36.

GRODEN, MICHAEL, 'Contemporary Textual and Literary Theory', in George Bornstein (ed.), *Representing Modernist Texts: Editing as Interpretation* (Ann Arbor: University of Michigan Press, 1991).

HANLEY, KEITH, 'Crossings Out: The Problem of Textual Passage in *The Prelude*', in Robert Brinkley and Keith Hanley (eds.), *Romantic Revisions* (Cambridge: Cambridge University Press, 1992).

HARTLEY, DAVID, *Observations on Man, His Frame, His Duty, and His Expectations*, facsimile and intro. Theodore L. Huguelet, 2 vols. (Gainsville, Fla.: Scholars' Facsimiles and Reprints, 1966).

HAUGHTON, HUGH, PHILLIPS, ADAM, and SUMMERFIELD, GEOFFREY (eds.), *John Clare in Context* (Cambridge: Cambridge University Press, 1994).

HAZLITT, WILLIAM, *The Collected Works of William Hazlitt*, ed. A. R. Waller and Arnold Glover, 13 vols. (London: J. M. Dent, 1902–6).

—— *The Complete Works of William Hazlitt*, ed. P. P. Howe, 21 vols. (London: J. M. Dent & Sons, 1930–4).

HEANEY, SEAMUS, 'John Clare: A Bi-centenary Lecture', in Hugh Haughton, Adam Phillips, and Geoffrey Summerfield (eds.), *John Clare in Context* (Cambridge: Cambridge University Press, 1994).

HEINZELMAN, KURT, 'Self-Interest and the Politics of Composition in Keats's *Isabella*', *English Literary History*, 55 (1988), 159–93.

HELSINGER, ELISABETH, 'John Clare and the Place of the Peasant Poet', *Critical Inquiry*, 13 (Spring 1987), 508–31.

HILLES, FREDERICK W., and BLOOM, HAROLD (eds.), *From Sensibility to Romanticism: Essays Presented to Frederick A. Pottle* (New York: Oxford University Press, 1965).

HIRSCH, E. D., JR., *Validity in Interpretation* (New Haven: Yale University Press, 1967).

HOBSBAUM, PHILIP, *Tradition and Experiment in English Poetry* (London: Macmillan, 1979).

HOFKOSH, SONIA, 'The Writer's Ravishment: Women and the Romantic Author—The Example of Byron', in Anne K. Mellor (ed.), *Romanticism and Feminism* (Bloomington, Ind.: Indiana University Press, 1988).

HOLMES, RICHARD, *Coleridge: Early Visions* (London: Hodder & Stoughton, 1989).

HOMANS, MARGARET, *Women Writers and Poetic Identity* (Princeton: Princeton University Press, 1980).

—— *Bearing the Word: Language and Female Experience in Nineteenth-Century Women's Writing* (Chicago: University of Chicago Press, 1986).

—— 'Keats Reading Women, Women Reading Keats', *Studies in Romanticism*, 29 (1990), 341–71.

HONIGMANN, E. A. J., *The Stability of Shakespeare's Text* (London: Edward Arnold, 1965).

HORNE, PHILIP, *Henry James and Revision* (Oxford: Clarendon Press, 1990).

HUME, DAVID, *A Treatise of Human Nature*, ed. L. A. Selby-Bigge, rev. edn. P. H. Nidditch (Oxford: Clarendon Press, 1978).

IOPPOLO, GRACE, *Revising Shakespeare* (Cambridge, Mass.: Harvard University Press, 1992).

JACK, IAN, *The Poet and His Audience* (Cambridge: Cambridge University Press, 1987).

JAMES, HENRY, *The Golden Bowl* (Harmondsworth: Penguin Books, 1979).

JARVIS, ROBIN, 'The Five Book *Prelude*: A Reconsideration', *Journal of English and German Philology*, 80 (1981), 528–51.

JONES, JOHN, *Attempts in Verse by John Jones, An Old Servant with Some Account of the Writer, Written by Himself and an Introductory Essay by Robert Southey, Esq. Poet Laureate*, 2nd edn. (1831; London: John Murray, 1834).

JORDAN, FRANK (ed.), *The English Romantic Poets: A Review of Research* (New York: Modern Language Association of America, 1985).

JOYCE, JAMES, *Ulysses. A Critical and Synoptic Edition*, ed. Hans Walter Gabler with Wolfhard Steppe and Claus Melchior, 3 vols. (New York: Garland Press, 1984).

KANT, IMMANUEL, *Kant's Critique of Aesthetic Judgement*, trans. J. C. Meredith (Oxford: Clarendon Press, 1911).
—— *Kant's Critique of Pure Reason*, trans. Norman Kemp Smith (New York: St Martin's Press, 1968).
KEATS, JOHN, *The Letters of John Keats, 1814–1821*, ed. Hyder Rollins, 2 vols. (Cambridge, Mass.: Harvard University Press, 1958).
—— *Keats: The Complete Poems*, ed. Miriam Allott (London: Longman, 1970).
—— *The Poems of John Keats*, ed. Jack Stillinger (Cambridge, Mass.: Harvard University Press, 1978).
—— *Endymion (1818): A Facsimile of Richard Woodhouse's Annotated Copy in the Berg Collection*, ed. Jack Stillinger (New York: Garland Publishing, 1985).
KELLEY, THERESA M., *Wordsworth's Revisionary Aesthetics* (Cambridge: Cambridge University Press, 1988).
—— 'Poetics and the Politics of Reception: Keats's "La Belle Dame Sans Merci"', *English Literary History*, 54 (1987), 333–62.
KESSLER, EDWARD, *Coleridge's Metaphors of Being* (Princeton: Princeton University Press, 1979).
KETTERER, DAVID, *Frankenstein's Creation: The Book, The Monster, and Human Reality*, English Studies Monograph Series, 16 (Victoria, BC: University of Victoria Press, 1979).
KLANCHER, JON P., *The Making of English Reading Audiences, 1790–1832* (Madison: University of Wisconsin Press, 1987).
—— 'English Romanticism and Cultural Production', in H. Aram Veeser (ed.), *The New Historicism* (London: Routledge, 1989).
LAMB, CHARLES, *The Life and Works of Charles Lamb*, ed. Alfred Ainger, 12 vols. (London: Macmillan, 1900).
LANGBAUER, LAURIE, 'Swayed by Contraries: Mary Shelley and the Everyday', in Audrey A. Fisch, Anne K. Mellor, and Esther H. Schor (eds.), *The Other Mary Shelley: Beyond 'Frankenstein'* (New York: Oxford University Press, 1993).
LANGBAUM, ROBERT, *The Mysteries of Identity: A Theme in Modern Literature* (New York: Oxford University Press, 1977).
LEADER, ZACHARY, *Reading Blake's 'Songs'* (London: Routledge & Kegan Paul, 1981).
—— *Writer's Block* (Baltimore: The Johns Hopkins University Press, 1990).
LEASK, NIGEL, *The Politics of Imagination in Coleridge's Critical Thought* (London: Macmillan, 1988).
—— *British Romantic Writers and the East: Anxieties of Empire* (Cambridge: Cambridge University Press, 1993).
LEVINE, GEORGE, and KNOEPFLMACHER, U. C. (eds.), *The Endurance of Frankenstein* (Berkeley: University of California Press, 1982).

LEVINSON, MARJORIE, *Keats's Life of Allegory: The Origins of a Style* (Oxford: Basil Blackwell, 1988).

LINDENBERGER, HERBERT, *On Wordsworth's 'Prelude'* (Princeton: Princeton University Press, 1963).

LIPKING, LAURENCE, 'The Marginal Gloss', *Critical Inquiry*, 3 (Summer 1977), 609–55.

LIU, ALAN, *Wordsworth: The Sense of History* (Stanford, Calif.: Stanford University Press, 1989).

LOCKE, JOHN, *An Essay Concerning Human Understanding*, ed. P. H. Nidditch (Oxford: Clarendon Press, 1975).

LOCKHART, JOHN GIBSON, *Memoirs of the Life of Sir Walter Scott*, 10 vols. (Boston: Houghton Mifflin, 1901).

LOVEJOY, ARTHUR O., 'On the Discrimination of Romanticisms', *PMLA* 39 (1924), 229–253.

LOVELL, ERNEST J., 'Byron and Mary Shelley', *Keats–Shelley Journal*, 2 (19 Jan. 1953), 35–49.

—— (ed.), *Medwin's Conversations of Lord Byron* (Princeton: Princeton University Press, 1966).

—— (ed.), *Lady Blessington's Conversations of Lord Byron* (Princeton: Princeton University Press, 1969).

LOWELL, AMY, *John Keats*, 2 vols. (Boston: Houghton Mifflin, 1925).

LUCAS, JOHN, *England and Englishness: Ideas of Nationhood in English Poetry, 1688–1900* (London: Chatto & Windus, 1990).

—— 'Revising Clare', in Robert Brinkley and Keith Hanley (eds.), *Romantic Revisions* (Cambridge: Cambridge University Press, 1992).

—— 'Clare's Politics', in Hugh Haughton, Adam Phillips, and Geoffrey Summerfield (eds.), *John Clare in Context* (Cambridge: Cambridge University Press, 1994).

—— *John Clare* (Plymouth: Northcote House, 1994).

LUKE HUGH J., 'The Publishing of Byron's *Don Juan*', *PMLA* 80 (1965), 198–209.

LYONS, J. O., *The Invention of the Self* (Carbondale, Ill.: Southern Illinois University Press, 1978).

McELDERRY, B. J, 'Coleridge's Revisions of "The Ancient Mariner"', *Studies in Philology*, 29 (1932), 68–94.

McGANN, JEROME J., 'Editing Byron's Poetry', *The Byron Journal*, 1/1 (1973), 5–10.

—— 'The Meaning of "The Ancient Mariner"', *Critical Inquiry*, 8 (Autumn 1981), 35–67.

—— *A Critique of Modern Textual Criticism* (Chicago: University of Chicago Press, 1983).

—— *The Romantic Ideology: A Critical Investigation* (Chicago: University of Chicago Press, 1983).

McGann, Jerome J., *The Beauty of Inflections: Literary Investigations in Historical Method and Theory* (Oxford: Clarendon Press, 1985).

—— *Social Values and Poetic Acts: The Historical Judgement of Literary Work* (Cambridge, Mass.: Harvard University Press, 1988).

—— *Towards a Literature of Knowledge* (Chicago: University of Chicago Press, 1989).

—— *The Textual Condition* (Princeton: Princeton University Press, 1991).

MacGillivray, J. R., 'The Three Forms of *The Prelude*', in *Wordsworth, 'The Prelude': A Casebook*, ed. W. J. Harvey and Richard Gravil (London: Macmillan, 1972).

McKusick, James, ' "A language that is ever green": The Ecological Vision of John Clare', *University of Toronto Quarterly*, 61 (Winter 1991–2), 30–52.

—— 'John Clare's London Journal: A Peasant Poet Encounters the Metropolis', *Wordsworth Circle*, 23 (1992), 172–5.

—— 'Beyond the Visionary Company: John Clare's Resistance to Romanticism', in Hugh Haughton, Adam Phillips, and Geoffrey Summerfield (eds.), *John Clare in Context* (Cambridge: Cambridge University Press, 1994).

—— 'John Clare and the Tyranny of Grammar', *Studies in Romanticism*, 33 (Summer 1994), 255–77.

Manning, Peter J., *Byron and His Fictions* (Detroit: Wayne State University Press, 1978).

—— ' "My Former Thoughts Returned": Wordsworth's "Resolution and Independence" ', *The Wordsworth Circle*, 9 (1978), 398–405.

—— *Reading Romantics: Texts and Contexts* (New York: Oxford University Press, 1990).

—— 'Cleansing the Images: Wordsworth, Rome and the Rise of Historicism', *Texas Studies in Literature and Language*, 73/2 (Summer 1991), 271–326.

—— '*Don Juan* and the Revisionary Self', in Robert Brinkley and Keith Hanley (eds.), *Romantic Revisions* (Cambridge: Cambridge University Press, 1992).

Marchand, Leslie A., *Byron: A Biography*, 3 vols. (New York: Alfred A. Knopf, 1957).

Marshall, David, *The Surprising Effects of Sympathy: Marivaux, Diderot, Rousseau and Mary Shelley* (Chicago: University of Chicago Press, 1988).

Matthews, G. M. (ed.), *Keats: The Critical Heritage* (London: Routledge & Kegan Paul, 1971).

Mays, J. C. C., 'Reflections on Having Edited Coleridge's Poems', in Robert Brinkley and Keith Hanley (eds.), *Romantic Revisions* (Cambridge: Cambridge University Press, 1992).

MAYS, J. C. C., 'Coleridge's "Love": "All he can manage, more than he could" ', in Tim Fulford and Morton D. Paley (eds.), *Coleridge's Visionary Languages: Essays in Honour of J. B. Beer* (Cambridge: D. S. Brewer, 1993).

MELLOR, ANNE K., *English Romantic Irony* (Cambridge, Mass.: Harvard University Press, 1980).

—— *Mary Shelley: Her Life, Her Fiction, Her Monsters* (New York: Routledge, 1988).

—— (ed.), *Romanticism and Feminism* (Bloomington, Ind.: Indiana University Press, 1988).

MENDELSON, EDWARD, *The English Auden* (London: Faber & Faber, 1977).

—— *Early Auden* (London: Faber & Faber, 1981).

—— 'The Two Audens and the Claims of History', in George Bornstein (ed.), *Representing Modernist Texts: Editing as Interpretation* (Ann Arbor: University of Michigan Press, 1991).

MEYER, CONRAD FERDINAND, *Sämtliche Werke. Historisch-kritische Ausgabe*, ed. Hans Keller and Alfred Zach (Berne: Benteli, 1958–63).

MILEUR, JEAN-PIERRE, *Vision and Revision: Coleridge's Art of Immanence* (Berkeley: University of California Press, 1982).

MITCHELL, W. J. T. (ed.), *Against Theory: Literary Studies and the New Pragmatism* (Chicago: University of Chicago Press, 1985).

MOERS, ELLEN, *Literary Women* (Garden City, NY: Doubleday, 1976).

MOI, TORIL, *Textual/Sexual Politics: Feminist Literary Theory* (London: Methuen, 1985).

MOON, MICHAEL, *Disseminating Whitman: Revision and Corporeality in 'Leaves of Grass'* (Cambridge, Mass.: Harvard University Press, 1991).

MORLEY, EDITH J. (ed.), *The Correspondence of H. C. Crabb Robinson with the Wordsworth Circle*, 2 vols. (Oxford: Clarendon Press, 1927).

MORRIS, JOHN N., *Versions of the Self: Studies in English Autobiography from John Bunyan to John Stuart Mill* (New York: Basic Books, 1966).

MURRAY, E. B., 'Shelley's Contribution to Mary's *Frankenstein*', in *Keats–Shelley Memorial Bulletin*, 29 (1978), 50–68.

NEHEMAS, ALEXANDER, 'The Postulated Author: Critical Monism as a Regulated Ideal', *Critical Inquiry*, 8 (1981), 133–49.

NITCHIE, ELIZABETH, *Mary Shelley: Author of Frankenstein* (New Brunswick, NJ: Rutgers University Press, 1953).

NUSSBAUM, FELICITY, *The Autobiographical Subject: Gender and Ideology in Eighteenth-Century England* (Baltimore: Johns Hopkins University Press, 1989).

ORWELL, GEORGE, *Inside the Whale* (London: Gollancz, 1940).

OWEN, W. J. B., 'Costs, Sales, and Profits of Longman's Editions of Wordsworth', *Library*, 12 (1957), 93–107.

PARFIT, DEREK, *Reasons and Persons* (Oxford: Clarendon Press, 1984).

PARKER, HERSHEL, *Flawed Texts and Verbal Icons: Literary Authority in American Fiction* (Evanston, Ill.: Northwestern University Press, 1984).

PARRISH, STEPHEN MAXFIELD, *The Art of the Lyrical Ballads* (Cambridge, Mass.: Harvard University Press, 1973).

—— 'The Worst of Wordsworth', *The Wordsworth Circle*, 7/2 (Spring 1976), 89–91.

—— 'The Editor as Archeologist', *Kentucky Review*, 4 (1983), 3–14.

—— 'The Whig Interpretation of Literature', *Text*, 4 (1988), 343–50.

PAUL, C. KEGAN, *William Godwin: Friends and Contemporaries*, 2 vols. (London: Henry S. King, 1876).

PAULIN, TOM (ed.), *The Faber Book of Vernacular Verse* (London: Faber & Faber, 1990).

—— *Minotaur: Poetry and the Nation State* (London: Faber & Faber, 1992).

PERKINS, DAVID, *The Quest for Permanence: The Symbolism of Wordsworth, Shelley, and Keats* (Cambridge, Mass.: Harvard University Press, 1959).

PHILLIPS, ADAM, 'The Exposure of John Clare', in Hugh Haughton, Adam Phillips, and Geoffrey Summerfield (eds.), *John Clare in Context* (Cambridge: Cambridge University Press, 1994).

PLOWMAN, EDWARD M., and HAMILTON, L. CLARK, *Copyright: Intellectual Property* (London: Routledge & Kegan Paul, 1980).

POLIDORI, JOHN WILLIAM, *The Diary of John William Polidori, 1816, Relating to Byron, Shelley, etc.*, ed. William Michael Rossetti (London: Elkin Mathews, 1911).

POOVEY, MARY, *The Proper Lady and the Woman Writer: Ideology as Style in the Works of Mary Wollstonecraft, Mary Shelley, and Jane Austen* (Chicago: University of Chicago Press, 1984).

POWELL, MARGARET KETCHUM, 'Keats and His Editor: The Manuscript of *Endymion*', *The Library*, 6 (1984), 139–52.

RABEN, JOSEPH, 'Shelley's "Invocation to Misery": An Expanded Text', *Journal of English and German Philology*, 65 (1966), 65–74.

RAJAN, TILOTTAMA, *Dark Interpreter: The Discourse of Romanticism* (Ithaca, NY: Cornell University Press, 1980).

REDPATH, THEODORE, *The Young Romantics and Critical Opinion, 1807–1824* (London: Harrap, 1973).

REID, THOMAS, *Essays on the Intellectual Powers of Man* (1785; rpt. New York: Garland Press, 1971).

REIMAN, DONALD H. (ed.), *The Romantics Reviewed: Contemporary Reviews of Romantic Writers*, 9 vols. (New York: Garland Press, 1972).

—— *Romantic Texts and Contexts* (Columbia, Miss.: University of Missouri Press, 1987).

—— 'Shelley's Manuscripts and the Web of Circumstance', in Robert Brinkley and Keith Hanley (eds.), *Romantic Revisions* (Cambridge: Cambridge University Press, 1992).

RICKS, CHRISTOPHER, *Keats and Embarrassment* (Oxford: Clarendon Press, 1974).

RIDENOUR, GEORGE, *The Style of Don Juan* (New Haven: Yale University Press, 1960).

—— '*Don Juan* and the Romantics', *Studies in Romanticism*, 16/3 (Fall 1977), 563–71.

RIVERS, ISABEL, *Books and Their Readers in Eighteenth-Century England* (New York: St Martin's Press, 1982).

ROBINSON, ERIC, and SUMMERFIELD, GEOFFREY, 'John Taylor's Editing of Clare's *The Shepherd's Calendar*', *Review of English Studies*, 14/56 (1963), 359–69.

ROE, NICHOLAS, *Wordsworth and Coleridge: The Radical Years* (Oxford: Clarendon Press, 1988).

—— 'Revising the Revolution: History and Imagination in *The Prelude*', in Robert Brinkley and Keith Hanley (eds.), *Romantic Revisions* (Cambridge: Cambridge University Press, 1992).

ROLLINS, HYDER E. (ed.), *The Keats Circle: Letters and Papers, 1816–1878*, 2 vols. (1948; Cambridge, Mass.: Harvard University Press, 1965).

RORTY, AMÉLIE (ed.), *The Identities of Persons* (Berkeley: University of California Press, 1976).

ROSS, MARLON B., 'Romantic Quest and Conquest: Troping Masculine Power in the Crisis of Poetic Identity', in Anne K. Mellor (ed.), *Romanticism and Feminism* (Bloomington, Ind.: Indiana University Press, 1988).

—— *The Contours of Masculine Desire: Romanticism and the Rise of Women's Poetry* (New York: Oxford University Press, 1989).

RUOFF, GENE W., *Wordsworth and Coleridge: The Making of the Major Lyrics, 1802–1804* (New Brunswick, NJ: Rutgers University Press, 1989).

RUTHERFORD, ANDREW (ed.), *Byron: The Critical Heritage* (New York: Barnes & Noble, 1970).

ST CLAIR, WILLIAM, *The Godwins and the Shelleys* (London: Faber & Faber, 1989).

SCHLEGEL, FRIEDRICH, *Friedrich Schlegel's Lucinde and the Fragments*, trans. Peter Firchow (Minneapolis: University of Minnesota Press, 1971).

SCHWARTZ, LEWIS M., 'Keat's Critical Reception in the Newspapers of His Day', in *Keats–Shelley Journal*, 21-2 (1972/3), 170–87.

SCOTT, WALTER, *The Letters of Sir Walter Scott*, ed. H. J. C. Grierson, 12 vols. (New York: Columbia University Press, 1932–7).

SHEATS, PAUL D., *The Making of Wordsworth's Poetry, 1785–1798* (Cambridge, Mass.: Harvard University Press, 1973).

SHELLEY, MARY WOLLSTONECRAFT, *Frankenstein or the Modern Prometheus: The 1818 Text*, ed. James Rieger (New York: Bobbs-Merill, 1974).

—— *The Letters of Mary Wollstonecraft Shelley*, ed. Betty T. Bennett, 3 vols. (Baltimore: Johns Hopkins University Press, 1980–8).

—— *The Journals of Mary Shelley: 1814–1844*, ed. Paula R. Feldman and Diana Scott-Kilvert, 2 vols. (Oxford: Clarendon Press, 1987).

—— *The Mary Shelley Reader*, ed. Betty T. Bennett and Charles E. Robinson (New York: Oxford University Press, 1990).

—— *Frankenstein* (New York: Everyman's Library edn., Alfred A. Knopf, 1992).

—— *Frankenstein*, ed. Maurice Hindle (Harmondsworth: Penguin, 1992).

—— *Frankenstein*, ed. Johanna M. Smith, in the series Case Studies in Contemporary Criticism (Boston: Bedford Books of St Martin's Press, 1992).

—— *Frankenstein or the Modern Prometheus: The 1818 Text*, ed. Marilyn Butler (London: William Pickering, 1993).

SHELLEY, PERCY BYSSHE, *The Poetical Works of Percy Bysshe Shelley*, ed. Mary Shelley, 4 vols. (London: Edward Moxon, 1839).

—— *The Letters of Percy Bysshe Shelley*, ed. Frederick L. Jones, 2 vols. (Oxford: Clarendon Press, 1964).

—— *Shelley's Prose or the Trumpet of a Prophecy*, ed. David Lee Clark (Albuquerque: University of New Mexico Press, 1966).

—— *Shelley: Poetical Works*, ed. Thomas Hutchinson, corr. G. M. Matthews (1905; London: Oxford University Press, 1970).

—— *Shelley's Poetry and Prose*, ed. Donald H. Reiman and Sharon B. Powers (New York: W. W. Norton, 1977).

—— *The Poems of Shelley*: i. *1804–1817*, ed. Geoffrey Matthews and Kelvin Everest (London: Longman, 1989).

SHILLINGSBURG, PETER L., *Scholarly Editing in the Computer Age: Theory and Practice* (Athens, Ga.: University of Georgia Press, 1986).

SHOEMAKER, SYDNEY, *Self-Knowledge and Self-Identity* (Ithaca, NY: Cornell University Press, 1963).

SIMPSON, DAVID, *Irony and Authority in Romantic Poetry* (Totowa, NJ: Rowan & Littlefield, 1979).

SIMPSON, DAVID, 'Criticism, Politics, and Style in Wordsworth's Poetry', *Critical Inquiry*, 2 (1984), 52–81.

SISKIN, CLIFFORD, *The Historicity of Romantic Discourse* (New York: Oxford University Press, 1988).

SMALL, CHRISTOPHER, *Ariel Like a Harpy: Shelley, Mary and Frankenstein* (London: Victor Gollancz, 1972).

SMILES, SAMUEL, *A Publisher and His Friends: Memoir and Correspondence of the Late John Murray*, 2 vols. (London: John Murray, 1891).

SMITH, DOROTHY E., *Everyday Life as Problematic: A Feminist Sociology* (Boston: Northeastern University Press, 1987).

SMITH, GAYLE, 'A Reappraisal of the Moral Stanzas in *The Rime of the Ancient Mariner*', *Studies in Romanticism*, 3 (1963), 42–52.

SPACKS, PATRICIA, *Imagining a Self: Autobiography and Novel in Eighteenth-Century England* (Cambridge, Mass.: Harvard University Press, 1976).

SPARK, MURIEL, *Mary Shelley* (London: Constable, 1988).

SPEARS, MONROE K., *The Poetry of W. H. Auden: The Disenchanted Island* (New York: Oxford University Press, 1963).

STERNE, LAURENCE, *Tristram Shandy*, ed. James A. Work (New York: Odyssey Press, 1940).

STILLINGER, JACK, *The Hoodwinking of Madeline and Other Essays on Keats's Poems* (Urbana, Ill.: University of Illinois Press, 1971).

—— *The Texts of Keats's Poems* (Cambridge, Mass.: Harvard University Press, 1974).

—— 'Textual Primitivism and the Editing of Wordsworth', *Studies in Romanticism*, 28/1 (Spring 1989), 3–28.

—— *Multiple Authorship and the Myth of Solitary Genius* (New York: Oxford University Press, 1991).

—— 'Keats's Extempore Effusions and the Question of Intentionality', in Robert Brinkley and Keith Hanley (eds.), *Romantic Revisions* (Cambridge: Cambridge University Press, 1992).

—— 'The Multiple Versions of Coleridge's Poems: How Many *Mariners* did Coleridge Write?', *Studies in Romanticism*, 31/2 (Summer 1992), 127–46.

—— *Coleridge and Textual Instability: The Multiple Versions of the Major Poems* (New York: Oxford University Press, 1994).

STOREY, EDWARD, *A Right to Song: The Life of John Clare* (London: Methuen, 1982).

STOREY, MARK (ed.), *Clare: The Critical Heritage* (London: Routledge & Kegan Paul, 1973).

—— *The Poetry of John Clare: A Critical Introduction* (London: Macmillan, 1974).

STRANG, BARBARA, 'John Clare's Language', in John Clare, *The Rural Muse*, ed. R. K. R. Thornton (Ashington: Mid-Northumberland Arts Group with Carcanet Press, 1982).

STRAWSON, P. F., 'The Parfit Connection', review of Derek Parfit, *Reasons and Persons*, New York Review of Books, 31 (1984), 42–5.

SUNSTEIN, EMILY W., *Mary Shelley: Romance and Reality* (Boston: Little Brown, 1989).

TANSELLE, G. THOMAS, 'The Editorial Problem of Final Authorial Intention', *Studies in Bibliography*, 29 (1976), 167–211.

—— *Selected Studies in Bibliography* (Charlottesville, Va.: University Press of Virginia, 1979).

—— *Textual Criticism since Greg: A Chronicle, 1950–1985* (Charlottesville, Va.: University Press of Virginia, 1987).

TAYLOR, CHARLES, *Sources of the Self* (Cambridge, Mass.: Harvard University Press, 1989).

TAYLOR, CHARLES H., JR., 'The Errata Leaf to Shelley's *Posthumous Poems* and Some Surprising Relationships Between the Earliest Collected Editions', *PMLA* 70 (June 1955), 408–16.

TENNYSON, ALFRED, LORD, *The Poems of Tennyson*, ed. Christopher Ricks (London: Longman, 1969).

THORPE, JAMES (ed.), *The Aims and Methods of Scholarship in Modern Languages and Literatures* (New York: Modern Language Association, 1963).

—— *Principles of Textual Criticism* (San Marino, Calif.: Huntington Library, 1972).

THORSLEV, PETER L., JR., *The Byronic Hero: Types and Prototypes* (Minneapolis: University of Minnesota Press, 1962).

—— *Romantic Contraries: Freedom versus Destiny* (New Haven: Yale University Press, 1984).

TIBBLE, J. W. and ANNE, *John Clare: A Life* (London: Michael Joseph, 1972).

TRELAWNY, EDWARD JOHN, *Letters of Edward John Trelawny*, ed. H. Buxton Forman (London: Oxford University Press, 1910).

—— *Adventures of a Younger Son*, ed. William St Clair (London: Oxford University Press, 1974).

TRILLING, LIONEL, *The Liberal Imagination: Essays on Literature and Society* (New York: Viking Press, 1950).

UNGER, PETER, *Identity, Consciousness and Value* (Oxford: Oxford University Press, 1991).

VEEDER, WILLIAM, *Mary Shelley and Frankenstein: The Fate of Androgyny* (Chicago: University of Chicago Press, 1986).

VENDLER, HELEN, *The Odes of John Keats* (Cambridge, Mass.: Harvard University Press, 1983).

VISCOMI, JOSEPH, *Blake and the Idea of the Book* (Princeton: Princeton University Press, 1993).

WADE, STEPHEN, 'John Clare's Use of Dialect', *Contemporary Review*, 223 (July–Dec. 1973), 81–4.

WALL, WENDY, 'Interpreting Poetic Shadows: The Gloss of "The Rime of the Ancient Mariner"', *Criticism*, 29/2 (Spring 1987), 179–95.

WALLEN, MARTIN, 'Return and Representation: The Revisions of "The Ancient Mariner"', *Wordsworth Circle*, 17 (1986), 148–56.

WALKER, ERIC C., '*Biographia Literaria* and Wordsworth's Revisions', *Studies in English Literature*, 28 (1988), 569–88.

WARREN, ROBERT PENN, *Selected Essays* (1941; repr. New York: Random House, 1958).

WASSERMAN, EARL, *The Finer Tone: Keats's Major Poems* (Baltimore: Johns Hopkins University Press, 1983).

WATSON, GEORGE, 'The Accuracy of Lord Byron', *Critical Quarterly*, 17/2 (Summer 1975), 135–48.

WELLEK, RENÉ, 'The Concept of Romanticism in Literary History', *Comparative Literature*, 1 (1949), 147–72.

WHEATLEY, KIM, 'The *Blackwood*'s Attacks on Leigh Hunt', *Nineteenth-Century Literature*, 47/1 (June 1992), 1–31.

WILLIAMS, BERNARD, *Problems of the Self* (Cambridge: Cambridge University Press, 1973).

WIMSATT, W. K., JR., *The Verbal Icon: Studies in the Meaning of Poetry* (Lexington, Ken.: University of Kentucky Press, 1954).

—— and BEARDSLEY, MONROE, 'The Intentional Fallacy', *Sewanee Review*, 54 (1946), 468–88.

WOLF, SUSAN, 'Self-Interest and Interest in Selves', *Ethics*, 96 (1986), 704–20.

WOLFSON, SUSAN J., 'The Illusion of Mastery: Wordsworth's Revisions of "The Drowned Man of Esthwaite", 1799, 1805, 1850', *PMLA* 99 (1984), 917–35.

—— '"Their She Condition": Cross-Dressing and the Politics of Gender in *Don Juan*', *English Literary History*, 54/3 (Autumn 1987), 585–617.

—— 'Editorial Privilege: Mary Shelley and Percy Shelley's Audiences', in Audrey A. Fisch, Anne K. Mellor, and Esther H. Schor (eds.), *The Other Mary Shelley: Beyond 'Frankenstein'* (New York: Oxford, 1993).

WOLLSTONECRAFT, MARY, *Mary and The Wrongs of Woman*, ed. Gary Kelley (London: Oxford University Press, 1976).

WORDSWORTH, JONATHAN, *The Music of Humanity: A Critical Study of Wordsworth's 'Ruined Cottage' Incorporating Texts from a Manuscript of 1799–1800* (New York: Harper & Row, 1969).

—— (ed.), *Bicentennial Wordsworth Essays in Memory of John Alban Finch* (Ithaca, NY: Cornell University Press, 1970).

WORDSWORTH, JONATHAN, 'The Five Book *Prelude* of Early Spring 1804', *Journal of English and German Philology*, 76 (1977), 1–25.
—— *William Wordsworth: The Borders of Vision* (Oxford: Clarendon Press, 1982).
—— 'Revision as Making: *The Prelude* and Its Peers', in Keith Hanley and Robert Brinkley (eds.), *Romantic Revisions* (Cambridge: Cambridge University Press, 1992).
WORDSWORTH, WILLIAM, *The Prose Works of William Wordsworth*, ed. Alexander B. Grosart, 3 vols. (London: E. Moxon, Son, & Co., 1876).
—— *Poetical Works of William Wordsworth*, ed. Edward Dowden, 7 vols. (London: George Bell & Sons, 1892–3).
—— *The Poetical Works of William Wordsworth, Edited from the Manuscripts, with Textual and Critical Notes*, ed. Ernest de Selincourt and Helen Darbishire, 5 vols. (Oxford: Clarendon Press, 1941–9).
—— *Poetical Works*, ed. Ernest de Selincourt, rev. edn. Thomas Hutchinson (Oxford: Oxford University Press, 1950).
—— *The Prelude*, ed. Ernest de Selincourt, rev. edn. Helen Darbishire (Oxford: Clarendon Press, 1959).
—— *Lyrical Ballads*, ed. R. L. Brett and A. R. Jones (London: Methuen, 1963).
—— *Selected Poetry and Prefaces of William Wordsworth*, ed. Jack Stillinger (Boston: Houghton Mifflin, 1965).
—— *The Selected Poetry and Prose of Wordsworth*, ed. Geoffrey Hartman (New York: New American Library, 1970).
—— *The Prose Works of William Wordsworth*, ed. W. J. B. Owen and Jane Smyser, 3 vols. (Oxford: Clarendon Press, 1974).
—— *The Salisbury Plain Poems of William Wordsworth*, ed. Stephen Gill (Ithaca, NY: Cornell University Press, 1975).
—— *Home at Grasmere*, ed. Beth Darlington (Ithaca, NY: Cornell University Press, 1977).
—— *The Prelude: A Parallel Text*, ed. J. C. Maxwell (Harmondsworth: Penguin Books, 1977).
—— *William Wordsworth: The Poems*, ed. John O. Hayden, 2 vols. (Harmondsworth: Penguin Books, 1977).
—— *The Letters of William and Dorothy Wordsworth*, ed. Ernest de Selincourt; *The Early Years, 1787–1805*, rev. edn. Chester L. Shaver (Oxford: Clarendon Press, 1967); *The Middle Years, 1806–11*, rev. edn. Mary Moorman (Oxford: Clarendon Press, 1969); *The Middle Years, 1812–1820*, rev. edn. Mary Moorman and Alan G. Hill (Oxford: Clarendon Press, 1970); *The Later Years, 1821–1853*, rev. edn., Alan G. Hill, 4 vols. (Oxford: Clarendon Press, 1978–88).

—— *The Prelude 1799, 1805, 1850*, ed. Jonathan Wordsworth, M. H. Abrams, and Stephen Gill (New York: W. W. Norton, 1979).

—— *William Wordsworth*, ed. Stephen Gill (Oxford: Oxford University Press, 1984).

—— *Selected Prose Writings*, ed. John O. Hayden (Harmondsworth: Penguin Books, 1988).

WRIGHT, HERBERT, *Boccaccio in England from Chaucer to Tennyson* (London: Athlone Press, 1957).

WU, DUNCAN, 'Editing Intentions', *Essays in Criticism*, 41/1 (Jan. 1991), 1–10.

—— 'Acts of Butchery: Wordsworth as Editor', *The Wordsworth Circle*, 23/3 (Summer 1992), 156–61.

YEATS, W. B., *Variorum Edition of the Poems of W. B. Yeats*, ed. Peter Allt and Russell K. Alspach (London: Macmillan, 1957).

YOUNG, EDWARD, *Conjectures on Original Composition*, ed. Edith J. Morley (Manchester: Manchester University Press, 1918).

ZELLER, HANS, 'A New Approach to the Critical Constitution of Literary Texts', *Studies in Bibliography*, 28 (1975), 231–64.

INDEX

354   INDEX

Wordsworth, William (*cont.*):
 115–16, 120–4, 127–8, 132–3,
 137–9, 141, 143, 145, 153–4,
 161, 167, 171–3, 185, 236, 246,
 270, 277, 282, 307–8, 314
 Cornell edition 20, 22, 25, 26–32,
  44, 74
 Fenwick Notes 51, 55–7
 French Revolution, Wordsworth
  and 60–1, 63, 72
 editor's obligation 72–7
 Prelude and revision 57–72
 revision as imposition 41–6

revision and personal identity 19–26
revision and theme of return 46–57
text as continuum 32–41
Wu, Duncan 73, 138, 139

'Yarrow Revisited' (Wordsworth) 14,
 52–5, 57
'Yarrow Unvisited' (Wordsworth)
 50–1
'Yarrow Visited' (Wordsworth) 51–2
Yeats, W. B. 4

Zeller, Hans 73, 142, 155